POLITICS IN THE ORDER OF SALVATION

POLITICS IN THE ORDER OF SALVATION

New Directions in Wesleyan Political Ethics

Theodore R. Weber

KINGSWOOD BOOKS
An Imprint of Abingdon Press
Nashville, Tennessee

POLITICS IN THE ORDER OF SALVATION
NEW DIRECTIONS IN WESLEYAN POLITICAL ETHICS

Copyright © 2001 by Abingdon Press

Library of Congress Cataloging-in-Publication Data

Weber, Theodore R.,
   Politics in the order of salvation : new directions in Wesleyan political ethics / Theodore R. Weber.
      p. cm.
   Includes bibliographical references (p.) and index.
   ISBN 0-687-31690-1 (alk. paper)
      1. Wesley, John, 1703-1791—Political and social views. 2. Wesley, John, 1703-1791—Ethics.
3. Christianity and politics. 4. Salvation. I. Title.

   BX8231 .W43 2002
   261.7'092—dc21

                                                                                2001045001

Scripture quotations are from the King James Version of the Bible.

Excerpts from *The Methodist Revolution* by Bernard Semmel. Copyright © 1973 by Basic Books, a member of Perseus Books Group. Reprinted by permission of Basic Books, a member of Perseus Books, L.L.C.

Excerpts from *Liberty and Property: Political Ideology in Eighteenth-Century Britain* by H. T. Dickinson. Copyright © 1977 by H. T. Dickinson. Reprinted by permission of Holmes & Meier.

Excerpts from "The American War" from *The Unpublished Poetry of Charles Wesley*, vol. 1, ed. S. T. Kimbrough Jr. and O. A. Beckerlegge. Copyright © 1988 by Abingdon Press. Used by permission.

Excerpts from *Methodism and Politics 1791–1851* by E. R. Taylor. Copyright © 1935 by Cambridge University Press. Reprinted with the permission of Cambridge University Press.

Excerpts from Leon O. Hynson "Human Liberty as Divine Right: A Study in the Political Maturation of John Wesley," *Journal of Church and State* 25 (1983): 57-85, are reprinted with the permission of *Journal of Church and State*.

Excerpts from *Laws of Ecclesiastical Politie*, vol. I, by Richard Hooker, edited by Georges Edelen and W. Speed Hill, Cambridge, Mass.: Harvard University Press. Copyright © 1977 by the President and Fellows of Harvard College. Reprinted by permission.

Excerpts from *Laws of Ecclesiastical Politie*, vol. III, by Richard Hooker, edited by Paul G. Stanwood and W. Speed Hill, Cambridge, Mass.: Harvard University Press. Copyright © 1981 by the President and Fellows of Harvard College. Reprinted by permission.

Excerpts from *The Works of John Welsey*, volumes 1, 2, 3, 9, 11, 20, 21, and 26. Copyright © 1982–92 by Abingdon Press. Used by permission.

For Mudie

ACKNOWLEDGMENTS

In the course of writing this book, I have been assisted, supported, and advised by various persons and institutions to whom or which I express my gratitude for their contributions and encouragement. Rex Matthews, erstwhile Academic Books Senior Editor for Abingdon Press, invited me to undertake this project. Ulrike Guthrie, his successor in that post, has seen it through to completion. Randy Maddox, chair of the Kingswood Books Committee for Abingdon Press, has applied his own impressive knowledge of John Wesley's thought and life to the editorial process. Persons who have read all or parts of the manuscript include academic colleagues Joseph L. Allen, Hendrik W. Boers, Stephen Gunter, Robin Lovin, Jong Chun Park, Theodore H. Runyon, and Pastor Robert A. Weber. Richard P. Heitzenrater and Henry Rack provided valuable information in the course of the research.

The resources of the following libraries were more than adequate to my research needs: the Pitts Theology Library and Woodruff General Library of Emory University, the New College Library and Main Library of Edinburgh University, the National Library of Scotland, and the Chung Chi College Library and Main Library of the Chinese University of Hong Kong. Their staff members proved always to be cooperative, prompt, and highly competent.

I began writing this book while Honorary Visiting Fellow of New College of Edinburgh University and member of the ministerial staff of St. Giles Cathedral—the great church in the Calvinist tradition from which John Knox led the sixteenth-century Scottish Reformation. I concluded writing most of it while a visiting professor in Chung Chi College of the Chinese University of Hong Kong. All writing in the interim took place while I was bringing to conclusion my thirty-nine years of teaching Christian social ethics in the Candler School of Theology of Emory University. I am grateful to all of those institutions for their support, and especially to their chief officers—Duncan Forrester, Principal of New College; Gilleasbuig Macmillan, Minister of St. Giles; Lo Lung-Kwong, Head of the Theology Division of Chung Chi College; and R. Kevin LaGree, then Dean of the Candler School of Theology.

Special thanks are due to Hendrik Boers for his encouragement, prompt responses, insightful comments, excellent technical advice, and especially his friendship, and to Eric Weber—an electronics engineer and not a theologian—for rescuing the project at the point of transferring from one computer system to another.

My gratitude to my wife, Mudie Overstrom Weber, is a response not to her contributions to this research and writing project—which in ways indirect have been quite considerable—but to her love and companionship through more than forty-five years of marriage. It cannot be measured or verbalized. I express it simply by dedicating this book to her.

CONTENTS

Abbreviations

Concise Eccles. History	John Wesley, *A Concise Ecclesiastical History from the Birth of Christ to the Beginning of the Present Century* (abridged from John L. Mosheim), 4 vols. (London: Paramore, 1781).
Concise History of England	John Wesley, *A Concise History of England from the Earliest Times to the Death of George II*, 4 vols. (London: R. Hawes, 1776).
Journal CW	*The Journal of the Rev. Charles Wesley, M.A.*, ed. Thomas Jackson, 2 vols. (London: Wesleyan-Methodist Book Room, 1849; reprinted Grand Rapids: Baker Book House, 1980).
Letters (Telford)	*The Letters of the Rev. John Wesley*, A.M., ed. John Telford, 8 vols. (London: Epworth Press, 1931) [NB: Use only for letters dated after 1755].
NT Notes	John Wesley, *Explanatory Notes upon the New Testament*, 3rd corrected ed. (Bristol: Graham & Pine, 1760–62; many later reprints).
OT Notes	John Wesley, *Explanatory Notes upon the Old Testament*, 3 vols. (Bristol: W. Pine,

1765; reprinted Salem, Ohio: Schmul, 1975).

Works

The Works of John Wesley; begun as *The Oxford Edition of The Works of John Wesley* (Oxford: Clarendon Press, 1975–83); continued as *The Bicentennial Edition of The Works of John Wesley* (Nashville: Abingdon Press, 1984–); 15 of 35 vols. published to date.

Works (Jackson)

The Works of John Wesley, ed. Thomas Jackson, 14 vols. (London, 1872; Grand Rapids: Zondervan, 1958).

Writings SW

Susanna Wesley: The Complete Writings, ed. Charles Wallace Jr. (New York: Oxford University Press, 1997).

PREFACE

My first venture into John Wesley's political thought was a long paper titled "A Comparison of Responses to the American Revolution: John Wesley and the American Methodist Preachers." I wrote it for Professor H. Richard Niebuhr's course in Christian Ethics, in the Yale Divinity School in the winter and spring quarters of 1949. One might wonder why—with that beginning—it took me more than fifty years to produce a book on the topic. The explanation is easy. When the Candler School of Theology of Emory University hired me in 1958 as a young instructor in the field of social ethics, its faculty was populated with persons who knew a great deal about Wesley and Methodism. Preeminent among them was Dean—later Bishop—William R. Cannon. When I suggested to someone that I might like to teach a course on Wesley's social thought, my request was greeted with a vacant stare and a kind of guttural noise that seemed to imply either that I was an impostor in a field of experts or that there was no such subject to be taught. Thus rebuffed, I contented myself with teaching broadly in the field of Christian social ethics, and specifically in historical and contemporary Christian political thought—but not in Wesley studies. Twenty-five years later, after all the experts had departed and I was a senior faculty person, I felt free to introduce a course on John Wesley's ethics. It may have been the only such course in existence at the time, but I am not sure. I have taught it almost every year since then, including a memorable semester in early 1999 spent inflicting it on Chinese and Indian students at the Chinese University of Hong Kong. This late-career teaching of John Wesley's ethics prompted me to end the delay in writing a book on Wesley's political thought.

As a result of this personal academic history, I approach the topic as a theological ethicist, not as a Wesley specialist, and specifically not as a Wesley historian. I am interested more in the theological and moral reasoning—present, absent, or implied—in Wesley's political thought than in the details and impact of his political history. That is why much of the book (chapters 6 through 11) is devoted to conceptual analyses of Wesley's thought on perennial political issues such as representation, authority, obligation, the state, rights, and war. Also, as a veteran teacher of many courses and seminars in Christian political thought, I have attempted to place Wesley's political thinking in the context of centuries of theological and political argument, as well as of English politics in the seventeenth and eighteenth centuries, and to show its relationship to the variety of viewpoints on and interpretations of these topics that have emerged and contended with each other in Christian history.[1]

Of course, historical inquiry is essential—especially in the case of someone like John Wesley, whose meager political writings were polemical missiles in the midst of struggle, and whose political thinking was contextual and historical rather than abstract and philosophical.[2] Therefore I devote chapters 2 through 5 of the book to historical study of his political development. However, readers interested in the political course and influence of the Methodist movement, the Halévy thesis concerning Methodism's impact on prospects for a French-type revolution in England, the internal politics of Wesleyan and post–Wesley Methodism, or the political thought of persons in the movement other than Wesley, should turn instead to the distinguished works of social historians such as Elie Halévy, E. R. Taylor, Wellman J. Warner, E. P. Thompson, Bernard Semmel, John Walsh, and David Hempton.[3] The concerns of this book are with Wesley himself and with the nature and content of his political thought.

It would not suffice for me to present a historical and analytical study of John Wesley's political thought without offering some theological engagement with both Wesley and the subject matter of politics. I do this mainly in the opening chapter, where I pose the problem of a Wesleyan political language, and in the concluding one, where I explore the prospects for recovering the political image of God as the principal means of *bringing politics into the order of salvation.* This exploration of the concept of the political image is my principal theological contribution to a Wesleyan discussion of political thought and ethics, as well as of other dimensions of Wesleyan theology. I advanced the concept of the political image in a paper presented to the Wesley Studies Group of the American Academy of Religion in November 1990, and published in 1995 under the title, "Political Order in *Ordo Salutis:* A Wesleyan Theory of Political Institutions."[4] At the Tenth Oxford Institute for Methodist Theological Studies (1997), I developed the concept further in a paper on "The 'Political Image' and Wesleyan Political Language." These two papers issued in the theological argument of the present volume.[5]

Both aspects of the book—the historical/analytical and the theological—reflect concerns of churchmanship, and not only those of academic scholarship. Although I write as an academic person, I write also as a Methodist pastor committed to the church, the quality of its common life, and its role in the serving and reconciling work of God. I have attempted to combine research into John Wesley's political thought with reflection on largely unexamined dimensions of his theology to the end of encouraging among all persons and denominations in the Wesleyan tradition experiments in formulating an authentic and efficacious Wesleyan political language. It is a language of service, not of the dominating uses of power. I hope also that these efforts will contribute to ecumenical discourse over the political vocation of humankind under God to care for the earth and all the inhabitants thereof.

Atlanta, Georgia
January 2000

CHAPTER ONE

THE PROBLEM OF A WESLEYAN POLITICAL LANGUAGE

The workshop on Global Mission and Political Economy of the Tenth Oxford Institute for Methodist Theological Studies (1997) opened under a serious handicap: Its members met as Wesleyans to consider issues of politics in a global context, but without a common Wesleyan political language with which to communicate with one another and to address their political agenda. Lutherans can speak the language of Two Kingdoms if they choose to do so, Roman Catholics that of natural law, Calvinists that of covenant and federalism, and Mennonites that of a community of faithful disciples living under the law of Christ, but Wesleyans have no common symbols of discourse deriving from their own theological tradition with which to think and speak as *Wesleyans* about the meaning of political reality and responsibility.

By *political language* I mean a form of communication that interprets political reality and sets expectations for political behavior. In the Christian traditions the political language is a distinctive idiom that embodies and expresses a communion's characteristic and fundamental theological perspectives. It is a *religious* language, to be sure, but it is simultaneously, coevally, and inherently a *political* language, permeated with understandings of state, people, authority, obedience, law, but integrated—more or less—with understandings of the saving work of God. Adherents of a given tradition may not always use their common language, and sometimes they may offend against its implications and requirements, but they have the language to use, and if they are brought up rightly in those traditions, they know how to speak it.

If there is a *Wesleyan* political language, it was not available to the members of the workshop because it does not seem to be in use in contemporary Methodist literature on political questions. When the United Methodist bishops declared themselves in *In Defense of Creation* and addressed issues of nuclear war and deterrence, their few scattered references to John Wesley mainly reiterated his claim that war was the chief manifestation of original sin.[1] At no time did they advise the Methodist faithful—and others who might be listening in—on how to think about such matters in a Wesleyan theological manner, nor did they employ and exemplify a characteristically Wesleyan approach in their own deliberations. When theological ethicist Paul Ramsey rebuked the bishops of his church for errors in theological and political thinking in *In Defense of Creation*, and challenged them to *Speak Up for Just War or Pacifism*, he made much more explicit use of Wesley, and more authentic and constructive use of Wesley's doctrine of original sin for thinking about the responsibilities of states in a fallen world.[2] But even Ramsey did not draw on *Wesley's* manner of thinking theologically about politics, or indeed on any historically developed and commonly accepted Wesleyan approach.

If we cast our view more widely, if we examine Methodist statements on social issues over the past fifty or so years, if we scan the writings on political questions of Methodist theologians and ethicists (in addition to Ramsey), we find much the same thing. References to Wesley are more a matter of claiming relationship than of drawing substance. Theologically informed writings on political questions reflect diverse and mixed theological influences—liberal, Niebuhrian, Barthian, evangelical, process, liberationist, black church, Mennonite. They do not communicate a sense of working within a Wesleyan tradition of political discourse. And if, furthermore, we ask laity in the Wesleyan family to identify themselves politically, they reach for secular symbols—conservative, liberal, socialist—not theological ones. It would not occur to most of them to interpret political choices and to understand and identify themselves in relation to those choices through the use of Wesleyan political language, or through the use of any theological language for that matter.

The reason that neither the United Methodist bishops nor United Methodist professor Paul Ramsey, nor other statements and writings from Methodist sources, draw on a specifically Wesleyan method and framework for interpreting political reality and determining political responsibility is that none exists in any form commonly acceptable among the spiritual legatees of John Wesley. There is no Wesleyan "political theology"—no political-moral doctrine expressive of Wesleyan theology manifest throughout Methodist history, taught universally in Methodist seminaries and church schools, sung in the hymns, preached from the pulpits, formative of the Social Principles of The United Methodist Church, motivationally powerful in the character of Methodists and others in the Wesleyan tradition. Wesleyanism does have strong social and humane commitments rising out of Wesley's concern for the poor and his history of establishing educational and charitable institutions, but it has no characteristic, commonly accepted, publicly recognizable symbols for contextualizing these commitments politically. It is true, of course, that Methodists and their Wesleyan kinfolk *do* politics in various and sundry contexts, including the church itself, but they do not *see* politics with a common clarifying vision and they do not *speak* politics with a common tongue.

I recall, by contrast, my experience some years ago of sharing a seminar with Professor Trutz Rendtorff of the theological faculty of the University of Munich. Professor Rendtorff's seminar was on "The Problem of the State in Protestant Thought." Quickly it became apparent that "Protestant" was to be translated as "Lutheran," or even more particularly, "*German* Lutheran." The seminar presupposed Luther's political thought, drew on the profound and extensive resources of German Lutheranism, and tested all the newer proposals against Luther's *Zweireichelehre*.[3] When I lectured on Reinhold Niebuhr's reformulation of democratic philosophy, the students were interested in Niebuhr's "Vindication of Democracy and Critique of Its Traditional Defense,"[4] but they insisted on drawing Niebuhr also into the Lutheran framework by reason of his Lutheran roots and the Lutheran elements in his theology (and his aggressively German name!). I have reflected subsequently, on several occasions, that I could not teach a similar seminar on Wesleyan political thought, not only because I would place the material in a wider and more ecumenical context, but also—and mainly—because there is no comparable tradition of political thought and ethics in Methodism. A Wesleyan political language once existed, but after the middle of the nineteenth century it disappeared into the sand. Even if it had continued, its conservative and repressive character was such that I could not give it such weight of authority. For the Protestant students in Munich, on the contrary, Lutheran language continued to be the way to speak theologically about politics—however strange their applications might have seemed to Luther.

THE RISE AND FALL OF A WESLEYAN POLITICAL LANGUAGE

In the decades following the death of John Wesley (1791), Methodist leaders in England deliberately—and to a great extent, successfully—created a Wesleyan political language, and made it a fundamental element of Methodist self-understanding. It was the language of passive obedience and nonresistance, of public order as the prime public value, of homage to a patriarchal monarch set in authority over the people by God and responsible for their welfare in ways that they were not. It discouraged ordinary people from political involvement, made political nonparticipation a virtue for Methodists, and instructed the faithful to attend not to public duties but to the duties of the stations to which God had appointed them. It was antirepublican, antidemocratic, aggressively respectful of the established order, and therefore thoroughly conservative. This language was adopted and enforced by the Methodist Conference, and given theoretical elaboration and wide publicity through the sermons and writings of Methodist leaders such as Jabez Bunting and Richard Watson. Increasingly it signaled identification with the Tory Party, especially in the struggle to retain legal discrimination against Roman Catholics.[5]

And it was demonstrably *Wesleyan* political language. The leaders who shaped this language did not create it out of nothing. All of the elements were present and prominent in the political thinking of John Wesley, the self-proclaimed Tory: reverence for monarchy, the notion of authority descending from God and not rising from the people, commitment to public order, obedience and nonresistance, professions of noninvolvement in political questions. In Wesley these elements were traditional and presuppositional, but not synthesized into a consistent political theory. The post-Wesley leaders of Methodism drew them together into a more conceptually organized, theologically supported set of symbols, and used the product to discipline the Methodists ecclesiastically and politically and to domesticate Methodism in English society. As David Hempton observed, partly with reference to this development, "Methodism converted Wesley's conservative tendencies into a conservative habit."[6] There were, to be sure, other aspects of Wesley's political thought—among them his passionate defense of religious and civil liberty and a strong constitutionalism that subordinated royal power to law. But these elements conflicted with tendencies toward passivity and autocracy, and were suppressed or subordinated in the post–Wesley formulation. They did not become dominant aspects of historic Wesleyan political language. The conservative, autocratic selection and synthesis became the concrete form the language took in history.

This language did not and could not establish itself as the enduring political idiom of the Methodist movement. To begin with, it had no universal applicability within Methodism. Factors peculiar to needs of English Methodism in the late eighteenth and early nineteenth centuries drove the process of its formation. Within the Methodist Connection, it was used to perpetuate in the connectional leadership the autocratic, clerical control that Wesley had established in his own person, but without Wesley's kindness and personal charisma. Within the wider context of English society, it was a means of protecting the Methodist movement from persecution and suppression. The second of these purposes actually was present from the early years of Wesley's evangelistic enterprise, but it received additional and special impetus in the nineteenth century for reasons deriving from the movement's success.

Bernard Semmel reports that in the years following the French Revolution the Methodist movement came under great suspicion because of the popular base of its membership, its egalitarian theological doctrines, its vitality and dynamism, its accelerating growth, and its disciplined organization.[7] Protectors of the social and political order wondered—often out loud and in print— whether Methodism would be, intentionally or otherwise, the social engine that would drive the British Revolution. Protectors of the national church, long convinced that Wesley and his unauthorized but successful ways were subversive of ecclesiastical order and control, became even more worried and threatening as Methodist evangelists moved from the mines and factories, where the church was a weak presence, to towns and cities, where it had traditional strength. For these reasons, the Methodist Connection came under vigorous attack.

The points of vulnerability for the Methodists were the itinerancy and the licensing of preachers. The movement depended for its success, if not its survival, on the mobility of its preachers and on the use of laypersons as preachers. Aware of this dependency, opponents of Methodism attempted to cripple it at both points. One tactic was to apply the Act of Toleration to the Methodists as Dissenters, rather than as members of the Church of England.[8] The Methodists would be allowed ministers as Dissenters, but their ministers would have to be settled clergy. That would end the itinerancy. Another tactic, begun by Lord Sidmouth in 1811, was to extend the Act of Toleration by tightening licensing requirements for preachers. He intended explicitly to exclude from licensing qualification persons "who were coblers [sic], tailors, pig-drovers, and chimney-sweepers, situations which disqualified them from being teachers and instructors of their fellow subjects."[9] Of course, these were precisely the "situations" from which the Methodists drew many of their preachers. To refuse them licenses would eliminate most of the candidates.

Eventually these efforts were defeated and the Methodists moved, perhaps unfortunately, to a position of respectability and influence. But their response to the threat had been an aggressive campaign to disarm their critics by establishing a public image of Methodism as politically neutered (but not neutralized), helpful, and subservient—a religious order of political eunuchs. They feared God and honored the king. They taught and required obedience to governing authorities, would offer no political interference, and would never countenance revolution. They were friends and beneficiaries of public order, not a threat to it. The Methodists were models of moral propriety, attentive to their duties, sober, reliable, always law-abiding. If all were Methodists, they contended, there would be no disorder.[10] When, in the course of supporting the resisters to liberalization of restrictions on Roman Catholics, the Methodists increasingly identified themselves as Tories, they gave their ideology a label and an institutional framework that supported inculcation and continuity.[11]

Wesleyan political language as it emerged in history was not a pedagogy for the Methodist movement existing and acting in diverse political venues. It was an *English Methodist* ideology designed for institutional control and denominational survival under conditions particular to England in the early nineteenth century. It was not transferable to other situations—even including England at a later time. Quite obviously, it was neither useful nor attractive to Methodists living in the new republic of the United States of America. The American colonies had repudiated loyalty to the king and allegiance to England through a war for independence. In place of royal authority and the governance of Parliament, they had established a republican form of government with authority from the people. John Wesley had opposed independence, republicanism, and popular authority. American Methodists suffered persecution because of Wesley's well-publicized views, whether they agreed with him or not. Most of the Loyalists among the Methodists—approximately one-third of the membership—left the colonies and moved to Canada. The remainder had to assure their fellow citizens and the officials of the government of their loyalty to the Constitution and the new republic. They confirmed this loyalty by adding to their twenty-four Articles of Religion one titled "Of the Rulers of the United States of America." It reads: "The President, the Congress, the general assemblies, the governors, and the councils of state, *as the delegates of the people,* are the rulers of the United States of America, according to the division of power made to them by the Constitution of the United States and by the constitutions of their respective states. And the said states are a sovereign and independent nation, and ought not to be subject to any foreign jurisdiction."[12] John Wesley, pragmatist and believer in divine providence, conceded to political reality and accepted this historic outcome. But the words of the article—especially those referring to officials as "delegates of the people"—did not represent the political convictions either of Wesley or of his clerical successors in English Methodism.

Methodists in the new United States spoke a different political language from the one developed for the English context. It was not *Wesleyan* political language.

One might infer, of course, that Wesleyan political language as developed in England remained the authoritative norm, and that the American Methodists—not for the first or last time—made an unorthodox departure from Wesleyan standards to serve their own particular needs. The problem with this inference is that tensions in English Methodist political orthodoxy appeared already in the eighteenth century, and accelerated to explosive force in the first half of the nineteenth. Within the Methodist ranks were persons who spoke the rights language of John Locke and Thomas Paine more fluently and fervently than the obedience language of John Wesley. The influence of the French Revolution as event and ideology encouraged their hopes and their activism, and thereby confirmed the suspicions of the conservatives. Many laity and some clergy demanded more openness and influence in the Conference, and resented and resisted the persistent efforts of "Methodist Pope" Bunting and others to consolidate and extend autocratic clerical control. In addition, laity increasingly wanted influence in British society and politics commensurate with their rising status and affluence, but were restrained by the political passivity and the "no politics" rule of Methodist teaching and practice. Because the established positions were defended with conservative Wesleyan political ideology, the laity and their clergy sympathizers turned more and more to the liberal rhetoric of rights, republicanism, and authorization of power from below to legitimate their claims. These tensions produced frequent and progressively serious defections from Wesleyan Methodist ranks, culminating in a massive split of the denomination in 1851. They produced also a transformation in Methodist political attitude and language. "By 1851," E. R. Taylor wrote, "there were two distinct political types in Methodism, one Conservative and one Liberal."[13] These types did not stabilize into Methodist alternatives; the liberal type won. According to Taylor, "As Methodism became more Nonconformist, it became more Liberal. Its desertion from an authoritarian system of Church government, and its progressive adoption of democratic ideals and a democratic constitution (especially in its 'schismatic'

THE PROBLEM OF A WESLEYAN POLITICAL LANGUAGE

branches), were accompanied by a change of political allegiance from Toryism to Liberalism."[14] The historic reign of Wesleyan political language was over.[15]

The history of this development and transformation falls outside our present interest. The point is that the departure from Wesleyan political language was an English Methodist transition and not simply an American aberration. Wesleyan political conservatism served a limited purpose of protection and control in a particular historical setting, but it failed to establish itself permanently as normative language for the Methodist movement. Obviously, it was not able to withstand the force of the liberal political philosophy that subsequently became the norm for vast sections of the modern world. But why did it lose out? Was this an accommodation to the impulses of modernity, driven by the desire to be large and influential rather than accept sectarian status and maintain the purity of the witness? Or were there theological reasons internal to Wesleyanism—specifically, conflicts within Wesley's own theology—that led to the repudiation of the historic political language without its being replaced with one that was theologically more defensible?

Both explanations apply. All of the great Christian traditions have found it necessary to adapt their political thinking to the emergence of democracy and republicanism in order to retain political influence and credibility. Such adaptation is at work clearly and explicitly in the social encyclicals of Pope Leo XIII (1878–1903),[16] and in Helmut Thielicke's efforts to show the contemporary relevance of Romans 13 and traditional Lutheran "Two Kingdoms" teaching.[17] Calvinism, already more "modern" than Roman Catholicism and Lutheranism, moved its covenantal and federal theology quite naturally into evolving constitutionalism with separation and balance of powers. It would be surprising if an expanding movement like nineteenth-century Methodism should fail to read the signs of the times and make its own accommodation to dominant political currents.

However, the three aforementioned traditions made their adaptations in the context of their characteristic theologies and with the use of their fundamental symbols for interpreting and relating to political reality. The Methodists, by contrast, rejected their own established political-theological symbols in their turn toward democracy and republicanism. On the surface, it appeared that they had rejected the traditional stance for nontheological reasons, and in its place had packaged a secular political orientation loosely with a pious, individualistic theology of salvation. To some extent that is true. But careful and insightful research has demonstrated that sources of the rejection of established Wesleyan political language are to be found also in Wesleyan theology itself.

For some time now interpreters of Methodism have argued that there is strong affinity between elements in the Wesleyan theology of salvation and basic aspects of liberal democratic political philosophy. In 1935 E. R. Taylor wrote, "Believers in a doctrine of Assurance found much in the democratic ideals of Liberalism which might be regarded as a natural corollary to their religion."[18] Taylor attributes the emergence and substance of Methodist liberalism more to Wesley's doctrines of salvation and assurance than to his social conscience and his own interventionist tendencies. By focusing on the political influences of these theological sources he clearly anticipated Bernard Semmel's thesis concerning the inherent democratic tendencies in Methodism. Semmel, in 1973, argued much more expansively in *The Methodist Revolution* that Wesley's "Arminian" doctrines of spiritual equality and the universal accessibility of salvation translated politically into democratizing elements in late-eighteenth- and early-nineteenth-century Methodism. This process of translation revealed a fundamental conflict between traditional Wesleyan political language and the most characteristic, most enduring aspects of Wesley's theology. Once that happened, the conservative political language no longer could have normative and canonical status within Methodism.[19]

Nevertheless, democracy and republicanism could not simply replace it and become established theologically as *Wesleyan* political language. They were not Wesley's politics. He personally did not infer them from "free grace and a dying love." To call this new political language *Wesleyan* in any historical sense would be simply to deny uncomfortable historical facts. Failing a more thoroughgoing integration of the theology of Wesley's politics with his theology of salvation, the Methodists were left with no political language of their own. But because they could not content themselves with being merely a pietistic sect focused on the life to come, they borrowed various languages from other sources—most commonly from liberal democratic philosophy. These political languages, to the extent that they had any theological affiliation at all, reflected optimistic Enlightenment views of human nature, rather than the orthodox Reformation view held by John Wesley. They believed in human goodness and its potentiality, but not in original sin.

PROSPECTS, PORTRAITS, AND PROBLEMS

This book was written on the premise that a Wesleyan political language is both necessary and possible. It is necessary for purposes of communication among Wesleyans on matters of political ethics, of guiding the translation of Wesleyan spirit and theology into political and social action, of completing the Wesleyan theological project, and of bringing something distinctively Wesleyan to the ecumenical table. It is possible because there are resources in John Wesley's theology—largely unnoticed by Wesley himself—that allow and enable the transcending of the limits of his eighteenth-century politics in the formulation of a political ethic and method dependent mainly on Wesleyan theology itself and not on the contingencies of political currents and conditions. With those concerns in mind, the book is both a historical and analytical inquiry into John Wesley's political thought and an attempt to provide new theological directions for political thinking in the Wesleyan tradition.

The focus on Wesley's political thought is essential, because John Wesley is the only specifically Wesleyan resource common to all branches of the Methodist family that may be usable for such a purpose. I have shown that there is no significant continuity in Wesleyan political language. It is not possible to address this topic by building on the history of Methodist political thought, as though one were adding another chapter to the progressive development of Methodist political doctrine. One must offer an invitation to reconnect directly with the founder of the movement—not as an act of filial piety or an exercise in antiquarianism, but as a necessity imposed by a history of abandonment and fragmentation in Methodist political thinking. This effort to reconnect cannot presume a simple recovery of John Wesley's political thought—as though it contained treasures of political dogma for the ages. Wesley's political thinking and acting were of the eighteenth century, contextualized in contemporary British struggles over absolutism, constitutionalism, and liberalism, and the unity or division of the empire. There are elements of general and permanent applicability, but the particular syntheses and the nuances bear the distinctive marks and scars of his time. It is an effort, rather, to gain greater understanding of the character and substance of Wesley's political thought in its concreteness, to challenge interpretations of his thought that distort its reality, and in particular to discern the relationship of his theology to his politics. The results will show us what is promising in Wesley's political thought, and what is inherently problematic.

Political Portraits: Tory, Liberal, Constitutionalist

Inherently problematic are some of the ideas and dispositions associated with the standard political portrait of John Wesley as *unreconstructed Tory.* They offer additional reasons for why a simple recovery of Wesley's political thought will not suffice to establish a Wesleyan political language. In this representation, Wesley was a thoroughly conservative man whose main political objective was to protect and preserve the institution of monarch ruling by divine right, and whose political ethic essentially was that of passive obedience to governing authority. He was Jacobite in political sympathies, at least for the first half of his life, and with that commitment or leaning opposed the liberal currents encouraged by John Locke's political philosophy, the "Glorious Revolution" of 1688–89, and the Hanoverian succession. On theological as well as practical grounds he excluded the people as such from political responsibility and participation, and most certainly from the process of authorizing offices and the uses of power. An opponent of natural right in political ethics and a patriotic supporter of the integral British community, he opposed the independence of the American colonies from England, and called the rebels to scriptural obedience to their rulers.[20]

This political portrait has been challenged in important respects by a revisionist line of Wesley interpretation of which Bernard Semmel and Leon Hynson are the most influential representatives. The revision links Wesley with the developing line of eighteenth-century political liberalism. Semmel and Hynson both argue that early in his career Wesley was a Jacobite, comfortable with divine right notions of indefeasible right of hereditary succession and passive obedience, but that in the course of his long life he moved from absolutism and theologically grounded monarchism to a position compatible in some respects with political commitments that previously he had opposed. Semmel contends that Wesley's evangelical theology of universal grace and individual responsibility showed affinities with liberal Enlightenment notions of individual rights and contractarian constitutionalism.[21] The coincidence of theological and political lines of development contributed to Methodism's appeal and influence and to what he calls the "Methodist Revolution." Hynson's central contention is that as Wesley matured politically, he affirmed liberty as the fundamental political value.[22] In opposing republicanism and the Americans' war for independence from England he was defending the conditions of individual liberty, not making the case for monarchism and the old order. According to Hynson, Wesley's stout preference for monarchy over aristocratic and especially democratic forms of government was based on the pragmatic judgment that monarchy provided the best guarantees of liberty, not on the theological judgment that monarchy was the form of government ordained by God. For both Semmel and Hynson, the conservative divine right ideology was one that Wesley outgrew as liberalizing tendencies became more prominent in his political thinking. His line of historical development was that of an *emergent liberal.*

Semmel and Hynson clearly are on the right track in replacing the hard-Tory picture of Wesley with one that affirms the central importance of liberty. However neither of them has made the proper identification of the political tradition or traditions that were fundamental for Wesley, and which therefore would provide the test case for linking a contemporary Wesleyan political language with Wesley's politics. The central conclusion of my own historical research is that in his fundamental political commitments John

Wesley was an *organic constitutionalist*. His constitutionalism had two sources: one was the ancient constitution with its reciprocating institutions of king, Lords, and Commons; its embedded historic rights; and its supporting and confirming traditions.[23] The other was the particular constitutional settlement of 1689, which retained the prominence of the king but without the Tory ideology that absolutized his power, demoted Parliament to an advisory body, and considered the king superior to the law (because he was the source of the law). These constitutional traditions provided the fundamental political culture in which John Wesley thought and acted. What they meant to him was that England should have a king, but that king and Parliament should rule together through a healthy coordination and limitation of branches of government. The king therefore is not absolute. He is not superior to the law, and his will is no law unless seconded by an act of Parliament. This constitutionalism was the primary context of Wesley's political thinking from the beginning of his life to its end. I find no sustainable evidence that he ever was a Jacobite, a nonjuror (in the political sense), a supporter of Stuart ambitions for recovery of the throne, or a believer in royal absolutism. To my knowledge he never used the term *divine right,* and certainly never advocated it in the sense of indefeasible right of hereditary succession. Mark John Wesley down as a constitutionalist—a believer in limited governmental power and in the primacy of law.

Wesley also held an organic view of the British community that placed him in a political tradition running from Richard Hooker to Edmund Burke, and therefore not in the tradition of individualistic liberalism. He believed that England was a unity of king (constitutional monarchy, which included Parliament), church, and people. This view is present in frequent allusions to "king and country," but it becomes explicit in "A Word to a Freeholder" (1747). In this tract Wesley is advising the readers how to vote: for the man who loves God, the king, the country's interest, and the church. Ultimately, he draws all of these loves together into a combined relationship:

> Above all, mark that man who talks of loving the Church, and does not love the King. If he does not love the King, he cannot love God. And if he does not love God, he cannot love the Church. He loves

the Church and the King just alike. For indeed he loves neither one nor the other.

O beware, you who truly love the Church, and therefore cannot but love the King; beware of dividing the King and the Church, any more than the King and country. Let others do as they will, what is that to you? Act you as an honest man, a loyal subject, a true Englishman, a lover of the country, a lover of the Church; in one word, a Christian![24]

Writers on Wesley's politics know this passage, but see it principally as evidence that Tory Wesley was suggesting implicitly that persons of good faith and judgment should vote for the Whig candidate.[25] The Tory candidate, who in fact might be a Jacobite, was far less likely to "love the king"—or at least a Hanoverian king. If that is Wesley's meaning, which I agree is the case, then he is offering further evidence of his support for the constitutional and successional arrangements of 1689. However, of equal if not greater significance is the evidence it presents of Wesley's organic style of political thinking, presupposing as it does (and celebrating) the integral unity of British people and institutions. With Wesley it is a constant from early in his career to the end of his life. One misunderstands his responses to the agitation for liberty and to the American War of Independence if one does not interpret them in the context of this organic, communitarian way of experiencing and explaining the political community.[26]

In important respects, this organic constitutionalism is a conservative tradition, but it is not the conservatism of autocracy and absolutism. Rather, it is a tradition that respects established institutions that protect the values of the people, while at the same time leaving the way open to change and improvement. This organic character of society coheres with and confirms both Wesley's constitutionalism and his commitment to liberty, but in ways different from those suggested by Semmel and Hynson. Semmel agrees that Wesley in the latter part of his career was a constitutional thinker, but saw his constitutionalism as essentially contractual, based as it was on the agreements of free individuals.[27] In Wesley's thinking, however, the constitution is more a historic growth and a web of relationships than a contractual agreement. It is a social reality, one not susceptible of reduction to the wills and agreements of individual members of the society. Similarly, his view of liberty is that it is a socially embedded reality, a capability or claim that is effective and assured insofar—and only insofar—as it is encompassed in supporting social relationships and paired reciprocally with corresponding duties and with the political value of order. Hynson may have this in mind in his treatment of Wesley's valuation of liberty, but his explanation of Wesley's politics as the pragmatics of liberty suggests a much less organic, more utilitarian concept. This *organic constitutionalism* with its component of embodied liberty is Wesley's primary political tradition.

The movement in Wesley research from portraying John Wesley as unreconstructed Tory ("fanatical Tory" in Albert Outler's unhappy phrase) to seeing him as emergent liberal raises the hope that further research into his politics will uncover a Wesley even more congenial to the prospects for a Wesleyan political language. The incorporation of Wesley's emphasis on rights and liberties into a concept of organic constitutionalism raises the hope even higher. Yet no amount or quality of research can exorcize the fundamental problem with Wesley's political thought, namely, his antidemocratic, antirepublican sentiments—his exclusion of the people from political responsibility and involvement and from any role in the conferring of authorization for the use of governmental power. No aggressive investigation, no artful revisionism can overcome the fact that Wesley denied a political role to the people, and that he never wavered from this conviction. What makes his stance especially intractable is that he grounded it theologically, and not only in the alleged lack of competence of the people to comprehend and prescribe for the complicated issues of public policy. In Wesley's unwavering view, authority for governing derives from God, is conferred by God on the one or ones at the peak of political responsibility in the society, and is delegated by them to lower functionaries. Authority moves from above to below, not from below to above. The people obey those set in authority over them; they do not authorize.[28] It is this inexorable conviction that later Wesleyans have found most offensive in his politics, and that has turned them away from Wesley as they have sought to work out their own political understanding as Methodist Christians. It is the reason the formulation of a Wesleyan political language requires theological reformulation, and not simply revisionist history.

Theological Language and Political Language

Any attempt at theological reformulation must reckon with the fact that a defining Wesleyan theological language already exists. It is the *ordo salutis*, the order or way of salvation—God's prevenient, justifying, sanctifying grace. It is the account of God's redeeming love, offered to all humankind freely and without exception, and of the empowerment to accept that love, so that "whosoever will, may come." Unfortunately, it is not a *political* language. As formulated by John Wesley, the *ordo salutis* is not comparable to Catholic natural law or the Lutheran Two Kingdoms as a device for attempting to account for both Christian and societal identity and action. Despite Wesley's insistence that "we know no holiness but social holiness," salvation language is spoken primarily of and for individuals in their relationship with God, not of the conditions of corporate existence, the nature of the state, the moral properties of collectives, or the meaning of societal power in the light of the work of God. Its symbolics convey neither a sense of political reality nor a design for Christian political vocation. It does not combine naturally with Wesley's political thought to form a coherent synthesis. Nevertheless it is there, and no one rightly can deny that it defines the theological heart of Methodism in its various forms. Any specifically *Wesleyan* theological reformulation, not excepting efforts to develop a Wesleyan *political* language, must either proceed from this language or at least be integrated with it.

Does a political language proceed from this Wesleyan theological language? Is the *ordo salutis* the source from which a Christian language of politics can be evoked and developed, even though as delineated by Wesley it is not itself political? The affinity observed by Taylor and Semmel between the liberal democratic philosophy of the Enlightenment and Wesley's doctrines of assurance, spiritual equality, and universal grace suggests that the *ordo salutis* contains an implicit political philosophy, requiring only the political exegesis of the grand themes of salvation to reveal it and prepare it for systematization. With sufficient inducement this evangelically derived politics will emerge armed with doctrines of universal suffrage, popular sovereignty, and representation.

There is affinity between the Wesleyan theology of salvation and the Enlightenment political philosophy. It helped inspire and support the Methodist rebellion against clerical and political conservatism and autocracy and the repudiation of the historic Wesleyan political language. But did the liberating theology give birth to the liberal politics? Did rebellious Methodists draw political conclusions from their language of salvation and then notice the affinity, or did they act from secular political inspiration and then find their rebellion confirmed by their doctrine and religious experience? If the former is the case, the Wesleyan political language should have been established theologically and ratified institutionally in this democratic idiom long ago. If the latter is the case, the affinity may be to some extent a historical accident—the selection of some elements out of the richness of religious experience while ignoring or suppressing others.

This affinity is more than mere historical accident. It is grounded christologically in the election of the human race, in the offer of pardon to all sinners, in the sanctifying power of transformation that arises out of the grace of justification. But the likely outcome of using the *ordo salutis* alone as the source of Wesleyan political language, especially given the affinity to eighteenth-century secular, democratic philosophy, is an emphatically individualistic politics. It does not support theologically Wesley's own strongly corporate sense of the British community and the social embodiment of rights and liberties. It seems to confirm the contention, offered above, that Wesley's order or way of salvation is oriented toward individual destiny and does not embody truly *political* thinking. It resonates well with the Lockean political philosophy that Wesley rejected, and with the views of the "warm men" for liberty whom Wesley opposed so vigorously. Much of the organic and corporate sense that Wesley might contribute to the enriching and stabilizing of democratic philosophy would be lost if a theory of and ethics for politics were to be deduced from Wesley's formulation of the order of salvation.

Even if the theological language of Methodism does not engender a political language that is sufficiently *political*, is it possible to achieve the desired linguistic results by integrating Wesley's actual political thought with his evangelical theology? Unfortunately not, because Wesley's politics and his understanding of *ordo salutis* are in direct contradiction on two fundamental points. One is the concept of God. The God of Wesley's politics is a hierarchical first person of the Trinity—above us, judging, dispensing, disposing. The God of the order of salvation, by contrast, reflects primarily the immanent second and third persons of the Trinity—God with us, not above us—sacrificing, sharing, participating, empowering. The second point is the contrasting roles of the people in politics and salvation. In politics the people have no role, whereas salvation is for all the people. The differences are theological, not practical. In politics divine authorization descends from above, electing those who are to rule, and excluding the rest. In the way of salvation God elects the entire human race, and offers to equip each person for participation in the work of God. These are fundamental differences, requiring in both cases a transformation of the understanding of the relationship of God to politics, and therefore of the understanding of politics itself.

THE PROMISE OF THE POLITICAL IMAGE

The possibilities for a Wesleyan political language depend on *bringing politics into the order of salvation,* not on integrating an autocratic concept of political authority with an egalitarian concept of access to redemption. Incorporating politics into the *ordo salutis* necessitates the democratization of the concept of political authority—unless of course one prefers to abandon the universal availability of saving grace. This democratizing consequence repudiates the central tenet of Wesley's political thought: the hierarchical descent of political authority from God to the rulers. To claim any authenticity in Wesleyan political language, such a transformation must be directed from within Wesley's theology itself, and not be imposed for reasons of preferred ideology. That inevitably implies using the language and concepts of the way of salvation—of prevenient, justifying, sanctifying grace. As we have seen, however, the *ordo salutis* as John Wesley developed it theologically does not suffice to support the corporate elements of a political language. Inferring liberty and equality from free and universal grace does not produce notions of either integral political society or political vocation.

All of these issues can be dealt with authentically and successfully through the development of a concept latent in Wesley's theology: the *political image of God*. John Wesley considered the political image to be of the essence of human nature. Human beings were constituted as such to image God politically—in the benevolent and productive care of the creation. *Political image* implies agency: humankind acts on behalf of God in the governing of the world. It is vocational: the political work of governing is the mission of humankind and the fulfillment of being human. It is corporate: this political vocation of imaging God is given to the whole of humankind, not to some selected or elected part thereof. It is authorizing: the authority to govern is given by God to the whole people (not first to the rulers), who then may confer limited authorization on persons and institutions to guide and assist them in the fulfillment of their common vocation. These implications are drawn justifiably from Wesley's own theology, but they have the effect of standing his concept of political authority on its head. At the same time, they both allow and require politics to be drawn into the order of salvation.

Recovering and developing the concept of the political image for a Wesleyan political language constitutes the constructive proposal of this book. Most of what I have to offer on the topic will appear in the final chapter. For the present I must point out that Wesley gave it very little attention, and never drew its revolutionary implications for his understanding of political authority. John Wesley set forth a concept of the *whole image of God* with three dimensions— *natural, political, moral*—and made the recovery of the whole image the focus of his evangelism and its supporting theology. In practice, however, he showed real and consistent interest only in the recovery of the moral image. His neglect of the political image blocked the integration of his politics and his understanding of the way of salvation. It hindered the formulation of a Wesleyan social ethic by focusing on an individualistic concept of Christian love largely incapable of dealing with questions of institution and power. It encouraged controversies over the meaning of Christian perfection and entire sanctification that often were sterile because their *moral image* concerns had no inherent or integral social and relational dimensions.

The recovery of the political image will address these problems, and in doing so will both clash with aspects of Wesley's politics and govern the formulation of a Wesleyan political language. The language it generates will function as do the political languages of other great Christian communions: it will require and enable Christians in the Wesleyan tradition to engage the political challenges of their own day; to discern with biblical and theological integrity the meanings of political reality and responsibility; and to confront in the light of those meanings the great and perennial issues of political authority and obligation, the nature and purpose of state and government, the grounds and definitions of rights and liberties, the mandates of justice, and the moral imperatives of peace and war. Moreover, it will authorize them to do so with confidence in the theological validity of their own representative and democratic political institutions—a point Wesley himself was not inclined to concede. On the other hand, it will not *require* democracy as a theologically necessary or preeminent system. The whole point of the political language is to incorporate Christians into the political work of God in whatever circumstances they find themselves.

None of the other established political languages is dogmatically exclusive. Each intends to express the fundamental theological orientation of its tradition, but all of them are available for borrowing and at times eclectic combination. So must it be with a prospective Wesleyan political language. It must bring to expression the fundamental elements of Wesleyan theology, and yet do so in such manner as to invite authentication wherever persons inquire into their responsibilities before God and humankind in the name and spirit of Christ.

Having sketched in preliminary fashion the theological route to the formulation of a Wesleyan political language, I now must turn to historical and analytical study of John Wesley's politics—first to a review of his development through eighteenth-century political controversies, and then to a conceptual analysis of particular political ideas and attitudes. In the final chapter, I return to explicitly theological method. The two methods are distinct, but nevertheless essential to each other. The historical approach in this case is not simply *non*theological, because part of its work is to discern the theology supporting Wesley's political attitudes. In that sense, theological inquiry belongs to the method of historical inquiry. The theological method in the formulation of a Wesleyan political language must connect with the politics of historic Methodism, because it addresses itself to a particular communion and not "to whom it may concern." It must draw honestly on the historical record, not changing it to serve its own aims, but also not accepting the historical record as the norm and limit of theology. A Wesleyan political language is, after all, a development in and from Wesley's *theology*, and not a reproduction of Wesley's politics.

As the course of its formulation proceeds, it will of necessity transcend the boundaries of politics narrowly defined. In doing so, it also will transform Wesleyan theology as such, and guide the completion of the Wesleyan theological project.

PART ONE

JOHN WESLEY'S POLITICAL DEVELOPMENT

CHAPTER TWO

READING THE POLITICAL RECORD: YOUNG MR. WESLEY'S POLITICS

To establish a reasonably accurate representation of John Wesley's politics one must analyze his political record, and not be diverted either by political labels ascribed to him or by his own protestations of political disinterest and incompetence. Wesley was a Tory, to be sure, but in eighteenth-century England Toryism was diverse and complex rather than singular and monolithic.[1] The label alone will not tell us what kind of Tory he was. While not denying that Wesley wore his Tory label to the end, Bernard Semmel and Leon Hynson have argued that Wesley was a late-emerging political liberal, and have offered as evidence the political implications of his Arminian theology (Semmel) and his concern for rights and liberties (Hynson).[2] However, whatever liberalism he may have revealed was not of the contemporaneous sort. It was neither individualistic nor contractarian, and it was expressed in the conservative cause of preserving the established constitutional order. On several occasions Wesley insisted that he was not a political person, that he had no special competence entitling him to make political judgments, and that his preachers should stay clear of politics.[3] In each of these cases, however, he sent a political message, thereby calling in question his claims to political innocency, unconcern, and impartiality, and confusing his political self-representation. These pointers to John Wesley's politics are worth investigating in their own right, but each of them risks distortion of the subject matter when taken as the starting point. What serves the purpose better is to examine Wesley's responses to particular contexts of political conflict, and let the pattern of his politics emerge. Having done that, we should have a better understanding of the relevance of political labels and the validity of self-definitions.[4]

John Wesley made public response to three major eighteenth-century situations of political conflict. The first was the Jacobite rebellion of the 1740s, which proposed to overthrow the Hanoverian monarchy and replace it with the Stuart heir of James II. The second was the democratic—at times republican—agitation of the 1760s and later, which argued in the name of liberty and popular sovereignty for expansion of the electorate, fundamental changes in the concept and allocation of representation, and, for some, the demolition of the monarchy. The third was the American War of Independence, which threatened the unity of the British community and abetted the inner turmoil of English politics. We shall examine each of these in succeeding chapters. In this chapter we must inquire into the nonpublic, largely undeclared politics of Wesley's early years. The view of some writers on Wesley is that the ingrained, conservative, coherent worldview of those years defined his politics forever, and informed and directed his later public responses. The view of others is that this conservative stance was the one from which he departed in order to make his public responses. Our first task is to attempt to discern what that early political orientation actually was, and whether the interpreters have represented it correctly.

WESLEY FAMILY POLITICS

The overriding British political issue for at least the first half of the eighteenth century was the consolidation of the events of 1688–89, in which the Catholic James II was driven from the throne and replaced, by Parliament, with the Protestants William III and Mary II. The political consequences of these events involved the question of royal succession, the relative power of king and Parliament, and the religion of the realm. Specifically to John Wesley's time, following the death of Queen Anne in 1714 the issue was the stability and continuity of the Hanoverian succession to the English throne. George, Elector of Hanover, who as George I succeeded Anne, was a great-grandson of James I, and therefore related to the Stuarts, but he was not in the Stuart line of succession. There were in existence male descendants of James II whose succession to the throne had been blocked by Parliament, but who nonetheless considered themselves the rightful rulers of England. They and their loyal supporters, called Jacobites, managed to promote uprisings in 1715 and 1745 which, although unsuccessful, threatened existing political constructions and reinforced serious divisions in English society. These divisions were present in Wesley's own family. His father, Samuel, was a champion of the Glorious Revolution and later a loyal supporter of the Hanoverians. His mother, Susanna, remained convinced of the indefeasible right of Stuart succession, and considered William III to be a usurper.

The highlighted incident, illustrative of the political conflict between Samuel and Susanna Wesley, is reported in almost all studies of John Wesley's politics, and must be included here. On one occasion early in 1702, Susanna did not say "Amen" to Samuel's prayer for King William III. Samuel noticed this omission, and according to Mrs. Wesley's account, "retired to his study, and calling me to him asked me the reason of my not saying Amen to the Prayer. I was a little surprised at the question and don't well know what I answered, but too too well I remember what followed: He immediately kneeled down and imprecated the divine Vengeance upon himself and all his posterity if ever he touched me more or came into a bed with me before I had begged God's pardon and his, for not saying Amen to the prayer for the Kg."[5] What she actually replied, according to their son John's account, was that "she could not [say Amen] for she did not believe the Prince of Orange was King."[6] Samuel's reported response was, "If that be the case . . . you and I must part: for if we have two kings, we must have two beds."[7] Having made his resolution, he then proceeded to make good on it. He lived in Epworth separate from his wife until Easter (5 April). Then he left for London to attend Convocation, vowing also to seek a naval chaplaincy. Susanna was no less adamant. In great distress over her husband's use of sexual deprivation as a political weapon, but mainly in distress over the profound financial threat to her six children and herself, she wrote to a friend and to an eminent nonjuring clergyman seeking advice. She complained "that since I'm willing to let him quietly enjoy his opinions, he ought not to deprive me of my little liberty of conscience." She stated that she "would submit to anything or do anything in the world to oblige him to live in the house with me," but she could not do what would "mock almighty God, by begging pardon for what I think no sin."[8]

Eventually there was a reconciliation. John Wesley's explanation for it is mistaken, however. He reported that King William's death and Queen Anne's accession to the throne put an end to the conflict, because both husband and wife could agree on the legitimacy of Anne's title.[9] Samuel continued to live apart from Susanna after William's death on 8 March 1702, because he had resolved before God never to touch or cohabit with her until she repented of her sin. What brought him back was not the change of monarchs, but a fire that destroyed two-thirds of the Epworth parsonage and most of their worldly goods, and almost took the lives of Susanna and some of their children. Apparently Samuel concluded that God had taken him seriously in his swearing of his rash and terrible oath, and had visited a wrathful divine vengeance well in excess of what he might have anticipated. He moved back into the remains of the parsonage with his wife and children. Less than a year later, another son was born. They named him John.[10]

Conjugal reconciliation produced more children, but no political agreement. In 1709 Susanna wrote: "Whether they did well in driving a prince from his hereditary throne, I leave to their own consciences to determine—though I cannot tell how to think that a king of England can ever be accountable to his subjects for any maladministrations or abuse of power, but, as he derives his power from God, so to him only must he answer for using it."[11] This is classic divine right language, widely spoken by Tories, but the mother tongue of Jacobites and nonjurors (persons who refused to swear an oath of allegiance to William III and subsequent monarchs not in the direct line of succession to James II). The king derives power from God, and therefore not from people or Parliament. Accordingly, the king is answerable only to God for whatever might be done in the exercise of the royal office. Because the right to govern is divine, it is indefeasible, that is, it cannot be revoked or abridged by anyone lower than God for any reason whatsoever. There is no doubt that Susanna Wesley held these views, and that her attitude toward oaths to William III were those of a nonjuror. However, there is no evidence that she supported active Jacobite efforts for a restoration of the male line of James II. Her opposition and resistance seem to have been in the realm of conscience. Apparently they were so completely in the realm of conscience that Samuel was not aware of them until the prayer incident—a prospect that stretches credibility.

In some basic respects, Samuel Wesley's political views at the theoretical level were not greatly different from those of his wife, even though they differed on the question of royal succession. Certainly as a Tory he believed in the divine origin of power and in passive obedience and nonresistance. In 1709 a High Church clergyman, Doctor Henry Sacheverell, was indicted by the Whigs in Parliament on charges of "high crimes and misdemeanours" against the state.[12] In 1710 he was tried before Parliament and convicted. Sacheverell had preached a sermon in which he warned that the church was in grave danger, and called for stringent measures against Dissenters. Whigs in government chose to interpret his remarks as an assault on the administration of Queen Anne, and in doing so to use Sacheverell as a means of attacking the Tories. The fact that Sacheverell, a man of known Jacobite sympathies, also had argued the case for absolute passive obedience to the king, allowed the Whigs to portray his words as a critique of the Glorious Revolution. Years later John Wesley reported that his father, Samuel Wesley, had written the speech that Sacheverell presented in his defense at his trial.[13] This intimate linkage has led to speculation that Samuel developed Jacobite leanings and moved away from his earlier stance. However, historians of the Sacheverell trial do not make much of John's claim that Samuel wrote the speech. Geoffrey Holmes and G. V. Bennett do not mention Samuel Wesley. Abbie Turner Scudi cites John Wesley as the source of this information, but neither accepts nor denies the claim. Writers on the Sacheverell case accept that he had some help with or advice on the speech, mainly from Francis Atterbury, but some find the language and style consistent with Sacheverell's other writings.[14]

Even if it were true that Samuel wrote the speech, or at least contributed to it, that would not mark him a Jacobite. Samuel also was a High Church Tory, a critic of Dissenters, and a believer in passive obedience—as were many other Tories who were not Jacobites. Moreover, four-fifths of the clergy and a majority of the laity supported Sacheverell, believing that in this trial the church itself was under fundamental attack. For them, the Jacobite cause was not the issue. Whatever Samuel's involvement in this affair, it does not constitute evidence of a change in basic political views. He supported the Glorious Revolution and therefore the parliamentary determination of royal succession.[15] That alone means that he could not hold to the notion of indefeasible hereditary right. When Anne died in 1714, he supported the Hanoverian claim to the throne. In 1730, he began the process of seeking permission to dedicate his book on Job to Queen Caroline, wife of George II—something he certainly would not have done had he thought George II to be a usurper.[16] The evidence shows that Samuel Wesley Sr. was neither a Jacobite nor a nonjuror, although he did share at least some basic Tory views with his wife.

However, the case is not so clear for Samuel Wesley Jr., a man twelve years senior to his brother John. Samuel Jr. was a close friend of Bishop Francis Atterbury, who certainly was a Jacobite.[17] In 1785, John Wesley defended his long-dead brother against the charge of Jacobitism, asserting that all the Wesley men (he did not mention his mother) were Tories, in that they believed "God, not the people, to be the origin of all civil power."[18] That belief clearly was characteristic of the Tories. How it distinguished them from the Jacobites, who also held that belief, is not made clear. John Wesley apparently felt that the distinction was a clear one, and that anyone who understood it would not make such an accusation. In view of Samuel Jr.'s associations, John may have pressed the distinction too far in his case. But the fact that the lines were not so distinct in the early part of the eighteenth century meant that one might interact with Jacobites and take on some degree of Jacobite coloring without actually being one. Most commentators on the relationship between Samuel Jr. and Atterbury report Samuel as being a High Churchman with rigid principles, but not, therefore, a Jacobite.[19]

In summary, the politics of the Wesley family was rooted deeply in late-seventeenth-century Tory ideology, but was divided, as in the case of many Tories, by the events of 1688–89. The mother held clearly and firmly to all the elements of divine right, and therefore to the legitimacy of the Stuart monarchy only. However, she kept her opposition in the realm of conscience and did not engage in active resistance. The father held belief in the divine source of authority and in passive obedience and nonresistance to the reigning monarch, but supported the expulsion of James II and the enthronement of William and Mary. Therefore he abandoned (implicitly if not explicitly) the essential notion of indefeasible hereditary divine right. What is most incredible in this conflict of loyalties is that Susanna's Jacobitism was so quiet and private that it took Samuel until 1702 to discover it!

JOHN WESLEY'S "JACOBITISM"

Where did the young John Wesley stand on this issue? The broad consensus of writers on this aspect of Wesley's life and thought is that early on he was "Jacobitish" to one degree or another. That is, he stood more to the Stuart than to the Hanoverian side of the question of succession, and espoused a political ideology supporting or requiring that expression of loyalty. If true, that means he sided more with his mother than with his father. It is necessary, however, to use cautionary words such as "broad" and "to one degree or another," because some writers identify young Wesley as a Jacobite without reservation, whereas others are much more guarded in their historical inferences. Elie Halévy states flatly that "John Wesley, at Oxford, was a Jacobite."[20] Bernard Semmel adds that early on he was a supporter of the exiled Stuarts,[21] and that his "early politics, the counterpart of his Laudian theological outlook, were . . . Tory and Jacobite, and like his mentor William Law, he had even been a nonjuror."[22] By contrast, V. H. H. Green, in his very thorough and careful The Young Mr. Wesley, states that "His High-Churchmanship carried with it a dislike of the Hanoverian regime which suggested an inclination to flirt with Jacobitism, but his inherent sense of loyalty and dislike of Roman Catholicism would never have made him a Jacobite in fact."[23] Reflecting Green's argument, Henry Rack observes cautiously that at Oxford Wesley "showed some tendency to flirt with Jacobitism or at least with opposition to the government by indulging in the kind of loose talk 'against King George' and 'evil speaking' of Walpole in 1725 which was common enough among young members of the university." Rack then adds, "There is nothing remarkable about this, and there is no sign of it continuing later."[24] In reviewing this literature, one notes that writers who are reserved about Wesley's alleged Jacobitism—such as Green and Rack—tend to devote much more attention to the evidence than do those who regard his alleged Jacobitism, Stuart support, and nonjuror stance as simple matters of fact.

What does that evidence tell us? It is easy to assume that young John Wesley had Jacobite tendencies, because Jacobite sympathies were pervasive at Oxford, and during his Oxford years Wesley certainly moved in Jacobite and nonjuror circles.[25] Wesley's happy frolickings with the Kirkhams and Granvilles in their Cotswold villages during those years also provided Jacobite and nonjuror associations.[26] However, it is not easy to know precisely what Jacobite inclinations meant in political context, or how deeply such commitments were felt. The period 1714–60 was a time of Whig ascendancy, when Tories largely were excluded from power in the state and from preferments—especially to the episcopacy—in the church.[27] Tory and High Church grumblings over Whig dominance and their own exclusion from rank and power could blend somewhat sympathetically with complaints about a German king of England who was not a proper Stuart and did not rule by divine right. The Whigs, for their part, did not miss the opportunity to paint their opponents with the Jacobite brush, thereby alleging treasonable attitudes. The lines and grounds of protest and differentiation were not always clear. That was especially true in Oxford University, which suffered discrimination from a perhaps overly suspicious Whig administration. Stuart sympathies persisted, but rhetorical Jacobite rumblings at times may have had more to do with agitation for university independence and with discriminatory patronage than with theologically grounded political ideology.[28] It is not possible simply to dismiss the Jacobite influences on young John Wesley, especially in view of the fact that his associates were serious and religiously grounded persons, but neither should one infer too much and too unqualifiedly from these environmental factors. Even among these associates there were several schools of thought on the matter, one of which, according to Martin Schmidt, "confined itself to a formal protest, and merely omitted the name of the king in the prayers from the Prayer Book."[29] Most complainers acknowledged the *de facto* Hanover rule, at least implicitly. The trend was more toward accommodation than toward opposition or rebellion.

Looking directly at John Wesley's own politics, one finds no record of his ever having declared himself a Jacobite or nonjuror, or having uttered or written anything that would show him in those early years lining up clearly on one side or the other on the central question of royal succession. Vivian Green, after deciphering Wesley's diary, observed that "after conversing with his friend Pollen of Corpus 'against King George' on 14th December, 1725, he had thought fit to include among his resolutions the following Saturday evening one not to detract 'against the King.' "[30] Apparently he had criticized the king, but the reason for doing so is not given, nor is the reason for the resolution not to do so again. The latter presumably reflects his strong convictions concerning passive obedience and nonresistance, a subject he discussed with Robin Griffiths on 5 November 1725 and with Sherman on 17 January 1726.[31] If so, the implication is that George was due this regard by reason at least of *de facto* if not *de jure* possession of the throne. Worthy of note is that Wesley refers to George I as the king and not as the usurper. Green reports also that in his first diary John Wesley copied out a contemporary rhyme that presumably reflected his own sympathies:

> In Cana's town our Lord was pleas'd
> With Bridal Folk to dine,
> And to compliment the Ruler's Feast
> Turn'd Water into Wine
> But when for joy of George's Birth
> Our Rulers mounted your Theatre
> Heaven would not countenance your Mirth,
> But turned the claret into water.[32]

Unfortunately, Green does not give the date of the entry; therefore, one cannot relate this inept attempt at poetry to the resolution not to detract against King George. These entries, however limited, indicate that young Wesley clearly was not enthusiastic about the reigning king, but they do not reveal the reasons for his criticisms or the nature or extent of his disaffection. Was he critical of King George because he was not a descendant of James II, or because he presided over a Whig government that proscribed the Tories from office and treated Oxford University as hostile territory? The report of "evil speaking of Walpole" suggests the latter, especially in the absence of any reference to the succession controversy or to the Stuart pretenders to the throne. Would a young Tory at Tory Oxford have "detracted" against King George had George's government been Tory and not Whig? Green implicitly lends weight to this argument when he records "the occasion a year previously, when he and others had been talking against the government in Burman's rooms."[33] In this case, it is the government rather than the king that is the object of criticism. One must concede that at this time government and king were not easily separated, if at all, and a firm believer in passive obedience might see the two as one. But if the government is the focus of criticism, the issue under reference almost surely is something other than that of royal succession and the legitimacy of the House of Hanover.

Green reports also Wesley's interest in two sermons, one in 1726 and one in 1727, both of which were commemorative of the death by beheading of Charles I on 31 January 1649. Charles, of course, was royal martyr to the Jacobites. Wesley was stimulated sufficiently by the second sermon—preached by Dr. George Coningsbury, Vice-Principal of St. Mary Hall—that he made an extensive summary of it in his diary. Green offers two citations from these notes. One is the statement that Charles "was a 'prince . . . not alien by birth' who 'preferred to dignities in the church men of true worth and learning.' "[34] The "alien by birth" comment surely is an allusion to the fact that King George was German and spoke no English. Probably Wesley resented this condition, as did most other natives of England. The second part of the quotation reflects resentment over ecclesiastical appointments controlled by the government, especially the appointment of Whig bishops. Neither of these complaints is inherently or exclusively a Jacobite issue.

Green's second citation from Wesley's summary undoubtedly is a statement of Jacobite ideology. It sets forth a theory of sovereignty that makes the "supreme governor" (in a temporal sense) answerable only to God, and therefore (by implication) not answerable to Parliament, people, or law.[35] The parliamentary supremacy of 1689 is a direct contravention of this view, as is the notion of the subordination of the king to the law. (The king rules according to the law, but as the source of law he is above the law.) In the absence of more extensive reportage from Wesley's diary, one cannot be sure whether Wesley wrote this down simply because it was part of the sermon or because he agreed with it. The latter is possible, but if so, it is at odds with other evidence from this period of John Wesley's belief in the limitation of royal power, the coordination of king and Parliament in the ancient constitution, and the supremacy of law.

Moreover, there is no political activity by John Wesley during this period, and specifically political activity identifiable as Jacobite—unless one includes under the rubric of such activity the (politically ambiguous) college bull sessions referred to above. The activities of the Wesleys' Oxford group were pious and eleemosynary, not political. They fed the hungry, clothed the naked, visited the sick and imprisoned—as the Scriptures required. They educated unschooled children and supported the families of prisoners. They rose early, prayed, read Scripture, communed often, pored over and discussed theological tomes. They led abstemious lives, and gave to the poor whatever money was not essential to their own support. Leon Hynson refers to them as the "nonjuring Holy Club,"[36] but at no time did they give themselves a particular political identification, express political motivation, or use their corporate existence for political purposes. Specifically, they never defined themselves or acted as a Jacobite or nonjuror group, even though many of these practices were those of the nonjurors and may have resulted to some extent from nonjuror influence. Their motivations, self-definition, and activities were strictly religious. They stayed out of politics, including the politics of royal succession. Whatever they may have thought politically, they apparently did not do anything political.

One item of evidence used heretofore to establish John Wesley's credentials as Jacobite and even nonjuror now can be dismissed on the basis of new or more careful research. It is the reference to a "Jacobite sermon," cited by Luke Tyerman, and noted by numerous other authors following Tyerman. "On June 11, 1734," Tyerman wrote, "Wesley preached before the university what his brother Charles called 'his Jacobite sermon,' for which he was 'much mauled and threatened.' He was prudent enough, however, before preaching it, to get the vice-chancellor to read and approve of it, and hence was able to set 'Wadham, Merton, Exeter, and Christ Church' objectors at defiance."[37] For many years it was assumed that this sermon no longer was in existence. With no document to correct Charles's characterization of the sermon as "Jacobite," the label and the missing sermon were used to confirm John Wesley's alleged Stuart sympathies. Recently however, Richard Heitzenrater has determined that it is the sermon titled "The One Thing Needful," which was transcribed by Charles Wesley and published under Charles's name by his widow.[38] There is nothing of explicit Jacobite character or reference in the text as we now have it. It is a nonpolitical, evangelical sermon on Wesley's central theme of the recovery of the image of God. If any words of the sermon were capable of stirring contextual angers, they would be the question at the beginning as to whether "riches, or honour, or power" could be proper ends of humankind, coupled with the one near the end as to whether the one thing needful could be "to obtain honour, power, reputation, or (as the phrase is) to get preferment?"[39] These were typical complaints of Tories-out-of-power versus Whigs-in-power, and of country versus court.[40] They recall the line from the Coningsbury sermon cited above to the effect that Charles I was a prince who "preferred to dignities in the church men of true worth and learning." That line, as we saw, was an implied criticism of Whig church appointment practices. These code words might well have provoked the numerous ambitious place-seekers in the Oxford environment. However, there is nothing overtly or obviously Jacobitic in these complaints—nothing that cannot be explained more directly with reference to other elements in the dynamics of British politics and ecclesiastical or university life. To call the sermon "Jacobite" was to use a standard contemporary device for smearing and discrediting one's enemies—comparable in our own time to labeling one's opponents "Communist." Probably that is what Charles Wesley was hearing when he characterized his brother's message as his "Jacobite sermon." It is interesting that Benjamin Ingham's diary entry for 11 June 1734 offered the simple statement that "John Wesley preached."[41] Ingham, a close associate of the Wesleys in the Holy Club at Oxford, made no reference to content or reaction. Apparently the "Jacobite sermon" dissolves as an item of evidence for John Wesley's alleged Jacobite tendencies.

One other item should be mentioned, although its importance easily can be exaggerated. In a letter to his mother written when he was an Oxford student, John Wesley referred to the "abdication" of King James II.[42] The claim that James had abdicated was a casuistic trick used by promoters and defenders of the revolution to obscure the reality of his expulsion by pretending that his departure was voluntary. The claim was false, and Wesley probably knew it was false. In using this particular expression, he simply may have been using careless language, or he may have been indicating support for the revolution and opposition to the Stuarts. In either case, Mrs. Wesley could not have been pleased with her son for using a word that she as a Jacobite sympathizer certainly would consider highly offensive.

NONJUROR ASSOCIATIONS

Maximin Piette states that John Wesley's intimate involvement with nonjurors in the early 1730s (he mentions the year 1735) resulted in the firming up of Jacobite convictions. He cites specifically the influence of William Law, himself a committed nonjuror, whose writings were of great importance to John, and whom both John and Charles Wesley looked upon as their spiritual director. "In addition," Piette writes, "his friend, Clayton, put him into personal contact with Dr. Thomas Deacon. Of all the Non-jurors he was the most fiery. Now Wesley, not satisfied with fighting in defence of the Methodists, took up a very definite position, as of late did his father and elder brother, in favour of the Stuarts. His new friends, Law, Clayton, and Deacon, could not do otherwise than confirm in his mind those sentiments which his mother had professed from the accession of William III."[43]

There is no doubt that Wesley had these nonjuror associations, and that they were of considerable importance to him. He read nonjuror theologians extensively, and resonated strongly with such nonjuror emphases as the ascetic and morally disciplined life, frequent communion and other regular religious practices, the reading of patristic literature, and the authority of the primitive Christian church.[44] The ministry to the poor and the prisoners also was a nonjuror practice, as I have acknowledged in referring to the Holy Club and its activities. These were some of the marks of High Churchmanship, and John Wesley was indeed a High Churchman. What is missing from these involvements, however, is any evidence of nonjuror political style or engagement, any discussion at all with nonjurors about questions of dynastic legitimacy. If the political results were what Piette says they were, namely, that John Wesley, his father, and his brother Samuel, "took up a very definite position . . . in favour of the Stuarts," surely there would be some identifiable manifestation to support this claim. Piette records none. Nor does he offer a single citation to back his assertion that the Wesley men supported the Stuarts in the 1730s, and that John was shaped strongly toward Jacobite sympathies through his nonjuror associations. Piette contends that John Wesley was influenced toward this nonjuror political stance by William Law. However, no mention of nonjuror political concerns appears in the correspondence with William Law or in other references to their relationship, or to Law's influence on the Wesleys.[45] Law openly and admittedly was a nonjuror in the fundamental sense: he refused to take an oath of allegiance to George I—a king whom he believed to be no king at all. But Wesley's correspondence with Law is altogether about theological issues and moral and religious practice. None of it is political. At no point does either writer raise the question of the propriety of taking the oath. The claim of nonjuror political influence, and especially of the political influence of William Law, clearly is without substance.

In 1735, during this period of nonjuror association, John and Charles Wesley sailed for Georgia. Piette says that all of the persons outside John's own family with whom he consulted about this proposed missionary venture were nonjurors.[46] That apparently was true. The substance of the inquiry and the advice, however, seems to have been spiritual and religious, not political. There is nothing in Wesley's account of the Georgia mission that suggests anything to the contrary. Everything that Wesley did on this mission, every representation of political loyalty, fell within the proper and existing lines of the English constitution. George II was king, and John Wesley acknowledged him as such. King, Lords, and Commons together were the governing authorities. Wesley did not think or act otherwise. He read and expounded to his congregation the Articles of Religion and the Homilies of the Church of England, as was required of every priest.[47] These documents included teachings on obedience to governing authorities. There is not the slightest evidence that Wesley presented these teachings on political obedience with Jacobite reservations and references. His religious practices may have been in the nonjuror mode, but his political sensibilities and actions were Loyalist.

Defenders of the Wesley-as-nonjuror thesis offer as conclusive evidence the definition of nonjurors in *A Concise Ecclesiastical History from the Birth of Christ to the Beginning of the Present Century*, a book listed bibliographically under John Wesley's name. Bernard Semmel writes that "Wesley distinguished nonjurors from 'the members of the episcopal church' in that the former believed '*that it is never lawful for the people, under any provocation or pretext whatever to resist the sovereign*,' i.e., '*passive obedience*,' and that '*the hereditary succession to the throne is of divine institution, and therefore, can never be interrupted, suspended, or annulled, on any pretext.*'"[48] Semmel precedes his citation of this passage with the statement that Wesley, "like his mentor William Law . . . had even been a nonjuror."[49] The definition, then, is cited both to establish Wesley as an adherent to this position and to show how he understood his own nonjuror politics. Leon Hynson summarizes Semmel's argument thusly: "It is this early position on divine right, passive obedience, and nonresistance to which Wesley alluded in the important Dartmouth-North correspondence. There is no reason to question the claim that this was the younger Wesley's political posture."[50] Hynson apparently accepts Semmel's conclusion, and does so without challenging Semmel's reading of the passage.

Of course there is reason to question the claim—especially the designation of Wesley as nonjuror—if it is based on this particular passage. John Wesley did not write the passage. As Semmel certainly is aware, it was written by a German scholar, J. L. Mosheim. Wesley abridged Archibald Maclaine's English translation of Mosheim's Latin text, and added a "Short History of the People Called Methodists" (because Maclaine's chronological tables of heretics included Wesley and George Whitefield!).[51] Probably Wesley agreed with the description of the nonjurors, as he should, but he did not write it. Moreover, the passage cited is descriptive only of the nonjurors as a group or movement. It does not pertain specifically to Wesley and his family, nor did Wesley make such an application. He clearly does not say or mean to say, "This is my position." Furthermore, the context does not favor the nonjurors. It commends the bishops and other clergy who refused to take the oath of allegiance to William III as men "eminently distinguished by their learning and virtue," but speaks of their "mistaken notion that James II, though banished from his dominion, remained, nevertheless, their rightful sovereign."[52] The passage is even more commendatory of the men who replaced them. Quite clearly it supports the Glorious Revolution, not the people who opposed it. Finally, the passage distinguishes the nonjurors from the "episcopal church" (i.e., the Church of England), and represents them as believing that the true church (themselves) is dependent on God alone and therefore independent of the jurisdiction of king and Parliament. This may have been the position of Thomas Deacon, with whom Wesley associated for awhile, but if so, Wesley did not follow Deacon by placing himself outside the established church or advocating its independence from the arms of government.[53] In short, the passage proves the opposite of what Semmel claims for it. Intended as an objective description of the nonjurors, it also dismisses the foundation of their position. In no sense can it be used to identify John Wesley as nonjuror.

The crucial questions are these: When did John Wesley ever refuse to take an oath of allegiance to a Hanoverian king? Why did he accept ordination at the hands of a bishop whose preferment moved through a Whig administration during the reign of a German George? The models for the real nonjurors were Archbishop of Canterbury Sancroft, several of his suffragan bishops, and approximately four hundred lower clergy, who accepted deprivation of their appointments rather than swear an oath of allegiance to William III, when James II—to whom they previously had sworn an oath—was still alive.[54] If John Wesley were in the same nonjuror mode, why did he not make the same witness? Why did he take the oath? Why did he seek and accept ordination from John Potter, Bishop of Oxford and later Archbishop of Canterbury, with no apparent qualms of conscience? It would not do to say that he came under these influences subsequent to ordination, because much of the case for his alleged Stuart political sympathies rests on suppositions concerning the influence of his nonjuring mother and the Oxford environment prior to his ordination as priest in 1728. The answer would seem to be that, despite his youthful fussing about the Hanoverians and their Whig governments, he was not seriously interested in the Stuart cause. In politics, at least, he was more his father's son than his mother's. He was a Tory and a High Churchman, but neither a real Jacobite nor an ideological nonjuror. In 1735, when his nonjuror involvement was most intense, he presented his late father's scholarly book on Job to Queen Caroline, apparently without any doubts that her husband, George II, was in fact and in law the king.[55]

John Wesley's attraction to the nonjurors was religious, not political. In saying this, I am mindful of Henry Rack's warning that in this period religion and politics could not be separated.[56] But Wesley's primary concern was the salvation of his own soul, not the issues and personalities of British politics. He believed the nonjurors served that primary concern with their commitments to primitive Christianity, the church fathers, and the disciplined religious and moral life. That was the basis of his interest in them. Gordon Rupp apparently agrees with this distinction when he writes, "At any rate the Non-Juring associations were continued in some of the positive stresses of the Holy Club: the search for Primitive Christianity; the concern for frequent, nay, constant communion, for the fasts and festivals of the Church—these were more important traits than ephemeral and anachronistic notions of passive obedience, of divine right, and of loyalty to the Stuart cause, for the sake of which Susanna provoked and endured the famous family row."[57] It can be argued, also, that by the 1730s questions of true church and right religious practice had superseded the question of dynastic loyalty in defining the nonjuror movement, and that the movement had divided into several parts distinguished from one another by religious, not political, differences.[58] In general, the nonjurors were more interested in defining themselves in relation to the Church of England than to the House of Hanover. If that is so, the transposition of foci would have made it possible for Wesley to engage the religious teachings and practices of the nonjurors without being challenged significantly by their political agenda. In any event, the religious effects on John Wesley loom large, whereas the political effects are obscure or nonexistent.

THE "HIGDEN CONVERSION" THEORY

Leon Hynson argues, as does Bernard Semmel, that early on John Wesley was both Jacobite and nonjuror, and held to fundamental belief in "divine hereditary right, with its correlatives of passive obedience and nonresistance."[59] Subsequently, Wesley endorsed the notion of limited monarchy, and became a champion of religious and civil liberties. Therefore, the conservative, monarchist politics with which Wesley usually is identified should be assigned only to this early period. In later years he was a liberal. Semmel's explanation of this change is that it was moved by pragmatic considerations pertinent to the vulnerability of the Methodist movement in the early 1740s. When the Pretender became more active in promoting rebellion at a time when the alleged usurper (George II) had become established more firmly on the throne, it became prudent to transfer loyalty—and with it passive obedience and nonresistance—to the House of Hanover, especially in view of the massive degree of violence that would be necessary to effect a change in ruling dynasties.[60] Although Hynson agrees that Wesley was a pragmatist, he sees the roots of reorientation at an earlier point and in a kind of intellectual conversion. The crucial factor, in Hynson's view, was Wesley's reading in 1733 of William Higden's *A View of the English Constitution*.[61] Higden, according to Hynson, was a repentant nonjuror who sought to reconcile himself to the Revolution of 1689 by reviewing the established distinction between monarchs *de jure* (by hereditary title) and *de facto*, and arguing that even the latter ruled with royal authority, because the legal enactments of their reigns were regarded as law by subsequent monarchs. "In his study," Hynson reports, "Higden came to the conclusion that the supreme authority of the English government rests in the king 'for the time being,' that is, in the reigning monarch. To this king the people owe allegiance, by requirement of both common and statute law, whether he was king de jure or de facto, or both."[62] Given that interpretation, Higden could regard all royal successors to James II as monarchs to whom oaths of loyalty were due even if they were not in the true line of hereditary succession. Therefore he could support, with justification, the Hanoverian line.

John Wesley's one reference to Higden's book appeared in a letter to Samuel Brewster, identified as "a friendly Non-Juror." In this letter of 22 February 1750, Wesley stated that, "With regard to my political principles, I have never had any doubt since I read Mr. Higden's View of the English Constitution which I look upon as one of the best-wrote books I have ever seen in the English tongue."[63] Hynson concludes that Higden's book "made a major contribution to Wesley's political maturation."[64] Other contributions came from his understanding of vocation, which led him to challenge the authority of bishops and by extension of the government, and his experience of the church-state struggle, which strengthened his appreciation for the religious protection offered by the Hanoverian monarchs. But the reading of Higden, in Hynson's view, was the principal catalyst for Wesley's shifting his loyalty from Stuart to Hanover, and for abandoning the divine right of hereditary succession in favor of the limited monarchy.

The principal defect in Hynson's interesting argument is that Wesley does not say that he changed his mind as a result of reading the book. He says he never has had any doubt with regard to his political principles since reading Higden's book. The more defensible inference from that choice of words surely is that Higden confirmed his views, not that he changed them. What Wesley read in Higden is what he believed already. If that is so, John Wesley could not have been a nonjuror in the original political sense when he read the book, if indeed he ever had been one. No nonjuror would accept the legitimacy of taking oaths to a monarch actually in possession of the throne without regard to whether he or she was monarch *de jure* or *de facto*. Recall, in this connection, that Susanna Wesley did not accept the *de facto* authority of William III, and therefore would not say Amen to a prayer for him. Higden may have removed some lingering uncertainties about royal authority, but that is not the same as being converted from one political orientation to another. The reading of Higden confirmed Wesley's existing political principles; it did not precipitate a shift of loyalty from the Stuarts to the Hanoverians.

Of greater and more enduring importance for Wesley's political thought is the manner in which Higden makes his case. What he does is appeal to the ancient constitution with its integrated combination of king and Parliament and its supporting culture of law and historic rights.[65] That concept acknowledges God as the ultimate source of authority, but not with the particular divine right notion fostered by the Stuarts, beginning with James I, in the seventeenth century. Stuart "divine right" made the king answerable only to God, and therefore not to people, Parliament, or law (or Pope). What establishes the legitimacy of Higden's *de facto* monarch is not direct divine authorization, or even simple possession of power, but the fact that the monarch's laws are acts of the king in Parliament recognized as law by subsequent monarchs. That is a constitutional argument imposing limiting conditions on royal power. It is not a divine right argument.

From what few scraps of commentary we have, and without convincing evidence to the contrary, we can assume that John Wesley held this constitutional view of royal authority. There is an item of correspondence from 22 May 1727 between John and Samuel Jr., which indicates that both of them believed in the subordination of the monarch to the law.[66] Moreover, two letters of 23 July 1736, written during his Georgia mission, confirm this constitutionalist interpretation. Both deal with a controversy between Carolina and Georgia over regulation of the Indian trade, and both include the following argument: "Is an act of the King in Council, in pursuance of an Act of Parliament, of any force within these bounds or not?"[67] The specification that an act of King in Council be pursuant to an Act of Parliament is constitutional language, not the language of divine right absolutism. There is no evidence that John Wesley ever held a different view. That these letters were written three years subsequent to his reading of Higden does not mean that he derived the ideas from that reading. To the contrary, these are the political principles that, according to Wesley, the reading of Higden's book confirmed.

HOW THE RECORD READS

In 1785, as we have noted, John Wesley distinguished between Jacobite and Tory by defining a Tory as "one that believes God, not the people, to be the origin of all civil power."[68] In that sense he declared his brother Samuel (whom he was defending), his father, and himself to be Tories, not Jacobites. That is something less than a clarifying distinction, because Jacobites also believed that God, not the people, was the source of civil power, and also because there was more to being a Tory than that particular definition. Moreover, no definition of "Jacobite" was offered. Nevertheless, it sufficed for the occasion, because he wanted to remove the taint of Jacobitism from the Wesley men while at the same time distinguishing them from those who believed the people to be the source of civil power. In that small but important way his definition established his position in contemporary disputes over issues of political authority. Earlier in the same year—in response to the same accusation against his brother Samuel—he wrote, "Both my father and all his sons have always praised God for the happy Revolution."[69] Certainly Samuel Sr. did that, but John may have stretched the truth slightly in his own case—after all, never in his young manhood did he ever record any praise or elation over the revolution's happy character, and his diary suggests some lack of affection for George I in the 1720s. But neither did he record any loyalty to the Stuarts, or any regret over the events of 1688–89. It is entirely possible, of course, that John Wesley may have praised the "happy Revolution" as did his father, yet been sour toward the German George and his Whig administration. If so, that would add strength to the argument that his "detracting against the King" was not an expression of Stuart loyalty and therefore not evidence of Jacobite sentiments.

Interpreters of Wesley often have dismissed these statements as the attempt of an old man with a Jacobite past to erase his tracks. They would not deny his claim concerning God and civil power, and would not need to, but they would argue that there is too much evidence of Jacobite leanings if not outright commitment in his early years to dismiss it so briskly. Our investigation of John Wesley's early political record suggests that his recollection at age eighty-two may be closer to the truth than the inferences of his interpreters. As we have seen, there is no direct, no overt, evidence of Jacobite or nonjuror political commitments. He did not identify himself as such, or engage in supportive political activity. He did not announce for the Stuarts or denounce the Hanoverians. He did not refuse to swear the oath of allegiance required for his own ordination or decline ordination at the hands of a Whig-appointed bishop. He acknowledged George I as king by resolving "not to detract against" him. He presented his father's study of the Book of Job to the queen of George II. His recorded occasions of criticizing king and Parliament (at age twenty-two) are not focused self-evidently on the dynastic question, and more likely reflect dissatisfaction with a German king and a Whig Parliament. He did not record any usage of the language of divine right, and in particular of the language of indefeasible hereditary right of succession to the throne. He was not a political absolutist, but believed royal power to be limited by law and constitution. As Vivian Green points out, he could not have been dedicated seriously to a Roman Catholic pretender to the throne. If he saw himself as Jacobite or nonjuror, he certainly was a quiet and equivocal—perhaps even sycophantic—one.[70]

Interpretations of John Wesley as Jacobite/nonjuror rest not on direct and overt evidences but on inferences from his associations, beginning with his mother. Susanna Annesley Wesley was a woman of extraordinary intelligence and determination who influenced her son, John, quite profoundly.[71] She also was one who believed that James II, whatever his faults (even including his allegiance to the Church of Rome), was the true and only king of England, that the rearrangements of 1688–89 were an offense against God, and that William III was a usurper and no rightful monarch of England. Advocates of the Jacobite/nonjuror theory of young Wesley's politics tend to infer his politics initially from his mother's influence. They do not necessarily rest the case there, but they find it a persuasive beginning. Hynson, for one, argues that John Wesley's earliest political stage "was shaped by his mother Susanna's influence and by the quietism of the Anglican articles of religion, the sixteenth-century homilies of the Church of England, and the seventeenth-century devotional book *The Whole Duty of Man.* This was the era of Wesley the nonjuror. The stage began at his mother's knee and continued through his education, through the years of the nonjuring Holy Club, through the American venture, and through the days and months following his religious experience at Aldersgate (24 May 1738)."[72] Hynson rightly identifies these other important influences on Wesley's political thinking, but sees the primary orientation as set by Susanna—a necessary move, because the other listed influences would not suffice to make him a nonjuror. (Many other persons came under the same influences, but only a minority of them became nonjurors.)

Bernard Semmel claims that, "Like his mother, Wesley had faith in such 'tangibles' as the blood royal, and although utilitarian grounds no doubt predominated in his transferring his loyalties from the Stuarts to the Hanoverians in the forties, he was sufficiently his mother's son to wish to satisfy his scruples by discovering some genealogical flaw as grounds for his new position— which he manages to do in the seventies."[73] Semmel offers no citations to support his claim concerning Wesley's "faith in such 'tangibles' as the blood royal." So far as I am aware, no such comments by him exist. Nor does he prove that Wesley had Stuart loyalties from which to transfer. Apparently, he simply assumes them. The mention of the "genealogical flaw" is a reference to a passage in *Concise History of England.*[74] There Wesley (or whoever the original writer was) denies the legitimacy of the Stuart monarchs by asserting the illegitimacy of the marriage of King John to Isabella, from which union the Stuarts were said to trace their descent. King George, the writer argues further, had a more defensible right to the throne, because he was descended lineally from Matilda, who had a prior claim. Whatever sense one may make of this argument, there is no evidence that it appears in this history for the purpose of satisfying Wesley's "scruples" in allegedly departing from his mother's Stuart loyalties. More likely, it was just one more opportunity to score points against the Jacobites in favor of the House of Hanover. Curiously, the folk who attribute dominant political influence to John's mother account little or none to his father, who was very much engaged politically, whereas his mother was not. On the rare occasions when John connects politics with his family, he cites agreement with his father, but says nothing of his mother.

Admittedly, there were other Jacobite and nonjuror associations—the Oxford milieu, the Cotswold friends, the Clayton-Deacon nonjurors. What I have argued is that, despite the intimacy of religion and politics, Wesley's interest and personal expression in these groups was almost wholly religious (allowing for romantic interests in the Cotswolds!), and apparently not at all political. His young women friends in the Cotswolds nicknamed him "primitive Christianity," not "the little Jacobite"! Spiritual and religious results from these associations abound, but no political results.

Weaknesses in these Jacobite/nonjuror inferences do not remove all suspicions, of course. Perhaps the primary result of Wesley's reading of Higden's *A View of the English Constitution* was to ease some residual uncertainties, even if not to change his mind. But the confident statements of Semmel, Hynson, and others that John Wesley was Jacobite and nonjuror during this period demand more evidence and more convincing argument than they provide. The record simply does not support that degree of characterization. The caution of scholars such as Green and Rack is much more defensible.

What we make of these Jacobite/nonjuror evidences depends in large part on which context of interpretation we accord primacy. If we accord primacy to the Susanna connection, we regard John Wesley as a congenital, second-generation Jacobite, and treat his Oxford, Cotswold, and other nonjuror associations as confirming and reinforcing factors. The later historical problem, then, is to explain how he became such an enthusiastic supporter of the House of Hanover and such a vigorous and at times emotional critic of the Jacobites. If, on the other hand, we accord primacy to Wesley's Tory and High Church identity, we recognize that some beliefs, tendencies, and associations that may appear Jacobite or nonjuror—when one is looking for such evidences—are open to a different and quite defensible interpretation. They do not have the inevitable political associations, and can be examined in the light of the priority of religious interest Wesley gave them. That is true especially of Wesley's nonjuror connections and religious practices.

Moreover, the Tory alternative does not necessarily imply particular dynastic loyalties. Although most Tories inclined toward James II, some Tories, among them Samuel Wesley Sr., supported both the Glorious Revolution and later the accession of George I. With the passage of time and the stabilizing of the Hanoverian regime, Tories increasingly accepted the political reality. To wear the label "Tory" during the reign of George I might imply opposition to the king because of his Whig government, but some Tories in opposition accepted and some rejected the legitimacy of the House of Hanover. This division in the Tory ranks allowed for ambivalence, which may have represented the real feelings of the young, essentially nonpolitical, John Wesley—especially in view of the opposed loyalties of his parents. It allowed also for accommodation to political reality without necessarily confronting the theological issues involved in transfers of fundamental political loyalties. The commitment to passive obedience and nonresistance, which were components of Toryism, was a hovering tendency that might attach to whoever was the incumbent of the throne.

The Tory context, not the Jacobite, is the one properly to be used to interpret the politics of young John Wesley. As we have seen, the actual record does not support the attributions of Jacobitism. Moreover, the broader process of Tory accommodation corresponds closely with what we know of John Wesley's early political development. What that process was early in the century is summarized by Harry T. Dickinson:

> The opposition or Country Tories, for their part, gradually severed all links with Jacobitism and all loyalty to divine ordination and indefeasible hereditary succession. . . . By the time the Tories joined the Country opposition to Walpole in the later 1720s they had fully reconciled themselves to both the Revolution settlement and the Hanoverian succession. Indeed, Bolingbroke was able to persuade most Tories to accept the ancient constitution, which held that a monarchy limited by Parliament was an immemorial right of the English nation, and to reconcile themselves to the Revolution settlement which had restored that constitution.[75]

Wesley may not have needed as much discontinuity and reconcili-ation as this passage describes. As we have seen, his "links with Jacobitism" were not self-evidently political, and he makes no mention of the right of indefeasible hereditary succession. But if he did need them, the general and gradual movement of Tories would have given him comfortable coverage for changing. His diary com-ments about opposing Walpole correspond in time to Dickinson's rough dating of the Tory-Country alliance against Walpole. Wesley's so-called "Jacobite sermon" of 1734 bears some marks of Country Tory ideology.

Potentially most significant for comparison is Dickinson's refer-ence to Tory acceptance of the ancient constitution with its parlia-mentary limits on monarchical power. That observation helps confirm our claim that Wesley already held a commitment to the ancient constitution when in 1733 he read William Higden's defense of the permissibility of taking oaths to a *de facto* monarch. Higden, we recall, held that the validating factor is historic consti-tutional recognition of the legitimacy of legislative acts of usurper kings. If most Tories, according to Dickinson, had accepted the ancient constitution by the late-1720s, we would expect the Tory John Wesley to bring this commitment to his reading of Higden's book a few years later. The ancient constitution comprehends Wesley's established political principles, which he said he never doubted after reading Higden in 1733. These were the principles of a reconciled Tory, not those of a Jacobite or nonjuror.

CONCLUSION: THE TORY CONSTITUTIONALIST

It is difficult to get a clear picture of John Wesley's early politics, because he left so few discernible traces. He was a young man with strong religious interests, but little evident interest in party politics, political issues, and political theory. Luke Tyerman records vigor-ous political activity at least within the scope of Wesley's peripher-al vision at the time of his ordination to the diaconate (1725): "Plotters . . . still plotted; among the chief of whom was Bishop Atterbury, the friend and patron of Wesley's brother Samuel. The prelate was arrested, was tried in the House of Lords, was deprived of his bishopric, was banished from his country, entered the service of the Pretender, and became his confidential agent."[76] While this was going on, according to Tyerman, John Wesley applied himself quietly to his studies. What we have learned of Wesley confirms this report. Wesley lived obscurely under Hanoverian rule without challenging it, and without provoking the authorities (except in Georgia, where the provocation was a young woman and the authority was her uncle).[77] He did not discuss regimes or political philosophies—at least in such a way that the discussion left a lasting record. The list of his early sermon titles carries no hint of political preaching.[78] With so little help from Wesley as principal, scholars have tended to infer his politics from his surroundings and associations. We have shown in this inquiry that the usual course of inferential reconstruction does not have sufficient supporting evidence to confirm the portrayal of Wesley as a Jacobite—or as a nonjuror, except with regard to religious practices.

It is clear, however, that John Wesley was a Tory, at minimum in the sense that he was not a Whig. What we have learned about his politics allows us to make some statements about his Toryism that not only will help clarify the stance of the young Mr. Wesley, but also may provide some clues to the understanding of his subsequent political development. There is, as we have seen, a suggestion of Country Tory sentiment, although it had no apparent theological or philosophical grounding, no organizational involvement, and no enduring significance.[79] The fundamental question is whether as a Tory Wesley was a theocratic divine right thinker, which would link him with the Stuart past, or a constitutionalist, which would link him with the Hanoverian future. The former is assumed by some noted interpreters of Wesley's politics, including Bernard Semmel and Leon Hynson. However, that characterization of Wesley is lacking in important elements of the divine right concept, principally the belief in indefeasible hereditary right of succession and the superiority of the king to law and Parliament. John Wesley did not speak of the former, which he surely would have done had he held that view, and he did not believe the latter. He also did not make much use if any of the term "divine right." That he believed in God as source of political authority and in passive obedience and nonresistance does not suffice to identify him as a divine right thinker without the inclusion of these other elements.[80]

The Wesley-as-Tory picture that emerges from our study is that of the Tory constitutionalist. Wesley's political thinking in this period proceeds in terms of the ancient constitution, an organic and historical concept that contrasts with liberal constitutional models, which tend to be rational, contractual, and even mechanical. In the young Wesley this concept does not rise to the level of theoretical reflection, possibly because it was a secure, presuppositional notion to which he felt no challenge. Nevertheless, it is implicit in his acknowledgment of Higden's book as confirming his political principles. It is manifest in fugitive statements concerning the supremacy of law and the authority of king and Parliament together. It is reinforced by Dickinson's portrayal of general Tory acceptance of the ancient constitution in the late-1720s.

When we look for lines of political development into Wesley's future, we should look for evidences of this Tory constitutionalism working its way beyond the dynastic oppositions of Stuart and Hanover to the interpretation of new challenges to English society. We should not give primacy to an alleged transition from divine right to liberal thinking. John Wesley's early political thinking never showed the absolutist tendencies that historic Stuart divine right formulations implied. His later public affirmations of rights and liberties never escaped the organic context of the ancient constitution.

CHAPTER THREE

PUBLIC POLITICAL
CONTROVERSIES I
JOHN WESLEY AND THE '45 REBELLION

John Wesley could afford the luxury of a nonpolitical religious ministry only so long as he was a quiet Anglican priest and Oxford tutor. When Methodism became a visible and influential movement, as it did beginning in 1739, he could not avoid public choices and stances. Even when he might have avoided them, he found himself drawn into political controversy by reason of social concern and increasing personal prominence. Wesley supported King George II and the House of Hanover openly and without reservation in the Jacobite rebellion of 1745, when Prince Charles Edward Stuart invaded Britain with the assistance of France, proclaimed his father king as James III, and sought forcibly to restore the Stuart monarchy. In the 1760s and later, Wesley supported the British constitution—especially its monarchic component—against widespread agitation for democratic reforms, including, among other proposals, the dissolution of the monarchy and the creation in England of a republican form of government. When in the 1770s the American colonies raised their complaints against king and Parliament, Wesley at first was sympathetic to the Americans. Soon, however, he turned against them—moderately, for awhile, when he saw the issue as the right of Parliament to tax the (directly) unrepresented colonies, but then more decisively when he perceived that their real intent was to sever their relationship with England. Each of these political moments raised different issues, and in doing so evoked different aspects of Wesley's political orientation. Taken together, they show that John Wesley was a constitutionalist and an English patriot, and neither a monarchist in the absolutist sense nor a liberal. Why those conclusions can be drawn, and what those terms meant in Wesley's case, will appear as we examine his responses to these three crises of eighteenth-century British history.

In this chapter, we shall investigate the first of these public political controversies. As a case study, it will enable us to test the argument that Wesley was a supporter of the House of Hanover from earlier days, against the claim that he was a Jacobite who changed his loyalty during the course of the conflict. It will enable us also to see whether constitutional considerations were more prominent in his political thinking at that stage than the divine right absolutism often attributed to him.

METHODISM IN THE '45

Jacobite supporters of the Stuart dynasty mounted two rebellions in the first half of the eighteenth century—in 1715 and again in 1745—known respectively as the '15 and the '45. Neither was successful in the objective to remove the German Georges and install on the throne a male heir to James II, although the second may have come closer to triumph than often is acknowledged.[1] Early in 1744 France assembled a fleet at Dunkirk to support a Stuart effort at restoration. The French fleet did not attack, however. The failure of this naval venture is attributed variously to dispersal of the armada by a storm, and to indecisiveness on the part of leading Tory Jacobites in providing clear signals of support. Undaunted by this failure of French backing, but with promises of future assistance, Prince Charles Stuart landed in Scotland in July 1745, assembled an army of 2,500 Scots, captured Edinburgh, and in September inflicted a crushing defeat on a British army at Prestonpans, Scotland. Instead of attacking Newcastle, as was expected, he moved inland with an army now swollen to 5,000 men and marched southward. The government was poorly prepared to resist. King George II was in Hanover, leading ministers of the Crown were divided as to the seriousness of the situation, and the small British standing army was deployed mainly on the continent. Not until 17 October 1745 did Parliament meet to provide funds to resist the Jacobites. In November Prince Charles captured Carlisle, and in December moved on Derby. However, failing to receive the degree of English support expected, Charles and his Scottish Jacobites decided not to march on London, but instead returned to

Scotland. On 16 April 1746, Charles and his army were defeated at Culloden in Scotland by a British army under the command of the Duke of Cumberland, second son of George II. The most serious Jacobite threat was at an end.[2]

Samuel Wesley Sr. had supported the House of Hanover and opposed the Jacobites on the occasion of the '15 rebellion. John Wesley, of course, was only twelve years old at the time, and—not surprisingly—recorded no impressions, nor did he reflect on the event subsequently. By 1744, however, the Methodist movement was up and running, John Wesley was becoming a known personality, and the Methodists were disturbing the peaceful control over church and society managed by bishops, priests, magistrates, and squires. General anxiety over the Jacobite threat focused at times on Wesley and the Methodists, and provided pretext and device for attacking them verbally, physically, and in print as enemies of king and church and subverters of the government.

Wesley records in his journal of 15 February 1744 that they had just learned of the imminent French invasion. His admonition to the congregation was, "Watch ye, and pray always, that ye may be accounted worthy to escape all these things and to stand before the Son of man" (Luke 21:36).[3] The message was nonpolitical—a typical Wesley advisory to get right with God in order to avert catastrophe, and to avoid political entanglements. His entry of 18 February indicates that he was more concerned with what he termed "another kind of invasion"—the violent riots against Methodists in Darlaston, Walsall, Wednesbury, and Aldridge.[4] Accounts of these riots offer no evidence that alleged Jacobite sympathies provided the excuse for attacking the Methodists, who for several years had been mob targets for reasons not directly related to Stuart ambitions and French invasion threats.[5]

However, political aspects of Methodist vulnerability came into focus on 27 February. Wesley was preparing to leave London to continue his work in other towns and cities when he learned of a proclamation requiring all "Papists" to get out of town. Although his leaving at that time was purely coincidental, it would offer his enemies the opportunity to accuse him of identifying with the departing Roman Catholics. To avoid the connection, Wesley delayed his trip for a week, commenting that he "was the more willing to stay, that I might procure more raiment for the poor before I left London."[6] Nevertheless, the Methodist societies and Wesley himself did not escape the hunt for "Papists," inspired and legitimated by the French and Jacobite threats, and conducted by local authorities and church officials. To protect his people and himself, on 5 March Wesley wrote to King George II, advising him that the Methodists were faithful members of the Church of England and loyal and obedient subjects of His Sovereign Majesty. We are, he wrote, "steadily attached to your Majesty's royal person and illustrious house. We cannot indeed say or do either more or less than we apprehend consistent with the written Word of God. But we are ready to obey your Majesty to the uttermost in all things which we conceive to be agreeable thereto. And we earnestly exhort all with whom we converse, as they fear God, to honour the king. . . . May he who hath bought us with his blood, the Prince of all the kings of the earth, fight against all the enemies of your Majesty with the two-edged sword that cometh out of his mouth!"[7] This letter never was sent, at least in part because Charles Wesley feared that John's writing on behalf of the Methodist societies would reinforce the impression that they were in reality a dissenting sect, contrary to John's explicit claim.[8] Charles's suspicions were confirmed on 11 April, when the minister of St. Ives preached against "'the new sect,' as enemies of the Church, Jacobites, Papists, and what not!"[9]

On 15 March, Charles Wesley was summoned before a magisterial court and charged with speaking "treasonable words, as praying for the banished, or for the Pretender." It seems that a witness had heard him praying that "the Lord would call home his banished," and understood the words as a prayer for the return of the Stuarts, rather than as preacher language used to call lost souls to return to God. Charles's explanation forced the witnesses to retract their testimony. Not satisfied simply to be cleared, Charles went on the offensive, asked the court to administer to him the oath of loyalty, demanded that his name be cleared, and defended the Methodists in language reminiscent of that which John had used in his aborted letter to George II. According to Tyerman's account, "At length, their worships reluctantly acknowledged, in explicit terms, that 'his loyalty was unquestionable.' "[10] The reluctance of the magistrates presumably meant that, although they could not convict Charles Wesley on the basis of the evidence given, they were not convinced by his passionate oration on Methodist loyalty. The suspicions remained, and were encouraged by rumor, resentment, and jealousy.

Five days later—20 March 1744—John Wesley was summoned by the Justices of Surrey to appear before their court at St. Margaret's Hill.[11] He did so, and learned that no one had filed charges against him, but that the judges wanted him to take the oath of loyalty to the king and to sign the declaration against popery. He complied, and was permitted to leave. However, nothing that either of the Wesleys did to affirm their loyalty and the ties of the movement to the Church of England sufficed to silence the accusations. John noted on 7 April 1744, that some residents of Rosemargay had asserted confidently that they had seen him recently in France with the Pretender (others said he was in prison in London!).[12] On 16 April, Degory Isbel informed him that some "vehemently asserted at St. Ives, of my bringing the Pretender with me thither last autumn, under the name of John Downes. It was that I called myself 'John Wesley'; whereas everybody knew Mr. Wesley was dead."[13] John Downes was one of Wesley's preachers, and Wesley was very much alive as his own pious self. When Charles Stuart's invasion became a reality, Wesley was informed (4 July 1745) by a friend in Cornwall that "All the gentlemen of these parts say that you have been a long time in France and Spain and are now sent hither by the Pretender, and that these societies are to join him."[14] In November of 1745, after Prince Charles had scored a considerable measure of success, someone started the rumor that Wesley was with the Pretender near Edinburgh.[15] One notes that the earlier vague association of Wesley and the Methodists with the Stuart cause soon became allegations of direct alliance and support. These misrepresentations and false statements, whether as innocent confusion or deliberate lies, were intended to discredit Methodism as a religious movement and John Wesley as a religious leader seemingly out of the control of the church. In legal terms, however, they amounted to deadly serious accusations of treason.

Throughout this crisis Wesley engaged in what today we would call damage control. Doubtless he saw his protestations of support for king and church as sincere expressions—obligated by the nature of the times—of the union of piety and loyalty. However, his choice of occasions for response and content of argument certainly reflect his awareness of Methodist vulnerability. I cited previously his letter to King George II of 5 March 1744, which was not sent, but the text of which survives. Its sentiments of loyalty are clear, as is its defensive nature. On 21 September 1745, Wesley wrote somewhat apologetically to the mayor of Newcastle-upon-Tyne, explaining his absence from a meeting of all householders called by the mayor, and affirming his loyalty to King George. "All I can do for his Majesty," Wesley wrote, "whom I honour and love—I think not less than I did my own father—is this: I cry unto God day by day, in public and private, to put all his enemies to confusion. And I exhort all that hear me to do the same, and in their several stations to exert themselves as loyal subjects, who so long as they fear God cannot but honour the king."[16] In a letter of 8 October to General John Husk, he put himself fully in compliance with Husk's orders to prepare for Jacobite assault by pulling down the battlements of his house: "I am ready, if it may be for his Majesty's service, to pull not only the battlements, but the house down; or to give up any part of it, or the whole, into your Excellency's hands."[17] A subsequent letter to the mayor of Newcastle began with sentiments of "The fear of God, the love of my country, and the regard I have for his Majesty King George," and concluded with the affirmation that "I should rejoice to serve, as I am able, my king and country." Wesley's conception of service in this case was defined by his perception of the moral degradation of the soldiers guarding the city. Wesley offered to spend his time—without pay—calling them to repentance. Their reformation, he argued was "in the interest of our country, as well as of these unhappy men themselves. For can it be expected that God should be on their side who are daily affronting him to his face? And if God be not on their side, how little will either their number or courage or strength avail!"[18]

A MIXTURE OF MOTIVATIONS

Some of Wesley's writings of the invasion period incorporate the interrelated themes of Methodist vulnerability, loyalty to King

George, and consequences to the nation of a Jacobite victory. His "Advice to the People Called Methodists" (10 October 1745) urges them to *"Consider, with deep and frequent attention, the peculiar circumstances wherein you stand."* After listing several other reasons why Methodists attract unwanted and hostile notice, he observes that "What makes even your *principles* more offensive is this *uniting* of yourselves *together,* because this union renders you more *conspicuous,* placing you more in the eye of men; more *suspicious,*—I mean, liable to be suspected of carrying on some sinister design (especially by those who do not, or *will* not, know your inviolable attachment to his present Majesty King George)."[19] In "A Word in Season: or, Advice to an Englishman" (15 October 1745) he asks consideration of the condition of the nation: It is in a civil war in which Scotland has been lost, British armies defeated, and the country is on the brink of return to tyranny.

> Think what is likely to follow, if an army of French also should blow the trumpet in our land! What desolation may we not then expect? what a wide-spread field of blood? And what can the end of these things be? If they prevail, what but Popery and slavery? Do you know what the spirit of Popery is? Did you never hear of that in Queen Mary's reign; and of the holy men who were then burned alive by the Papists, because they did not dare do as they did; to worship angels and saints, to pray to the Virgin Mary, to bow down to images, and the like? If we had a King of this spirit, whose life would be safe? at least, what honest man's? A knave indeed might turn with the times. But what a dreadful thing would this be to a man of conscience: "Either turn or burn: Either go into that fire, or into 'the fire that never shall be quenched?' "
>
> And can you dream that your property would be any safer than your conscience? Nay, how should that be? Nothing is plainer than that the Pretender cannot be King of England, unless it be by conquest. But every conqueror may do what he will; the laws of the land are no laws to him. And who can doubt, but one who should conquer England by the assistance of France, would copy after the French rules of government?[20]

A victory of the Jacobites and their French allies not only would bring dreadful carnage upon the land, but also would result in the imposition of Catholicism and arbitrary rule—even "slavery"—

with inevitable consequences of loss of liberty of conscience and rights of property. It is unmistakably clear from this passage that John Wesley fervently opposed the restoration of Stuart rule and just as fervently supported the Hanoverian establishment with the constitutional provisions and protections that it represented. To drive home the point, Wesley appended a hymn "For His Majesty King George," in which he prayed,

> The Spirit of thy grace
> Thy heavenly unction, shed,
> And hosts of guardian angels place
> Around his sacred head.
>
> Confound whoe'er oppose,
> Or force them to retire;
> Be thou a tower against his foes,
> Be thou a wall of fire.[21]

It is also clear from the totality of his response that his support of the Hanoverian monarchy was not reducible to his concern to protect the Methodists, however massively important that protection was to him.

METHODISM'S POLITICAL VALUE

Wesley's "A Farther Appeal to Men of Reason and Religion," published 18 December 1745, asserts the political value of Methodist evangelism, and implicitly accuses of treason those who have hindered the work of the "new sect." Resistance to Methodist work and message has deprived king and country of thousands who would have been inspired to serve them by reason of the sense of political obligation, which arises from religious devotion:

> Yea, had they only *not opposed* the work of God, had they only *refrained from* his messengers, might not the trumpet of God have been heard long since in every corner of our land? And thousands of sinners in every county been brought to "fear God and honour the King."
> Judge of what immense service we might have been, even in this

single point, both to our king and country. All who hear and regard the Word we preach, "honour the king" for God's sake. They "render unto Caesar the things that are Caesar's," as well as "unto God the things that are God's." They have no conception of *piety* without *loyalty*, knowing "the powers that be are ordained of God." I pray God to strengthen all that are of this mind, how many soever they be. But might there not have been at this day a hundred thousand in England thus minded more than are now? Yea, verily, even by *our* ministry, had not they who should have strengthened us weakened our hands.[22]

Wesley concludes the "Farther Appeal" by stating that "The plain religion now propagated is love," and asking, "And can you oppose this without being an enemy to mankind? No; nor without being an enemy to your king and country; especially at such a time as this." Wesley asserts that the country is on the brink of destruction. The explanation for this disaster is that it is a visitation of God for the sins of the people—a typically Wesleyan inference. But specifically it is a visitation

> because to all our other abominations we have added the open fighting against God; the not only rejecting, but even denying, yea, blaspheming his last offers of mercy; the hindering others who were desirous to close therewith; the despitefully using his messengers, and the variously troubling and oppressing those who did accept of his grace, break off their sins, and turn to him with their whole heart. I cannot but believe it is chiefly on this account that God hath now "a controversy with our land."[23]

The issue no longer is simply whether Wesley and the Methodists are loyal to King George. The Methodist movement now is represented as a primary generator of loyalty and obedience. Resistance to and oppression of the Methodists is the principal ground for divine punishment inflicted in the form of this war. Those who attack the Methodists as papists and Jacobites are the real traitors to king and country!

Admittedly, the "Advice" and the "Farther Appeal" deal only marginally with the political situation. Wesley is concerned much more directly and vocationally with soul-winning and moral reform than with political issues, and the political references in these documents are set in the context of more general advisories and defenses of the movement. This marginality of political interest may encourage those who contend that Wesley was a Stuart supporter who shifted his loyalty to the House of Hanover to protect his vulnerable Methodists. If that was his motive, it did not seem to help much. Not only did riots against Methodists continue, but press-gangs persisted in efforts to force the Methodist preachers—and Wesley himself—into military service.[24] However, there is nothing in this review of the evidence to support the theory of a change in loyalties. John Wesley offered no reflection on alternative claims, no hesitancy, no second thoughts. All of the citations show that he was devoted to George II as king and to the House of Hanover before, during, and after the crisis of '45. All of his references to a possible Jacobite-French victory reveal his horror at the probable consequences. He wrote in his journal of 9 November 1746, that "The day of Public Thanksgiving for the victory at Culloden was to us a day of solemn joy."[25] No wistfulness, no regrets, no tinges of hyprocrisy qualify that declaration. Wesley's behavior throughout the '45 confirms our contention in the previous chapter that he was a Hanoverian like his father, not a Jacobite like his mother.[26]

WHY THE JACOBITE ACCUSATIONS?

Why, then, was he accused constantly of Jacobitism? At one level, the charge simply was a convenient device for attempting to dispose of a movement suspected and resented for reasons other than those related to royal succession. After all, the problems of the Methodists in English society antedated the immediate crisis of the '45. In 1739 in Bath, for example, Beau Nash accused him of violating the Act of Parliament prohibiting conventicles. Wesley replied that "the conventicles mentioned in that Act (as the Preamble shows) are *seditious* meetings. But this is not such. Here is no shadow of sedition. Therefore it is not contrary to that Act."[27] This attempt to frighten Wesley away failed, but it illustrated the difficulty of Wesley's distinguishing the Methodists from Dissenters at a time when Dissenters suffered severe legal restrictions and were subject to hostile and aggressive treatment. Some of the suspicion of and antipathy toward the Methodists reflected a genuine fear of social chaos and conflict rooted in the memory of the revolutionary disorders of the 1640s. Some of it was pure jealousy on the part of pastors and bishops who resented Methodist successes that exposed the inadequacies of established church practice or the downright laziness and lack of concern of some clergy. Accusations of Methodist services drawing communicants away from parish church services were false but frequent. (Wesley argued that attendance at parish communion services increased where the Methodists were active, and that Methodist preaching was not conducted at the same times as parish services.) Bishops worried about religious enthusiasm, the teaching of heretical doctrine, and violations of church order.[28] Factory owners complained that workers were drawn away from their jobs to attend preaching services (they were not, according to Wesley—he held services before and after work hours). Pimps and bar owners raged over the conversion of prostitutes and drunkards (they got that right, Wesley agreed). In short, there were numerous grounds—real or fancied—for social anger and anxiety aimed at Methodists without connecting Wesley and his followers to the dynastic struggle between the Houses of Stuart and Hanover. The crisis of the '45 gave all these complainants a political weapon to use against the troublers of their peace.

At another level, however, there were factors that connected Wesley and the Methodists more immediately to the dynastic controversy, and provided more credible grounds for accusations of Jacobite and Stuart associations. The repeated allegations that Wesley was a papist, and therefore in league with the Roman Catholic Pretender to the throne, doubtless reflected his reputation for devotion to nonjuror religious practices of frequent communion and ascetic discipline. Also, John Wesley clearly was Tory in political identification. The government was Whig, the Tories were proscribed from power, and the Whigs used the Jacobite label to brand the Tories as Stuart loyalists and threats to the House of Hanover. Inasmuch as many Tories were in fact Jacobites—or at least had Jacobite memories—the accusation carried considerable political weight. Linda Colley reports that Wesley and the Tories-out-of-power had programmatic and constituency similarities. "The Wesleyan religious and social critique had much in common with the tory appeal. Tory M.P.s attacked placemen and rotten boroughs; so did Wesley. Tories condemned press-gangs, turnpikes and the wastefulness of whig aristocrats; so did Wesley. Given Wesley's own origins and politics it was to be expected that the whig authorities would make their usual ideological conflation and that in 1744–45 these quasi-tory evangelicals should have been accused of Jacobinism."[29] Additionally, according to Colley, the coal miners to whom Wesley and Whitefield preached had been recruited since 1714 for political and religious purposes—presumably as mobs for protest and violence. She refers to them as "High Church colliers."[30] To the nervous guardians of the establishment of 1689 they were Jacobites, as some of them indeed were—if they had any political understanding at all. All of these more explicitly political connections combined with nondynastic fears and complaints that had been in place before the crisis of the '45 to lend credibility to the accusations of Jacobite politics and Stuart loyalties.

Yet none of these arguments singly, nor all of them together, suffice to confirm Wesley in Jacobite sympathies at any time during this period, nor even to allow a serious hypothesis of Jacobite leanings. John Wesley was an unambiguous supporter of King George II and an ardent opponent of Stuart restoration. He did not want a Roman Catholic on the throne of England. He did not want to risk the loss of liberties guaranteed in the constitutional establishment of 1689. There is not the slightest evidence of Jacobite leanings during this period. Nor is there any trace of change from Jacobite to Hanoverian loyalty. Bernard Semmel asserted that "During the early years of the Revival, with the threat of the Pretender mounting, Wesley began to preach absolute loyalty to George II. In this he followed the path of other Jacobites, who, as the usurper became better established, extended the principles of nonresistance and passive obedience to him, and, as a final gesture, gave him divine right as well. Since a restoration of the Stuarts could occur only as a result of a violent upheaval, Wesley could not continue to be a Jacobite."[31] Semmel's observation may apply to many Jacobites, but it does not apply to John Wesley. The argument that Wesley converted gradually during the crisis of the '45 from Jacobite to Hanoverian—for pragmatic reasons related to the protection of the Methodists, or for other reasons—is without foundation. The evidence simply does not support that claim. It is true, of course, that Wesley spoke up to protect the Methodists and himself. It is possible, certainly, that he would have protested his loyalty less frequently and fervently had the Methodist movement not been at risk, especially given that his interests were religious and not political. But nothing in that line of reasoning invites the inference of a shift in loyalty. In 1744 (and earlier) Wesley was praying for the king by name, which his Oxford Jacobite confederates declined to do in the 1720s. In 1744 he and Charles took the oath of loyalty to the king (Charles demanded to be given the oath), without any hint of nonjuror hesitation or reservation. The crisis of the '45 did not rearrange John Wesley's fundamental political loyalties. He was a supporter of the constitution and the reigning king before this crisis arose, and his words and actions simply confirmed and expressed that fact. (One must add, also, that John Wesley never gave absolute loyalty to any temporal sovereign.)

For our purposes, of course, we must be more interested in what Wesley's loyalties represented in political substance than in what they actually were in dynastic attachment. Loyalty to the House of Hanover clearly implied acceptance of the limited monarchy and the coordination of king and Parliament in the constitutional settlement of 1689. It implied also at least tacit acceptance of the end of the legitimating principle of indefeasible right of hereditary succession to the throne. Wesley did not reflect openly and at length on these matters, but his "Advice to an Englishman" indicates that he understood the issues. He did not want to risk a return to absolutism, and he did not want a Catholic monarch, however clear the hereditary title might be. The depth of his commitment is reflected not only in his public words and deeds, but also in the fact that as a Tory he supported a king who evidently preferred his Whig Parliament to one that would have been dominated by Tories.

One must stress these points concerning political substance to counter some implications of the claim that Wesley was a monarchist. Monarchy as such was not the issue in the '45. George II and Charles Stuart disagreed as to who should be monarch, but not as to whether there should or should not be a monarchy. The central substantive issue—alongside of and related to the question of religious confession—was the kind of monarchy that England would have. Indeed Wesley was a monarchist, but on the question of the nature of monarchy there is no doubt that he sided with the constitutionalists against the absolutists. The fact that he may have had strong convictions concerning passive obedience did not incline him to the latter against the former. Already by this time in his political development, one can see that John Wesley was at least implicitly a constitutionalist. His monarchist sentiments were informed and circumscribed by the notion of limited monarchy.

PERSISTENCE OF THE JACOBITE MYTH

The linking of John Wesley and Methodism with the Jacobite question did not end with the defeat of the '45 rebellion. This linkage continued to dog Wesley for the rest of his life, although never again did it require the degree of public attention he was forced to give it in the period 1744–46. On 18 July 1747, he wrote to Ebenezer Blackwell that "A great door and effectual is opened now, almost in every corner of this country. Here is such a change within these two years as has hardly been seen in any other part of England. Wherever we went we used to carry our lives in our hands; and now there is not a dog to wag his tongue." The implication is that Methodists are able to move throughout the land more freely and securely because the burden of association with the Jacobites has been lifted. Nevertheless the accusations continue, but from a surprising source: "The most violent Jacobites among these are continually crying out that we are bringing the Pretender, and some of these worthy men bear his Majesty's commission as justices of the peace."[32] The "most violent Jacobites" are accusing the Methodists of behaving like Jacobites! Wesley's journal of 2 April 1755 records a positive evaluation of the Methodist presence in Stanley, with the further observation that "The warmest opposers are the Jacobites, who do not love us because we love King George. But they profit nothing, for more and more people 'fear God and honour the King.' "[33] A letter of 4 March 1756 to Blackwell indicates Wesley's support for the Whig candidate for Parliament, John Spenser.[34] The main issue in this case was that Spenser supported the king, and the principal opponent was a Jacobite. The Jacobite won (most of Wesley's candidates seemed to lose), much to Wesley's discomfiture. These citations indicate reciprocal antagonism between Methodists and Jacobites, and not only accusations of Jacobitism by others hostile to Wesley and the Methodists.

Yet the accusations of Jacobite association continued, and in some hostile situations were implied—or at least were in the background—even when not stated. These occasions compelled Wesley to reassert his loyalty to King George. On 6 July 1749, Wesley penned "A Short Address to the Inhabitants of Ireland, Occasioned by Some Late Occurrences."[35] This piece was a vigorous defense of the Methodists, and an attempt to explain them to the Irish. In his address he found it necessary to point out that

> on all proper occasions [the Methodists] strongly recommend, on the one hand, the most intense love of our country; on the other, the firmest loyalty to our Prince, abstracted from all views of private interest. . . . Hence those who were before of quite the opposite temper, are now generous, disinterested lovers of their country; and faithful, loyal subjects to their Prince, His sacred Majesty King George. . . . These are plain, glaring, undeniable facts, whereof, if any Magistrate will be at the trouble to take them, numerous affidavits may be made, in Dublin, Cork, Limerick, and many other places.[36]

The horrendous attacks on Methodists in Ireland, which created the context both for this address and for Wesley's oft-quoted letter of 27 May 1750 to the mayor of Cork, were propelled in part by accusations of Jacobitism and disloyalty.[37] On 5 January 1761, he wrote to the author (editor?) of the *Westminster Journal*, responding to a wide-ranging diatribe against the Methodists, which included the old charge that their "enthusiasm" endangered the government by subverting loyalty to the king. "The enthusiasm which has lately gone abroad is faith which worketh by love," Wesley replied. "Does this 'endanger government itself?' Just the reverse. Fearing God, it honours the king. It teaches all men to be subject to the higher powers, not for wrath but for conscience' sake."[38] Wesley (again) denied the authority of the Pope (and popes), and affirmed the Protestant government. But "Have not the minds of the vulgar been darkened to a total neglect of their civil and social duties?" the critic continued. "Just the contrary," Wesley replied. "Thousands in London, as well as elsewhere, have been enlightened to understand, and prevailed on to practise those duties, as they never did before."[39]

In these public challenges, Wesley was pressured over and again to affirm his loyalty and that of the Methodists to the Hanoverian king and to his country. The Methodists were no Jacobites, no subversives. To the contrary, Methodist theology and discipline moved the adherents beyond conversion and piety to biblically grounded devotion to and support for the governing authorities. Doubtless the vulnerability of the Methodists matched by the king's support for religious liberty encouraged this tendency, but they were not the primary source of it—at least not in the case of Wesley himself. Wesley was in the camp of the Hanoverians to begin with. He learned from Scripture that he was to "be subject to the governing authorities," and to "Fear God and honour the King." The protection the Protestant monarchy provided for his vulnerable Methodists reinforced these other grounds for his love of and loyalty to King George.

Wesley's protests and affirmations to the contrary notwithstanding, he never was able to get entirely clear of the Jacobite issue. As late as 1785, as we saw previously, John had to defend his late brother Samuel, and indeed all the men in the Wesley family, against the accusation of Jacobitism.[40] During the conflict with the American colonies, Wesley was charged with ideological Jacobitism. Caleb Evans, a pro-American Baptist minister in Bristol, claimed that Wesley "under an artful disguise . . . revived the good old Jacobite doctrines of hereditary, indefeasible, divine right, and of passive obedience and non-resistance."[41] We shall discuss this matter in subsequent chapters. At this point we should note that the ideological identifications proved more durable than the accusations of disloyalty. Wesley's strong stand for the monarchy during the Wilkite agitations and the colonial rebellion should have removed any serious doubts as to where his loyalty lay. Correlatively, the Stuart pretensions came to an effective and practical end when the last of their male heirs, Prince Henry, claimed the throne in 1788 as Henry IX. Henry Stuart, regarded by himself and the Jacobites as Duke of York, also was a cardinal in the Roman Catholic Church—an impossible combination for Britain at the end of the eighteenth century.[42] On 25 May 1788, Wesley noted in his journal that "This was the day on which all the Nonjuring congregations in Scotland began, by common agreement, to pray in all their public worship for King George and his family."[43] The accusations of loyalty to the Stuarts now could come to an end. However, the perceptions of Jacobite "divine right" ideology would persist—encouraged and abetted by British Methodist Tory conservatism in the first half of the nineteenth century.

CHAPTER FOUR

PUBLIC POLITICAL CONTROVERSIES II
RADICAL AGITATION AND CONSTITUTIONAL CRISIS

Although monarchy as such may not have been an issue during the Jacobite rebellion known as the '45, it became so later in the century as the Jacobite threat subsided and the more radical implications of John Locke's political philosophy came to the fore. In 1760, George III ascended the throne of England, succeeding his grandfather, George II. Beginning in that year the Whig dominance of British politics was broken, control of Parliament was contested more actively and equally, administrations served often with less tenure and greater instability, and the legislative process became more active and productive. Also, during the remainder of the century large-scale problems such as African slavery, domestic poverty, and the integrity of the empire rose to demand attention. The relative stability of the reign of the first two Hanoverians no longer set the context for that of the third of the line. John Brewer, H. T. Dickinson, and others have argued that the focus of political criticism changed during this period, and with it the approaches to the reforming of Parliament.[1] Through most of the decades of Whig supremacy (1714–60), complaints about government centered on corruption, patronage, placemen, and the maintenance of standing armies. These were characteristic complaints of Country against Court that encouraged Whigs-out-of-power to make common cause with Country Tories against Whigs-in-power. None of these points of conflict touched the constitution itself—the 1689 arrangement of a legislative power that combined king, Lords, and Commons. This was the limited monarchy with both royal prerogative and ultimate parliamentary supremacy, based on the notion that men of property (hence, men of virtue and wisdom) should govern and that the chief end of government should be the protection of property and the propertied system. Neither Whig nor Tory conceded to the people as such a role in government or in the authorization of governors. In the last third of the century, however, major foci of political conflict shifted to primary concern with the arrangement itself—the institutions, the balance of power among the components, the source of authority, and the purposes of government. The thrust was toward democratization, with arguments for the primacy of Parliament over monarchy, of Commons over Lords, of popular will over parliamentary authority, of the natural rights of the individual over historically acquired prescriptive rights. Of perhaps greatest importance was the shift from intraparliamentary debate and opposition to extraparliamentary agitation as the primary means of reforming Parliament itself.

Dickinson describes the change as follows:

Under the first two Hanoverians the Country opposition had been directed from within Parliament or by spokesmen with very close ties with the parliamentary classes. Starting with the Wilkite petitioning movement of the late 1760s, however, the most important and vociferous opposition to the establishment was extra-parliamentary and was directed by men who were not among the parliamentary élite even when, like Wilkes himself, they sometimes sat in Parliament. This shift from an opposition campaign largely waged by men sitting in Parliament to one conducted by men outside the governing élite was accompanied by a significant change in the arguments and demands put forward by the critics of the establishment. Whereas the Country opposition had largely accepted the virtues of the constitutional settlement achieved by the Glorious Revolution and merely complained that a corrupt Court was not allowing the balanced constitution to operate as it should, the more radical extra-parliamentary opposition began to claim that the Revolution settlement was far from satisfactory and to assert that liberty could only be secured if there were a major reform of the whole system of representation. Instead, therefore, of concentrating on reducing the Court's influence over the House of Commons as the best means of preserving the balanced constitution, the radicals began to press for an extensive measure of parliamentary reform that would make the House of Commons more responsive to public opinion at large. The radicals showed far less interest in Place and Pension bills, although these were still desired. They eventually aimed instead to extend the franchise to all adult males.[2]

For various reasons, much of the animus of this struggle was directed at King George III, who was charged, together with some of his ministers, with plotting to overthrow the balancing and limiting constitutional arrangements and install a form of absolutism.[3] This way of construing the issues—whatever its merit—allowed those who intended constitutional changes to represent themselves as defenders of the constitution by portraying the king and his supporters as the principal threat to it. Most of the critics had no intention of doing away with the limited monarchy; however, the movement in its most radical form advocated the abolition of the monarchy in favor of a republic. In its most disintegrative form, where natural rights and libertarian rhetoric challenged prescriptive rights, and republicanism predominated over commitments to monarchy, and where the arguments and charges were spread by way of unprincipled and inflammatory journalism, the movement risked the ascendancy of mob and demagogic rule over established forms of authority.

Proponents of the reform of Parliament by extraparliamentary forces (contrasted with reform of Parliament by itself) appealed to the writings of John Locke for support. Interpreters of these developments are quick to point out that Locke himself never was so radical. Locke supported the limited monarchy, the protection of property, and the limitation of office and electorate to propertied persons, and did not advocate popular authorization and control of governments. Nevertheless, the notions of individual rights and social contract associated with Locke provided the line of argument for the dismantling of the 1689 constitutional arrangements for which Locke had provided the ideological justification.[4]

In this conflictive situation, John Wesley rose to a new level of political consciousness, expression, and engagement. Heretofore his public political statements were limited to a defense of King George II against the pretensions of the Stuarts and their Jacobite supporters. Collectively they could be read—rightly or not—as a pragmatic maneuver to protect his vulnerable Methodists and the Methodist evangelistic movement. Now Wesley emerged as a champion of the beleaguered constitutional establishment as such and an opponent of the proposals for popular participation and control. Doubtless he saw the protection of the constitutional order as essential to the protection of the Methodists, but it is clear from the tenor and content of his writings on political issues that he valued the political order in its own right, and not only or even primarily as an instrument of Methodist survival. His principal writings on the constitutional challenges, prior to the onset of the American colonial war, are "Free Thoughts on the Present State of Public Affairs: In a Letter to a Friend" (1768, 1770),[5] "Thoughts upon Liberty" (1772),[6] and "Thoughts concerning the Origin of Power" (1772).[7] These are argumentative tracts, not systematic political theory. Nevertheless, they provide reasonably clear windows to John Wesley's political thinking and loyalties, and they are more expansive and revelatory as political documents than anything he wrote previously. We shall have occasion in later chapters to return to issues treated in these documents, but for the present we must sketch their arguments as a way of understanding Wesley's political development. We want to know exactly what he was defending and why, what he saw as major threats to his constellation of political values, which political concepts were important to his line of argumentation, and whether theological thinking influenced his political thinking on these matters.

WESLEY AND WILKES

Wesley wrote the first two tracts in response to widespread disturbances associated with and promoted by John Wilkes. Wilkes emerged in the 1760s as a champion of liberty of the press and of the right of the electorate to choose its own representatives without interference from Parliament. In fact, he was a profligate debauched gambler, a man with no apparent inner sense of moral limitation who squandered his Methodist wife's fortune and then used political journalism and activism as means to recoup what he had lost. His great art was as a manipulative, demagogic writer, who managed to gain support for his personal interests by identifying them with major issues of public concern. Wilkes was elected to Parliament from Aylesbury in 1757. In 1763 he published a scathing attack on the king in No. 45 of his newspaper, the *North Briton*, accusing the king of lying in one of his speeches.

Responding to this provocation, the king's ministers issued a general warrant (one that did not specify who was to be arrested) and had him committed to the Tower of London. Shortly he was released on grounds of breach of parliamentary privilege, then charged again in Commons with seditious libel. Subsequently he fled to France. Returning in 1768, he was elected to Parliament from Middlesex, expelled, and reelected twice after repeated expulsions. Ultimately the Commons declared his opponent Colonel Henry Luttrel (supported by the king's ministers) the incumbent of the seat, despite Wilkes's huge vote margin over Luttrel of 1,143 to 296. Their argument was that Wilkes was not a qualified candidate. Therefore, the 1,143 electors who chose him simply wasted their votes, leaving Luttrel with a majority of 296. Of course, Wilkes did not accept this result quietly. He continued his rousing of public opinion and street crowds against the king and his ministers, extended his campaign to the nation as a whole, and organized the Society for the Supporters of the Bill of Rights to formalize and extend his efforts.[8]

In 1768, when Wesley wrote the first draft of his "Free Thoughts," the Wilkite movement was powerful and threatening, and the cry of "Wilkes and liberty" at times filled the streets. Wesley professed neutrality with regard to the conflicts of the time, and evenhandedness in commenting on them. Nevertheless, he came down solidly on the side of the establishment, its personnel, and its institutions. In the specific case of the expulsion of Wilkes from the House of Commons and the refusal to recognize his election, he wrote, "I do not defend the measures which have been taken relative to the Middlesex election." Yet he supported the actions against Wilkes and embraced the standard justifications for them.[9] The House of Commons, Wesley insisted, had the right to expel and therefore to exclude. It acted correctly both in expelling and in excluding Wilkes, because he was not fit to hold the seat to which he had been elected. Moreover, Commons acted correctly in seating Luttrel, because in effect the 296 votes he received were the only ones cast for a qualified candidate. That was an argument offered to the House of Lords by Lord Chief Justice Mansfield in opposing Lord Chatham's motion to overturn the action of the House of Commons in seating Luttrel. Wesley quoted Mansfield at length, and also stated the argument as his own.

CAUSES OF THE PRESENT DISORDER

On the broader question of the causes of the present turbulence, Wesley examined to his own satisfaction the published and rumored charges against the monarch, his ministers, and Parliament, and dismissed them—with a few minor admissions. "We have removed the imaginary causes of the present commotions," he wrote. "It plainly appears, they are not owing to the extraordinary badness, either of the King, of his Parliament, of his Ministers, or of the measures which they have taken."[10] Of the king, he observed:

> His Majesty's character . . . after all the pains which have been taken to make him odious, as well as contemptible, remains unimpeached; and therefore cannot be, in any degree, the cause of the present commotions. His whole conduct, both in public and private, ever since he began his reign, the uniform tenor of his behaviour, the general course both of his words and actions, has been worthy of an Englishman, worthy of a Christian, and worthy of a King.[11]

And of the members of Parliament he asks, "Are not the present members, generally speaking, men of the greatest property in the land? And are they not, the greater part of them at least, as honest and wise as their neighbours?"[12]

To what, then, do we attribute the unrest? To covetousness (French gold, English gold), ambition, pride and envy, resentment—personal vices of the disrupters of an otherwise stable and satisfied political society. In his primary approach to explanation, Wesley works at the level of individual character and morality—where he is confident both of exonerating those whom he supports and of winning the contest of comparisons. He does not risk sustained and substantive political or socioeconomic analysis, nor does he treat with any philosophical rigor the issues of political justice that Wilkes exploited for his own purposes. When Wesley goes beyond these approvals and comparisons, it is to evaluate relative performance with regard to the protection of liberty. On that score he rates the monarch and his administration the best ever and anywhere, and the disruptive, irrational popular movements the greatest threat.

ORDER AND LIBERTY

But Wesley's attention to the achievements and conditions of liberty is an important qualification of what otherwise comes across as a simplistic, moralistic, individualistic explanation of the dissensions coursing through England. It embodies the two political values of fundamental importance to John Wesley: order and liberty. One cannot read this tract (and others by Wesley) without recognizing that he places a high premium on civil order as a condition of individual and corporate existence, and without sensing also the profound anxiety that he feels over the risks to that order both explicit and implicit in the lunging and thrusting course of events. Wesley defends the standing order against the raging disorder that threatened institutions, life, civil unity, and liberty, and which had begun to move from local to national in its range of disturbance and disruption. He denies that conditions in England in the 1760s were the same as those in the 1640s, which had led to civil war and the beheading of King Charles I, but he argues that they might be perceived as similar, and therefore lead to the same results:

> The people will be inflamed more and more; the torrent will swell higher and higher, till at length it bursts through all opposition, and overflows the land. The consequences of these commotions will be (unless an higher hand interpose) exactly the same as those of the like commotions in the last century. First, the land will become a field of blood; many thousands of poor Englishmen will sheathe their swords in each other's bowels, for the diversion of their good neighbours. Then either a commonwealth will ensue, or else a second Cromwell. One must be; but it cannot be determined which, King W——, or King Mob.[13]

Wesley's fearful predictions were not generated solely by the corporate memory of the bloody and chaotic 1640s, nor were they simply a political device for putting the opposition on the defensive. They rose out of his own experience: the riots against the Methodists in England and Ireland, which began decades previously, and persisted sporadically even through the time of this writing; and the '45 Jacobite rebellion, which gave a taste of the terrors and destruction of civil war even without developing into general and protracted conflict. In the former case Wesley urged the enforcement of the law by responsible authorities against the rioters; in the latter, the defense of the reigning monarch against the usurper. These were appeals to implement and reinforce the ordering, supportive, protective institutions of the society. Once again Wesley found it necessary to appeal to the confirmation of the existing protective order against the forces which, in his view, were either bent on its destruction or likely to destroy it even with no intent to do so.

When Wesley wonders what is to be done specifically, he asks:

> If any [method] is more likely, would it not be, vigorously to execute the laws against incendiaries; against those who, by spreading all manner of lies, inflame the people even to madness; to teach them, that there is a difference between liberty, which is the glory of Englishmen, and licentiousness, a wanton abuse of liberty, in contempt of all laws, divine and human? Ought they not to feel, if they will not see, that *scandalum regis*, "scandalizing the King," is as punishable as *scandalum magnatum* [scandalizing the nobility]? that for the future none may dare to slander the King, any more than one of his nobles; much less to print and spread that deadly poison among His Majesty's liege subjects? Is not this little less than high treason? Is it not sowing the seeds of rebellion?[14]

We are back to moralism, with some addition of paternalistic pedagogy. Criticisms of the king are lies. Persons who tell such lies should be punished, both because what they say is slanderous and because it is socially incendiary and therefore treasonable. Also, both the liars and those inflamed by them must be taught the difference between true liberty and licentiousness. Presumably they are unaware of the distinction, as well as of the fact that they are contending for licentiousness, not liberty. Here again we see no inclination on Wesley's part to take seriously either the rhetoric of liberty or the criticisms of the establishment. The civil order is under threat, and for no justifiable reasons. It is necessary to reaffirm and stabilize the order, through education where possible, but through the enforcement of law where necessary.

Wesley, however, was not simply defending order as such against disorder. He was defending what he saw as an order of liberty against a tyrannical order that surely would take its place after a terribly destructive period of disorder. The civil order of England that was under attack for alleged hostility to liberty offered—in his view—the highest achievements and protection of liberty ever seen.

> What then can we think of the violent outcry, that the nation is oppressed, deprived of that liberty which their ancestors bought with so much treasure and blood, and delivered down through so many generations? Do those who raise this cry believe what they say? If so, are they not under the highest infatuation? seeing that England, from the time of William the Conqueror, yea, of Julius Caesar, never enjoyed such liberty, civil and religious, as it does at this day. Nor do we know of any other kingdom or state in Europe or in the world, which enjoys the like.[15]

Wesley invites the critics to replace personnel and institutions with better ones if they can. This proposal encourages Hynson to read Wesley as a pragmatist for liberty—a person for whom liberty is the highest political value, and who is willing to contemplate major political exchanges and replacements for the purpose of restoring or maximizing liberty. Wesley's strong support of monarchy, according to Hynson, is grounded not in theological convictions about monarchy, but solely in the pragmatic assessment that it is the best form of government for protecting and preserving liberty. If you can find a better one, make the swap.[16] I shall discuss Wesley's views of monarchy in a subsequent chapter. At this point I must acknowledge that Hynson is correct in recognizing both Wesley's solid commitment to liberty and his pragmatism in analysis and decision making. However it does not follow that Wesley was as loosely connected to the established order as this proposal makes him seem. Wesley is not proposing seriously that anyone should look for a viable alternative to the present government. He means to say that they cannot possibly find anything better. What exists has some defects, to be sure, but it nonetheless is very good by any honest and informed appraisal, and if it were to be dismantled it would be replaced by something far worse. His pragmatic argument is conservative: improve on what you have already. It is not radical: tear down what exists and replace it with something new and better. In particular, he wants to stress that the present constitutional order is the best protection for liberty. If it is destroyed in the name of liberty, the results will be not greater liberty but mob rule, demagoguery, and tyranny.

We miss the main point if we understand Wesley to think only in terms of the quality of personnel or even the abstract, relative quality of institutions. Although his political rhetoric tends to be moralistic and individualistic, his sense of political reality is more systemic and organic. He quotes an unidentified writer to the effect that "The House supported its decisions against the current of popular prejudice; and, in defending their own judicial rights, secured the most solid part of the liberties of their constituents."[17] Rights may be individual, but fundamentally they are socially constructed and defended. Rights that are embedded in institutions, and which enable the effective functioning of those institutions, are better guarantors of the rights of individuals than naked appeals to individual rights—especially when the appeals are driven by waves of popular sentiment. Wesley thinks in terms of organic connectedness, even though he seems to speak in terms of interchangeable parts. Personnel and offices do not stand apart from institutions, and institutions do not stand apart from their historical development and their enwebbing in the society. Neither are liberty and order separable political values. The political culture of England is an ordering of liberty that survives and prospers because there is liberty in the order. Liberty is not an abstraction; it is a constituent of a particular political-legal order. To set liberty against the order of its embodiment is to threaten the foundations of liberty. This may be a form of pragmatism for liberty, but if so, it is a deeply organic pragmatism.

THE ROLE OF THE PEOPLE IN POLITICS

If anything should confirm Wesley's lack of interest in liberty as a free-floating political value, it is his resistance to the role of the people in politics. At the outset of "Free Thoughts" he pled insufficient competence to comment on public events, by reason of inadequate knowledge of both facts and motives (which did not stop him from offering his views as though he were fully competent not only to render but also to publish an opinion). Wesley's statement of his alleged lack of competence to comment may have been an attempt at modesty and objectivity, but it was also his way of setting up the argument that ordinary people did not have the knowledge requisite to political participation. With typical Wesley sarcasm he remarks, "I grant, every cobbler, tinker, porter, and hackney-coachman can do this; but I am not so deep learned: While they are sure of everything, I am in a manner sure of nothing; except of that very little which I see with my own eyes, or hear with my own ears."[18] Inventing a hypothetical speech for William Pitt, Wesley has him say:

> How came these colliers and keelmen to be so well acquainted with affairs of State? How long have they been judges of public administration? of naval and military operations? How came they to understand the propriety or impropriety of the measures I take? Do they comprehend the balance of Europe? Do they know the weakness and strength of its several kingdoms; the characters of the Monarchs and their Ministers; the springs of this and that public motion? Else, why do they take upon them to scan my conduct? *Ne sutor ultra crepidam!* "Let them mind their own work," keep to their pits and keels, and leave State affairs to me.[19]

Wesley concedes that the citizens of London are not on the same low level as the colliers of Newcastle, but adds:

> And yet I suppose they were equally incompetent judges of the measures which Mr. Pitt took. And I doubt they are full as incompetent judges of the measures taken by the present ministry. To form a tolerable judgment of them requires, not only a good understanding, but more time than common tradesmen can spare, and better information than they can possibly procure. I think, therefore, that

the encouraging them to pass their verdict on Ministers of State, yea, on King, Lords, and Commons, is not only putting them out of their way, but doing them more mischief than you are aware of.[20]

However greatly Mr. Wesley may have loved the common people, he clearly did not respect their aptitude for political commentary, and he certainly did not want to entrust to them a role in political decision making. His remarks in this case, we should note, were not simply observations on relative facility for political judgment, nor were they pertinent only to the merits of the Wilkes case. They represented a strong position on the question of whether political judgment should be limited to king, Lords, and Commons—in effect to the political class—or whether it should be extended to extraparliamentary forces, including the forces of public opinion. Should the constitutional arrangements of 1689 be left in place and confirmed once again, or should they be democratized? Should the political class—essentially the propertied class—continue to govern, or should the adult male population as a whole become the political class? Should prescriptive right remain the criterion of political judgment, or should it be replaced by appeals to natural rights? On these questions, Wesley stood with the conservative defenders of the constitutional arrangements of 1689, and against those who sought to change them. He might have answered them quite differently had he been a champion of liberty as such, rather than of the liberty ingredient in and protected by the established order.

The constitutional arrangements of 1689 were designed to protect property relations and men of property. We should note, therefore, that in defending these arrangements Wesley did not enter this conflict as a supporter of the property system. It is true that he spoke comfortably and approvingly of the members of Parliament being "generally speaking, men of the greatest property in the land," but that is by way of expressing his confidence in their responsibility by contrast with people like Wilkes, not of arguing—as they might— that the main purpose of government is to protect the property system. Wesley certainly believed that government should protect property ownership as a civil liberty, but his evident motivation in this pamphlet is the protection of the constitutional system itself and with it the necessary conditions for both order and liberty.

Inevitably, however, his partisanship to the constitution as a protector of order and liberty also had the effect of confirming the central role of property and men of property in the political system.

THREATS TO MONARCH AND MONARCHY

Wesley's "Thoughts upon Liberty," dated 24 February 1772, is another response to the continuing prominence of John Wilkes and to the perceived threat from his aggressive campaign of democratization and self-promotion. Wesley refers to Wilkes sarcastically as "our great patriot." He notes the various ways in which the image of Wilkes is displayed and the demand that windows be illuminated in his honor. The intimidating practices of the Wilkes mobs, countered only lightly by the authorities, confirm Wesley's insistence that Wilkes, his mobs, and his methods are destroyers of liberty, not saviors of it.

In this pamphlet Wesley is concerned primarily to counter threats to King George III and the monarchy arising from this mass phenomenon and its unrelenting, morally unlimited use of journalistic character attacks and accusations. Recent historians of the period have argued that although the king was attacked savagely in the journalistic media, the institution of monarchy was not at risk, and most critics were unlikely to take action against the monarch that would jeopardize the monarchy itself. John Brewer, for example, has written that "the [Wilkite] movement—despite the occasional cry such as, 'No Wilkes. No King . . . This is the most glorious opportunity for a Revolution that ever offered,' was remarkably loyalist. Almost every Wilkite ballad maintained, in a way that we perhaps would regard as incongruous, the compatibility of ardent support for the Crown with allegiance to 'Wilkes and Liberty.' "[21] Wesley, however, saw the matter differently. The rage that has been stirred up, the flame that has been kindled till it has become an inferno, is moving out of control, and will not stop short of destruction of monarch and monarchy. "How long have the public papers," he wrote,

represented one of the best of Princes as if he had been one of the worst, as little better than Caligula, Nero, or Domitian! These were followed by pamphlets of the same kind, and aiming at the same point,—to make the King appear odious as well as contemptible in the eyes of his subjects. Letters succeed, wrote in fine language, and with exquisite art, but filled with the gall of bitterness. "Yes, but not against the King; Junius does not strike at him, but at the evil administration." Thin pretence! Does not every one see the blow is aimed at the King through the sides of his Ministers? All these are conveyed, week after week, through all London and all the nation. Can any man wonder at the effect of this? What can be more natural? What can be expected, but that they who drink in these papers and letters with all greediness, will be thoroughly embittered and inflamed thereby? will first despise and then abhor the King? What can we expect, but that by the repeated doses of this poison they will be perfectly intoxicated, and only wait for a convenient season to tear in pieces the royal monster, as they think him, and all his adherents?[22]

What hinders this result is the presence of Parliament and the army. Of the two, the latter is the more necessary stabilizing force, because it protects the Parliament as well as the king, and the crowd will not dare challenge it. For this reason the king is urged to dissolve the Parliament and disband the army. "But . . . King George has too much understanding, to throw himself into the hands of those men who have given full proof that they bear him no great good-will. Nor has he reason to believe that they are much more fond of monarchy itself, whoever the Monarch be."[23] To Wesley, the protestations of loyalty are a sham. The real intention— veiled only thinly—is to eliminate both king and Crown.

LIBERTY AND LICENTIOUSNESS

Wesley establishes common ground with Wilkes and his supporters at the outset by affirming liberty as a constituent of human nature, a natural instinct that is also a rational instinct. "The love of liberty is then the glory of rational beings; and it is the glory of Britons in particular."[24] Britons throughout their history have struggled to preserve their liberty, and have shown a willingness to sacrifice everything else in order to keep it. But the meaning of liberty and its moral quality are not self-evident. There is liberty rightly understood, and there is licentiousness. The latter is egoistic willfulness, unrestrained by any considerations of law, morality, or religion. It is the liberty to murder, loot, and rape, and to execute monarchs. Liberty rightly understood, however, is concretized as religious and civil liberty. Religious liberty is "a liberty to choose our own religion, to worship God according to our own conscience, according to the best light we have."[25] Civil liberty is "a liberty to enjoy our lives and fortunes in our own way; to use our property, whatever is legally our own, according to our own choice."[26] Britons, according to Wesley, have religious and civil liberty—more than at any time since William the Conqueror, more than any other country in the world. It is absurd for the critics to argue otherwise. What the Wilkites obviously want is liberty as licentiousness. That is what their efforts to change the constitutional system will produce. If and when they succeed, religious and civil liberty will be at an end.

Neither religious nor civil liberty, Wesley argues, is under any threat from the reigning king. To the contrary, the king is the guarantor of liberties—especially of religious liberty. Wesley asks:

> Are we abridged of our religious liberty? His late Majesty [George II] was desired, about thirty years ago, to take a step of this kind. But his answer was worthy of a King, yea, the King of a free people: "I tell you, while I sit on the English throne, no man shall be persecuted for conscience' sake." And it is certain he made his promise good from the beginning of his reign to the end. But perhaps the case is altered now. Does His present Majesty tread in his steps? He does: He persecutes no man for conscience' sake. If he does, where is the man?[27]

Wesley drives the point home with a comparison of George III with his Tudor and Stuart predecessors: the "horrid fires" of Queen Mary's years, the hangings—even for religion—of Queen Elizabeth's reign, persecution of the Puritans by James I, the Act of Uniformity and the Acts against Conventicles under Charles II. None of these atrocities happens now. "O, compare King Charles, gracious Charles the Second, with King George, and you will know the value of the liberty you enjoy."[28]

One must not mistake these comparisons as pertaining only to the persons and penchants of the monarchs themselves. Wesley is comparing the arbitrary and absolutizing power of the Tudors and Stuarts with the limited power of the Georges. This is a constitutional argument, not in essence a personal one. Arbitrary power, characteristic of the Tudor and Stuart reigns, offended against historic individual liberties. Limited, constitutional power, characteristic of the Hanoverians, protects them. The outcome of the campaign of the "warm men for liberty" will be to destroy the constitutional balances, thereby replacing limited power with power even less limited than that of the Tudors and Stuarts, and leaving individual liberties completely unprotected. The outcome of these approaches to democratization will be chaos and tyranny.

THE "DIET OF POISON"

When Wesley asks for an explanation for such crass stupidity, such irrational argumentation as is found in this mass movement, he feints at first with the suggestion that the devil is behind it, but withdraws that suggestion quickly, acknowledging that his readers are far too sophisticated to buy it. Reaching for a more empirical explanation, he argues that for years the people of England have been fed a diet of poison through the various print media. In this respect he recognizes fully what Brewer and other historians have identified and studied as the most important empowering factor in the Wilkite movement: the developing facilities for spreading the message, the accusations, and the caricatures quickly and effectively across the nation and beyond. Given his analysis and his recognition of the power of journalism, Wesley draws the one conclusion that seems to him obvious, and the same one that he drew at the end of "Free Thoughts on Public Affairs": if anything can stop the willful, unreasoning destruction of king, constitution, and English liberty it is the enactment of laws punishing the publishing of lies that stir up dissension between the king and his subjects. Wesley is not comfortable with this solution. As a writer and publisher himself, and as a priest-evangelist often at odds with the religious and political establishment, he knows the value of the free dissemination of controversial and contrary views. But he is confident that the attacks on the king are lies, that lies deserve no protection, that these particular lies are profoundly damaging to the public good as represented in the institutions of the constitution, especially the monarchy. If the spreading of lies can be stopped by legal means, there may be some hope for preserving the political goods achieved through centuries of struggle—unless, of course, God "has a controversy" with this people!

The contrast between liberty and licentiousness is valid and appropriate. It is a distinction to which Wesley would return— rightly—in other writings. It was also pertinent to the prevailing situation, because John Wilkes was not inclined to make the same distinction in manipulating popular passions and using the rhetoric of liberty to advance his personal interests. The distinction between truth and falsehood in political discourse also is valid and appropriate—and continues to be so. We should balk, however, at accepting Wesley's superficial explanation for the disorder; namely, that there were no seriously justifiable complaints, only lies. For that reason and for others we should balk also at his proposal to stop the process of disintegration by suppressing the lies. If Wesley understood fully what was happening in British society, he shows only partial awareness in these two tracts. The long era of Whig dominance—or of dominance by a particular group of Whigs— was coming to an end, and the demise of this oligarchic rule was being abetted actively by George III. Accusations of arbitrary rule by the king and of his grasping for more power arose out of the group of demoted political potentates. They did not derive solely from the Wilkite movement. Some of the politicians-now-out-of-power sought to co-opt the Wilkite movement for their own purposes, as did persons with strong egalitarian commitments and with concerns to open up a closed political system. This diversity led to a division within the movement between those persons who had serious political and ideological concerns and those who—like Wilkes himself—were concerned mainly with personal advancement and political theater. Wesley either did not see this complexity, or chose for strategic reasons to ignore it. Instead he focused on Wilkes and rabid journalism as the problem—on the contrast of the man of good character (George III) with the man of bad character (Wilkes), of the reasoned governing by a sober and responsible king with the raving and rampaging of an unprincipled, irresponsible "King Mob." Other highly important elements in the mix receive no recognition.

Moreover, at least in these tracts, Wesley does not deal with the complaint that the maintenance of British liberties depends on the extension of the franchise—on a right to vote grounded in natural right, and therefore on greater adequacy of representation. In defending the existing constitution, Wesley saw himself as supporting the principal guarantor of British liberties. What he also was defending was a political oligarchy that maintained its power by rules of exclusion. During the years of Whig dominance the Tories were excluded, as were some of the (Country) Whigs. Now persons formerly in power were being excluded and were looking for ideological arguments as well as political alliances and mechanisms to support their return to power. None of these folks seriously intended extending the franchise to unpropertied persons, to say nothing of women or youth. Most extraparliamentary forces also intended no really radical extension of the franchise, but they did advocate reform of parliamentary representation and some degree of franchise extension sufficient to begin the opening up of the closed political system. John Wesley was aware of these arguments, but chose not to address the fullness of the claims for liberty in either publication.

THE SOURCE OF POLITICAL AUTHORITY

In "Thoughts concerning the Origin of Power," also from 1772, Wesley attacks the doctrines of right of individual consent to government and societal conferring of power and authority. His purpose obviously is to undercut the philosophical support that these ideas provided for the democratizing movement. One might argue, of course, that his main purpose is to reassert the sovereignty of God over the political process, because he restates the contention of Romans 13 that all authority derives from God. That he means to do that is true, but he does not develop the theological point, and he establishes his biblical position not by systematic argument but by eliminating the popular alternatives. Most of the essay is devoted to his demolition of the case for popular sovereignty. It is clear that he is continuing his defense of the established constitutional order and his opposition to republican and democratic alternatives by moving from questions of comparative character and relative performance on behalf of liberty to those having to do with ideological justification.

Wesley does not examine and dismiss the concept of natural right. Instead he draws the logical consequences of using the concept as the basis of a theory of governmental authorization. If one derives authority from natural right by way of consent of the governed, he asks, how can the circle of consenting persons be limited to adult, propertied males? Do not women have the same natural rights as men? youth the same as adults? unpropertied persons the same as propertied? How, then, can they be denied the franchise and the right to consent to being governed and given laws? Specifically with regard to women, he asks, "By what argument do you prove that women are not naturally as free as men? And if they are, why have they not as good a right as we have to choose their own Governors? Who can have any power over free, rational creatures, but by their own consent? And are they not free by nature, as well as we? Are they not rational creatures?"[29] Clearly Wesley does not mean to say that women, youth, and unpropertied males should be given the franchise. Rather, he is drawing obvious conclusions that he knows the advocates themselves do not accept, and thereby is exposing the hypocrisy of their philosophical pretensions. Moreover, Wesley does not name and examine the social contract theory, nor does he identify it with John Locke. He merely asks for historical evidence that such a collective transfer of power ever happened. He does a quick review of English history looking for evidence, but finds nothing to support the theory of popular conferral of authority.[30] He concedes that in the previous century the people of Naples appear to have acted in unity to confer authority on one particular person, but denies that this single occasion suffices to support a general theory. Having thus disposed of the below-to-above arguments for authorization of power, Wesley feels satisfied that nothing remains but an above-to-below argument. Because God is what ultimately is above, the inference is clear: All authority derives from God.

Wesley's views on political authority will be examined more fully later on. Here we need observe only that he is not giving the topic full theoretical examination; he is engaging in a polemic of logic that supports the stand taken in the other two tracts. This is partisan argument, not political philosophy. The essay is both different from and complementary to the other tracts, but the differences support the complementarity. Here Wesley introduces God-talk for the first time. His argument discloses a theological dimension of thinking about politics that made no appearance in the previous two essays—if one excuses the timid effort to attribute England's political disturbances to the devil. Wesley offered no theological defense of king, monarchy, or established order in those essays. The defense was based exclusively on empirical factors of comparative moral character and the reading of the record, and on projections of probable results from the destruction of the present order and its replacement by a different one. Now we see him moving from an empirical to a logical and ultimately to a theological mode of argumentation. As I have argued, however, his primary purpose in doing so is not to develop a theological understanding of political authority, but to deny philosophical legitimation to the democratizing movements. In this respect the essay is both different from and complementary to the others.

There is no explicit defense of king, Parliament, and constitution in this essay—by contrast with the others. The defense is implicit: those who hold and exercise power in Britain have their authorization for doing so from God, not the people. Therefore, when reform of policies and constitutional institutions becomes necessary, they should see to the reforms themselves, and not be beholden or responsive to extraparliamentary initiatives and demands. That line of argument confirms John Wesley's support of the constitutional arrangements of 1689. It is not monarchism, even though it includes enthusiastic defense of monarch and monarchy. It is not Toryism, even though it is anchored in belief in God as sovereign source of authority, and even though Wesley continued to identify himself as a Tory. It is constitutionalism—the legislative unity of king and Parliament enacting laws for kingdom and empire with reference to concepts of public good and historic rights and not to popular agitation or abstract concepts of natural right.

Perhaps the most interesting and intriguing aspect of "Origins of Power" is Wesley's application of his concept of authority to the classical threefold typology of forms of government: monarchy, aristocracy, democracy. All of these forms are acknowledged as authoritative in their own times and places, so long as there is recognition that their authority comes from God and not the people. That might seem to imply the ultimate "dethroning" of monarchy as the preferred if not exclusively legitimated form of government, the test of preference being only the pragmatic one of which best serves the cause of liberty. However, Wesley did not mean to say that all forms of government are inherently equal. He meant to say only that wherever you find established government, its authority comes from God, not the people. That contention served his purpose of confirming the established limited monarchy of England. In this respect also, his essay on "Origins of Power" is complementary to the two preceding tracts, even though it is different from them.

THE CONSERVATIVE CONSTITUTIONALIST

Interpreters of John Wesley's public political interventions often read the three essays of this period as evidences of his residual Toryism. In "Free Thoughts on Public Affairs" and "Thoughts upon Liberty" he defends monarch and monarchy—firm confirmation, apparently, of his "ingrained monarchism." In "Thoughts concerning the Origin of Power," according to this view, he discloses the remnants of his Jacobitic, divine right thinking by attributing political authority ultimately to God. That is an incorrect reading of Wesley's effort. It relies, usually, on the flawed supposition that he was a Jacobite from his mother's influence, and carried residual Jacobitism into his response to this major internal domestic conflict. Wesley indeed defends monarch and monarchy in these essays, but as integral elements of the constitution—not as institutions to be regarded and conserved separately. Because the king is under direct attack, he defends the king. Because he is convinced that wild Wilkites and others intend to destroy the monarchy and create a republic, he defends the monarchy. In every instance, however, he is defending the British constitution, and therefore king and monarchy, as constituents of that organic, institutional arrangement.

One should note that he defends the Parliament as well. At times it may seem that Wesley speaks up for the Parliament primarily because he sees it as a bulwark protecting the king from the mob, just as he speaks up for the army as a protector of Parliament. But that does not detract from his regard for Parliament as an ingredient of the constitution with its own proper constitutional functions. Wesley defends the Parliament as an institution existing in supportive reciprocity with the monarchy, and not as a mere instrument or extension of the monarchy.[31] Parliament has its own work and integrity, as do each of its two houses.[32] King, Lords, and Commons, acting together with mutual confirmation and limitation, constitute the political and legal reality that Wesley defends against the radical threats—republican, democratic, libertarian. These are the sentiments of an eighteenth-century British constitutionalist, not of a Jacobite monarchist, not even of an advocate of liberty as the dominant political value.

Wesley stated also that authority comes from God, not the people. Although some would take that as evidence of Jacobite leanings, Wesley himself insisted that it meant he was a Tory, not a Jacobite. Even that claim may be too restrictive, because many Whigs also believed that authority came from God and not from the people—despite their inclination to identify as the people not the generality of folk, but the remnant of Parliament that installed William and Mary on the throne of England. Wesley made this argument about the divine source of authority for two principal reasons—one theological, the other practical. The theological reason was simply that he read it in the Bible, preeminently in Romans 13. The practical reason was that empowering the people through attribution of authority would—in his estimate—threaten the constitution, and with it the combination of order and liberty that he treasured and celebrated. As I have noted, however, Wesley never made the specifically Jacobitic arguments normally associated with the claim that political authority derives from God. He did not use the language of divine right, did not argue for indefeasible hereditary right of succession, and most definitely did not place the king above the law or above parliamentary confirmation of royal acts. When he allowed that divine authorization might descend on an aristocracy and even a democracy, and not necessarily on a monarchy, he quite obviously was not limiting this theological claim to the service of monarchical absolutism.

The proper context for understanding Wesley's response to this raging public controversy is neither Jacobitism, nor Toryism, nor liberalism. It is the conservative reaction to the radicalism of the latter part of the eighteenth century. "Conservative" in this case meant protective of the constitutional arrangements deriving from the settlement of 1688–89. It did not refer to reactionary Jacobitism. Dickinson describes the conservative stance as follows:

> The conservatism of the late eighteenth century may have had its roots in an almost unthinking acceptance of the existing constitution and an instinctive fear of change, but these attitudes were firmly grounded in the realities of the situation and in unshakeable assumptions about the nature of politics and society. Once these attitudes and assumptions came under challenge from the radicals the defenders of the prevailing order began to develop a conservative ideology of considerable appeal, endurance and intellectual power. The first constituent element in the conservative campaign was to persuade the public of the practical virtues of the existing political system and to point out the dangerous consequences of reform. The second was to mount an attack on the intellectual foundations of the radical case and to formulate an ideology which would provide a strong buttress to the existing order. These two approaches were then combined in order to argue that those in power under the existing constitution also happened to be those who *ought* to exercise authority in a well constituted State.[33]

Wesley's own expressed ideology did not fit that of the conservative reaction in all respects. Conservatives focused their politics on the preservation of the property system. Wesley's defense of order and liberty may have implied or presupposed a defense of the property system, but that system as such was not his central concern. Conservatives believed that natural inequalities existed and should translate into political inequality. If Wesley held that belief, which is unlikely, he did not publish it. Wesley offered no support to conservative rationalizations of inequitable representation and political payoffs.[34] Neither did he show any interest in employing conservative ideology to confirm particular persons in power. But his arguments fit exactly with the two constituent elements that Dickinson describes: he trumpeted the virtues of the existing system and projected disaster if it were destroyed and replaced; and he attacked the radical (liberal) ideology with its arguments for natural rights, popular sovereignty, and social contract. In these two fundamental respects he was obviously and undeniably a constitutional conservative. That is the political Wesley who comes to expression in his responses to radical—democratic and republican—agitation following the accession of George III.

CHAPTER FIVE

PUBLIC POLITICAL CONTROVERSIES III
LIBERTY AND INDEPENDENCE: THE AMERICAN COLONIAL REBELLION

The rebellion of the American colonies against England, George III, and the rule of Parliament provided the third major crisis context for the disclosure and development of John Wesley's political thought. This case was continuous with the domestic struggle over democratization through the presence of familiar motifs that remained at the center of political discourse and were reaffirmed sharply: defense of the British constitution, of king and monarchy, of ordered liberty; rejection of the natural rights basis of political participation and of popular consent as the source of governmental authorization; reaffirmation of both historic, prescriptive authority and of the divine origin of political authority. New, however, was the broadened context of political engagement and reflection: the British community itself was at risk of dissolution as the rebels sought independence from England. This quest for independence, played out on a transoceanic stage, opened wider parameters for the interaction of destructive tendencies, threatened the organic solidarity of the community, and heightened the danger to fundamental institutions and liberties. Opposition to independence and to the dissolution of the British community ultimately became the primary factor, though by no means the only one, in Wesley's response to this crisis.

John Wesley was fully and acutely aware of the values at stake in this struggle and of its potential for destroying life, property, and the fabric of society. Throughout the conflict Wesley saw himself as a peacemaker and reconciler, and wrote political tracts, which (in his view) were intended to calm the roiling passions on both sides. However, his representation of himself as a neutral peacemaker was inaccurate and self-deceptive. He was, in reality, an ardent partisan and patriot whose idea of peace was acceptance of obedience to the king and the king's laws, and whose contribution to political discourse mainly took the forms of arguing the case for royal and parliamentary authority and exposing as lies the arguments against king and government made by the American rebels and their English supporters. He was accused widely of writing his political tracts with government prompting and encouragement and in hope of rewards of pension and elevation to the episcopacy, and found it necessary to deny and refute these accusations publicly and in print.[1]

EARLY ADVOCACY FOR THE AMERICANS

Wesley's self-representation as neutral peacemaker was not simply wrong, and it was neither cynical nor hypocritical. In the early stages of the controversy he was sympathetic to the plight and claims of the colonists, believing as he did that they had been treated badly in some ways, and that they were seeking nothing more than redress of grievances based on their rights as English people. In 1768 he wrote, "I do not defend the measures which have been taken with regard to America: I doubt whether any man can defend them, either on the foot of law, equity, or prudence."[2] He does not specify what the measures were, but presumably they pertained to the taxing of the American colonies, for he attributes them to George Grenville. As First Lord of the Treasury (Prime Minister), Grenville was responsible for the Revenue Act of 1764 and the Stamp Act of 1765—laws the Americans considered offensive and oppressive, and which provoked and legitimated their serious opposition. Wesley makes a point of identifying the measures with Grenville in order to absolve of blame both the present ministry and the king.[3] Subsequently, Wesley would defend the same tax laws as mild and justifiable means of getting the colonists to help pay for their own defense. In 1768, however, he agreed with their critics.

Wesley's strongest statement of support for the colonists was his letter of 14 June 1775 to the Earl of Dartmouth, Lord Privy Seal and formerly Secretary of State for the colonies. The following day he sent the same letter, with minor changes, to Lord North, the Prime

Minister. Wesley sets the stage for his appeal with these oft-quoted words: "All my prejudices are against the Americans. For I am an High Churchman, the son of an High Churchman, bred up from my childhood in the highest notions of passive obedience and non-resistance. And yet, in spite of all my rooted prejudice, I cannot avoid thinking (if I think at all) that an oppressed people asked for nothing more than their legal rights, and that in the most modest and inoffensive manner which the nature of the thing would allow."[4] Evidently the agitation for independence and the support-ing natural rights argumentation have not come to his attention, for he defines the conflict in terms of legal rights—rights English peo-ple are entitled to by law or custom, but which have been illegally or unwisely restricted in the case of the American colonies ("an oppressed people"). Apparently also, he does not view the colonial activity on behalf of these rights as a serious breach of passive obe-dience and nonresistance, because he refers to the "modest and inoffensive manner" of their contention.

However, Wesley does not examine and argue these claims. Instead, he turns to prudential reasons for restraint by the govern-ment in pressing the case against the colonies: the Americans are highly motivated, fighting for hearth and home, whereas the British troops mainly are mercenaries fighting for nothing more than money. The Americans also are unafraid; are better equipped, trained, and disciplined than we have let ourselves believe; and they are united—despite the rumors of their divisions. Moreover, England's heavy investment of troops, resources, and attention in America leaves it seriously vulnerable to foreign and domestic ene-mies. Foreign countries will not overlook the significance of the relocation of the British army to another continent, leaving the motherland protected only by a weak and timid militia. Wales, Scotland, and Ireland may seize the opportunity to remove them-selves from the control and governance of English power. English dissidents, active already for years with inflammatory propaganda against the king and the monarchy, will discern the internal weak-ness as the occasion for overthrowing the constitutional institu-tions and replacing them with a republic. Social unrest will mix with political dissent: there is a decay in trade, and a scarcity of provisions.[5] These latter conditions in particular suggest not only a volatile sociopolitical mix, but also the prospect of divine punishment because of the country's sins: "When I consider (to say nothing of ten thousand other vices shocking to human nature) the astonishing *luxury* of the rich and the *profaneness* of rich and poor, I doubt whether general dissoluteness of manners does not demand a general visitation. Perhaps the decree is already gone forth from the Governor of the world."[6] Having sketched out these dire prospects deliberately by comparison with the unrest of the 1640s, Wesley concludes with the ominous admonition (omitted from the draft sent to Lord North): "O my Lord, if your Lordship can do anything let it not be wanting! For God's sake, for the sake of the King, of the nation, of your lovely family, remember Rehoboam! Remember Philip the Second! Remember King Charles the First!"[7]

FROM ADVOCACY TO OPPOSITION

Shortly thereafter Wesley began a migration from advocate to opponent of the colonists' claims, and in attitude from sympathy and compassion to suspicion and hostility. The usual interpretation of this move is that he came to perceive that what the Americans were after was not legal English rights, but independence from England. The former he could countenance and endorse; the latter he would have to oppose. This interpretation is essentially correct. However, it is important to recognize that there were at least three aspects of—or stages in—the transition. First, under the influence of Samuel Johnson, Wesley turned against the "taxation without representation" arguments of the Americans (and their English sympathizers). Second, he changed his view of the source of the conflict. Initially he believed that the American agitation was English in origin: the Wilkite crowd and other fellow travelers in the movement for democratization and republican institutions, having failed to achieve their ends in the context of English politics, now sought leverage by generating opposition to the government in the colonies.[8] Without surrendering his accusations of the English opponents of the government, Wesley now came to see that the Americans had initiatives and motives of their own that were not explicable simply as provocations from abroad. Third, he became convinced that what the Americans really were after was separation from the mother country—literally, the destruction of the British community. Agitation for legal English constitutional rights was merely a subterfuge used to confuse and divert the opposition while developing strength and support for prosecuting the plans for independence. The second and third of these aspects were not really separable in time, and therefore probably should not be spoken of as "stages." The last point—perception of the drive for independence—clearly was the weightiest factor in changing John Wesley from a sympathizer to an opponent of the political activities of the American colonists.

The "Calm Address"

Wesley's first major statement in opposition to the Americans was "A Calm Address to Our American Colonies."[9] The main purpose of the pamphlet was to counter the Americans' argument concerning taxation, especially the leading slogan "no taxation without representation." American agitators and their English supporters had been arguing since the midsixties that Parliament had no right to tax the colonies because they were not represented in that legislative body. Taxation was justifiable only with the consent of those being taxed. The Americans had given no consent, and were not represented institutionally for the purpose of doing so. Therefore the taxes levied by Parliament were unconstitutional and unjust. Moreover, in the absence of parliamentary representation, the Americans were entitled by natural right to enact their own laws and impose their own taxes.

In his response Wesley asserts the full authority of king and Parliament to tax the colonies. Colonies exist by grant of royal charter; they have no authority deriving from any other source. Specifically, they have no justifiable appeal to a natural right of self-government to support a claim to be taxed only with their own consent. Whatever original right the colonists—or anyone else—may have possessed in nature was lost with the transition to civil society and civil government. The colonists are members of the British Empire, subjects of the king. They have no independent political existence, and no grounds for claiming such. Their seat of government is in London. This government has constitutional authority as well as divine authorization. It fixes the rights of the colonies in their charters, and in doing so does not surrender its constitutional authority over them. The point is confirmed by the history of tax legislation going back at least to Charles II, which shows that Parliament always has exercised tax authority over the colonies.[10] Furthermore, if Parliament has the right to enact laws that govern the colonies, it has the right to tax them. If it has no right to tax them, neither does it have the right to enact any laws affecting them. The colonists do not dispute the right of the government to enact laws; therefore they should not challenge its right to impose taxes. "Considering this," he insists, "nothing can be more plain, than that the supreme power in England has a legal right of laying any tax upon them for any end beneficial to the whole empire."[11]

Wesley does not deny that colonists may have rights other than those specified in the charters. Although he does not use the term *prescriptive right*, he seems to be implying that concept when he speaks of rights that the colonists have as English people, rights—including the right to vote—that they have because their ancestors had them.[12] These are rights derived from English historical experience, not from human nature. He argues that they have made these rights of no effect by moving across the ocean, where they have no possibility of exercising them. In doing so, however, they did not delegitimize the legislative authority of those for whom they no longer can vote. But his main point is that they are not entitled to claim a natural right of suffrage and representation to replace the historic rights they rendered ineffective by their migration. Supposed natural rights of individuals are not the basis of governmental authority. The government in place has the authority to legislate for the empire because it is the government in place, because it is constitutional, and because God delivers authority from above to the governors. It need not consult the electorate or the people at large, for it is not obligated to them. It is obligated to God and to the public good, to king and country, but not to the presumed natural rights of the citizens. Wesley's position on these matters—specifically on natural rights, consent, and governmental authority—is consistent with his views advanced in previous writings, especially "Thoughts concerning the Origin of Power."[13]

Wesley also does not use the term *virtual representation*, but that is how his position can be characterized. The colonists, he insists, are represented in Parliament even though they do not vote for members and send them to London. The few qualified men who sit in Parliament virtually represent all of the king's subjects. They look after the interests of everyone in the empire, including the colonists. There is no defensible right of direct representation with its correlative of necessary consent to the enactment of laws and the imposition of taxes. Laws enacted in the absence of direct representation are laws nonetheless, and they require the obedience of the subjects. Taxation presupposes representation, but not direct representation. That is the meaning of the British constitution.

Proponents of direct representation argued that not to be represented directly was tantamount to slavery. Wesley dismissed that argument as self-evident nonsense. "I have no representative in Parliament; but I am taxed; yet I am no slave. Yea, nine in ten throughout England have no representative, no vote; yet they are no slaves; they enjoy both civil and religious liberty to the utmost extent."[14] Persons who whine that they are in slavery because they are not allowed to elect representatives to Parliament are maliciously distorting the meaning of the term. If they want to know what slavery is, they should consider the condition of the Africans in America. They are the real slaves. Their owners are not in slavery simply because they cannot consent to the taxes that they must pay.

> "Who then is a slave?" Look into America, and you may easily see. See that Negro, fainting under the load, bleeding under the lash! He is a slave. And is there "no difference" between him and his master? Yes; the one is screaming, "Murder! Slavery!" the other silently bleeds and dies!
>
> "But wherein then consists the difference between liberty and slavery?" Herein: You and I, and the English in general, go where we will, and enjoy the fruit of our labours: This is liberty. The Negro does not: This is slavery.[15]

Liberty is freedom of movement, freedom to use and dispose of our property. Elsewhere he includes and stresses freedom to worship God according to our own understanding and inclination.[16] The colonists enjoy all these liberties. But liberty has no necessary implications for electoral politics and governmental authority. Therefore the argument that absence of franchise and of direct representation has made them slaves is demonstrably false.

To his own satisfaction, then, Wesley demolishes the link between slavery and absence of representation, as well as the argument for a natural right to representation. His position on the fundamental issues of political theory is clear: there is a government that has the authority to impose taxes on its subjects. Although its seat is in London, it is the government for the entire British Empire. The colonists are members of the British Empire whose political existence and rights are defined in charters granted to them by the government in London. Therefore the government has the constitutional right to tax them, and they have the constitutional obligation to obey and to pay the taxes. The only relevant rights in this case are the ones established in historical prescription or granted by the government through charter. There are no relevant rights of human nature, in particular no right to representation, to be set in opposition to these prescriptive and legal rights. The claim of "no taxation without representation" is disallowed.

Having dealt with the theoretical issues, Wesley turns to a reasoned explanation for the particular taxes that presumably have caused the uproar.

> A few years ago, you were assaulted by enemies, whom you were not able to resist. You represented this to your mother-country, and desired her assistance. You was largely assisted, and by that means wholly delivered from all your enemies. After a time, your mother-country, desiring to be re-imbursed for some part of the large expense she had been at, laid a small tax (which she had always a right to do) on one of her colonies.[17]

This argument is the same one offered by Grenville and other supporters of the policy of taxing the colonies. Presumably it is the same one that Wesley could not defend in 1768: the colonies initiated the situation by seeking protection from the British government, which granted it. Subsequently the government, seeking some relief from the heavy expenses of this protection, asked the colonies to share the burden. Hence the taxes, which were justified both in the right to impose and in the justice of the particular imposition. Wesley treats the support of the colonies by the government as a matter of benevolence and maternal care. He does not consider that the colonies represented a projection of imperial policy, and that the assistance given was also an instrument of imperial self-interest—even though he was fully aware of English imperial expansionist realities. Brewer acknowledges that the American situation can be and was interpreted in various ways, but argues that the geopolitical and strategic perspective dominated discussions of the colonies in the peace negotiations following the Seven Years' War. "The government's decision to plump for hegemony on the North American continent by retaining the whole of Canada, and to content itself with a holding operation in the West Indies, placed the Americans at the very centre of the British imperial design."[18] Quite clearly, the inclination of the British government to help the colonies was not driven by pure generosity. Wesley's disposition to ignore this element of imperial politics allowed him to seem more like an apologist for governmental policy than the fair and even-handed commentator he took himself to be.

Wesley published this pamphlet in two editions. In the revised edition he states that "I was of a different judgment on this head, till I read a tract entitled, 'Taxation no Tyranny.' But as soon as I received more light myself, I judged it my duty to impart it to others. I therefore extracted the chief arguments from that treatise, and added an application to those whom it most concerns. I was well aware of the treatment this would bring upon myself; but let it be, so I may in any degree serve my King and country."[19] This admission in the revised form of the pamphlet reveals the fact that most of the writing was not Wesley's own but a severely edited form of Samuel Johnson's tract. It reflects the harsh public criticism that Wesley drew for plagiarizing Johnson's work, to which he now gives credit not only for changing his mind on the taxation issue, but also for providing the substance of the "address," which he published under his own name. Apparently Johnson himself did not object to Wesley's using his work in this fashion, and may even have been pleased that Wesley's version—improved by editing—gave his ideas much wider publicity.[20]

Public Forgetting and Remembering

There is no doubt that Wesley did an about-face on the issue of taxing the Americans, and that Johnson's tract convinced him to do so. Wesley apparently had been so convinced of the rightness of the American cause that he had recommended strongly to others a book titled *An Argument in Defence of the Exclusive Right claimed by the Colonies to Tax Themselves*.[21] Following the first publication of "A Calm Address," in which Wesley attacked the American position, Caleb Evans, a Calvinist Baptist minister in Bristol, wrote a public letter to Wesley reminding him of this recommendation and of his support the previous year of a candidate in Bristol who was sympathetic to the Americans.[22] Evans used this evidence to impugn the honesty of Wesley's sudden conversion to the government's position, and accused him of covert Jacobitism and desire for personal gain. At this point, Wesley engaged in some public forgetting. In the preface to the revised edition of "A Calm Address" he insisted: "The book which this writer says I so strongly recommend, I never yet saw with my eyes. And the words which he says I spoke, never came out of my lips."[23] Writing to Charles Wesley on 3 November 1775, he remarked that this public response should be "a sufficient answer to Mr. Evans's letter."[24] In fact, as James Rouquet wrote to Wesley, John had urged his brother Charles to read the book. This had happened at Rouquet's house.[25] Wesley responded, "I say, I remember nothing of that book, neither of the title nor of the argument. But I will send to the bookseller's to-morrow for the book; and if I have read, I cannot but remember when I see it again."[26]

An even more vigorous if not brutal jog to John's memory was provided by William Pine, Wesley's printer and publisher. According to John Telford's editorial note, "Pine had written to say that in September 1774 Wesley gave him the pamphlet on the right claimed by the Colonies to tax themselves, and advised him to put it into his newspaper as the best thing that had been written on the subject."[27] By the time of Pine's subsequent letter, Wesley had separated himself from his printer, because—as John wrote to

Charles—Pine (an ardent supporter of the colonies' cause) "every week publishes barefaced treason."[28] Nevertheless, Wesley could not ignore this mounting evidence. On November 12 he wrote again to Rouquet, "I will now simply tell you the thing as it is. As I was returning from the Leeds Conference, one gave me the tract which you refer to, part of which I read on my journey. The spirit of it I observed to be admirably good; and I *then* thought the arguments conclusive. In consequence of which, I suppose (though I do not remember it), I recommended it both to you and to others; but I had so entirely forgotten it, that even when it was brought to me the other day I could not recollect that I had ever seen it."[29]

Having confessed to this remarkable feat of forgetting, Wesley then wrote to Caleb Evans these grudging admissions:

REVEREND SIR,—You affirm (1) that I once "doubted whether the measures taken with respect to America could be defended either on the foot of law, equity, or prudence." I did doubt of these five years, nay indeed five months ago.

You affirm (2) that I "declared" (last year) "the Americans were an oppressed, injured people." I do not remember that I did; but very possibly I might.

You affirm (3) that I then "strongly recommended *An Argument for the Exclusive Right of the Colonies to Tax Themselves.*" I believe I did; but I am now of another mind.

You affirm (4) "You say in the Preface, *I never saw that book.*" I did say so. The plain case was, I had so entirely forgotten it that even when I saw it again I recollected nothing of it till I had read several pages. If I had, I might have observed that you borrowed more from Mr. Parker than I did from Dr. Johnson. Though I know not whether I should have observed it, as it does not affect the merits of the cause.[30]

The remainder of the letter deals with issues of personal integrity, beyond what already had been implied. Although Wesley had the courage—or felt the necessity—to reply publicly to Evans, admitting many of his charges, he could not resist introducing the published response with the observation that he was answering "a very angry letter," nor did he forgo the opportunity to accuse Evans of plagiarism of Parker's tract in return.[31]

Differences with Samuel Johnson

Despite Wesley's heavy reliance on Johnson's tract, there are significant differences of emphasis between the two works. Johnson is quite fully aware of the efforts of English agitators to turn the American conflict to their own purposes, but he tends to attribute initiative to the Americans, "who tried to infect the people of England with their disloyalty."[32] This focus of blame is implied in the subtitle of his tract: "An Answer to the Resolution and Address of the American Congress." In tandem with that charge he indicts the Americans with striving for independency, and not only or primarily for redress of grievances based on their rights as English people. Wesley, by contrast, concentrates on the taxation issue, as though he wanted to continue to see the matter as a resolvable dispute within a family united as to basics. When he offers his views on who is responsible, he writes:

> My opinion is this: We have a few men in England who are determined enemies to monarchy. Whether they hate His present Majesty on any other ground than because he is a King, I know not. But they cordially hate his office, and have for some years been undermining it with all diligence, in hopes of erecting their grand idol, their dear commonwealth, upon its ruins. I believe they have let very few into their design; (although many forward it, without knowing anything of the matter;) but they are steadily pursuing it, as by various other means, so in particular by inflammatory papers, which are industriously and continually dispersed throughout the town and country; by this method they have already wrought thousands of people even to the pitch of madness. By the same, only varied according to your circumstances, they have likewise inflamed America. I make no doubt but these very men are the original cause of the present breach between England and her colonies. And they are still pouring oil into the flame, studiously incensing each against the other, and opposing, under a variety of pretences, all measures of accommodation. So that, although the Americans in general love the English, and the English in general love the Americans, (all, I mean, that are not yet cheated and exasperated by these artful men,) yet the rupture is growing wider every day, and none can tell where it will end.[33]

With these words Wesley signals continuity with the positions taken on domestic English politics in "Free Thoughts on the

Present State of Public Affairs"[34] and "Thoughts upon Liberty,"[35] and extends their application to the colonial dispute. The troubles, he contends, are the work of English conspirators, who deliberately have inflamed America to serve their own (English) political purposes. He is not ready to follow Johnson in laying primary blame on the Americans, although he will do so in subsequent writings. Wesley minimizes the issue of independency as well. He deals with it marginally and by implication in the course of reminding his readers that already they have more liberty than any other country in the world, and certainly more than they would have under a republic.[36] He does so again more pointedly in an appendix to his tract, where he responds to a sermon by Dr. Smith of Philadelphia, accusing Smith and his confederates of desiring "a liberty from obeying your rightful Sovereign, and from keeping the fundamental laws of your country."[37] Nevertheless, his worries over independency in this document are muted by comparison with Johnson's sharp accusations, and are much less direct and judgmental than in Wesley's own subsequent writings.

On 1 March 1775, Wesley had written to Thomas Rankin, one of his preachers in America, "It is not unlikely that peace will be reestablished between England and the Colonies."[38] This comment reveals Wesley's frame of mind in writing: he hopes for resolution and reconciliation, for quieting the attacks on the government in England, for avoiding an irreparable split in the British community. That last point clearly was prominent in his concern, even if he was more sensitive immediately to the implications of the conflict for English public order and governmental authority. On April 21 he wrote to Rankin that these are "critical times . . . if the storm once begins in America, it will soon spread to Great Britain."[39] On June 2, less than two weeks before writing to Dartmouth and North, he wrote his brother Charles, "Just what I thought at first, I still think of American affairs. If a blow is struck, I give *America* up for lost, and perhaps *England* too. Our part is, to continue instant in prayer."[40] So long as Wesley entertained these fears and reviewed them in a context of modest hopefulness for a healing outcome, he kept under control any inclinations to sharp partisanship and repressed any analyses that might forecast a divorce. Doubtless that is why he was slower than Samuel Johnson to blame the

Americans for the conflict, and less inclined to recognize their drive toward independency—even though otherwise he drew heavily on the words of Johnson's tract to set forth his own views on the taxation issue.

Wesley's letter to Rankin of 28 July 1775, urged this content of preaching "till these troubles are at an end": "The universal corruption of all orders and degrees of men loudly calls for the vengeance of God; and inasmuch as all other nations are equally corrupt, it seems God will punish us by one another. What can prevent this but an universal, or at least a general, repentance? Otherwise we have great reason to fear God will soon say, 'Sword, go through that land and destroy it.' "[41] This evenhandedness of judgment draws back from political analysis and from the identification of particular causes of conflict and the attribution of responsibility. It fits the mood of someone not yet ready to take sides in some radical sense. On the other hand, we should not overlook the fact that by rejecting the colonists' arguments on taxation and representation, Wesley had moved to the government's side in the controversy even without accusing the Americans of initiating the conflict and aiming for separation from England. From that point on Wesley was perceived publicly as the government's man.

AMERICAN REPERCUSSIONS OF WESLEY'S POLITICS

Methodists in the colonies suffered for Wesley's intervention in the controversy. They were divided among themselves over loyalty to the Crown or to the new nation and its emergent government, but with most members siding with the latter. However, because of Wesley's public stance in opposition to the colonial cause, they were labeled collectively as Tories, and subjected to physical and verbal abuse and governmental repression. The preachers in particular were vulnerable to hostile action by the "patriots." According to historian William Warren Sweet, "The extent of the persecution endured by the Methodist preachers, especially in Maryland, was not inconsiderable. A number were committed to jail in Annapolis, several were beaten by mobs, others were given coats of tar and feathers."[42] As a result of this treatment many

Methodists removed to safer locations. A large portion of the membership moved eventually to Canada, and some went west.[43] All of the English-born preachers returned to England, except for Francis Asbury, who continued the Methodist work in America. Asbury himself was hounded by the authorities and by revolutionary vigilantes, and spent part of the war in hiding. Unhappy with Wesley because of the trouble brought on the American Methodists by his public opposition to the American cause, Asbury wrote in his journal of 19 March 1776:

> I . . . am truly sorry that the venerable man ever dipped into the politics of America. My desire is to live at peace with all men; to do them no harm, but all the good I can. However, it discovers Mr. Wesley's conscientious attachment to the government under which he lived. Had he been a subject of America, no doubt he would have been as zealous an advocate of the American cause. But some inconsiderate persons have taken occasion to censure the Methodists in America on account of Mr. Wesley's political sentiments.[44]

Wesley had urged his preachers in America to adopt a stance of neutrality and stay out of politics. Of course, he did not follow his own advice, and his failure to do so cost the colonial Methodists dearly.

TRACING THE TRANSITIONS

One cannot be precise in establishing the point at which Wesley turned decisively against the colonists, because he began to broaden his attribution of responsibility for the conflict while simultaneously offering conciliatory words. He notes in his journal on 7 September 1775 that "Understanding some of our friends here [Plymouth] were deeply prejudiced against the king and all his ministers, I spoke freely and largely on the subject at the meeting of the society. God applied it to their hearts, and I think there is not one of them now who does not see things in another light."[45] This intervention on behalf of king and government shows where he stands in terms of loyalty, but in the absence of specific reference to the colonial controversy it is no different from his long-standing position on domestic English conflict. However, his letter to Charles Wesley of 17 October 1775 shows a definite inclination to attribute blame to the American leaders, although not yet to the American people. "I find a danger now of a new kind—a danger of losing my love for the Americans: I mean for their miserable leaders; for the poor sheep are 'more sinned against than sinning,' especially since the amazing informations which I have received from James Ireland."[46] John Wesley does not disclose the nature of the "amazing informations," which led him to make this new and somewhat startling accusation. But it is evident that he was being fed news, of whatever reliability, which encouraged him to rethink his interpretation, and to assign some initiating responsibility to American leaders while not excusing the domestic English enemies of the king and the monarchy. Nevertheless, three days later he could write to Thomas Rankin, dismissing a paper that had been sent to him as "abundantly too tart; and nothing of that kind will be of service now. All parties are already too much sharpened against each other; we must pour water, not oil, into the flame." He defends his "Calm Address," presumably from the charge that it was inflammatory. He wrote it "before I knew the American ports were shut up," and adds, "I think there is not one sharp word therein; I did not design that there should." Yet he acknowledges that it was perceived as inflammatory, and admits that it was provocative: "Many are excessively angry, and would willingly burn me and it together." With some apparent satisfaction he notes that "above forty thousand of them have been printed in three weeks, and still the demand for them is as great as ever."[47] (Subsequently he would put the number at fifty to one hundred thousand.)[48] Wesley concludes the letter by stating, "I am persuaded love and tender measures will do far more than violence. And if I should have an interview with a great man (which seems to be not unlikely), I will by the grace of God tell him so without any circumlocution. Our time is in God's hands; Let us stand ready for all things!"[49]

The Hopper Correspondence

Wesley's tone changes in the course of his correspondence with Christopher Hopper. In his letter of 11 November 1775, Wesley observes, "For the one question is, 'Have we a right to tax or no?' If we have, they are rebels, and accountable to God and man for the blood that is shed. If we have not, they are innocent, and the blood lies at our door. Will they allow this right? or can we give it up?"[50] On the surface, at least, that comment is moderate and rather matter-of-fact—apparently leaving the question open. However, his letter to Hopper on 26 December 1775 manifests his increasing frustration and exasperation with the Americans:

> I see no possibility of accommodation. The one point is, Has the Supreme Power a right to tax or not? If they have, they cannot, they ought not to give it up. But I say, as Dean Tucker, "Let them drop." Cut off all other connexion with them than we have with Holland or Germany. Four-and-thirty millions they have cost us to support them since Queen Anne died. Let them cost us no more. Let them have their desire and support themselves.[51]

The apparent moderation of the first letter obscures the fact that Wesley had made clear his belief that the English government had a full constitutional right to tax the colonies. The implication is that the colonists in refusing to pay the tax had positioned themselves as rebels. The second letter leaves no doubt as to his view of the constitutional issue or to his attitude toward the Americans. The Americans are both rebels and ingrates. They deserve no further support from England, and should get none. That will teach them a lesson. Wesley's interest in reconciliation appears to be at an end.

On the other hand, it seems clear that Wesley's thinking about the conflict focuses on constitutional issues—especially the right to tax—and not on the issue of independence. Even with his increasing tendency to scold and upbraid the Americans, he nevertheless sees the matter in terms of its interrelationships with and impact on English politics, and persists in faulting the English opponents of king and government.

"National Sins and Miseries"

Two additional documents of this period shed light on these continuities in Wesley's thinking. One is the sermon on "National Sins and Miseries" preached at Bethnal-Green on 12 November 1775, as part of a fund-raiser for widows and orphans of English soldiers killed at the Battle of Bunker Hill.[52] Contrary to his usual practice, Wesley wrote this sermon out in advance, partly to have a text with which to refute later misrepresentations by his critics, partly because he intended to publish the sermon. In the sermon, Wesley turns the tragic event into a theodicy question: Why do the innocent ones—the relatives of the fallen, especially the children—have to suffer? Wesley makes no effort to answer the question through political analysis of factors leading to the violent exchange. Instead, he explains the event as divine punishment for the general wickedness of the English people. Comparing England with King David's Israel, Wesley writes, "General wickedness then occasioned a general visitation; and does not the same cause now produce the same effect? We likewise have sinned, and we are punished."[53] In the course of this general visitation, the suffering of the innocent becomes unavoidable. Wesley gives prominence to several types of sin—injustice, lying, overindulgence, sloth—and adds a catalog of others. The two societal calamities that result from the visitation are unemployment with its companions, poverty and hunger, and the "lunacy" of crying out for unbridled liberty. The latter is especially pertinent to the understanding of his political thinking at this time. Wesley interprets the demand for liberty in both England and America as a form of madness, of mob psychosis, of complete loss of rational control in social behavior:

> Widespread poverty (though not in so high a degree) I have seen several years ago. But such widespread a lunacy I never saw, nor I believe the oldest man alive. Thousands of plain, honest people throughout the land are driven utterly out of their senses by means of the poison which is so diligently spread through every city and town in the kingdom. They are screaming out for liberty while they have it in their hands, while they actually possess it; and to so great an extent that the like is not known in any other nation under heaven; whether we mean civil liberty, a liberty of enjoying all our legal property, or religious liberty, a liberty of worshipping God according to the dictates of our own conscience. Therefore all those who are either passionately or dolefully crying out, "Bondage! Slavery!" while there is no more danger of any such thing than there is of the sky falling upon their head, are utterly distracted; their reason is gone; their intellects are quite confounded. Indeed many of these

have lately recovered their senses; yet are there multitudes still remaining who are in this respect as perfectly mad as any of the inhabitants of Bedlam.[54]

This "lunacy" manifests itself in the dissolution of social order and manners. Persons who normally are quiet, friendly, and cooperative, now rage and swear at, threaten, and attack one another. Once orderly subjects, who feared God and honored the king, now breathe treason and rebellion.

When Wesley turns from England to the colonies, he sees the same phenomenon. In commenting on this case, however, he shows the necessary linkage of liberty to established, constitutional government, and exposes the political consequences when the link is broken:

> Here is *slavery*, real slavery indeed, most properly so called. For the regular, legal, constitutional form of government is no more. Here is real, not imaginary, bondage; not the shadow of English liberty is left. Not only no *liberty of the press* is allowed—none dare print a page or a line unless it be exactly conformable to the sentiments of our lords, the people—but no *liberty of speech*. Their "tongue" is not "their own." None must dare to utter one word either in favour of King George, or in disfavour of the idol they have set up—the new, illegal, unconstitutional government, utterly unknown to us and to our forefathers. Here is no *religious liberty;* no liberty of conscience for them that "honour the King," and whom consequently a sense of duty prompts them to defend from the vile calumnies continually vented against him. Here is no *civil liberty;* no enjoying the fruit of their labour any further than the populace pleases. A man has no security for his trade, his house, his property, unless he will swim with the stream. Nay, he has no security for his life if his popular neighbour has a mind to cut his throat. For there is no law, no legal magistrate to take cognizance of offenses. There is the gulf of tyranny—of arbitrary power on one hand, and of anarchy on the other. And, as if all this were not misery enough, see likewise the fell monster, war![55]

We need not examine the accuracy of Wesley's representation of political conditions in the colonies. Our concern here is with what and how he thought politically, not with the accuracy of his observations. In terms of political sentiment and understanding, there is nothing in this sermon that he could not have written before the problems with the colonies became so massive and demanding of attention. Wesley is writing about England primarily, not about the colonies. He is writing about the conditions of social order and the inevitable results of disregarding those conditions, not about the dismembering of the empire. Obviously the situation in the colonies concerns him greatly, but he continues to see that situation from the standpoint of English politics. America is another and indeed frightening and bloody example of what he is forecasting for England if the English people forsake the established constitutional order for the abstractions of liberty, and turn from the rule of constituted and divinely ordained officials to the authority of popular mandate. Now they have before them a live and vivid portrayal of the consequences: confident and secure liberties are destroyed by the passion for absolute liberty, predictable and responsible governing gives way to the whims and swings of mob rule, social order dissolves into anarchy and tyranny and ultimately into the terror and destruction of war. Slavery as a political condition comes into existence, because of the absence of government—especially of balanced, restraining, constitutional government—not because of the absence of direct representation. The sermon probably was small comfort, if any, to the persons for whom it was intended, but it manifests both the effort of Wesley the evangelist to require the people to get right before God, and the perception of Wesley the preacher that there is a political component to public and personal repentance. However, it offers no evidence that he has shifted priority of blame for the conflict to the Americans, or that he has come to think of independence as the controlling political issue.

The Motive for Writing

A second document pertinent to continuities in Wesley's thinking about the colonial situation is his letter of 29 November 1775 to the editor of *Lloyd's Evening Post*. Wesley wrote in response to Augustus Toplady's "An Old Fox Tarred and Feathered," published by *Lloyd's* in October 1775, in which Toplady accused Wesley of having base, personal motives for publishing his "Calm

Address." In this letter Wesley denies that his motive was to get money or preferment for himself or his brother's children, or "to please any man living, high or low," or to inflame anyone.[56] Rather,

> I contributed my mite toward putting out the flame which rages all over the land. . . . Now, there is no possible way to put out this flame or hinder its rising higher and higher but to show that the Americans are not used either cruelly or unjustly; that they are not injured at all, seeing they are not contending for liberty (this they had even in its full extent, both civil and religious); neither for any legal privileges, for they enjoy all that their Charters grant. But what they contend for is the illegal privilege of being exempt from parliamentary taxation;—a privilege this which no charter ever gave to any American colony yet; which no charter can give, unless it be confirmed by both King, Lords, and Commons; which, in fact, our Colonies never had, which they never claimed till the present reign, and probably they would not have claimed it now had they not been incited thereto by letters from England. One of these was read, according to the desire of the writer, not only at the Continental Congress, but likewise in many congregations throughout the combined Provinces. It advised them to seize upon all the King's officers; and exhorted them, "Stand valiantly only for six months, and in that time there will be such commotions in England that you may have your own terms."
>
> This being the real state of the question without any colouring or aggravation, what impartial man can either blame the King or commend the Americans? With this view, to quench the fire, by laying the blame where it was due, the "Calm Address" was written.[57]

With an inclination to backbiting and a capacity for vitriolic language that he decried in others, Wesley added: "As to reviewers, newswriters, *London Magazines,* and all that kind of gentlemen, they behave just as I expected they would. And let them lick up Mr. Toplady's spittle still, a champion worthy of their cause."[58] That aside, of most importance for our present interest is that as late as 29 November, Wesley was blaming English politicians and publicists for inciting the Americans, and was defining the primary issue in terms of the right of parliamentary taxation—a constitutional question—and not in terms of a clear move toward independence.

In the context of the Hopper correspondence, these two additional items confirm that Wesley was in clear agreement with Samuel Johnson on the constitutional right of taxation, but had not reached the same degree of clarity on centering the blame for the conflict or charging the Americans with committing themselves to a goal of independence from England. No longer is he willing to regard the colonists as simply dupes of the English Wilkites and their allies. The colonists bear responsibility for what they are doing. At the same time, however, he wants to press the case against the English dissidents for inciting the Americans. On the question of independence, he continues to regard the colonists as Englishmen subject to the Crown, and he strives to convince them that they are mistaken intellectually on their interpretation of the constitutional status of right of taxation, and factually on their claim to having been denied their liberties. Yet he has drawn the line by defining them as rebels for refusing the parliamentary right. However, even that is not clear in its implications. The separation of the Americans seems in his mind to be a consequence of their dissenting view of the constitutional question, rather than of their determination to become independent. Wesley's December 26 letter advising Hopper to "Let them drop" may have been the signal that his uncertainties and ambivalence on issues other than the right of taxation had come to an end. Or it may have been simply a moment of impatience and exasperation.

The Declaration Against Independence

After this letter to Hopper there is nothing for several months in Wesley's correspondence or journal that reflects developments in his thinking on these matters.[59] On 4 April 1776, however, he notes in his journal that "I began an answer to that dangerous tract, Dr. Price's *Observations on Liberty;* which if practised would overturn all government and bring in universal anarchy."[60] That response will prove decisive in setting Wesley fully against the American cause by defining the primary motive of their actions as a desire for independence, and by tracing the origin of their agitation to a time earlier than the incitements of the English dissidents. It will manifest a turn also in Wesley's personal attitude toward the colonists from an inclination toward sympathetic understanding and reconciliation to partisan hostility and denunciation. By the time Wesley wrote "Some Observations on Liberty: Occasioned by a Late Tract,"[61] he indeed had decided to "Let them drop."

At the outset of his response, Wesley goes right to the point: Price and the Americans are agitating for independence, not liberty.[62] They insist the two are the same thing, but they are mistaken. Liberty is religious and civil—as he has declared on previous occasions. The Americans as well as the English have plenty of both, guaranteed increasingly and firmly by the British government since the Revolution. Independence, by contrast, is separation from governmental authority with the intent of creating a new and different authority. Liberty requires the support and protection of government; independence is the antithesis of government. Wesley agrees that everyone has a right to liberty, but there is no right to independence once persons exist in civil society and have come under the rule of an established government.

> "Nay, not only the Americans [Price wrote], but all men, have a right to be self-governed and independent." You mean, they had a right thereto, before any civil societies were formed. But when was that time, when no civil societies were formed? I doubt hardly since the flood; and, wherever such societies exist, no man is independent. Whoever is born in any civilized country, is, so long as he continues therein, whether he chooses it or no, subject to the laws and to the supreme governors of that country. Whoever is born in England, France, or Holland, is subject to their respective Governors; and "must needs be subject to the power, as to the ordinance of God, not only for wrath, but for conscience' sake." He has no right at all to be independent, or governed only by himself; but is in duty bound to be governed by the powers that be, according to the laws of the country.[63]

Price argues—in a manner typical of persons of his persuasion— that the absence of independence and self-government is a condition of slavery. Wesley replies, as he has done before, that such a claim changes the meaning of slavery and trivializes the reality. Can it be argued seriously that persons who enjoy religious and civil liberty in such abundance are slaves? Can one speak of the masters in America as slaves in the same sense as the Africans whom they own? To the contrary, government by laws enacted by competent authority beyond popular control is not slavery; such government, and not independence, is the condition of freedom:

> And he that is thus governed, not by himself, but the laws, is, in the general sense of mankind, a free man; not that there ever existed any original compact between them and those Governors. But the want of this does not make him a slave, nor is any impeachment to his liberty; and yet this free man is, by virtue of those laws, liable to be deprived, in some cases of his goods; in others, of his personal freedom, or even of his life. And all this time he enjoys such a measure of liberty, as the condition of civilized nations allows; but no independency: That chimera is not found; no, not in the wilds of Africa or America.[64]

Price's argument for independence leads, in Wesley's view, to the end of all responsible government and therefore to the end of liberty.

Wesley presses the theoretical argument by incorporating into this tract most of the text of his "Thoughts concerning the Origin of Power," the main thrust of which was to deny the claim that authority to govern derived from a consenting people.[65] Who are the people?—he asked once again. For purposes of franchise, do they include women, young males, persons without property? If not, how does the concept establish the case for self-government and representation? Outside the main lines of political theory, he noted and sought to refute other bases for claiming a right of independency. Price and others argued that the colonies gained a right to independence when the British government seized smugglers and carried them to England for trial, rather than allowing them to be tried in American courts. Wesley responded that the American courts were rigged to favor the smugglers, including John Hancock. There would be no honest process and outcome unless the accused felons were tried in England. Price noted the growing size of the colonial population, which he stated was already half the size of that of England, and argued that such mass in itself established grounds for independence. Wesley denied the principled claim that population size justifies independence, and disputed the population estimate. Price appealed for examples to the Corsicans defending against the Genoese, the United Provinces of

Holland rebelling against Spain, and the Romans fighting against the allied states of Italy. Wesley answered that these were examples of separate states struggling against subjugation, not territories of a single political entity seeking to separate from that entity and its sovereign government. If states exist separately and in their own right they are entitled to the full liberty implied in such national existence, but no natural liberty generates a right of independence from a people's legal government.

Wesley's "Some Observations on Liberty" finalizes the shift in his attitude toward the American colonists and their cause. Now he stands clearly in opposition, with little if any of the conciliatory attitude manifest in the letter to Lords Dartmouth and North. Independence becomes for him the defining issue, and with its ascendancy, the parliamentary right to tax fades into the background (but does not disappear). The tract reveals nothing new in his political thinking. In fact, he repeats here much of what he wrote previously that expressed his fundamental political views. However, the issue of independency provides a new focus for his constitutionalism and his opposition to political doctrines of popular sovereignty based on natural rights theories. Also, it provides a specific context for the application of his implicit and at times explicit views of the organic solidarity of the British community. The British people are one people under the one government of king, Lords, and Commons. No claim to independency by one segment of the people can be allowed to supersede that solidarity; no appeal to natural rights can be allowed to set aside the authority of an established government, supported by historical prescription and effective in its fulfillment of constitutional responsibilities.

A Change in Attitudes

With independency now identified as the controlling issue, Wesley signals a change in his view of who is responsible for initiating the conflict.

> I once thought those measures had been originally concerted in our own kingdom; but I am now persuaded they were not. I allow that the Americans were strongly exhorted by letters from England,

"never to yield or lay down their arms till they had their own terms, which the Government would be constrained to give them in a short time." But those measures were concerted long before this; long before either the Tea Act or the Stamp Act existed; only they were not digested into form,—that was reserved for the good Congress. Forty years ago, when my brother was in Boston, it was the general language there, "We must shake off the yoke; we never shall be a free people till we shake off the English yoke." These, you see, were even then for "trying the question," just as you are now; "not by charters," but by what you call, "the general principles of liberty." And the late Acts of Parliament were not the cause of what they have since done, but barely the occasion they laid hold on.[66]

This assignment of original responsibility, coupled with the motive of seeking independence, allows Wesley to judge that military action by the British government to resist the colonies' campaign for independence and to restore the authority of the government is a use of force in a just cause.[67] It encourages him also to reverse his opinion of the Americans. In the Dartmouth-North letter he had spoken with admiration of the Americans, of their inspired devotion to home and hearth, of their willingness to fight and to sacrifice, of the superior advantage of fighting on their own territory, and at the same time called in question the effectiveness of British forces fighting as mercenaries. Now the patriot Wesley plays down the numbers, strength, commitment, and courage of the American forces, and trumpets the superior capability and resourcefulness of the British.[68] He is especially doubtful "Whether a quarter of the American fighting men, are determined to fight in so bad a cause; to fight, not for liberty, which they have long enjoyed, but for independency."[69] From this point on, Wesley will report American motives and behavior in negative and disparaging terms.

To see how sharp the change is in Wesley's attitude toward the American conflict, one should compare "Some Observations on Liberty" with his "A Seasonable Address to the More Serious Part of the Inhabitants of Great Britain, Respecting the Unhappy Context Between Us and Our American Brethren, by a Lover of Peace."[70] In the latter, the mood of reconciliation dominates. The conflict is an "unnatural civil war," reciprocal destruction within the family of Englishmen, brother slaying brother—with the further consequence of weakening the people and thereby exposing them to external enemies. Every effort should be made to "quench the flame," before it consumes both the English and their American relatives. Wesley identifies and minimizes the central issue by declaring it "a matter . . . in dispute relative to the mode of taxation."[71] He states further, "To be plain, the present melancholy dispute either is, or is not, founded in a constitutional right on the one part, and a constitutional opposition on the other. So far is certain. Therefore, till the entire nature of both constitutions is well and fully understood, it is utterly impossible to decide thereon."[72] Not only does he not raise the issue of independence, he declines even to take a position on the taxation question! Moreover, he is not disposed to say who is to blame, to answer the questions, "Who was first in the transgression? Who began this dreadful strife?"[73] Others have answered the question more ably than he. Also, he does not want to cloud the inquiry into a complicated case any more than has been done already.

Ultimately, Wesley turns to the concept of a divine judicial inquiry and action to try to explain this fratricidal condition. Possibly we have well-nigh filled up "the measure of our iniquity," and therefore can expect the fate of other peoples who have incurred the wrath of God. "But it is certain," he writes, "that iniquity of every kind, and amongst all ranks and orders of men, has and does abound; and as we are punished with the sword, it is not improbable but one principal sin of our nation is, the blood that we have shed in Asia, Africa, and America."[74] He mentions specifically the African trade, presumably in slaves, and claims that the East Indian trade is no better. To these sins he adds "an astonishing contempt and neglect of truly sacred things; especially the solemn worship of Almighty God: And herein our Nobility and Gentry almost universally distinguish themselves." The outcome: "We seem indeed to have been at our meridian height of power, greatness, &c.; (not of holiness unto the Lord;) and it is to be feared that the glory has begun to depart."[75] He calls on both "Ye friends of America" and "Ye friends of Government" to "turn your eyes therefore, for a moment, from those you suspect to be the only authors of the present evil,"[76] to contemplate the universality of wickedness in the country, and to inquire into their own responsi-bility for it.[77] The polarizing issues are comprehended and subor-dinated under the common judgment of God.

In the Jackson edition of Wesley's works, this address is placed after "Some Observations on Liberty" and before other tracts deal-ing with the American war. It certainly is out of place there. One cannot imagine that Wesley would be so irenic, so tentative, so evenhanded after writing the "Liberty" tract, and so forgetful of the strong positions he took therein. Frank Baker assigns the date of February 1776.[78] It is far preferable to the Jackson arrangement, because it places it two months before the commencement of "Some Observations on Liberty." But even that relocation does not seem early enough. The mood of "Seasonable Address" is com-pletely contrary to the hostility and resignation of the second let-ter to Christopher Hopper (26 December 1775). The appeal to a general judgment on the people is reminiscent of the sermon on "National Sins and Miseries" (November 1775). And what is most compelling, the unwillingness to take a stand on the taxation ques-tion implies that it predates even the "Calm Address" (September 1775), where Wesley takes an unambiguous stand, publishes it, and distributes it broadly. But precision on the question of dating is of no great significance once it is clear that it predates "Some Observations on Liberty." Assuming that Wesley indeed wrote the "Seasonable Address," the comparison of the two tracts allows us to see with striking clarity the shift in Wesley's thinking that remained unchanged and unqualified for the remainder of the war.

The Patriotic Ideologue

In 1777, Wesley published "A Calm Address to the Inhabitants of England."[79] At the outset he recalls his "Calm Address to our American Colonies," written a year and a half previously, which was distributed widely and exercised considerable influence despite the reality that he could not send it immediately through the closed American ports. That success encourages him to write once again, this time to his countrymen who remain in England. His purpose—he insists once again—is not that of seeking advan-tage for himself, but of contributing "all that in me lies to the public welfare and tranquility. A flame was studiously kindled some time since," he continues, "which threatened to involve the whole nation. By the blessing of God, it is greatly checked; it does not spread, or blaze as formerly. But it is not quite put out. I wish to quench the remains of that evil fire."[80]

Doubtless Wesley understood his own motives in such noble terms, but on reading the document it is difficult to take him seriously. What he attempts is a descriptive-analytical account of the American struggle for independence. What he achieves is a heavily pro-British interpretation of causes and events. From the beginning the colonies grew and prospered. "This was the natural effect of the unparalleled lenity of the Government they were under, and the perfect liberty they enjoyed, civil as well as religious. Through the same causes, from the smallness of their taxes, and the large bounties continually received from their mother country, (which also protected them from all their enemies,) their wealth increased as fast as their numbers."[81] The benefits received from the benign mother country were answered by regular and systematic defrauding of king and government of customs revenues, a practice that added greatly to colonial fortunes and impaired the revenues of the Crown. To recoup some of these expenses and losses, "the English Government a few years ago thought it equitable to lay a small duty upon the stamps in America, in order, if not to bear themselves harmless, yet to lessen their burden."[82] The Americans protested loudly, and with the support of ambitious and boisterous friends in England succeeded in having the Stamp Act repealed.

The account continues through the rising aspirations and machinations of the Americans, their reciprocity with the English republicans, the attempt of Parliament to lay a small duty on tea "that every part of the British empire should furnish its share of the general expense," the American response in the form of the Boston Tea Party, and the early days of the war in which British ships and stores were seized and British forces were set at sore disadvantage. Throughout this recitation the British government is reasonable, moderate, benevolent, protective; the Americans are dissembling, conspiratorial, dishonest, fraudulent. Then "At length the King published a Proclamation for a General Fast in

England, that we might 'humble ourselves before God, and implore his blessing and assistance.' "[83] (Late in 1775 Wesley had urged Lord Dartmouth to propose such a proclamation to the king.)[84] From that point on, the king's troops scored one success after another, "and everywhere drove the rebels before them like a flock of sheep."[85] It was clear to John Wesley that God was on the side of the British government.

Substantively, this tract also contributes nothing new to the understanding of Wesley's political thinking. He reiterates the distinction between liberty and independence, and illustrates the destruction of liberty through independency with what he takes to be evidence from the American experience.

> Do you not immediately observe, that after this huge outcry for liberty, which has echoed through America, there is not the very shadow of liberty left in the confederate provinces? There is no liberty of the press. A man may more safely print against the Church in Italy or Spain, than publish a tittle against the Congress in New-England or Pennsylvania. There is no religious liberty. What Minister is permitted to follow his own conscience in the execution of his office? to put man in mind to be "subject to principalities and powers?" to "fear God and honour the King?" Who is suffered (whatever his conscience may dictate) to "pray for the King, and all that are in authority?" There is no civil liberty. No man hath any security, either for his goods, or for his person; but is daily liable to have his goods spoiled or taken away, without either law or form of law, and to suffer the most cruel outrage as to his person, such as many would account worse than death. And there is no legal method wherein he can obtain redress for whatever loss or outrage he has sustained.[86]

This condition is set in direct and stark contrast to "the perfect liberty which we enjoy"[87]—in England, where it is guaranteed by law and historic precedent, and is not corrupted and threatened by natural rights claims to independency and popular consent.

If the essay reveals nothing new in Wesley's political thinking, it nonetheless confirms both the decisiveness of his position and the trend of his thinking. The American cause is independence, not redress of grievances as Englishmen. That is the main reason for turning against them and supporting the suppression of their rebellion. It is an issue that transcends and is qualitatively different from an argument over the constitutionality of taxation, because it rejects the unity of the people governed by the constitution. This lust for independence is an American idea, one that predates the actions of the British government, which allegedly provoked it. It is not a product of English agitation against Crown and Parliament, although once visible it entered into a relationship of reciprocity with English republican dissent. Futhermore, it comes to expression in actions that manifest the destruction of civilized behavior. Of the American forces, for example, Wesley writes, "they can rob, and plunder and destroy, and turn a well-peopled and fruitful land into a wilderness. They can burn houses, and drive men, women, and children into the wild woods, in the depth of winter. Yea, they can burn whole towns, without any regard for the sick or aged, that necessarily perished in the flame."[88] Throughout the colonial war for independence, Wesley will report incidents that in his view demonstrate the moral degradation and cynicism of the Americans. His sympathetic portrayal in the letter to Lords Dartmouth and North will make no further appearance.

Wesley's sermon of 1778, titled "The Late Work of God in North-America," underscores the continuity in his thinking about the American war.[89] The sermon purports to show the interaction of divine providence and human action in the rise and fall of both American prosperity and American religious commitment. The pattern of the relationship between religion and economics basically is the one found in other writings by Wesley on the topic: Persons of little or no wealth find God and come under religious discipline; this discipline encourages frugality and industriousness, which leads to prosperity; prosperity brings spiritual temptations that weaken and dissipate religious commitment; loss of religious commitment and moral righteousness leads to loss of wealth; loss of wealth allows the recovery of humility and return to religion. Such is "the adorable providence of God."[90] What is different with the treatment of the cycle in this sermon is Wesley's linking it with the rise and fall of colonial prosperity. The colonies prospered greatly—in no small measure because of the benevolence and protection of Mother England. This prosperity intersected the great American religious revival, and undercut its power with greed, sloth, luxury, wantonness, and idleness. Colonial prosperity in turn was brought low by numerous bad consequences resulting from the lusting after independency and the resulting conflict with England. With the loss of prosperity came new opportunities for the work of God.

At one point Wesley expands his analysis of the American defection: he traces the spirit of independency not only to the 1730s, but all the way back to the English experience of persons who left for the New World.

> It may reasonably be supposed that the colonies in New England had from their very beginning an hankering after independency. It could not be expected to be otherwise, considering their families, their education, their relations, and the connections they had formed before they left their native country. They were farther inclined to it by the severe and unjust treatment which many of them had met with in England. This might well create in them a fear lest they should meet with the like again, a jealousy of their governors, and a desire of shaking off that dependence to which they were never thoroughly reconciled. The same spirit they communicated to their children, from whom it descended to the present generation. Nor could it be effaced by all the favours and benefits which they continually received from the English Government.[91]

With these observations, Wesley is almost at the point of suggesting that the Americans, though related closely to the English, are a different people by reason of a different historical experience. That acknowledgment would establish some provisional grounds for independence closer to Wesley's manner of historical thinking, and would even open the possibility of claiming the natural rights of national groups. Of course, he does not take that step. His words may constitute a more ample and sympathetic explanation, in accordance with his image of himself as a fair and evenhanded commentator, but they do not amount to justification. Independence is wrong, and through the providence of God the Americans pay a terrible price for their arrogance and ingratitude in seeking it. Ultimately, however, the defeat of their efforts and the resulting distress work to the glory of God by enabling a return to religion.

Calming Words of Assurance

Two other addresses of 1778 relate to the events of the time, although once again neither indicates a change in Wesley's thinking about the war with the colonies. His "A Serious Address to The People of England, with Regard to the State of the Nation," is dated 20 February 1778.[92] Designed mainly to reassure the people that the state of the nation is healthy, that it is not on the brink of ruin, that the country and its economy are well managed, it cites extensively some remarks by the Dean of Gloucester to show that England is improving in population, agriculture, trade, and several other indexes. There are no references to the colonial conflict, but the effort to calm the people fits Wesley's political strategy of restraining public fears and passions and deflecting criticism from the king.

Connection with the American situation is implied in a subsequent tract, in which Wesley makes reference to a "general panic" that has prevailed for several months and is spreading—even to Ireland. Wesley's "A Compassionate Address to the Inhabitants of Ireland," dated 10 May 1778, speaks directly to the condition of conflict in yet another effort to deal with public fears of disaster.[93] The people need not worry over the course of events in the war: Washington's troops are few and diminishing, untrained, weak in commitment. They will not stand and fight a superior, seasoned, well-provisioned British army. "Will these dead-doing men, do you think, be in haste to cut off all the old, weather-beaten Englishmen? Otherwise they will not have made an end of them, before the time comes for their returning home!"[94] Neither should they fear Britain's European neighbors. A French invasion of England or intervention in the colonial war is not a serious possibility, because of the strength of the British navy: "And while we are indisputably masters at sea, what can the French do but gnash their teeth at us?"[95] Should they attempt to join with the American army, "there is no doubt but General Howe would give a good account of them all."[96] Spain is unlikely to meddle, and Portugal dare not because of the risks of exposing itself to attack by Spain. But what about " 'those intestine vipers, who are always ready to tear out their mother's bowels. And how should we defend ourselves against these, if they made a general insurrection?' "[97] Wesley allows that the question of domestic revolutionary plots is worth considering, but proceeds to dismiss the prospect. The English people would have to be fast asleep to allow such conspiratorial success. Moreover, the forces in the homeland—both regular and independent—are easily sufficient to defeat any such attempt. It is a strange conclusion, considering that revolution in England was one of Wesley's persistent and driving fears.

This tract is a work of arrogant, self-assured patriotism that reverses the sentiments and estimates of the Dartmouth-North letter of three years previously. It is confident, triumphal, and smug. Even the question concerning divine judgment on the nation because of the sins of the people is diluted—uncharacteristically—by the claim that neither England nor Ireland "have yet 'filled up the measures of their iniquities.' "[98] Also, scriptural religion "is continually increasing in every part of the kingdom," and he knows of "no instance in all history . . . of the Governor of the world delivering up a kingdom to destruction, while religion was increasing in it."[99] The judgmental warnings of "National Sins and Miseries" and other documents seem to have been set aside, presumably because they did not serve Wesley's political efforts of the moment.

Wesley's attitude toward the Americans remained hostile and condemnatory throughout the war. His journal of 2 March 1777 records the treachery and murder with which an American sea captain, Arthur Crawford, rewarded the kindness, openness, and Christian charity of an English seaman, Captain Bell.[100] On 1 August 1777 he writes, "I desired as many as could to join together in fasting and prayer that God would restore the spirit of love and of a sound mind, to the poor deluded rebels in America."[101] On 29 December 1779 he reports the case of the Collector of Customs for the eastern ports of Maryland, a man who was "zealous for King George." This Loyalist was hunted persistently by rebel bands who proposed to kill him on the spot, until he was rescued by deserters from the American army who rowed him out to a waiting English ship.[102]

INTERPRETING THE WAR'S OUTCOME

The ending of the war with an American victory brought little or nothing in published comment in John Wesley's own words.

However, he did publish several items written by other persons, which criticized sharply the conduct of the war, and especially the leadership of General Howe.[103] Howe, we recall, was the general in whom Wesley placed great confidence earlier on as being fully able and prepared to "take care" of the French should they dare intervene. Charles Wesley's reaction was more direct, emotional, and angry than that of John. In a long poem titled "The American War," Charles raged against Howe, Howe's brother, and other commanders, charging them with treason as well as incompetence. In Charles's view the war could have been won easily had Howe prosecuted it with reasonable competence and energy, or worse, if he had not sold out to the enemy. A selection of but two verses from this lenthy composition conveys Charles's cynicism and outrage:

> Th' Americans we all allow,
>> Were conquer'd by Immortal Howe,
> The younger of th' Illustrious Pair,
>> The British Thunderbolt of war.
> As oft as met, as oft as seen,
>> Agen he beat them, and agen
> (Whene'er he thought it worth his while);
>> As sheep he drove them from the Isle,
> Resistless on their armies fell,
>> And stormed their Forts impregnable,
> Scatter'd their fugitive remains,
>> (But not pursued them) on the Plains:
> With ease their Provinces he took,
>> Their Provinces with ease forsook,
> And threw them wantonly away.
>> As if he took them but in play.[104]

> What now has our great Captain done?
>> Wilfully lost whate'er he won,
> Done to his friends as little good
>> And as much mischief as he could;
> Our army and their Chief forsook,
>> And made them pass beneath the yoke,
> (Branding us with eternal shame);
>> Blown up the spark into a flame;
> The Loyalists *alone* subdued,
>> And prodigal of British blood,

Wasted our lives with wanton pleasure,
And twenty millions of our treasure:
His Sovereign basely disobey'd;
His trust perfidiously betray'd;
His Country sold; his duty slighted;
The Colonies with France united;
Made our amazing Efforts vain;
Imbroil'd us both with France and Spain;
Gain'd his own Party the ascendant,
And made AMERICA independent![105]

Because John Wesley published commentaries critical of Howe and the conduct of the war, we can assume that, in general, he shared his brother's opinions—even if he was not as passionate and unrestrained in expressing his patriotism and his disgust. When the war was over, however, John desired to move ahead with the Methodist work in America. He chose a favorite theological device to reconcile himself to the unwelcome outcome. On 10 September 1784 he wrote to Our Brethren in America:

By a very uncommon train of providences many of the Provinces of North America are totally disjoined from their Mother Country and erected into independent States. The English Government has no authority over them, either civil or ecclesiastical, any more than over the States of Holland. A civil authority is exercised over them, partly by the Congress, partly by the Provincial Assemblies. But no one either exercises or claims any ecclesiastical authority at all.[106]

Wesley's principal objective was to clear the way formally for his ordination of ministers and appointment of superintendents for America. He did this by declaring that the English state and church no longer had ecclesiastical authority in that part of the world. In doing so, however, he declared also that the United States was a nation separate from England, governed by its own civil authorities and not by Crown and Parliament. He recognized frankly and publicly the independence of America that he had fought so strenuously to prevent. In offering this admission he departed from his practice of recriminations and political-economic explanations, and attributed the result to "an uncommon train of providences." If, despite all Wesley's certainties about the conflict, God in God's eternal wisdom decided otherwise, there was nothing for John Wesley to do but accept the political reality as divinely decreed and get on with the work of saving souls. Moreover, the result should be permanent, should be accepted as such by the Methodists, and recognized as a form of providential deliverance: "As our American brethren are now totally disentangled both from the State and the English hierarchy, we dare not entangle them again either with the one or the other. They are now at full liberty simply to follow the Scriptures and the Primitive church."[107]

But Wesley could not shed his resentments completely, despite this process of accommodation. As late as 29 March 1786 he could write in his journal: "We came to our old steady friends at Burslem. But he with whom I used to lodge is no more seen. He trusted the Americans with all his substance, and they cheated him out of all."[108]

MODES OF ARGUMENTATION

Throughout the conflict with America, most of Wesley's argumentation is nontheological. He boasts the superiority of the British constitution, and insists on its authority—specifically, in this case, in matters of taxation. He repudiates theories of natural rights and popular consent, and affirms historical and prescriptive rights and virtual representation. He distinguishes independency and liberty, rejecting the former and celebrating the latter. He examines the provisions of charters pertaining to colonial governance. He inquires into the origins of conflicts, analyzes motives, and assigns responsibility. Occasionally he invokes a theological mode of argument, as he does in explaining war as punishment for sin, and in his appeals to providential ordering to explain something not fully clear to him on empirical and historical terms. Or having made his case primarily on nontheological terms, he may cap off the treatise with a theological coda, as he does in his "Calm Address to the Inhabitants of England." There he follows the listing of government-protected benefits with an invitation to be thankful to God for these things. Then he adds, "And as long as we fear God, shall we not 'honour the King?' looking upon him with a love mixed with reverence? Should we not remember him before God in prayer, that his throne may be established in righteousness? that he, and all which are in authority under him, may duly administer justice, to the punishment of wickedness and vice, and the maintenance of true religion and virtue? And is it not our part carefully to abstain from speaking evil of the ruler of our people; and to study to 'lead a quiet and peaceable life, in all godliness and honesty?' "[109] But that is not his usual practice in arguing issues under dispute. For the most part, in his defense of government and government policies in public argumentative tracts, Wesley appeals to reason, common sense, experience, and findings of fact. Theological language plays a subordinate and reinforcing role.

Yet when Wesley speaks his mind most directly, he invokes the divine authorization of civil authority at the outset and establishes as first principle that his listeners or readers should "fear God and honour the King!" That was his exhortation in Newbury on 18 October 1775, because of the presence there of "many red-hot patriots."[110] Or he would put them in mind to "be subject to the higher powers, for they are ordained of God," as he did with Church of England Dissenters and Methodists at the end of the aforementioned "Calm Address to the Inhabitants of England." There he advised them to do so to avoid the wrath of the rulers, but only after he had admonished them to be subject for the sake of conscience.[111] Or he would require them to "Render unto Caesar the things that are Caesar's, and unto God the things that are God's," as he did in London at St. Vedast's on 10 November 1776 (the Gospel for the day),[112] in Sunderland on 3 May 1777,[113] to soldiers in Tullamore on 16 April 1778,[114] and in Halifax on 26 July of that year.[115] These references establish the primacy for Wesley of the theologically defined grounds for obedience to the government over the nontheological considerations. Yet the former receive little if any exposition and argumentation by contrast with the latter. Wesley's extended political thinking on issues of the time was made public primarily in secular language, even though his fundamental belief was that persons should obey rulers because of the divine origin of civil authority.

The explanation is not difficult to find. Across his career John Wesley made a practice of speaking in direct scriptural terms to persons whose Christian commitment he could assume, especially when speaking in his role as preacher. Extensive explanation to them was not necessary; if they truly were Christians, they would believe the Scripture and act on it. It should suffice to quote the Tribute Passage or Romans 13 for Christian believers to get the point and understand what was required of them. However, when he could not assume genuine Christian conviction, his practice was to speak in rational and empirical terms—to convince the mind with argument and findings of fact. That was his method, for example, in the famous essay "Thoughts upon Slavery," where he made only minimal use of religious argument.[116] Inasmuch as most of his public statements during the American War of Independence worked with the latter assumption rather than the former, he wrote in the manner of a political advocate rather than a Christian preacher and counselor. Religious allusions were present in his writings, but as a rule they were employed to support the other form of argumentation rather than to define the foundation and substance of political responsibility. As a result, we have a fairly clear delineation of Wesley's political thought in relation to contemporary political alternatives, but we do not have from him a theologically integrated understanding of political reality and approach to political action.

JOHN WESLEY, CONSTITUTIONALIST

This distinction is of some importance, because it helps dispose of the notion that John Wesley was a residual divine right thinker who had not quite gotten over his earlier alleged Jacobitism. Caleb Evans, Augustus Toplady, and others accused him of Jacobitism during the time of this political struggle. Evans claimed that Wesley in his "Calm Address" had "under an artful disguise . . . revived the good old Jacobite doctrines of hereditary, indefeasible, divine right, and of passive obedience and non-resistance."[117] He certainly was wrong on the Jacobitic "divine right" accusation, as was Toplady in making similar charges. Wesley—as I argued earlier—was essentially a constitutionalist who took his political bearings from the settlement of 1688–89, and who praised the benefits he received from it during his lifetime. When he wrote, "English liberty commenced at the Revolution,"[118] he was not expressing an original thought, and he certainly was not speaking as a Tory. Rather, he was reciting a slogan of the conservative Whigs who wanted to keep the constitutional arrangements intact, and with them their own threatened positions of power.[119] Wesley showed little interest in the personal fortunes of individual politicians, but he showed great interest in the stability and durability of the British constitution. It was the guarantor of both order and liberty, the heart of the social fabric, the defender against enemies foreign and domestic. The appeal to the divine authorization of rulers confirms the constitutional order of king and Parliament ruling together, not the sovereign authority of kings, including their sovereign authority over Parliament. If Wesley could write, as he did, that the king could act only in accordance with law,[120] that he could not grant an exemption from the power of Parliament,[121] and that "the will of the King is not their law any more than it is ours,"[122] he was writing as a constitutionalist, not as a Jacobitic divine right thinker.

John Fletcher was designated by Wesley as his successor, but died before Wesley did. In a response to Evans, Fletcher offered the following classification: "The strong Whigs are for the republican government which obtained in the days of Cromwell and the Rump, the strong Tories contend for the high, monarchical government, which prevailed in the day of King James II. You and I, sir, are for the government which has obtained since the revolution."[123] Those were John Wesley's sentiments exactly. In "The Doctrine of Original Sin," he wrote, "We are under an excellent constitution, which secures both our religious and civil liberty."[124]

One must not conclude, however, that Wesley's appeal to the divine source of civil authority was nothing more than a theological rationalization for what he believed on other grounds. It was a conviction, deeply held, that constituted a visible and enduring remnant of his Toryism. As we saw earlier, he defined himself as a Tory in this specific way, although in this way only.[125] It was also a natural outcome of his reading of Scripture. However, it does not establish him as a divine right thinker in the contemporary meaning of that term, and it does not make him a classical Tory on all counts. Its practical political applications were to set him intentionally in opposition to Lockean theories of natural rights and popular sovereignty, and to confirm the historical fact of the continuing Constitution of 1689. He did not use it to endorse royal absolutism—something in which he did not believe. Certainly he defended the king, but as an element of the constitution coordinate with the Parliament, not as a power above the Parliament. Wesley's appeal to divine authorization of civil power affirmed the authority of the constitution, of king and Parliament ruling together, not vulnerable to challenges from other sources of authority. In this respect his response to the American conflict confirmed the political portrait of Wesley the constitutionalist that became clearly visible in the domestic conflict with the Wilkites and their allies.

Wesley's public engagement in the conflict with America was thus an episode in his continuing effort to stabilize and protect the British constitution, which he believed essential to both liberty and order in Britain and the rest of the empire. However, the conflict also posed in direct fashion the integrity of the empire itself. As Wesley addressed the prospect of its dissolution, he exposed once again the organic elements in his thinking. The empire was the totality of the British community. This community was one people with one constitution, one king, one Parliament. The Americans were Englishmen abroad, not foreigners. Turmoil in America threatened the political and social stability of the homeland, but more immediately and directly it threatened the destruction of the inclusive community. That community could not be allowed to dissolve in a passion for individualistic natural rights.

CALVINISTS AND POLITICS

John Wesley did not need additional assurance that his political views were correct, but he felt reinforced nonetheless by the fact that many of his critics, such as Evans and Toplady, were Calvinists. On 29 November 1775, he wrote to Mrs. Crosby that those "who are the avowed enemies of Christian Perfection are in general the warmest enemies of King George and of all that are in authority under him; yet the counsel of the Lord shall stand, and

He will turn the counsel of Ahitophel into foolishness."[126] Wesley routinely accused the Calvinists of antinomianism. Inasmuch as the Calvinists tended to support both the English dissidents and the American rebels, that confirmed his view of the "predestinarians" and also his political commitments. Opposition to constitution and government was a form of antinomianism. It was theologically and morally—as well as politically and legally—insupportable. If the Calvinists were critical of him, he had to be right.

A COURT THEOLOGIAN?

One of the most distressing aspects of Wesley's intervention in the conflict with America was the appearance he gave of being a religious propagandist for the government. After the plaintive letters to Dartmouth and North of June 1775, on behalf of the colonists, there is no evidence of critical distance on his part that would allow him to review the policies of the government without always supporting them. Samuel Johnson had written *Taxation no Tyranny* at the urging of the government, and had submitted that and other writings to cabinet officers for their review and for some degree of censorship. Wesley subsequently copied or paraphrased large portions of Johnson's pamphlet into his own "Calm Address." An appreciative government "was evidently pleased to have Wesley's support," wrote W. W. Sweet, "for an edition was purchased and distributed at all the church doors in London." Moreover, continues Sweet, "one of the officials of state waited upon him and asked whether there was anything the government could do to assist either Wesley or his people. To this Wesley replied that 'he looked for no favors, and only desired the continuance of civil and religious privileges.' He did, however, finally accept fifty pounds from the privy purse to apply toward some of his charities."[127] Wesley's response was honest and characteristic. However, it was also naive. He failed to recognize that his defense of policy coupled with the government's attention to him gave credence to his critics' public portrayal of him as a priest in the pay of the court. Was he seeking a bishop's mitre or a pension—or both?

Surely he was not, but why should a man who apparently was so intimately involved with the government be believed?

Perhaps the most serious and grievous compromise involved John Fletcher. Fletcher had written a *Vindication of the "Calm Address"* in response to Caleb Evans's attack, and some other pieces defending Wesley's intervention.[128] Incredibly—it would seem to us today—Fletcher submitted them to Lord Dartmouth for review and editing. Evans claimed that Dartmouth made many changes. Fletcher insisted that the changes were few and insignificant, but did not deny the nobleman's editing of his writings.[129] Telford reports that "One was immediately commissioned to ask Mr. Fletcher whether any preferment in the Church would be acceptable; or whether he (the Chancellor) could do any service. He answered, 'I want nothing but more grace.' "[130] Fletcher's response was even more pious and less demanding than Wesley's, but it did not override the gravity of his willing concession. Wesley then compounded the compromise by writing to Lord Dartmouth: "My Lord,—The corrections made in Mr. Fletcher's papers which your Lordship was so kind as to make, as well as those made by the gentlemen who perused them, will prevent several objections."[131] Perhaps, but they surely raised others. Wesley was impressed that a cabinet minister should show interest in these writings; he was even more impressed that the minister was an evangelical Christian. Apparently it did not occur to him that he and Fletcher were creating a situation that would allow their opponents to pillory them as tools of the administration, regardless of their own intentions, and regardless of how honorable and God-fearing the nobleman might be.

That is another reason why Wesley probably should have followed his own advice, and stayed out of politics. Not only was he too sure of the rightness of his position and of the cynical and sinister motives of his opponents; he was too trusting of authorities with whom he felt comfortable. He lacked the self-awareness of either the prophet or the Machiavellian politician. He was not a prophet, suspicious of all constellations of human power; he was not a Machiavellian, shrewdly using religion and morality to play the political game. Because he knew that his views were right and his motives pure, he did not have sufficient sense of how a prominent clergyman like himself could be politically engaged while at the same time presuming to be nonpolitical.

Nevertheless, the critics were wrong in charging him with cynical self-interest on the one hand and unreconstructed Jacobitism on the other. What this review of Wesley's response to the American War of Independence shows is that he was motivated by substantive political commitments that fit his rubric of the public good, and that these commitments were to a politics of effective but limited power. Wesley had a strong affinity for King George III, and sought to defend him, but it was for George as a limited monarch, not an absolute one. He was for king and country, for the constitution of king, Lords, and Commons, for the British community, for the rule of law, for the reciprocity of public order and individual liberty, for historical precedent and continuity, for the acknowledgment of God as ultimate source of authority. This listing of political values is not in order of priority. Wesley's political sensibility was so organic that there could be no priority. All of these elements were integrated in the totality of political existence. To threaten any one of them, such as the monarchy, or to overemphasize any one, such as liberty, would be to threaten their unity and therefore each of them individually.

PART TWO
ASPECTS OF WESLEY'S POLITICAL THOUGHT

CHAPTER SIX

POLITICAL AUTHORITY I
REPRESENTATION AS ORGANIZATION FOR ACTION IN HISTORY

Political authority as the right to exercise power over a political society is the central problem in John Wesley's political thought. It was the political issue with which he contended most often and in most depth throughout his life, because it was the central problem of English politics throughout the eighteenth century. It is also the central problem *with* John Wesley's political thought. His severely and deliberately antidemocratic, antirepublican view of authority in governing creates major difficulties for subsequent generations of Wesleyans who would like to have usable political as well as theological guidance from the principal founder of the Methodist movement. For those reasons it is necessary to accord this problem more attention than other aspects of Wesley's political thought, and in doing so to extend the inquiry through more than one chapter.

What were Wesley's views on political authority? A simple summary answer is that authority to govern comes from God, not from the people. That answer doubtless is the one John Wesley would give, for he surely believed that authority was handed down by God to the topmost level of political society, and did not rise up from below.[1] He made that point over and over again in essays and sermons in which he denied the consent basis of authority and the contractual character of society, and enforced the pious, biblical duties to "be subject to the governing authorities, for they are ordained of God" and to "render unto Caesar the things that are Caesar's." Wesley's view of political authority certainly is grounded in God as source, and just as certainly rejects the people as source, but it is otherwise not so monochromatic. It includes the subordination of all governmental power to law, the coordination and reciprocity of royal and parliamentary authority, notions of prescriptive right and virtual representation, the testing of regimes and institutions by their ability to protect rights and liberties and to provide order and defense, and—at least implicitly—the weight of the ancient constitution. If it is not a republican and democratic view, and intentionally it is not, it nevertheless is limited and constitutional rather than absolute and arbitrary. Moreover, its constitutional sense is organic and historical, not individualistic and contractual.

If the God/people summary is insufficient, there is methodological risk in focusing the study on particular conflicts in which that polarity was salient, and abstracting from Wesley's longer history of political engagement with its variety of issues and its wider examination of the moral rights and limits of the exercise of political power. Wellman J. Warner runs that risk in his *The Wesleyan Movement in the Industrial Revolution.*[2] He begins his inquiry into Wesley on political authority with Wesley's opposition to late-eighteenth-century radical uses of John Locke's natural rights and social contract concepts. Warner's book justly is celebrated as a contribution to the history of the Wesleyan movement, and he obviously is correct in giving prominence to Wesley's opposition to Lockean theories. However, the decision to use this particular historical moment as both the starting point for and the dominant element in Wesley's understanding of political authority dislodges or obscures other elements of considerable significance.

To understand John Wesley on political authority rightly, one must identify broader contexts of inquiry. One of these, obviously, is the history of English politics in the eighteenth century. Another is the long and rich history of Christian political thought, especially the history of theological reflection on the grounds, rights, and limits of the exercise of power. These two contexts, viewed concretely, are not separate. The former is in part a chapter of the latter. It depends on it for the shaping of alternatives in the self-representation of English society. Moreover, it carries the latter history along into new and often contradictory syntheses. I shall begin the contextual inquiry into Wesley's understanding of political authority with the identification of concepts and images that develop through the history of Christian political thought and reach a particular form of historic expression in the political world that confronted John Wesley, and to which he felt obliged to respond.

As an interpretive device I shall use the concept of representation that is central to Eric Voegelin's *The New Science of Politics.*[3] Representation, according to Voegelin, is "the form by which a political society gains existence for action in history."[4] Societies articulate themselves into institutional structures that give them the capacity for historical action which, simply as undifferentiated societies, they do not have. This articulation is more than a set of power relationships; it is also a set of symbols—a representation of meaning—in terms of which the society understands itself politically, and confers on the rulers whatever authority they may have to act over and on behalf of the society—to legislate, command, require, and expect obedience. Moreover, the articulation of a society is not static. It develops through the competition of forces and symbols, and—in Western civilization, at least—tends toward the inclusion of all societal elements. The course of representational articulation that constituted the history of English politics into the eighteenth century was informed massively by Christian symbols of meaning and ordering developed in the history of Christian political thought. These symbols were used to establish and confirm the arrangements of power and to endow with sanctity the lines and limits of political authority. The delineation of this process of articulation to Wesley's time, however briefly sketched, will help us understand the frameworks within which he addressed the questions of political authority.

Obviously, this concept of representation is different from our usual understanding of the term, which pertains to "representative institutions" and to the designation of some persons to act as agents of the whole society, or certain elements thereof. Voegelin argues that the latter concept is found mainly in European societal articulations, whereas the notion of representation as the form taken for action in history is fundamental to all societies in their development. Moreover, the former includes the latter as a particular mode of articulation. We have encountered Wesley's response to this secondary concept of representation in the historical review chapters, and shall do so again in a subsequent analytical one, but for the present we shall use the concept in Voegelin's primary sense.

The present chapter—a historical inquiry into Wesley's location in the struggle over political articulation and organization in eighteenth-century England—does not exhaust the inquiry into John Wesley's understanding of political authority. The next chapter is an analytical study of the theory explicit and implicit in Wesley's understanding of the authority of governments. The study of Wesley on political authority concludes with a topical chapter on political obligation and obedience.

REGNUM *AND* SACERDOTIUM *AND* THEIR ENGLISH *MUTATIONS*

The articulation of European political society in the course of Christian history involved the interaction of two coordinate and often conflicting modes of organizing society—*regnum* (kingly or temporal power) and *sacerdotium* (priesthood)—and appeals to two sources of authority—God and the people or community. In A.D. 494 Pope Gelasius I wrote to Emperor Anastasius, attempting both to define the separate roles and to establish the coordination of temporal authorities and the priesthood in the organization of society:

> For Christ, mindful of human frailty, regulated with an excellent disposition what pertained to the salvation of his people. Thus he distinguished between the offices of both powers according to their own proper activities and separate dignities, wanting his people to be saved by healthful humility and not carried away again by human pride, so that Christian emperors would need priests for attaining eternal life and priests would avail themselves of imperial regulations in the conduct of temporal affairs. In this fashion spiritual activity would be set apart from worldly encroachments and the "soldier of God" (2 Timothy 2:4) would not be involved in secular affairs, while on the other hand he who was involved in secular affairs would not seem to preside over divine matters. Thus the humility of each order would be preserved, neither being exalted by the subservience of the other, and each profession would be especially fitted for its appropriate functions.[5]

Gelasius did not balance the scales quite as evenly as this quotation suggests, because he insisted that—the distinction and separation notwithstanding—the spiritual responsibilities of the priests were weightier than the temporal responsibilities of the emperors. Moreover, he allowed some space for priests in "the conduct of temporal affairs." Throughout the Middle Ages emperors and popes, and later kings and popes, struggled with one another over matters of primacy and control. Prominent in this struggle was the question of divine authorization of the exercise of power. No one doubted that God was the preeminent source of authority—everyone knew the admonition of Paul to be subject to governing authorities (or higher powers) by reason of their divine ordination (see Romans 13:1). But popes argued that the authority of temporal rule was mediated through the papacy, thereby establishing ultimate ecclesiastical control, whereas emperors and kings argued that their authority came directly from God and therefore was not subject to sacerdotal mediation and regulation. According to J. N. Figgis, this papal-imperial or papal-regal contest was the source of the notion of the divine right of kings, which played such a significant role in subsequent British history.[6] According to the medieval formulation promoted by imperial and regal publicists, kings who ruled by divine right had spiritual obligations to the pope, but no political obligations. As temporal sovereigns, they were answerable to God alone. By the time of James I and VI, with the monarch as head of both church and state, they acknowledged no obligations to the pope.

The form in which these issues of representation and authority confronted John Wesley in the eighteenth century was set in the determinative events of 1688, when the Catholic James II (1685–88) was expelled from the throne of England, and 1689, when the Protestants Mary Stuart and William of Orange ascended the throne as Mary II (1689–94) and William III (1689–1702)—by parliamentary decision, not by indefeasible divine right. In the early sixteenth century, King Henry VIII (1509–47) had attempted to resolve the duality of authority in church and state by renouncing the authority of the pope and declaring himself head of the Church of England and Defender of the Faith. However, Henry's Erastian combination failed at two major points. First, it did not assure the continuance of his royal successors in loyalty to the Protestant faith. His daughter, Mary I (1553–58), was openly, aggressively, and murderously Catholic, and the Stuart monarchs of the succeeding century flirted back and forth with Catholicism until James II actively sought to turn the Church of England again toward Rome. Second, despite the theological grounding of the monarchy that accompanied this resolution, it did not finally subdue Parliament as an institution wrestling with the monarchy for influence if not supremacy in the governing of the realm. Parliament emerged as an increasingly significant dimension of the continuing articulation of English society, claiming an ever more prominent place in the existential reality of representation. James I (1603–25) sought to counter this competition by ruling unilaterally without reference to Parliament, and by deciding civil and criminal cases that belonged in the courts. His justification was the divine right of kings to rule without answering to anyone but God. What, according to Figgis, had originated as a symbolic measure for protecting the rule of emperors and kings from papal interference now became a weapon of the Stuart kings in the internal English struggle with Parliament.[7] James's son, Charles I (1625–49), dismissed Parliament and sought to rule alone, thereby precipitating civil wars that led to his execution and the establishment of the Commonwealth under Oliver Cromwell.

Toward the end of the seventeenth century, English political sentiment polarized around two alternative modes of representation as the form that English society should take for action in history. Tories supported the notion of the monarch ruling by divine indefeasible hereditary right—above the law because he or she was the source of law, answerable to no one but God, due passive obedience and nonresistance from all subjects, and head of the church as an institution coterminous with the society—the only legally established and privileged religious organization. Whigs supported the concept of a government of king and Parliament together, with predominance of power on the parliamentary side. The justification for such an arrangement was not divine right, but (most commonly) the concept of the ancient constitution supported at times by natural right. The purpose of government was to defend life, liberty, and property—with heavy emphasis on property. There should be a national church with the monarch as its head, and it should be Protestant, but more toleration should be granted to Dissenters than most Tories were willing to allow. Neither Tories nor Whigs had any interest in allowing to ordinary people a role in the conduct of government. The articulation of English society to such a degree of inclusiveness did not yet reach that far.

The expulsion of James II in 1688, followed by the constitutional arrangements of 1689, appeared to resolve these fundamental conflicts over the representational articulation of English society. Parliamentary supremacy was established, because Parliament had assumed the authority to determine the royal succession. The idea of indefeasible hereditary right, that is, the notion that no impediment of any kind could possibly render the rightful heir ineligible or unfit to occupy the throne, effectively was at an end. There would be monarchs, and rules of biological succession would be observed, but the rules would be set by Parliament. Specifically, no Catholics need apply. The daughters of James II, Mary and Anne (1702–14), would become reigning queens because they were Protestants and posed no risk of perpetuating the religious struggle at the level of royal power and prerogative. However, the son of James II by a second marriage, also named James, could not succeed his father, because he was Roman Catholic, and Parliament had blocked the Catholic succession. Monarchs would continue to have power, but their power would be exercised under the law and in collaboration with the Lords and Commons. If the religious question had been resolved, so had the question of the form of representational articulation: it would be limited, constitutional monarchy, with ultimate parliamentary authority—not absolute monarchy with Parliament as an instrument of the will of the ruler. On the terms of this settlement, Mary Stuart and her spouse and first cousin, William of Orange, came to the throne in 1689. When William died in 1702 (Mary had died in 1694), he was succeeded by Anne, the second daughter of James II. Anne died in 1714, without surviving children. The throne of England then passed to George, Elector of Hanover, great-grandson of James I. George was a German who spoke German and French but no English. He loved Hanover, and tolerated England.

WESLEY'S STANDPOINT: THE CONSTITUTIONALIST PHASE OF ARTICULATION

Our study of John Wesley's political development has determined that he made a clear stand in favor of limited monarchy and constitutional government, and against royal absolutism and the divine right of kings as the representational form in which the British community should organize itself for action in history. Wesley supported the Hanoverian monarchy against Stuart pretensions, endorsed the parity and reciprocity of royal and parliamentary authority in the making of laws, and insisted on the subordination of the royal will to established law. These positions were manifest to one degree or another in all of his public political exposures and involvements: the Jacobite rebellion of '45, the agitation for constitutional changes and extraparliamentary political influence, and the American colonial war for independence. Despite Wesley's Tory self-identification, they were more Whiggish than Tory, and they certainly were not Jacobitic. As formal expressions of representation, they were constitutional. As specific historical expressions, they embodied and attempted to perpetuate the particular constitutional settlement of 1689. Implicitly in Wesley's case, explicitly with others, they were grounded in the tradition of an ancient constitution with its representational coordination of royal and parliamentary institutions and its incorporation and protection of English liberties.

In attempting to understand John Wesley's politics it is essential to begin with the recognition that he had accepted the constitutional phase of the articulation of English society, and was not occupying the ground of the absolutist phase. If one starts elsewhere, one may find that the explanatory connections break down. Theodore Jennings, for example, works with the assumption that Wesley's politics was shaped by the royalist political theology of the sixteenth-century Homilies of the Church of England.[8] He insists that "the political theology of the Homilies plays a privileged role in the articulation of [Wesley's] own political views."[9] Nevertheless, Jennings comes quickly to the (appropriate but apparently opposite) conclusion that "The remarkable thing about the much longer and more monarchist Elizabethan

Homily for our purposes is the insignificant role it plays in Wesley's own thought."[10] With regard to the royal theology as a whole, Jennings writes that "it is remarkable how little use Wesley makes of it."[11] I take that to mean that the political theology of the Homilies does not play a "privileged role" in Wesley's political views. It is a conclusion to which one comes if one examines Wesley's views from the standpoint of what he actually did and said politically, and not from what he is supposed to have believed as a priest of the established church. With the former approach, one can see that Wesley is defending a constitution of which the monarchy is an essential but limited element. He is not defending a theology of monarchy more appropriate to Jacobite and high Tory commitments to a monarch answerable only to God. Moreover, one can see that when the biblical language incorporated into this royal theology appears in Wesley's dealings with political crises, it is not—as Jennings supposes—the directive force. It is an ideological weapon to which Wesley resorts in order to require acceptance of the constitutional order that he defends mainly with practical and constitutional—not biblical and theological—arguments. With the latter—royalist political theology—approach, one is at a loss to explain the limitation of royal power and authority that is so evident in Wesley's public political statements.

ROYALIST/ABSOLUTIST SYMBOLS OF REPRESENTATION

That Wesley carried along some of the symbolic rhetoric of the absolutist phase is true. Historical transitions rarely are completely disjunctive in either social or individual consciousness. Wesley did in fact fear God and honor the king. However, that is not evidence in his case of a fundamentally royalist orientation to politics. Wesley's establishment in the traditions, values, and assumptions of the settlement of 1689, and his loyalty to the Hanoverian (not the Stuart) monarchy, are clear and incontrovertible. They have been reviewed and documented throughout the preceding historical study, and need not be repeated here. What must be done at this point is to investigate prominent symbols of the Jacobite or high

Tory political formulations to see whether and to what extent they established and sustained some influence on Wesley's political thinking.

The Homilies of the Church of England

As Jennings rightly observed, Wesley knew the Homilies of the Church of England as official statements of the theology of that church, binding on priests and believers along with the Articles of Religion and the Canons. Priests were required to read them to their congregations in order to teach correct doctrine to all members and to enforce loyalty to the Crown and obedience to the monarch and other magistrates. Although the Homilies were documents reflecting struggles of the sixteenth century, they remained in force in the eighteenth century. John Wesley—a learned, fully ordained clergyman—dutifully read them to persons under his priestly care, even though they were intended originally and primarily for parishes where clergy were unlicensed and/or unlearned in theology. Two Homilies in particular set forth correct political doctrine. The first is "An Exhortation Concerning Good Order and Obedience to Rulers and Magistrates." It was initiated during the reign of Henry VIII, and published in 1547 during the reign of Edward VI. The second is "An Homily Against Disobedience and wilful Rebellion," published in 1570 in the reign of Elizabeth I (1558–1603).[12] One would expect the political theology of these Homilies to provide the ideational substance for Wesley's political thinking. Was that in fact the case?

In attempting to answer this question we must bear in mind that our concern here is with the symbols of representation, of the organization of a society for action in history, and not with the related but different issue of political obligation. The first thing to notice with regard to symbolic representation is that the two Homilies have different theological explanations of the origin of government. According to the Homily of 1547, government is part of the original design of creation:

> Almighty God hath created and appointed all things in heaven, earth, and waters, in a most excellent and perfect order. In heaven he appointed distinct and several orders and states of archangels and

angels. In earth he hath assigned and appointed kings, princes, with other governers under them, in all good and necessary order.[13]

Moreover, all the relationships of superordination and subordination throughout humankind are arrangements of this creational design. Human beings are assigned their responsibilities through a grand societal application of what appears to be Martin Luthers's threefold distinction of *Beruf, Stand, Amt:*

> . . . every degree of people in their vocation, calling and office, hath appointed to them their duty and order: some are in high degree, some are in low, some kings and princes, some inferiors and subjects, priests and laymen, masters and servants, fathers and children, husbands and wives, rich and poor; and every one have need of other; so that in all things is to be lauded and praised the goodly order of God, without the which no house, no city, no commonwealth can continue and endure, or last.[14]

Whatever influence of Luther may lie behind this concept, there is no suggestion in the text that the order is a result of the Fall and not an original plan of the Creator.

The Homily of 1570 has a different theological understanding of the origin of political authority and of relationships of superordination and subordination. They are not elements of original divine creation, but are responses of God to human disobedience, that is, to the fall of humankind. In this mythic reconstruction of creation there is no mention of kings and magistrates. "Man"—a corporate symbol of humankind—is required to obey and serve God, and is given God's law as a means of doing so. Furthermore, "man," collectively, is accorded a relationship of dominance over all other earthly creatures. Nothing is said in this creational context of any differentiation of roles and functions in the administration of this responsibility. Offices, statuses, and social ranks with their attendant duties are not part of creation's order.

> As God the creator and lord of all things appointed his angels and heavenly creatures in all obedience to serve and to honour his majesty; so was it his will that man, his chief creature upon the earth, should live under the obedience of his creator and lord: and for that cause, God, as soon as he had created man, gave unto him a certain

precept and law, which he (being yet in the state of innocency, and remaining in paradise) should observe as a pledge and token of his due and bounden obedience, with denunciation of death, if he did transgress and break the said law and commandment. And as God would have man to be his obedient subject, so did he make all earthly creatures subject unto man, who kept their due obedience unto man, so long as man remained in his obedience unto God: in the which obedience if man had continued still, there had been no poverty, no diseases, no sickness, no death, nor other miseries, wherewith mankind is now infinitely and most miserably afflicted and oppressed.[15]

In this blessed and harmonious ordering, "obedience is the principal virtue of all virtues, and indeed the very root of all virtues, and the cause of all felicity."[16] Disobedience as rebellion against God and God's law entered this paradise and destroyed or distorted every form of relationship and all health that existed in the whole system of relationships. In response to this disaster, God acted to recover some degree of order, and in doing so introduced the human patterns of rule, command, and obedience.

After this breach of obedience to God, and rebellion against his majesty, all mischiefs and miseries breaking in therewith, and overflowing the world, lest all things should come unto confusion and utter ruin, God forthwith, by laws given unto mankind, repaired again the rule and order of obedience thus by rebellion overthrown; and, besides the obedience due unto his majesty, he not only ordained, that, in families and households, the wife should be obedient unto her husband, the children unto their parents, the servants unto their masters; but also, when mankind increased, and spread itself more largely over the world, he by his holy word did constitute and ordain in cities and countries several special governors and rulers, unto whom the residue of his people should be obedient.[17]

According to this interpretation, God reintroduces order into the disordered creation, first, by requiring obedience to himself (the foundation of all order), and second, by introducing patterns of obedience into the relationships of the household. God's provision for the ordering institutions of governors and rulers comes only later—in response to the growing size of world population.

Governmental institutions and all human relationships of authority and obedience are effects of the fall of humankind into sin; they are not endowments of creation. Quite obviously the political theology of the second Homily differs from that of the first on this fundamental point.

The second thing to notice follows from the first: in the Homily of 1547, monarchy is a theologically necessary institution by reason of its specification in the order of creation. Given that provision, no other form of government could be theologically acceptable. The same conclusion is not drawn in the Homily of 1570. In that one, government as such, not a particular form of government, is God's response to the disorder of sin: "[God] by his holy word did constitute and ordain. . . special governors and rulers."[18] At this point there is no specific mention of monarchs, an omission that seems to undercut the theological necessity of monarchy and leave the way open to the acceptance of other forms of government.

One can make too much of this difference, of course. Both Homilies are defending the present monarch and the institution of monarchy. The second no more than the first shows any inclination to apply legitimation to other forms of government, or even to discuss them. Moreover, the second Homily sees the princely government of kingdoms as an analogy of the divine governance of the universe, and argues that earthly kingdoms are rightly governed to the degree that the prince conforms to the example of God's governance:

And as God himself, being of an infinite majesty, power, and wisdom, ruleth and governeth all things in heaven and in earth, as the universal monarch and only king and emperor over all, as being only able to take and bear the charge of all; so hath he constituted, ordained, and set earthly princes over particular kingdoms and dominions in earth, both for the avoiding of all confusion, which else would be in the world, if it should be without such governors, and for the great quiet and benefit of earthly men their subjects, and also that the princes themselves, in authority, power, wisdom, providence, and righteousness, in government of people and countries committed to their charge, should resemble his heavenly governance, as the majesty of heavenly things may by the baseness of earthly things be shadowed and resembled. And for that similitude that is between the heavenly monarchy and earthly kingdoms well governed, our saviour Christ in sundry parables saith, that the kingdom of heaven is resembled unto a man, a king: and as the name of the king is very often attributed and given unto God in the holy scriptures; so doth God himself in the same scriptures sometime vouchsafe to communicate his name with earthly princes, terming them gods: doubtless for that similitude of heavenly government, the nearer and nearer that an earthly prince doth come in his regiment, the greater blessing of God's mercy is he unto that country and people, over whom he reigneth: and the further and further that an earthly prince doth swerve from the example of the heavenly government, the greater plague he is of God's wrath, and punishment by God's justice into that country and people, over whom God for their sins hath placed such a prince and governor.[19]

The analogy of divine governance does not have the same ease and congruence of application to aristocracies and democracies that it has to monarchies. It would appear therefore to carry some implication of special theological status for monarchy even if that is not made explicit, and even if no reference is made to other forms of government. On the other hand, the argument for similitude seems to be the practical one of the functional utility of monarchical rule, not the ontological one of inherent imaging coherence between divine rule and the institution of monarchy. Also, the similitude varies with the relative conformity of princely behavior to God's ruling action. We may conclude that the analogical construal of monarchy—although powerful and suggestive—lacks the force and exclusiveness of the ontological, that is, of the construal of monarchy as an element of original creation. On this point the second Homily, albeit unintentionally, leaves some latitude for later Anglicans to accept the theological explanation for government while avoiding the theological necessity of kingship. The first Homily does not.

John Wesley probably would have read the Homilies as basically in agreement on obedience to governing authorities, but clearly not on the theological explanation for the origin and nature of government. On that point the two diverged—obviously and fundamentally. For that reason he could not have taken his political theology directly and unreflectively from the Homilies as though they offered a unified account of symbolic representation.

Inevitably he would have had to decide for one against the other on some matters, and in doing so would have to appeal to authorities other than the Homilies themselves. There is no evidence, of which I am aware, that Wesley ever held or advocated the view of the Homily of 1547—that government with its enforcement functions and its relationships of command and obedience was part of the plan of creation. He did believe that humankind was created in the political image of God, with the responsibility of governing the nonhuman creation. That responsibility, however, was a corporate commissioning of all human beings. It did not involve or imply the subordination of some human beings to others. It made no creational provision for kings and other governors. By inference, as well as for lack of evidence to the contrary, one can conclude that he did not consider monarchy to be a theologically necessary element of the original divine plan. Whatever may be said about Wesley's attachment to kingship and to particular kings, he was not a royalist or a monarchist in that sense. Nor did he think of social roles and relationships in the static terms of the 1547 Homily.

Did he then accept the representational symbolism of the Homily of 1570? Certain aspects of Wesley's political thinking are in fact closer to this Homily than to the earlier one. His occasional statements about the actual work of government reflect the view that explains it as God's provision for the ordering of sin in the world. Governments should maintain order, enforce the law, and protect the Methodists from the mobs. Without government, "every man does what is right in his own eyes." Also, Wesley, like the 1570 Homily, makes use of the analogy of divine action to develop some moral content for the conduct of political office—a matter to be examined in more detail in a later chapter. Even so, one must be cautious in making close comparisons. Wesley's statements about the role and function of government suggest a more comprehensive view of its work—one symbolized by the broad rubric of the "public good"; not one limited to protection, preservation, and punishment. Furthermore, Wesley uses the analogy of God (and of the angels) essentially to suggest how public officials should conduct themselves; he does not use it to generate a theology of political institutions, and specifically one of kingship imaging the divine rule. And finally, this "order of preservation" view of government cannot be traced solely to the second political Homily. It was an ancient theological interpretation of the origin and nature of the state, widely held, restated and reinforced by Luther, and available to Wesley from other sources in addition to this one.

Perhaps the clearest distinction between Wesley's attitude toward political institutions and that of the two Homilies appears in the short essay "The Origins of Power," where he allows that God might bestow governing authority on aristocracies and democracies as well as on monarchies.[20] Nothing of the sort appears in the Homilies, which are exclusively monarchist in their symbolic representation (although the second Homily allowed the pragmatic possibility of other forms of government). Wesley certainly was committed to monarchy and particular monarchs, but there was more openness on his part than on that of the Homilies to alternative modes of symbolization, and no conformity to the limits they imposed. Even without this citation, however, there is enough evidence from the analysis of the Homilies—along with the evidence of Wesley's constitutionalism—to establish that he was not dependent on them in any fundamental sense for his political thinking. I have pointed to the explanation already: Wesley engaged English politics in the context of the constitutionalist phase of the articulation of societal representation. He did not engage it in the royalist/absolutist phase. His alleged "monarchism" must be interpreted in constitutional, not absolutist, terms.

Robert Filmer's Patriarchalism

Sir Robert Filmer's *Patriarcha* and other writings of his presented the strongest and most influential seventeenth-century case for the absoluteness of royal power.[21] Filmer argued that all authority derived by natural right from parental authority, and more specifically, from the authority of the father. Both Scripture and historical experience, according to Filmer, made clear that fathers had full authority over their children, including the power of life and death. This power was to be used in benign and beneficial fashion, namely, for the welfare of the children. Moreover, it was to be used with responsibility to God, who was the ultimate and original bestower of power and authority. But otherwise it was arbitrary, in the sense that the father's will was law, and that it was not subject to other controlling considerations. Political authority, in Filmer's view, was a form of paternal authority, for the king was the father of the family that constituted the nation. God had given dominion over the world to Adam, the father of the human race. Kings were descendants of Adam, and as fathers of their nations held the same rights over their people as Adam held—by divine commission— over the human family. Thus Filmer could speak of "the natural power which kings have over their people by right of father-hood."[22]

Filmer wrote *Patriarcha* between 1628 and 1648 (the exact date is uncertain). It was the time of intense struggle between royalists and republicans following the death of James I in 1625 and leading to the execution of Charles I in 1649. Filmer sought to establish the sole and unlimited authority of the monarchy by showing its origin in God and nature, refuting natural right theories of the location of authorization with the people, and demonstrating the derivative—from the Crown—character of all parliamentary and legal authority. He laid the basis for the royalist case, as we have seen, in the patriarchal theory of paternal right and Adamic royal descent. He dismissed the argument for popular origins by asking when such a transfer ever took place in history, and by insisting that if all have a natural right to confer authority, then conferral by a lesser—presumably representative—number is a usurpation. Neither common law nor statute law, he contended, binds the royal will, "For as kingly power is by the law of God, so it hath no inferior law to limit it,"[23] and "the prerogative of a king is to be above all laws."[24] Parliament has no authority or even existence apart from the king, and it most definitely has no authority over him in the making of laws. "The parliament is the king's court, for so all the oldest statutes call it, 'The king in his parliament.' But neither of the two houses are that supreme court, nor yet both of them together. They are only members of a part of the body, whereof the king is the head and ruler."[25] Parliament has no claim by right against the king, because all parliamentary rights and privileges derive from the king, and not from any other source. "For all those liberties that are claimed in parliaments are the liberties of grace from the king, and not the liberties of nature to the people."[26] Moreover, "in parliament all statutes or laws are made properly by the king alone at the rogation of the people."[27] Parliament does not make laws. The king in Parliament makes laws, and the authority of the laws is the authority of the king. The Lords advise the king, and the Commons give consent, but the king alone is the lawmaker. What the king enacts, the king can repeal, set aside, or revise.

Filmer also makes a point of demonstrating that monarchy is a superior and highly effective form of government, whereas democracy is inferior, ineffective, and indeed disastrous. This pragmatic argument may serve his polemical purposes, but theoretically it is irrelevant. Once he has established political authority in the absolute paternal rights of the father, he has made the case for monarchy as the sole authoritative form of government and needs no demonstration of its relative efficacy. The theoretical argument, not the practical one, establishes royal absolutism and excludes any justification for claiming that the people have the right to choose their form of government and also to choose and control their governors.

Although several of Filmer's writings were in print in the middle of the seventeenth century, his main work, *Patriarcha*, was not published until 1680.[28] The occasion was the Exclusion Controversy, in which the Whigs sought to exclude James, Duke of York and brother of Charles II, from succession to the throne. The Tories, to gain a propaganda advantage, countered by republishing Filmer's previously published works and then bringing out the *Patriarcha* for the first time. This ploy was enormously successful. Filmer's theories attained such prominence and influence in the struggle as to prompt published rebuttals by James Tyrrell and John Locke, among others. The title page of Locke's *Two Treatises of Government* announces that in the *First Treatise*, "The False Principles of Sir Robert Filmer, and His Followers, Are Detected and Overthrown."[29] Filmer's influence waned with the passage of time, but persisted with some strength into the eighteenth century, and informed the Jacobite ideology that John Wesley was alleged to have espoused.[30]

Robert Filmer and his patriarchal theory come into the picture in this study of John Wesley because of the enduring implications of these Jacobite allegations, and because some writers see strong similarities between Filmer and Wesley. Peter Lee states that "[Wesley] had a paternalistic idea of government, like 'the learned Sir Robert Filmer, Baronet.' "[31] Robert Hole, commenting on William Paley's use of the notion that the state's power over life and death derives from God, adds, "Wesley and William Jones had both used this argument, taken from Filmer, to stress the divine nature of government."[32]

One can see similarities between Filmer's thought and Wesley's, which suggest some influence of the former on the latter, whether direct or indirect. Both of them insist that authority in society comes from the top down: God delivers authority to the topmost point in society, which then delegates to lower officials. Accordingly, both attack the argument that authority derives by natural right from the people. Both ask for historical evidence of an original contract and transfer of authority, and both demand to know why ordinary people should be considered competent to make political decisions. Both of them argue the superiority and efficaciousness of monarchy and the inferiority and destructiveness of democracy as forms of government.

However, once one has registered these similarities one must acknowledge some striking and decisive differences. Wesley's case against the authority and political competence of the people is a defense of the constitutional arrangement of 1689 against republicanism, not of absolute monarchy against Parliament. For Wesley the legitimate and effective government is the combination of king and Parliament. He does not subordinate one arm of government to the other, nor does he believe one element of government to be the source of the other's authority, rights, and privileges. Both king and Parliament, in his view, are involved in the making of laws. If he leans more to one side than to the other, it is toward Parliament.[33] The will of the king is not authoritative unless supported by a law made in the Parliament. Wesley clearly does not agree with Filmer that the king is the sole lawmaker, that the Lords merely advise, and that the Commons merely register consent. He does not believe that the king is above the law in any sense. Also, in Wesley the concept of individual liberty has a considerable political presence that it does not have in Filmer. Even though this liberty is not the source of governmental authority, it is a limit to governmental power, and its protection is a provision of governmental responsibility.

Wesley never, to my knowledge, mentions Robert Filmer or his works. He does not use Filmer's theory of Adamic origin and natural paternal right to explain the origin of royal—or any other political—authority. To the contrary, implicitly he rejects Filmer's fundamental position by distinguishing between parental and royal authority, as well as by subordinating the royal will to the law. In his sermon "On Obedience to Parents," Wesley writes:

> Do everything which your father or mother bids, be it great or small, provided it be not contrary to any command of God. Herein God has given a power to parents, which even sovereign princes have not. The King of England, for instance, is a sovereign prince; yet he has not power to bid me do the least thing unless the law of the land requires me so to do; for he has no power but to execute the law. The will of the king is no law to the subject. But the will of the parent is a law to the child, who is bound in conscience to submit thereto unless it be contrary to the law of God.[34]

We should not overlook that Wesley is contrasting royal authority with parental authority, not paternal authority. When he speaks of father or mother in this regard, he is destroying the foundation of Filmer's case for the absolute natural right of the father, on which Filmer's theory of royal patriarchy is built. When he goes on to distinguish between parental and royal authority, and to argue the constitutional subordination of the king to the law, he is simply widening the gap that exists between Filmer's political thought and his own.

Against the backdrop of these differences, we must examine Peter Lee's assertion that Wesley's paternalistic idea of government was like Filmer's. Indeed Wesley did think of kings—at least of George II and George III—as father figures, and his concept of government was broadly paternalistic. However, there are very few "fatherly" references in his published writings, and none is used to develop fundamental concepts of authority. Perhaps the most noticeable is found in his "A Word to a Smuggler." There he compares smuggling to other forms of thievery, except that it is a case of stealing from our father, the king.

Open smugglers are worse than common highwaymen, and private smugglers are worse than common pickpockets. For it is undoubtedly worse to rob our father than one we have no obligation to. And it is worse still, far worse, to rob a good father, one who sincerely loves us, and is at that very time doing all he can to provide for us and to make us happy. Now, this is exactly the present case. King George is the father of all his subjects; and not only so, but he is a good father. He shows his love to them on all occasions; and is continually doing all that is in his power to make his subjects happy. An honest man therefore would be ashamed to ask, Where is the harm in robbing such a father?[35]

One can imagine that Filmer would agree with these sentiments, yet not be satisfied with them as a vindication of his basic point. The "father" references in this passage tell us how a king should act toward his subjects, but they do not touch the question of the king's right to rule. They belong to the genre of "image of princes" literature, not to that of political authority. Moreover, there probably is nothing of a substantive nature in this passage that would be different if Wesley were writing during the reign of Queen Anne, and speaking of her as the "mother" of her people. Yet Filmer's theory is based on the specific notion of patriarchy, not on the more general one of monarchical benevolence. Wesley's paternalistic idea of government was not like Filmer's with regard to the fundamental issue of paternal authority and royal patriarchy. Evidently, Peter Lee was not sufficiently discriminating in his comparison.

Although Wesley did not refer to Filmer by name, and did not discuss or employ his patriarchal theory, it is unlikely that he did not know of them. John Fletcher, his close friend and designated successor, defended Wesley in the controversy over the American War of Independence in terms that at first reflected Filmer clearly, before modifying his views in subsequent publications. Robert Hole describes this movement in Fletcher's writing on political authority:

Fletcher made three attempts to define Methodist views on the nature of authority before getting them right. Initially, he adopted a position which was almost undiluted Filmer: power came from God to Adam and so to his royal descendants; national governments grew out of family government. A few months later, he qualified this view in two ways. He explained that the heirs of Adam might not only be monarchs but could include other forms of government— king and parliament, doge and senate, emperor and diet. That was in line with Wesley's view, but Fletcher went beyond this to argue that God-given authority was operative and binding only if the government "retains that power by the consent of the majority." Only in his third attempt did Fletcher describe Wesley's position accurately. Government is the creation of God, not of the people. Its authority is of divine not human origin. Its right to govern is independent of the people. However, the consent of the majority is necessary to support civil government, as is the consent of soldiers in an army. It is a tacit, not a formal act of consent, and it is not the source of authority, merely the requisite without which that authority cannot be exercised.[36]

Actually, Wesley gave less weight to this form of consent than does Hole in bringing Fletcher around to Wesley's position. Also, he did not see governors of any kind as "heirs of Adam." However, Hole's sketch of the changes in Fletcher's position is correct in most respects. The main point for our purpose is that Fletcher knew Filmer's patriarchal theory and endorsed it, but had to modify and eventually give it up in order to be true to Wesley. That supports the notion that Wesley knew of Filmer and his theory, even though he did not refer to them. It supports also the argument that Wesley's position on authority was not Filmer's, despite the fact that they agreed on the basic tenet that authority came from God, not the people.

The differences between Wesley and Filmer reinforce our claim that they occupied divergent standpoints in relation to the representational articulation of English society. Filmer was in the tradition of royal absolutism; Wesley was in the constitutionalist tradition. Both men should be understood primarily from these differing standpoints; therefore, Wesley should not be interpreted with heavy reliance on his similarities with Filmer, even though they shared some convictions. The similarities suggest in part that Wesley was holding on to some ideas that fit more comfortably with the position that Filmer represented, but somewhat less so with his own constitutionalism. Filmer could speak confidently of authority from God delivered to a monarch who ruled absolutely by original paternal right. Wesley also spoke confidently but less convincingly of authority that descended to a monarch whose power was limited by Parliament, law, and historic and natural liberties. Wesley referred to the king as a "sovereign prince," but it was clear that his prince was no sovereign. Filmer, who published a collection of quotations from Jean Bodin's *Six Books of the Republic*, certainly was comfortable with Bodin's definition of sovereignty: "the absolute and perpetual power of the state, that is the greatest power to command."[37] Filmer's sovereign prince was the sole locus of that power; Wesley's was not. In Wesley's thought, sovereignty belonged to the constitutional order of government—not to the king above, and separate from the other elements of government. It was a view he shared with William Higden. Authority descended to that constitutional order, whatever it might be. In Filmer's thought, the king was the only rightful recipient of authority, and therefore the only true sovereign. These differences, which derive from differing orientations to the articulation of societal representation, are of much greater significance than the similarities. They make it clear that the two men viewed the articulation of English society differently. Wesley's views are neither continuous with nor modified from Filmer's.

The Divine Right of Kings

Did John Wesley believe in the political-theological doctrine of the divine right of kings? William Warren Sweet states flatly that "he certainly believed in the divine right of kings and repudiated the idea of the sovereignty of the people."[38] Bernard Semmel and Leon Hynson are more guarded, arguing that early on Wesley believed in divine right, but changed or surrendered this emphasis later in life. Semmel sees Wesley as holding on to the doctrine for practical purposes of resisting revolutionary turmoil, but yielding it to natural right on the theoretical level under the pressure of his liberalizing theology. "Wesley was a Laudian Churchman," Semmel wrote, "who feared lest Protestant Enthusiasm be led into the paths of speculative Antinomianism, and from thence into the fiery cauldrons of revolution. To avoid such a calamity, he preached the doctrines of the divine right of kings and of nonresistance as essential to the Christian persuasion, although we recall that he had on occasion described both civil and religious liberty as natural rights. But, having set aside in his later life the 'narrow spirit of Laud,' would he move from a Laudian Toryianism to a Grotian Arminian Whiggery, from divine right more unequivocally to natural right? In one further matter, this was to prove the case."[39] Hynson focuses more clearly and directly on the contradictions between the doctrine and Wesley's politics: "Wesley's commitment to the limited monarchy which the Glorious Revolution brought must be seen as a precise opposition to the divine right argument; Wesley supported kingly authority which undergirded human rights, not all or any kingly authority; and . . . Wesley's powerful assertion of liberty of conscience undercut the old passive obedience and non-resistance appeals."[40]

To attempt to clarify Wesley's views on this important question, I shall review his political attitudes in the light of J. N. Figgis's statement of the elements of the doctrine. Figgis wrote:

The theory of the Divine right of Kings in its completest form involves the following propositions:—

(1) Monarchy is a divinely ordained institution.

(2) Hereditary right is indefeasible. The succession to monarchy is regulated by the law of primogeniture. The right acquired by birth cannot be forfeited through any acts of usurpation, of however long continuance, by any incapacity in the heir, or by any act of deposition. So long as the heir lives, he is king by hereditary right, even though the usurping dynasty has reigned for a thousand years.

(3) Kings are accountable to God alone. Monarchy is pure, the sovereignty being entirely vested in the king, whose power is incapable of legal limitation. All law is a mere concession to his will, and all constitutional forms and assemblies exist entirely at his pleasure. He cannot limit or divide or alienate the sovereignty, so as in any way to prejudice the right of his successor to its complete exercise. A mixed or limited monarchy is a contradiction in terms.

(4) Non-resistance and passive obedience are enjoined by God. Under any circumstances resistance to a king is sin, and ensures damnation. Whenever the king issues a command directly contrary to God's law, God is to be obeyed rather than man, but the example of the primitive Christians is to be followed and all penalties attached to the breach of the law are to be patiently endured.[41]

How do Wesley's own views compare with the historic meaning of divine right?

(1) Wesley believed that government was a divinely ordained institution, but he did not make the same case specifically for monarchy. As we have seen, he did not follow the Homily of 1547 in claiming that monarchy was an establishment of original creation. Indeed, he did not argue that government as superordination and domination was a provision of original creation. To be more precise, he did not make much of a theoretical case one way or the other on the origins of government, but he seemed to be more in accord with the 1570 Homily's contention that government was given by God to counteract the disorder produced by human sin. His acceptance of the ancient trilogy of monarchy, aristocracy, and democracy implied that none of these, including monarchy, was theologically necessary and theologically superior to the others. Monarchs rule by divine ordination, but so do other governors. His clear preference for monarchy over other forms of government was based partly on an inclination to accept the historical order as given, and partly on his appreciation for the moderate reign of the Hanoverians. It was a sentimental and pragmatic preference, not one determined by theological considerations.

On the other hand, one must acknowledge religious elements in Wesley's attitude toward the incumbents of the throne. He could speak of "his sacred majesty King George,"[42] and declare that "a King is a lovely, sacred name."[43] Those attributions suggest more than a mere pragmatic justification of and preference for the institution. They convey the residual power of the Tory sentiments of Wesley's parents, and warn against too precise distinctions between religious and pragmatic attitudes toward monarchy. Wesley would not have used the terms "sacred" and "majesty" to refer to types of governors who were not royal. Doubtless this religious sense helps explain his defense of Richard III, Mary of Scotland, and Charles I.[44] Nevertheless, Wesley's monarchs were human creatures subject to his severe criticism—especially in the cases of the Tudors and Stuarts—for abuses of power and for bad character. He could speak of Henry VIII as not having "a grain of virtue or public spirit,"[45] and exclaim sarcastically, "O what a blessed governor was that *good-natured man*, so called, King

Charles the Second! Bloody Queen Mary was a lamb, a mere dove, in comparison of him!"[46] His comments on the other Tudors and Stuarts were equally complimentary. However passive and deferential toward royalty—on religious grounds—he may have been as a young man, in his later and politically more active years he evaluated monarchs in a more secular and pragmatic context, with special attention to their support or repression of religious liberty. He used scriptural texts to require obedience to the Georges, whom he perceived as good rulers and protectors of liberty, but not to analyze or defend the institution of monarchy in religious terms. Moreover, he believed that the same scriptural texts required obedience to rulers who were not royal. Wesley believed in the divine provision for government, the divine source of authority, and the divine ordination of rulers, but not in monarchy as a divine institution with a theological status different from and superior to other types of political institution.

(2) Wesley never spoke of the indefeasible right of hereditary succession to the throne, and never defended it in print—if at all. On one occasion when he used the term "indefeasible right," it was in reference to religious liberty, not to the occupancy of the throne or the legitimacy of succession.[47] He always supported the Hanoverians against the Stuart pretenders, most notably in the Jacobite rebellion of '45. The disjunctive events of 1688–89, which dismissed the principle of indefeasible hereditary right, were for him the "happy Revolution." Although he did not publish his disagreements with his mother, it is clear that he did not follow her in affirming this fundamental element of divine right.

(3) Wesley certainly believed that monarchs were accountable to God, but not to God alone. Monarchs are accountable also to the constitution and to the law, and they have no authority to act unilaterally and without parliamentary approval. In rejecting the American colonial claim that the king's charter had granted the colonies an exemption from parliamentary taxation, he wrote, "For to say, that the King can grant an exemption from the power of Parliament, is saying in other words, that one branch of the legislature can grant away the power of the others. This is so far from being true, that if there is, in the charter of any colony, a clause exempting them from taxes for ever, yet, unless it were confirmed

by an act of the whole Legislature, that clause is void in itself. The King (to use the phrase of the law) was 'deceived in his grant,' as having given that which he had no right to bestow."[48] That passage is consistent with everything Wesley ever wrote on the powers of the monarch and the relationship of the monarch to Parliament. He was committed to limited monarchy, to constitutional monarchy, not to absolute monarchical sovereignty. His position on the question of limits to royal power and authority stood in clear opposition to that of the theory of divine right.

(4) Wesley's views on obedience to authority will be considered in a later chapter. Here it must suffice to say that in broad outline he was committed to the proposition that one must obey governing authorities unless they commanded something contrary to the command of God. That was consistent with the theory of divine right on this issue, but also with Christian teaching on political obligation for centuries before the divine right concept was fully formulated. However, Wesley added the further proviso that what the authorities commanded also must be in accord with the law. What we shall see in a subsequent chapter is that Wesley developed an approach to the obedience question that was more active and dynamic than the passive position of traditional Christian, Tory, and divine right teaching. Nevertheless, in the context of republican dissent and American rebellion, his employment of Romans 13 and other "obedience" texts was distinctly restrictive and conservative. It looked to his contemporaries like divine right, and his opponents were quick to make that accusation.

This comparative analysis makes clear that Wesley did not believe in divine right in the precise sense in which it was understood at the time. The tendency of some writers on Wesley's politics to hang the "divine right" label on him suggests that they equate the doctrine with the historically dominant themes of the divine source of political authority and the requirement of obedience to governing authority, and do not pay attention to the concrete and explicit historical meaning that emerged in the seventeenth century and was still a matter of contention well into the eighteenth century. Central to this historical meaning are the elements of indefeasible right of hereditary succession and the responsibility of the monarch to God alone. The divine source of authority and political obligation are necessary elements, but they are not peculiar to the historic concept of divine right, inasmuch as they were shared much more widely. Wesley's politics, as expressed both in his writings and in his loyalties, repudiates the central tenets of indefeasible hereditary right and the supremacy of the king to law, constitution, and Parliament. He should not be referred to as a "divine right" thinker, if the concept is understood and used properly. He was a constitutionalist, and that is something quite different.

So far, we might anticipate general assent from Semmel and Hynson. However, both of these very able writers on Wesley's politics argue that he made a transition from divine right to more liberal politics. Hynson wrote that "by 1770 he no longer was fighting a battle for the divine right monarchy but for the divine origin of power."[49] Semmel says that "he preached the doctrines of the divine right of kings and of non-resistance."[50] I can find no evidence that John Wesley fought a battle for divine right monarchy or preached the doctrine of the divine right of kings. As I have indicated in the historical inquiry chapters, I find no evidence that he ever used the term "divine right," and evidence of only one or two (nonapplicable) references to indefeasible right. What I find is that he accepted the Glorious Revolution either "happily" or at least as *fait accompli.* His reading of William Higden's book confirmed his political principles; it did not change them. His support of King George II against the Stuart pretenders was out of conviction; it did not represent a conversion or a mere practical concession to protect the Methodists. If the term "divine right" is used in its proper historical sense, there is no compelling reason to assign it to John Wesley.

This comparative review of royalist and absolutist symbolizations of representation makes clear that John Wesley did not locate himself in that historic option for the organization of English society for action in history, however much he may have used its terminology. His political location was in the next stage of articulation, namely, that of constitutional government. Wesley was a constitutionalist in the historical sense: he accepted, celebrated, and defended the constitutional settlement of 1689 with its abrogation of indefeasible hereditary divine right and its establishment of parliamentary authority beyond the confines of royal prerogative. He was a constitutionalist also in the theoretical sense: he supported the limitation of governmental power; its division, balance, and reciprocity; its subordination to law at all levels; and its respect for and protection of individual liberties. Constitutionalism, in Wesley's view, was consistent with his belief that authority is from God, not the people. Nevertheless, he embraced a different understanding of political authority in practice from that of the high Tories and Jacobites who also used that formula. It should be clear, therefore, that we must set aside the symbolizations of "John Wesley, Tory," or divine right, monarchism, royalism, and absolutism when attempting to understand Wesley politically. Whatever residual overlappings in consciousness these symbols may have, they do not represent his placement in the process of English political articulation. They distort our efforts to discern his understanding of political authority.

A THIRD PHASE OF REPRESENTATION: THE PEOPLE AND THEIR AGENTS

Of course, the articulation of English political society did not come to an end with the consolidation of the results of the Glorious Revolution. Early in the reign of George III it was evident that the process was moving toward wider inclusion of excluded elements of the society, supported by the symbolic language of natural rights and social contract. The more radical elements of John Locke's philosophy, which earlier in the century had been subordinated to his defense of property, now were called into service to challenge the control of government and society by men of property, to demand more equitable representation in Parliament, and in some cases even to press for an end to the monarchy. This movement of the process was manifest in the Wilkite movement, in the agitation in both England and America for "no taxation without representation," in critiques of "rotten boroughs" and the nonrepresentation or underrepresentation of large cities, and ultimately in the rebellion of the American colonies against England in the name of liberty and independence.

John Wesley opposed this next step in the process of articulation in all of its forms and manifestations. He was content quite fully for English society to be organized for action in history with a limited monarchy, parliamentary institutions for the enactment of laws, and a preeminent constitution grounded in history and precedent and embodying and protecting the liberties of the English people. He saw no need in theory or practice for the mode of representation to be resymbolized and restructured in democratic and republican terms, or for the people to have any role in authorizing governmental power or participating in its exercise.[51] Quite to the contrary, he insisted, any change in that direction would have disastrous consequences for the country as a whole and even for those rights and liberties whose enhancement was sought by means of these changes. "The greater share the people have in the Government," he wrote, "the less liberty, either civil or religious, does the nation in general enjoy. Accordingly, there is most liberty of all, civil and religious, under a limited monarchy; there is usually less under an aristocracy, and least of all under a democracy."[52] Those words established both his affirmation of the present stage of articulation of English society and his resistance to transition to the next.

Wesley offered several arguments against the democratization of politics. All of them rest ultimately on the hierarchical nature of authority deriving from God and descending from above to below, but some are of a practical nature, and some are pertinent to the ideology of the republican and democratic movements. By now they are thoroughly familiar.

First, in Wesley's view there is no defensible normative basis for the claim that governments are authorized by popular consent. Authority comes from God—as the Bible says. If it comes from God, it cannot come from the people. Coming from God, it descends from above. It cannot arise from below. That should settle the matter, and eliminate the necessity of further argument. However, Wesley was not interested merely in declaring revealed truth; he wanted to defend the constitution—the established political and legal order—by disarming and defeating the opposition. Therefore he assailed the principal normative claim of the democratizing opposition, namely, that authority to govern derives from the natural right of individual self-government, and is conferred on governments when individuals consent to be governed. This argument obviously is defective because it is reduced easily to absurdity: If all individuals must consent to government, then women, youth, and persons without property must give their individual consent—and with the same weight as mature, propertied males. However, that prospect is patently so absurd that not even the proponents of the theory believe or propose it (certainly Wesley himself did not). Therefore the argument is without merit.

> The supposition, then, that the people are the origin of power, is in every way indefensible. It is absolutely overturned by the very principle on which it is supposed to stand; namely, that a right of choosing his Governors belongs to every partaker of human nature. If this be so, then it belongs to every individual of the human species; consequently, not to freeholders alone, but to all men; not to men only, but to women also; nor only to adult men and women, to those who have lived one-and-twenty years, but to those who have lived eighteen or twenty, as well as those who have lived threescore. But none ever did maintain this, nor probably ever will. Therefore the boasted principle falls to the ground, and the whole superstructure with it. So common sense brings us back to the grand truth, "There is no power but of God."[53]

Common sense, of course, does not bring us back necessarily to God as the source of authority, once Wesley has demolished the case for the popular sources. It may bring us simply to the arbitrariness of power. That was a consequence Wesley chose to ignore, presumably because he was more interested in destroying the arguments of the radical (not Jacobite, in this case) opposition to the constitution and defending the status of the government than he was in developing a theoretically consistent and defensible argument for the nature of governmental authority. As a supporter of the Revolution, he wanted to make clear that its authority did not come from popular consent. That conclusion would allow him then to defend the resulting constitutional institutions against the consent-theory demand that they should be revised drastically in the direction of greater democratization.

Second, the people as a whole are not political agents. They do not as a body institute and authorize governments, nor do they as a body execute significant changes in government. As to the first exclusion, there is no significant historical evidence that governments originate when a people acting as a whole create a social compact; establish a government; identify its purpose, powers, and limitations; and transfer authority from themselves to their governors. Specifically British history is empty of records of common authorizing action, at least for the preceding seven hundred years. The notions of a historical transfer by an entire people acting together, and its companion the social contract, are fictions. Such things never happened.[54]

As to the second exclusion, the major political disruptions and realignments in history are the work of the few, not the many. Moreover, the acting few are not the agents or delegates of the people as a whole.

> Perhaps you will say, "But if the people did not give King Charles the supreme power, at least they took it away from him. Surely, you will not deny this." Indeed I will; I deny it utterly. The people of England no more took away his power, than they cut off his head. "Yes, the Parliament did, and they are the people." No; the Parliament did not. The lower House, the House of Commons, is not the Parliament, any more than it is the nation. Neither were those who then sat the House of Commons; no; nor one quarter of them. But suppose they had been the whole House of Commons, yea, or the whole Parliament; by what rule of logic will you prove that seven or eight hundred persons are the people of England? "Why, they are the delegates of the people; they are chosen by them." No; not by one half, not by a quarter, not by a tenth part, of them. So that the people, in the only proper sense of the word, were innocent of the whole affair.[55]

By similar reasoning Wesley dismisses the claim that the people restored power to King Charles II and later conferred power on William III at the time of the Revolution. William III did not obtain royal power

> as William the First did; although he did not claim it by right of conquest, which would have been an odious title; yet certain it is, that he did not receive it by any act or deed of the people. Their consent was neither obtained nor asked; they were never consulted in the

matter. It was not therefore the people that gave him the power; no, nor even the Parliament. It was the Convention, and none else. "Who were the Convention?" They were a few hundred Lords and gentlemen, who, observing the desperate state of public affairs, met together on that important occasion. So that still we have no single instance in above seven hundred years of the people of England's conveying the supreme power either to one or more persons.[56]

In neither case did the people, as a whole, act. Nor did those who engaged in effective action do so as the delegates of the people. By what he takes to be a simple and honest review of the facts, Wesley dismisses the arguments for both direct action by the people, including conferral of authority, and indirect conferral through delegated representation.

Third, despite any connection of the people as a whole with these stunning changes, the outcome was authoritative power. Government resulted from these actions, and as government it had the right to make laws and require obedience. Governmental authority exists with full effectiveness in the present governmental institutions—or to put it in the language of the theme of this chapter, in the particular institutional mode in which English society is organized for action in history. In that sense it is representational authority. It does not require transition to a more inclusive, more democratic, mode.

Fourth, if the people are not the source of governmental authority, neither should they participate in government. To follow Wesley's arguments we must note that he is using the concept "people" in different ways in different contexts. In the broadest sense he means all who are not officeholders. The "people," thus understood, cannot claim a right to participate. The moral grounding for participation in government comes from above and descends to particular persons; it is not inherent in human nature as such. In another sense, "people" means "ordinary folk." Ordinary English folk are not qualified by education and experience to formulate governmental policy and make political decisions. Here we should recall Wesley's musings, cited in a previous chapter, over whether the colliers and keelmen of Newcastle knew enough about public administration, naval operations, and the balance of Europe to advise Mr. Pitt on his choice of cabinet ministers, or whether even the politically more sophisticated and intellectually more competent citizens of London had that capability.[57]

However, the concept that made Wesley most nervous and confirmed his resistance to democratization was the one that equated "people" with the "mob." That was the meaning contextualized and made manifest for him in the Wilkite and related movements, which in his view threatened the order of society and the basic liberties of the English people. That was his view also of political tendencies in the American colonies. It was clear to Wesley that this mindless, emotional, manipulated crowd should not be allowed into either the process of authorization or the practice of governing. To permit such a thing would be to invite and assure the destruction not only of particular governments, but of government itself. It was this picture of political dissolution, irrationality, and irresponsibly that he had in mind when pronouncing democracy the worst form of government—the one most inimical to liberty.

We should note in passing that Wesley had no direct acquaintance with democratic government to support this generalization, but tended to equate democracy with what he experienced as social disintegration. We should note also that the logic of his contention—"The greater share the people have in the Government, the less liberty, either civil and religious, does the nation in general enjoy"—implied an absolute monarchy, not a limited one, as the most liberty-supportive form of government.[58] But these observations are beside the point. Wesley was not reporting a political science survey or making a scholarly comparison of various political forms. He was defending an established constitutional order against a movement that was thrusting English society into the next stage in societal articulation. That stage required greater inclusiveness in its representational work of organizing the society for action in history. Wesley's conservative arguments in defense of the constitutional order focused on the risks of greater inclusiveness to the basic societal values of order and liberty. It was clear to him that acceptance of the principle of public participation would threaten those values, whatever the justification for the principle might be.

One final comment: Wesley did not defend the constitutionalist stage of political articulation against democratization by appealing to political disablement resulting from original sin. Allen Lamar Cooper contended that "just as man was incapacitated to act spiritually for himself, he was incapacitated to govern himself."[59] This strongly Lutheran argument does not represent John Wesley's view. It is true that Wesley understood one of the purposes of government to be a dike against sin, but the theological argument he used to seal the exclusion of the people from politics was not original sin but the divine origin of political authority. He allowed democracy as a possibly legitimate form of government, which he could not have done had he drawn from sinful human nature a general inference of political incapability. However, in the context of history, he could defend an existing political system by resisting democratization primarily on grounds that those outside the political process had no divinely given right to gain entry.

THE CHURCH IN SOCIETAL ARTICULATION

We cannot conclude this inquiry into John Wesley's views on representation as the organization of the political society for action in history without some attention to the role of the church in that organization. In that specific context Wesley accepted the Protestant establishment with its Erastian arrangement whereby the monarch was head of church as well as state, and crown and Parliament exercised legal control over most aspects of the church's life and work.[60] His admonition in "A Word to a Freeholder" (1747) to "beware of dividing the King and the Church, any more than the King and country" was addressed to voters in a particular election, but it represented his lifelong conviction concerning the organic unity of crown, church, and people.[61] As a young man Wesley fussed about the favoritism of the Whig administration in episcopal and other preferments, and he fraternized with Thomas Deacon and other nonjurors who opposed their "true church" to the Church of England, but he never considered leaving the Church of England and never directly contested the ingredient relationship of the church to the English polity. His adamant insistence on remaining in the church despite immense pressures for Methodist separation is well known and need not be reviewed here. When his Methodists were attacked by mobs stirred up by parish clergymen, he called for enforcement of the law to protect the innocent and punish the guilty, but not for the separation of church and state. Maurice Woods wrote that for Toryism the Crown was "the visible symbol of patriotic unity and religious faith."[62] In that respect John Wesley certainly was a Tory, however Whiggish his politics might have been otherwise.

Yet there is some evidence of less than full commitment to this Erastian model on Wesley's part. On several occasions he spoke critically, cynically, and even bitterly of what he took to be the dubious conversion to Christianity of the emperor Constantine, but especially of the detriment to the church resulting from the Constantinian settlement with its integration of political and religious forces and fortunes. In the sermon "Of Former Times," he wrote:

> I have been long convinced from the whole tenor of ancient history that this very event—Constantine's calling himself a Christian, and pouring that flood of wealth and power on the Christian church, the clergy in particular—was productive of more evil to the church than all the ten persecutions put together. From the time that power, riches, and honour of all kinds were heaped upon the Christians, vice of all kinds came in like a flood, both on the clergy and laity. From the time that the church and state, the kingdoms of Christ and of the world, were so strangely and unnaturally blended together, Christianity and heathenism were so thoroughly incorporated with each other that they will hardly ever be divided till Christ comes to reign upon earth. So that instead of fancying that the glory of the new Jerusalem covered the earth at that period, we have terrible proof that it was then, and has ever since been, covered with the smoke of the bottomless pit.[63]

This passage could have been written by an Anabaptist discussing the fall of the church and assigning the time and occasion of its fall to its union with the state under Constantine. The church is the kingdom of Christ; the state is the kingdom of the world. The two apparently have nothing inherently to do with each other, and when they come together the blend is strange and unnatural. Moreover, the penetration of the church by the state brings a heavy injection of heathenism that will continue to infect and corrupt the church until the return of Christ. This viewpoint, presented so forcefully here and in other passages, strikes at the root of the English Protestant establishment, which Wesley accepted as a matter of course and defended with great certainty and flourishing scriptural weaponry.

Wesley also showed ambivalence toward the concept of a national church—a notion integral to the English establishment. The minutes of the conference of 1747 record these pertinent questions and answers:

Q. Does a church in the New Testament always mean "a single congregation"?
A. We believe it does. We do not recollect any instance to the contrary.
Q. What instance or ground is there in the New Testament for a national church?
A. We know none at all. We apprehend it to be a mere political institution.[64]

In his sermon on "The Cure of Evil-Speaking," Wesley refers to "the national church, the whole body of men termed 'the Church of England.' " This empirical definition, he notes, does not fit the meaning of "church" as used in the text. Then he adds—dismissively—"Neither would it answer any Christian end if you could [define it in this manner]."[65] In his sermon "Of the Church," he is much more accepting of the concept of a national church. "That part of this great body, of the universal church, which inhabits any one kingdom or nation, we may properly term a 'national' church; as, the Church of France, the Church of England, the Church of Scotland." This concept, together with churches visible in much smaller combinations, he finds "exactly agreeable to the nineteenth Article of our Church, the Church of England: 'The visible church of Christ is a congregation of faithful men, in which the pure word of God is preached, and the sacraments be duly administered.' " Having established the scriptural validity of the concept "national church," he finds it "easy to answer that question, What is 'the Church of England'? It is that part, those members, of the universal church, who are inhabitants of England. The Church of England is that 'body' of men in England in whom 'there is one Spirit, one hope, one Lord, one faith,' which have 'one baptism,' and 'one God and Father of all.' This and this alone is the Church of England, according to the doctrine of the Apostle."[66] Even this supracongregational view differs, however, from the organic, institutional concept of national church. Potentially it includes some who are not formal members of the Church of England, and excludes some who are. It is a view of the church that sits loose from its institutional reality and from the comprehensiveness of the establishment concept.

Whatever latent explosive charges these reservations may have carried, they did not detonate to demolish Wesley's own profound loyalty to the English Protestant establishment with its particular combination of religious and political elements. His primary concern in his anti-Constantine comments was the harm to the church arising from the power and affluence that the new relationship with the empire delivered, not the political aspects of the relationship or the religious benefits to the empire. The church lost spiritual gifts, the clergy became corrupt, the various callings of ministry were unified in one man as the leader of a congregation, the church lost the will to endure persecution, and Christian faith became permeated with heathenism. It seems obvious that if Wesley wanted to see the church rid itself of these harmful effects and recover its integrity and spiritual power he should have urged it to renounce all legal and political involvements. Yet however much he may have deplored these effects on the church, he did not counsel separation and the renunciation of support. Nor did he challenge the theological validity of an office that was at once head of state and head of church, or charge that civil governance was corrupted by religious and ecclesiastical associations. To the contrary, he celebrated the role of religion in government and the combination of piety and loyalty in king and commoner. Moreover, he always repudiated the charge that he and his Methodists were Dissenters from the English establishment.

Wesley also did not draw the conclusions for church-state separation implicit in his reservations concerning the idea of a national church. In the first place, he held these reservations in tension, and at times contradiction, with unwavering commitment to the church defined in national and institutional terms. He set forth a low-church, congregationalist view of the reality of the church, but remained a priest of the Church of England with sufficient High Church identity to be labeled at times a Jacobite and even a papist. He dismissed the national church as "a merely political institution," but honored the institution and claimed to observe and to teach its requirements and procedures. He resorted to unauthorized practices such as field preaching, extemporaneous prayer, and the ordination of clergy for America and Scotland, but refused to allow his preachers to administer the sacraments, urged attendance at parish services, and emphasized the authority and staying power of his own priesthood.

In an oft-cited passage, Frank Baker has noted that

> throughout his adult life Wesley responded with varying degrees of enthusiasm to two fundamentally different views of the church. One was that of an historic institution, organically linked to the apostolic church by a succession of bishops and inherited customs, served by a priestly caste who duly expounded the Bible and administered the sacraments in such a way as to preserve the ancient traditions on behalf of all who were made members by baptism. According to the other view the church was a fellowship of believers who shared both the apostolic experience of God's living presence and also a desire to bring others into this same personal experience by whatever methods of worship and evangelism seemed most promising to those among them whom the Holy Spirit had endowed with special gifts of prophecy and leadership.[67]

In this uneasy cohabitation, the deeply rooted, family-nurtured character of the churchly elements—the historical, institutional, sacerdotal—prevented the more dynamic sectarian elements from providing the defining view of the nature of the church. In doing so it stemmed the fragmentation or dissipation of the notion of national religious membership, which was an essential element of British community consciousness.

In the second place, if we consider these issues from the standpoint of Wesley's view of the English polity and community rather from that of his evangelistic mission, there is no significant contest. The religious-political establishment prevails; it is simply taken for granted in his way of regarding the organization of English society for action in history. That claim is confirmed amply in "Ought We to Separate from the Church of England?"—a paper prepared by John Wesley for submission to the Conference of 1755.[68] In this document Wesley defends adherence to most of the institutional regularities of the Church of England—to the doctrines, rubrics, sacraments, prayers, public services, and governing authorities.[69] More important for our present purpose, he accepts without question the authority of Parliament in confirming the rubrics and constituting bishops as governors of the church, and of magistrates in regulating divine worship.

Responding to the charge that Methodists should not submit to any "ordinance of man," because Christ is the only lawgiver in his church and the Bible the only rule of worship, he argues:

> The Jewish Church was Christ's as really as the Christian. And he was the only lawgiver in the Jewish as well as in the Christian Church. Yet King Jehoshaphat proclaimed a fast without any derogation to Christ's authority. Yet King Josiah commanded the law to be read, and gave many other directions to that church. Yet Nehemiah ordained the whole form of divine worship, and Christ was honoured, not injured, thereby. . . . It plainly follows that magistrates may regulate divine worship without any infringement of the supreme authority, and that although Christ is the only *supreme* lawgiver therein, yet magistrates are *subordinate* lawgivers, even to the Church.[70]

To the question whether Methodists should separate from the Church of England because "the church is only a creature of the state," he responds:

> If you mean only that King Edward the Sixth required several priests in the then Church of England to "search into the law of God and teach it the people"; that afterwards he restored the scriptural worship of God to the utmost of his knowledge and power, and (like Josiah and Nehemiah) gave several rules for the more decent and orderly performance of it—if you mean this only by saying "the Church is a creature of the state"—we allow it is, and praise God for it. But this is no reason at all why we should separate from it.
>
> Neither is this, that "the king is the supreme governor of the Church of England." We think the king ought to be the supreme governor of his subjects. And all of the Church of England are

his subjects. Therefore (unless he should command anything contrary to the law of God) we willingly obey him as our supreme (visible) governor.[71]

Whatever negative thoughts Wesley may have had about Constantine's conversion and the debilitating effects on the church of its deal with the Roman Empire, they do not extend to the English pattern of church-state relationships. In these passages Wesley takes his stand—unrelentingly, unapologetically—as a defender of English Erastianism. Tensions in the Gelasian duality of *regnum* and *sacerdotium* are resolved by subordinating the latter to the former. Wesley apparently has no theological objections to this arrangement. In fact, he establishes a theological framework for state control of religious matters and institutions by regarding the political community as church, and assigning the monarch the role of lawgiver for the church under the extended rule of Christ. That is clear from his reference to the "Jewish church," for which the kings can proclaim fasts, command the law to be read, and ordain the form of worship without in any way usurping the functions of the priests or challenging the law-giving authority of Christ. Kings and other magistrates are divinely ordained officials of an integral community at once political and religious. Their preeminent authority in the political community—under the transcending authority of Christ—allows and requires them to make and enforce religious as well as civil laws for both church and state. They are not suffered to make laws contrary to the law of God, or otherwise violate the divine command, but their roles in enacting laws for the church, confirming the bishops, revising the prayerbook, and establishing the pattern of worship are in fulfillment of a divine commission, not a usurpation of ecclesiastical commission.

This is not a general theory of church-state relationships. It is a theological reaffirmation of the English establishment. It holds for Wesley despite the separationist concept set forth in the anti-Constantine passage quoted earlier. In that passage, Wesley separated the church as the kingdom of Christ from the state as the kingdom of the world. However, he directed the critique of Constantinianism against the church, and did not draw its obvious implications for the relationship of church with state, or for the religious pretensions and responsibilities of the civil power. In the passage acknowledging the king as supreme governor of the church, Wesley places the temporal power under the kingship of Christ (as supreme lawgiver), but in doing so subordinates the church to the state. Ultimately this pattern of Erastian predominance, this commitment to the English Protestant establishment with the king as head of the church, was stronger in his thought and practice than the christological framework of temporal power or the anti-Constantinian criticisms that supported the emergent sectarian impulses of the Methodist revival. It was the religiously political—or politically religious—form in which English society was organized for action in history. John Wesley accepted it as the theologically defensible providential ordering of God.[72]

TRINITARIAN THEOLOGY AND THE POLITICS OF SYMBOLIZATION

Our inquiry has shown that John Wesley affirmed the constitutional order of eighteenth-century England as the normative mode of representation, that is, as the form in which the society should organize itself for action in history. He rejected the other two modes of representation that strove for dominance in his lifetime. To understand Wesley's views on political authority rightly, one must begin with this historical location, not with the summary statement that authority is from God, not the people, nor with a reconceptualization of Wesley as an emergent natural rights or human rights thinker.[73] In practical terms, political authority for John Wesley is the authority of the established political order, the authority of law over power and position, of the separate but balanced and coordinated offices of king, Lords, and Commons, of the customary procedures and values that came to expression in the ancient and unwritten constitution. It is constitutional authority. Moreover, this constitutionalism is organic and historical, not contractual. There is nothing mechanical or atomistic in Wesley's view of the constitution, nothing to suggest that it arises from the agreement of contracting individual wills. To the contrary, the constitution as historical reality is antecedent and superior to the wills of the members of the society. Although—and because—it antedates them, it requires their allegiance and obedience. That is why the constitution is authoritative and the members are not.

To be sure, Wesley confirms the constitutional arrangement with ultimate authority derived from God. Like Robert Filmer, Wesley insists that authority, derived from above, follows the same flow and descends from the topmost level of the political structure to those that are lower. For Filmer, however, that pattern established the authority of the absolute monarch over his subordinate and instrumental Parliament, and even over the law. For Wesley, by contrast, the pattern protects the limited monarchy and its parliamentary companions against demands for constitutional change to promote greater inclusiveness. Filmer used the theological argument to resist movement from the absolutist to the parliamentary mode of representation; Wesley used it to resist transformation of the parliamentary or limited monarchy mode into one that was more republican and democratic.

These similarities, taken together with the differences, illustrate the possibilities and problems of relating theology to politics. Filmer's royalist absolutism allowed the clear coordination of his theology and his politics. God rules absolutely and the king does also—under God and by God's revealed and natural design. Wesley's theocratic view of authority coupled with his constitutionalism and his openness to forms of government other than absolute monarchy is not as logically coherent, and it is somewhat awkward by comparison. Royal rule is not simply an image of divine rule; the monarch rules coordinately with Parliament and is limited by Parliament. The pattern of top-down derivation of authority should make the monarch the primary recipient and ultimate dispenser of all governing authorization, but that is not so in a limited, constitutional monarchy. As we have noted previously, authority from God descends to the constitutional order in which monarch and Parliament are institutional partners, not to the monarch as superior to Parliament. Moreover, the monarch is subordinate to the law, a provision that gives the law authority over the monarch. Something in this arrangement interferes with the clear notion of authorization from above: the separation and balance of powers, the role of electors, and the subordination of royal will to the primacy of law suggest some loci of authorization that do not fit the hierarchical theological model Wesley attempts to share with Filmer.

Constitutionalism in eighteenth-century England represented not only an articulation of English society beyond absolutism; it represented also a form of symbolization not inherently dependent on theological language. That is, it expressed a process of secularization as well as a process of political development. It is evident from Wesley's manner of political discourse that he was caught up in the secularizing process as well as in the political transition. Despite his appeals to scriptural texts to establish political authority, his political argument rests only lightly on theological considerations. I have noted previously that Wesley makes little use of God-talk in his political tracts. Most of his argumentation involves legal, theoretical, and especially practical considerations. The uses of Romans 13 and other scriptural texts arrive on the scene mainly to reinforce conclusions reached on other grounds. Hynson and Semmel, in particular, have argued that Wesley changed his political theology from divine right to human rights and natural rights, largely in response to the liberalizing and democratizing elements of his evangelical theology. However, except for his largely theistic arguments for religious liberty, his rights language mainly was philosophical, political, and practical—not theological. He does not say much about natural rights, by contrast with historic rights. What he does say is protected from descent into radical individualism more by his organic and historical sensibilities than by any development of Wesleyan theology to accommodate and support his views. His rights language provides further evidence of his participation in the secularization of politics, and of the instrumental rather than fundamental relationship of his theology to his political thought.

In concluding that Wesley established himself firmly in the constitutionalist mode of representation, one must conclude also that he did not develop the theological language to give symbolic expression to his political commitments. A hierarchical theology of politics that ordains the peak of power in society with supreme authority does not cohere with a political system designed to control dominant power and diversify authority, that is to say, a constitutional system. If constitutionalism is to be interpreted in theological terms, the theology cannot be simply hierarchical. It must begin to derive authority from below, not only from above. Failure to adjust the theological enterprise away from its hierarchical mode results inevitably in reactionary or irrelevant political theology and the secularization of constitutional thought.

What the attempt to combine top-down authority with constitutionalism reveals in Wesley's case is a failure to think through the political implications of his trinitarian theology. Bestowal of authority from above suggests the first person of the Trinity. Wesley's insertion of Christ into the political process was mainly if not exclusively in the form of judge and lawgiver, roles that retain the hierarchical relation of the first person. The principal work of the second person of the Trinity—the work of salvation—suggests the empowerment of all people to engage the fullness of their humanity, including their recovery of the political image of God. The full involvement of trinitarian theology in political thinking becomes possible only with the opening of participation and the process of authorization to those who are outside the system, namely, to those who are "below." Viewing the matter from the other (i.e., the political) side, Wesley could not support his constitutionalist politics solely with hierarchical, first-person-of-the-Trinity theology, even when assisted by the second person in hierarchical, nonsalvific relationships. He needed to engage the nonhierarchical elements—the second and third persons of the Trinity in their primary roles. However, had he taken that step, he would have been driven by trinitarian logic to make his politics more inclusive. Because he did not do that, his political arguments became increasingly secular, and his appeals to divine authorization of political power encouraged others to represent him as an old-line Tory monarchist—if not Jacobite.

CHAPTER SEVEN

POLITICAL AUTHORITY II
THEORETICAL ELEMENTS AND
MISSED OPPORTUNITIES

Our investigation in the preceding chapter showed that John Wesley's concept of political authority cannot be reduced to the theologically driven formula—authority is from God, not the people. Central to his thinking on the topic are elements of constitutionalism, which he expresses constantly in nontheological terms and which are not necessarily implied in the formula. In fact, when viewed in the context of Wesley's involvement in eighteenth-century political conflicts, the nontheological terminology of constitutionalism establishes his basic position, and the theological arguments are brought in to confirm it. Our investigation in the present chapter shows a different relationship of the theological and nontheological elements. Wesley's declaration that God is the one true source of political authority establishes a general theory that makes no inherent provision for temporal limits to sovereign power. His constitutionalism, which essentially is a theory of limited power, runs the risk, then, of standing simply as one historical example among others of a way to arrange political power, and not as a normative ideal for and critique of all other forms. Wesley's failure to integrate his theology with his constitutional politics enhances the normative vulnerability of the latter and invites the former to the ideological role of defender of established power. The exodus from this dilemma requires a transformation of the formula to read: *authority is from God through the people*. Certainly that is not what Wesley had in mind, but it is the only way to confirm the representational movement from absolutism to structural and organic limits to power, and it is a legitimate inference from historical resources and aspects of his theology that he chose to ignore.

This chapter examines the nature and implications of what can be characterized rather loosely as Wesley's "general theory" of political authority, and then compares it with the particular theory of limited power stated or implied in his interventions in political conflicts. The last part of the chapter will consider alternative ways Wesley might have chosen to relate the general and particular theories, and therefore the theological and nontheological elements—which in effect is to show how he might have come up with a different (though nevertheless Wesleyan) theory of political authority.

A GENERAL THEORY: POLITICAL AUTHORITY IN THE BEING OF GOVERNMENT

Wesley begins his "Thoughts on the Origin of Power" with this statement: "By power, I here mean supreme power, the power over life and death, and consequently over our liberty and property, and all things of an inferior nature."[1] The reference to *origin* in the title is to the ultimate source of the authority of supreme power, to the fundamental validation of its right to command and its expectation to be obeyed (i.e., not to the course of history by which the power became supreme). Wesley assumes, of course, that the exercise of power must be authorized. Political obligation is moral obligation. Obedience is for the sake of conscience, and not only to avoid the wrath of government. His answer to the question of origin, understood in these terms, is predictable—authority derives from God: "'there is no power but from God: The powers that be are ordained of God' (Rom. xiii.1.)." His reasoning: "I cannot but acknowledge, I believe an old book, commonly called the Bible, to be true."[2]

Perhaps one dignifies this sketch of an idea too much by referring to it as a *theory* of political authority. After all, most of the tract is devoted not to the development of Wesley's theologically grounded views on the topic, but to a refutation of the claim that authority to govern derives from the people by way of consent expressed through elections and social contracts. It is polemic—not a reflective, systematic, self-critical reaching for and elaboration of first principles, either theological or philosophical. Nevertheless, it is clear that Wesley intends this inquiry and its conclusion to be a general explanation of the authority of all governments of any description wherever and whenever they are to be found. He covers the classical typology of monarchy, aristocracy, and democracy, and cites examples of supreme power in various countries and different centuries. In that sense, therefore, this brief outline is a general theory of political authority—one that explains the authority of all loci of supreme power.

An immediate question is whether there is any supreme power that is not authorized, or whether the existence and possession of such power constitute *prima facie* evidence of authorization. Wesley's "general theory" includes no criteria for answering this question—for distinguishing governments that are divinely ordained to exercise supreme power from those that are not. Government *in its being* as supreme power apparently is authorized government. Where there is government, there is divine authorization of its power. Particular actions of a government may be legally or morally wrong, but they nonetheless are actions of a government with the right to command obedience as the institutional embodiment of supreme power.[3] Presumably God ordains whatever power achieves supremacy by whatever methods. The theory itself does not discriminate. (Of course, one could suppose, as Wesley might have, that arrival at supremacy was evidence of providential ordering.)

A related question, or perhaps a different way of putting the same question, is whether the general theory requires limitations to power that are political or constitutional in nature and not solely moral limits addressed to the conscience. That does not appear to be the case. When Wesley centers his inquiry on *supreme power* his choice of terms suggests and may even reflect Bodin's concept of sovereignty as the locus of absolute and perpetual power in a society. Wesley employs the term and endorses the concept in affirming the inherent right of the English government to tax the American colonies without regard to whether they are represented in Parliament. In "A Calm Address to Our American Colonies," he argued against the claim of "Dr. Smith in Philadelphia," who contended that " 'No power on earth has a right to grant our property without our consent.' " Wesley replied, "Then you have no Sovereign; for every Sovereign under heaven has a right to tax his subjects; that is 'to grant their property, with or without their consent.' Our Sovereign* has a right to tax me, and all other

Englishmen, whether we have votes for Parliament-men or no."[4] Sovereignty, in Wesley's view, is an irreducible attribute of government as supreme power. It means that the government is authorized only from above and not from below, that it has rightful entitlement to tax the people and enact other legislation without consulting them or seeking their approval, that it is not answerable to or restricted by other political powers or jurisdictions. Wesley's general theory of governmental authorization, resting as it does on the concept of sovereignty, is a theory that imposes no political or constitutional limits on authorized governments.

Certain provisions in Wesley's political writings confirm this conclusion. One is that absolute monarchies are included with numerous examples in his list of supreme powers with divine authorization.[5] Their absolutism apparently has no bearing on their status as authorized powers. With reference to that point, Wesley never doubted that the Tudors and Stuarts exercised royal authority, however grievous their pretensions to absolutism and however much he may have criticized their abuse of liberties.[6] Another provision is his statement concerning the derivation of other levels and loci of authority from the supreme power. "There is no subordinate power in any nation, but what is derived from the supreme power therein. So in England the King, in the United Provinces the States are the fountain of all power. And there is no supreme power, no power of the sword, of life and death, but what is derived from God, the Sovereign of all."[7] In this hierarchical scheme—suggestive of Filmer, if not copied from him—the lower levels of power (i.e., of authority) derive from the higher levels and do not qualify or limit them.

Yet another confirming provision is the preexistent or presuppositional character of governmental authority. Wherever we meet government, we meet authoritative power. Persons born into a society are born obligated to laws of the society enacted before their births. They do not become obligated when they are old enough to consent to the laws. When infants emerge into consciousness of responsibility, they emerge to awareness of existent political obligation. Obligation is neither created by nor contingent upon their awareness and affirmation. "And how," Wesley asks, "has any man consented to those laws which were made before he was born? Our consent to these, nay, and to the laws now made even in England, is purely passive. And in every place, as all men are born the subjects of some state or other, so they are born, passively, as it were, consenting to the laws of that state. Any other than this kind of consent, the condition of civil life does not allow."[8] Passive consent, or tacit consent as it is called by other writers, essentially means that one's remaining in a society and not leaving it implies consent to the rule of the government and therefore to the legitimacy of its actions. This passive consent may provide important assistance to the government's ability to govern without unusual friction and instability, but it has nothing to do with its authority—its right to govern. The authority of the government is independent of any consent, whether active or passive.

What separates Wesley from High Tories and Jacobites in this regard is the fact that he offers a general theory of governmental authority, and not a defense specifically of monarchical authority. Especially noteworthy is his acceptance of democratic governments as having their authority from God, considering his antipathy to democracy in both Methodism and English politics, and his insistence that democracies were the governments most inimical to civil and religious liberties. Of course, he does not mean that democracy is a divinely authorized *form of government*. What he means is that where one finds government *existing in democratic form* one must acknowledge that as the supreme power it wields its power with divine authority, and that its officers are ministers of God. For Wesley, that result is to be accounted to the strange and inscrutable workings of God's providence—like the successful establishment of the new republic in America despite his certainty that the colonies could not justifiably make themselves independent of England. Nevertheless, it is intriguing that Wesley could concede legitimation to a form of government dependent on authorization from the people governed (i.e., from below), while insisting, without any apparent sense of contradiction, that its authorization came from above. Yet that is a necessary implication of his view that divine authorization attends the being of government, and is the theological basis of the moral element in political obligation.

Of course, there are some limits established for a general theory rooted in divine authorization. A government may not require what is contrary to the law or command of God. Wesley also believed that a government should not require what was contrary to natural law, although he did not develop a full theory of natural law as part of a political ethic.[9] These religious and moral limits on supreme power are consistent, certainly, with Wesley's affirmation that all authority is from God. Indeed, they are implied if not expressed in it. Most of them are limits acknowledged also by Jean Bodin, the philosophical originator of the theory of sovereignty. However, they are religious and moral limits binding on conscience but not expressed necessarily in constitutional arrangements or other forms of political or legal restraint. Wesley's general theory of political authority has no such inherent power-limiting provisions.

SUPREME POWER AND CONSTITUTIONALLY LIMITED POWER

Wesley's so-called general theory requires no constitutional or political limits—or even aspiration to such limits—for the predication of divine authorization to supreme power. His actual political commitments, however, were to limited government in a constitutional context. Was his limited government simply a historical example of the general theory with no universal application, or was it latently a challenge to the theory?

Wesley gives us no direct help with this question. To the contrary, he leaves a trail of confusing leads—probably because he was interested in polemical witness and not in theoretical clarification, probably also because his self-certainty allowed no sense of conflict. To begin with, there is confusion in his use of the term *sovereign*. When he speaks of the sovereign, he means the king, but his king quite clearly is not *sovereign*. That is, he is not the supreme power. In the response to "Dr. Smith in Philadelphia," cited previously, Wesley placed an asterisk next to the word "Sovereign." The asterisk is significant. He used it to add this footnote qualification to the inherent right of the sovereign to lay taxes: "That is, in connexion with the Lords and Commons."[10] Once he had done that he had denied implicitly but effectively the sovereignty of the royal person. Applying the term to the monarch thereafter is simply an archaism; the real sovereign in English society is the mixed constitutional government, consisting of king, Lords, and Commons. Wesley confirms this consequence in "Some Observations on Liberty" by referring to king and Parliament together as "the supreme power of my country."[11]

In view of this development, it is strange that in "Origins of Power" he could refer to the king as the supreme power in England, and claim that all other locations of power in the society were derived hierarchically from him. If the supreme power is the king and Parliament together, it cannot be the king alone. In the limited monarchy, which he supported without reservation, the powers of monarch and Parliament are separated and balanced. Parliament does not receive its authority from the monarch, and is not subordinate to the monarch. To the contrary, the will of the monarch, according to Wesley, has no authority unless supported by an act of Parliament. When Wesley spoke of members of Parliament as representatives, he declared that they were representatives of God.[12] In context, of course, he meant that they were not representatives of the people. It is significant, however, that he did not call them representatives of the king. In fact, they were not representatives of the king. They did not derive authority by delegation from the king. Wesley's affirmation of the mixed and balanced constitution is at odds with his other affirmation of the king as supreme power and proximate source of other political power.

Wesley's typology of governments in "Origins of Power" includes no place for limited monarchy—the only form of monarchy he supported directly. All his monarchical examples are of absolute monarchs. Apparently he was not interested at that point in the relationship of a general theory of temporally unlimited political authority to the particular historical experience of authority in a constitutionally limited government. His efforts were consumed with refuting the arguments of the Lockeans, not with making his own position fully consistent and coherent.

However, one must not conclude that Wesley's general theory had no bearing on his particular contextual political commitments. After all, he continued to use the term *supreme power,* and to use it in such ways as to invoke sovereignty and its rights. The point was that for Wesley the mixed and balanced government of king, Lords, and Commons, collectively, was supreme power and therefore truly *sovereign*, even though he continued to refer to the monarch equivocally as "the Sovereign." He made the point especially in two contexts. One was the authority of the government to impose taxes even in the absence of representational consent. Taxation legislation, like legislation generally, was an inherent right of supreme power and therefore not a limited or contingent right. The second was the sovereign power of the government in London over the several parts of the empire. English colonies were creations of the English government. If their charters issued by the king through acts of Parliament granted them certain rights to tax themselves, or to legislate on other specific matters, they held those rights under the terms of the charters. As colonies they had no rights that were not contractual, especially natural rights to serve as authoritative bases for claims against the sovereign government. In these respects the general theory of supreme power and its authority applied to Wesley's particular historical experience. The limitations, which he honored and on which he insisted, were internal to the government as supreme power; they were not limitations on the supreme power itself. His constitutional convictions with their doctrines of limited power did not result in a modification of the general theory.

Understood solely as the right to command and to expect obedience, the authority of government as defined in Wesley's theory of sovereignty and supreme power is compatible with constitutionalism as an internally limiting system of government. However, it is incompatibile with constitutionalism understood as authoritative and effective restraints on supreme power. That is especially true if the restraints are located in the consent of the governed, regardless of how that consent may be delivered. His general theory of authority served, therefore, as a limiting principle for his constitutionalism, confining it essentially to the supremacy of law and the reciprocity and balance of royal and parliamentary power, and excluding the need for greater diffusion of participation and control. That limitation was exactly what Wesley wanted.

A more difficult question concerns the limits to exercise of supreme power presented by historically developed values and norms, specifically English liberties and the provisions of the ancient constitution. Does the authority of supreme power extend over these socially organic claims on and limits to the power of government? Do the rights of sovereignty overrule their normative force?

Wesley does not address the question of liberties as limits to power with such directness that one can infer a conclusive answer. Dr. Price, according to Wesley, claimed that the king and Parliament could take all our liberties away. "But they do not"; Wesley responded, "and, till it is done, they are freemen. The supreme power of my country can take away either my religious or civil liberty; but, till they do, I am free in both respects."[13] Does Wesley mean simply that the government has sufficient force to take liberties away, or that it is *entitled* to take them away as a matter of sovereign right? The opening argument of "Origins of Power" appears to support the case for sovereign right. The supreme power has power "over our liberty and property," among other things, and this supreme power is exercised with authority from God. On the other hand, his criticisms of the Tudors and Stuarts for their abuse of rights, his celebration of the revolution of 1688 because of its establishment of English liberties, and his praise of George II and George III for protecting religious liberty point to the interpretation that the taking away of liberties would be an unjustified exercise of superior force and not an entitlement of divinely authorized power. That interpretation is confirmed by his setting the "indefeasible right" to religious liberty as a limit to the authoritative exercise of power: "And God did never give authority to any man, or number of men, to deprive any child of man thereof, under any colour of pretence whatever."[14] Nevertheless, Wesley is counting on the government to respect English liberties as a *moral* limit to action by the supreme power. His theory requires no *constitutional* limit to that power's abrogation of the liberties. In that regard, Dr. Price appears to have the stronger argument.

A similar question pertains to the ancient constitution itself. Is this historically developed combination of provisions and expectations binding on the government as supreme power, or does *supreme power* imply that the government has divinely given authority to alter or even dismiss the constitution? William Higden had argued that one who was a king *de facto* but not *de jure* established authority in the eyes of nobles and people by fitting his acts as king into long-established practices, and especially by gaining acceptance for his laws in the history of royal legislation.[15] That argument implies that supreme power can establish itself *de novo* by unconstitutional means, but that once established it acquires legitimacy by accommodating itself to historical constitutional expectations. In other words, the constitution plays a fundamental, indeed necessary, role in the process of legitimation. Wesley stated that Higden's views were his own. The revolution of 1688 changed the constitution by abolishing the indefeasible hereditary right of succession to the throne. Some of the makers and supporters of the revolution justified this fundamental change by claiming that the revolution had restored the ancient constitution.[16] Wesley celebrated the "happy revolution," and did not criticize it. What one sees in these arguments or cases is not support for a sovereign right to change the constitution, but the priority of constitution as norm, together with acknowledgment that breaks in constitutional regularity occur, and the insistence that when these breaks occur they must be justified with reference to the constitution. If that interpretation is correct, it means either that the constitution—not the government—is the supreme power and therefore the bearer of sovereign right, or that the notion of supreme power as expressed in the general theory is a defective rendering of the concept of political authority. Both of these possibilities point away from the notion of temporally unlimited power as the recipient of divine ordination.

If more is to be said descriptively and analytically about this awkward combination of two approaches to political authority, it would begin with the observation that the general theory of unlimited supreme power carried to its logical conclusion issues in the triumph of sovereign right over both liberty and constitution. It is difficult to imagine that John Wesley would be satisfied with that conclusion, however much he might defend the sovereign authority of the government in matters of taxes and colonies. The next thing to be said is that the role of Parliament vis-à-vis the monarch, the claims of organically embedded liberties, and the majestic appeal of the ancient constitution suggest relationships of authority that cannot be delineated in hierarchical fashion. They run laterally, or from below to above, but not from above to below. Wesley's theological approach to political authority, which clearly is hierarchical in character, cannot account for these relationships. Unfortunately, he does not ask how they might be accounted for theologically, and how his understanding of political authority might be recast constructively in terms of his wider theological perspective. Theologically, he establishes and maintains the primacy of the general theory of temporally unlimited authority, with its implication that his constitutionalism is simply another historical example with no claims to universal or at least wider applicability. Practically speaking, his actual political commitments imply relationships of authority that call the general theory in question. However, these commitments and their implications have no apparent theological grounding.

AUTHORITY FOR THE "HAPPY REVOLUTION"

So far in this chapter I have sought to understand the substance of Wesley's understanding of political authority by comparing and contrasting his theologically grounded general theory with his not theologically grounded constitutionalism. At this point I shall consider Wesley's response to a particular case that evoked strident and searching arguments over authorization, and ask what may be learned from it directly or by inference concerning his views on political authority. The case in question is the expulsion from the throne of England of James II and the installation of William III and Mary II. This transition was more than a change of monarchs; it was a major disjunction in the authorizing procedures of English politics. Effectively it terminated the indefeasible right of hereditary succession, and established the supremacy of Parliament in determining the criteria for succession to the throne. Wesley accepted the change enthusiastically, celebrated the "happy revolution," hailed the revolution as the true beginning of English liberties, and supported the House of Hanover against the Jacobite pretenders. But how did this man who stoutly demanded obedience to governing authorities justify both the dethroning of the ruler of the English people and this profound alteration in authorizing procedures? Regrettably, Wesley affords us only glimpses of his moral reasoning in this case—no sustained and systematic analysis—and leaves it to us to infer and construct his more comprehensive and coherent view.[17]

Wesley's most direct and most revelatory statement on the justification for the revolutionary action is one from "Thoughts Concerning the Origin of Power," quoted in a previous chapter.[18] It reads as an explanatory statement rather than as a justificatory one; yet one cannot avoid the impression that Wesley constructs the explanation in order to confer approval. William III did not gain the throne as did William I: by seizing it forcibly and then claiming right of conquest. That would have provided him with an "odious title." (Wesley may have been unaware of the fact that William of Orange was prepared to invade England and seize the throne if it were not offered to him.) Nor was the title conferred on him by the people or by Parliament. "It was the Convention, and none else . . . a few hundred Lords and gentlemen, who, observing the desperate state of public affairs, met together on that important occasion."[19]

One may be tempted to suppose that Wesley saw some authority in the Convention that exceeded parliamentary authority, but that probably was not his view and in any event it is not the point. Wesley's focus is not on the Convention as such, but on the "few hundred Lords and gentlemen." These were the persons of substance and responsibility in England, who met together to deal with a profound crisis and did the right thing. Because of who they were they saw themselves as representing the society as a whole and acting in the best interests of all the people. Cynically—or realistically—one can argue that they consulted their own interests and acted to maintain the property system and control by propertied interests. However true that may be, it does not displace their self-perception—which includes some degree of self-deception—of *noblesse oblige*. They saw themselves obligated by reason of their positions in society to set aside the awesome principle of indefeasible hereditary right and select a monarch—or monarchs—more likely to serve the true and enduring interests of the English people than the reigning monarch. The Parliament, then, through appropriate legislation, could confirm this action by redefining the laws of succession. Apparently that is how Wesley viewed them also, for there is no suggestion on his part that he disapproved of their extralegal—or simply illegal—action. To the contrary, his manner of reporting the event implies approval, even though he does not work through a process of moral or legal reasoning to justify and defend their arrogation to themselves of the authority to effect such a momentous transition. It may have occurred to him that this presumption of propriety, which we suppose the "Lords and gentlemen" to have felt, corresponded in important respects to his own sense of justification in undertaking his evangelistic mission often in defiance of church authorities. If so, he did not make the connection publicly.

Assuming that these men did the right thing, even without constitutional or legal authority, their action does not establish the title to the throne of the new monarchs in the absence of the right of hereditary succession and without further criteria of legitimation. True, William and Mary—or in proper order Mary and then William—were of the Stuart family, but they were not in the line of succession so long as a son of James II was alive. Why should they be considered rightful monarchs and not usurpers—as indeed they were considered by Susanna Wesley and all other Jacobites? Wesley commented that if William had taken the throne by force he would have had an "odious title." It may have been odious indeed, but not therefore invalid. After all, Wesley notes that William I took the throne by force, but he regarded him as king nonetheless, as he did others in subsequent English history who seized the crown and did not simply inherit it. What, in Wesley's view, established royal authority when it no longer was certified by indefeasible hereditary right and when the action of the leading citizens in conferring the title did not in and of itself confirm the title?

One criterion of confirmation is the notion of *prescriptive right*—a term Wesley did not use, but which describes his political thinking nonetheless. Prescriptive right is a kind of "squatter's rights" that is, if one holds the office over a period of time and exercises the power successfully, one is entitled to the office even if the entitlement is not grounded in other forms of right. Wesley's characterization of 1688–89 as the "happy revolution," his enthusiasm for George II and George III, and most notably his conviction that the revolution established or reestablished English liberties imply that he accepted this criterion. Whether he would have allowed the same legitimacy of royal title to monarchs of whom he disapproved is something we shall never know. His pertinent statements amount to ideological defenses of the approved kings, not inquiries into the nature of prescriptive right and its legitimizing application to William and Mary and succeeding monarchs.

A second criterion of confirmation, and one that overlaps the first, is the one proposed by William Higden, affirmed by John Wesley, and helpfully brought to our attention by Leon Hynson. It is that monarchs currently occupying the throne, even though *de facto* and not *de jure*, are kings or queens nonetheless, because their legislative acts are accepted and recognized as law by subsequent monarchs. There is an element of prescriptive right in this argument, because the monarchs *de facto* would have to maintain possession of the throne over a period of time in order to legislate. However, the main condition of this criterion is that the legislative activity that signals the legitimacy of the monarchy takes place within a constitutional structure and under its terms, and not outside of or in spite of the constitutional structure. That is why some Whigs in the latter part of the eighteenth century sought to defend the revolution as a restoration of the ancient constitution. Wesley never used that argument directly and explicitly. His one venture in that general neighborhood was—as has been noted—to repeat the Whiggish claim that English liberties began at the revolution. Nevertheless, his acceptance of Higden's proposal implies acknowledgment of the preeminence of inherited constitutional procedures in legitimizing the titles of monarchs, however they may have come to the throne.

Either or both of these criteria probably would have satisfied Wesley, given the distance in time from which he viewed the event and the favor with which he regarded the Hanoverian monarchy. Neither of them, of course, would have sufficed to define legitimacy for William and Mary—and especially for William—at the time of their ascent to the throne. Both prescriptive right and legislative acknowledgment require some passage of time to establish authority by some right other than that of conquest or consent. If in the absence of Wesley's own thoroughgoing analysis we construct some pattern of authorization, using elements of Wesley's political thought and inclinations, it should look something like this: (1) there is an element of consent in the conferring of the title, but it is the consent of the men of substance and responsibility, not the consent of the people—either directly or indirectly; (2) there is a very prominent element of public interest or public good, inasmuch as James II was perceived as damaging fundamental interests of the British people to a substantial degree, whereas William and Mary were expected to protect and advance them; (3) the conferral honors the legitimist principle of hereditary succession by anointing members of the Stuart line, even though they are not the Stuarts directed to the throne by indefeasible right; (4) the new monarchs are placed within a constitutional tradition and framework, which limits their power and provides procedures for its exercise.[20]

One might characterize the action of the "Lords and gentlemen" as a pragmatic reaction to a situation of severe crisis (which it was, of course). In that case, the governing criterion of authorization would be whether the transfer of power was successful in establishing a stable and productive regime. Eventually that criterion would create the entitlement of prescriptive right. The need for that entitlement—and its function in the political process—would imply that the criterion of pragmatic success did not suffice for authorization, however important to the process it might be. That conclusion would be true to Wesley's thought and action in both political and ecclesiastical matters. Writers on Wesley have noted that his evangelistic initiatives required not a few pragmatic decisions and departures. Some have seen evidences of this pragmatism in his politics, most especially in his repudiation of the defensible claims of the Stuart pretenders in favor of the preferred Hanoverians. However, Wesley's thinking in neither politics nor religious activity was ever simply pragmatic. It was always a mixture of aims and constraints, of goals, limiting rules, and responsibilities. The packaging of elements, which I have suggested as authorizing the conferring of legitimate title on the new monarchs, combines the pragmatic with the traditional, the procedural, and the institutional. This combination of elements in the process of authorization and justification characterizes Wesley's moral reasoning in this case, whereas a simple pragmatism does not.

It is conceivable, of course, that Wesley might have regarded the placement of William and Mary on the throne of England simply as a work of divine providence. Many persons in the Tory tradition believed not only that God appointed that there should be kings, but also that God appointed particular kings to particular thrones—a concept somewhat difficult to maintain together with the indefeasible right of hereditary biological succession. Wesley, in arguing against Deist notions of predictable universal regularity, sometimes maintained a kind of divine positivism—all events occur not only with the knowledge of God, but also by the hand of God. It was another point at which he was less than "a hair's breadth from Calvinism." However, whatever may be the case with regard to Wesley's not fully consistent views in this matter, he did not apply this particular theological explanation to the revolution and the enthronement of William and Mary. As was usually the case with his political arguments, this one also was practical, pragmatic, and constitutional—not theological. Nor did he attribute any divine leading or sense of divine leading to the Lords and gentlemen who collectively carried off this fundamental change. In Wesley's view, they simply did what they thought to be right.

A RETURN TO THE STATE OF NATURE?

Because of Wesley's unrelenting rejection of both individual natural right as a source of political authority and its companion, the social contract theory of the origin of government, one does not expect him to appeal to these notions in justifying the revolution of 1688 and its resulting political and constitutional arrangements. However, Hynson suggests that he might have done so. He asks, "How then did Wesley come to accept the revolution of 1688? Did a restoration to a state of nature occur in 1688? Does a natural state ever come to exist in a society that has operated under a charter? For Wesley, revolution apparently restores the state of nature."[21] Hynson notes that in "Some Observations on Liberty" (1776), "Wesley again argued that persons have a right to self-government prior to the founding of civil societies."[22] Referring to Wesley's acceptance of the new American republic, Hynson observes further, "Resisting revolution in its uncertain course, Wesley, influenced by Higden, could accept the new state as fait accompli. When revolution is consummated, there is an apparent return to the state of nature in which the people (of America in this instance) enter into an original compact with those who become their governors. Evidently an original contract had been achieved in England with the success of the Glorious Revolution in 1689. For both revolutions, Wesley's acceptance was based primarily on pragmatic political arguments, although one must observe his reference to divine providence."[23]

It is true that in "Some Observations on Liberty" Wesley acknowledged a right to self-government before societies were formed.[24] He did the same in "A Calm Address to Our American Colonies."[25] In both cases, however, his words seemed more a concession for the sake of moving the argument along than an active contention for rights in a state of nature. In neither case did he argue that societies and governments were created in an original compact by consenting right of persons living in a presocial condition. His point, rather, was to make a clear distinction between the social and presocial conditions of human beings, and to insist that persons in society are governed by the laws of their societies and have no natural rights claims of a political sort to press against their governments. Whatever may have been the case for "naked sons of nature," entrance into society implied the loss of presumptive natural rights with no implications for continuing or resuming their authority. Moreover, in the passage from "Some Observations on Liberty," Wesley expressed doubt that any such presocietal conditions had ever existed—at least "since the flood." His further statement is explicit: "not that there ever existed any original compact between them and those Governors."[26]

What Wesley seems to be saying is this: If you can imagine persons living in a completely presocial condition, then certainly they have a right to self-government, because no one else has it. If, however, persons live in society, then they have no such right, because all rights pertaining to government belong to the sovereign. The sovereign has the right to dispose of life, liberty, and property without asking the consent of the subject. Of course, life in a presocial condition is a purely mythic construction. No one lives in such a condition, and no one has at least since Noah's flood. Therefore the appeal to natural rights has no bearing on matters pertaining to political authority.

In the "Calm Address," where Wesley is dependent on Samuel Johnson, he refers to the ancestors having "ceded to the King and Parliament the power of disposing, without their consent, of both their lives, liberties, and properties."[27] The reference to ceding to the king and Parliament carries no implication of authorization, reciprocity, or control. It means nothing more than that they handed over the power. Wesley's concessive statements on rights in a presocial condition were made for the purpose of arguing the irrelevance of natural rights to political authority. He did not mean to suggest the notion of an "original compact" to recreate society and government after a revolution.

Furthermore, Wesley's comments about rights in a state of nature were offered in the context of the American struggle for representation and independence. Did he understand them to have some bearing on the events of 1688–89? It is true that during the time of Wesley's writing the argument was current that the disruption in English society had returned the society to a state of nature from which the active agents rescued it by restoring civil society. But there is no evidence that Wesley held that view, no statements by him—to my knowledge—in which he applied this argument to the Glorious Revolution. His claim, in the passage cited, that never since the flood had there been a time when civil societies were formed, excludes the possibility that he saw William and Mary's ascension to the throne as the contractual creation of a new society out of a state of nature. His firm denial in "Origins of Power" and elsewhere that the people as such had anything to do with the radical transitions, and his denial also that the Lords and gentlemen were representatives of the people in effecting the revolution, imply with certainty that in his view the populace as a whole was not party directly or indirectly to any such contract. Conceivably he would have seen some contradiction in claiming a completely new beginning while striving to maintain continuity with the past by finding a Stuart monarch of some sort and by appealing for justification to the ancient constitution.

Wesley did not apply the "state of nature" argument even to the creation of the American republic. What he saw there was simply "a very uncommon train of providences." Hynson is right when he interprets Wesley's explanations and justification with reference to pragmatic political arguments and to divine providence. His claim that Wesley interpreted the revolutions as returns to the state of nature has no comparable support.

In a later chapter I shall analyze Wesley's concept of rights more thoroughly. At this point, where the central interest is in the substance of his understanding of political authority, it suffices to point out that his accepting language concerning rights in a state of noncivil existence implies nothing concerning the right to exercise power in civil society. He demarcates a clear and impenetrable boundary between the two conditions.

A FURTHER NOTE ON REPRESENTATION

The preceding chapter set forth the distinction between representation as organization of a people for action in history, and representation as agency. In that chapter I dealt with the former meaning; in this chapter, and in this section, I must explain Wesley's views of the latter. Most of this explanation will present nothing new, because it has been necessary to touch on this point in several places throughout the book. Mainly what we have seen thus far is that representation as agency is not necessary to the establishment and protection of freedom, nor is it a condition of governmental authority. A benign government honors and protects the liberties of the people without the need for monitoring and control from below. A sovereign government has the authority to tax and to dispose of life, liberty, and property without deriving that authority from the consent of the people. Essentially, the government functions authoritatively and functions well without the particular concept of representation urged upon it by the Americans and the English radicals.

However, the English government was a parliamentary system to which the members were elected as representatives. On several occasions John Wesley voted in elections for members of Parliament (usually with unfavorable results). Moreover, at times he noted the irrationality or unfairness (i.e., the unrepresentative-ness) of the distribution of seats in Parliament. He wrote in his jour-nal of 2 October 1754, "I walked to Old Sarum, which, in spite of *common sense*, without house or inhabitant, still sends in members to the Parliament."[28] In his entry of 25 August 1755 he reported, "I rode over the mountains close by the sea to Looe, a town near half as large as Islington, which sends *four* members to the Parliament! And each county in North Wales sends *one!*"[29] It seems odd that he would show even that degree of interest in a system whose repre-sentational reason for being had so little relevance to either liberty or authority.

Wesley, of course, supported the parliamentary system, and therefore he accepted the electoral procedures for selecting the members. What he objected to were the notions, first, that election conferred authority, and second, that the members of Parliament were answerable in some primary sense to the persons who elected them. Dr. Price had argued, "Government is a trust, and all its powers a delegation." Wesley responded, "It is a trust, but not from the people: 'There is no power but of God.' It is a delegation, namely, from God; for 'rulers are God's ministers,' or delegates."[30] Members of Parliament are elected by a particular constituency, but their authority in office comes from God, not from the constituen-cy or the electoral process. Once in office they are answerable to God, not to the people who chose them.

Nevertheless, Wesley could speak of the members of Parliament as representatives of the people. The concept is present in his oft-quoted but somewhat off-the-mark response to Price's observation that " 'All your freehold land is represented; but not a foot of theirs . . . there is not a blade of grass in England but is represented.' " Wesley shot back, "I really thought, not the grass, or corn, or trees, but the men of England, were represented in Parliament. . . . Here is Mr. Burke; pray, what does he represent? 'Why, the city of Bristol.' What, the buildings so called; or the ground whereon they stand? Nay, the inhabitants of it."[31]

Wesley is not simply equivocating when he denies that members of Parliament represent the people, while allowing that they repre-sent the "men of England" and that Mr. Burke represents the inhab-itants of Bristol. What he means is that Edmund Burke and other members look after the interests of their constituents, even though they do not receive their authority as representatives from the constituents and are not answerable to them. Even if they have no actual constituencies, as apparently was the case with the members from Old Sarum, they are representatives nonetheless, for they represent all of the people in considering the good of the empire. This grand concept, when taken seriously, assures that the members will not be swayed by narrow, parochial interests, but will legislate for the benefit of everyone.

Wesley does not use the term *virtual representation* to characterize his position, but that is what he means. He quotes Evans as claiming that the English are virtually represented, and apparently accepts it for the English, while extending it to the Americans to answer their objection that they are not represented.[32] What he means is that the members of Parliament in effect represent all the peoples of the empire, whether elected directly by them or not, by virtue of that they are entrusted by God with the good of the entire political society. That argument protects the sovereignty of the government while establishing expectations of responsibility, benevolence, and evenhandedness.

In Wesley's case, we should extend the concept of virtual representation, if only by inference from his attitudes and stances. His understanding of virtual in one sense is similar to Machiavelli's concept of *virtú*, in that it implies a high level of capability with several dimensions. Persons chosen as delegates to Parliament should possess a combination of qualities that would enable them to fulfill their trusts with competence, reliability, and distinction. They should be men of wisdom, insight, and discretion; able to understand the mysteries and complications of policy and politics to a degree unlikely for ordinary folks. They should be men of property, not because protection of property—in Wesley's view, at least—is the first end of government, but because as persons with heavy material investments in the society they will come equipped, one hopes, with a strong sense of responsibility for its general welfare. Moreover, they should be men of virtue, in the sense of *moral* virtue: honorable, reliable, trustworthy; lovers of God, king, and country—quite unlike Machiavelli's *Prince*, in that respect. Wesley's conviction that the country in fact is represented virtually in these ways, and his concern that such representation continue, allow him to trust that a sovereign government with the authority to take away life, liberty, and property will not do so. The representational protection for the people is not rightly a procedure for controlling the governors and calling them to account. It is a moral form of protection, embedded in the ethos of the society and manifest in the character of the rulers. If this historically generated moral order is undermined, or if the good rulers are replaced with bad ones, all rights will be at risk. Therefore one should fear God and honor the king, that the established order not be shaken and destroyed.

PATHS NOT TAKEN

At the beginning of this chapter, I stated that Wesley established his general theory of political authority theologically. That statement remains true, but now I must modify it to say that in his general theory Wesley combined the notion of divine ordination of power taken from Romans 13 with the concept of sovereignty taken at least indirectly from Bodin, and in doing so limited the ways of thinking about God as the source of political authority. Theologically, it was not necessary to dichotomize God and the people as alternative sources of authority. Other writers before Wesley—persons more profound than he in both theological and political understanding—had overcome the dichotomy by incorporating the people into the process of authorization without, in their view, compromising the primacy of God. If Wesley knew of their work, he did not cite them and argue with them. He simply assumed that Romans 13 established a logical disjunction: If God is the source, the people are not; if the people are the source, then God is not. His conclusion, however, was not solely a matter of logic, or even of simplistic reading of Scripture. He was driven to this conclusion by two factors not in themselves theological. One was his own historical positioning in defense of the constitutional arrangements of 1689, and therefore against any opening to democratizing currents. The other was his acceptance and employment of the concept of sovereignty, a political doctrine with theological roots that by Wesley's time had been effectively and influentially secularized. His practical political commitments told him that the people should not be the source of authority. His concept of sovereignty told him that with supreme power, and only with supreme power, came entitlement to use the power. In consequence, his reading of the Scripture provided him with a confirmation of governmental authority that seemed to him self-evident.

Our task in the remainder of this chapter is to show that other theologically defined paths lay open to him. Had he taken one or more of them, his view of political authority would have been different, and so also would important dimensions of his larger theological project.

Divine Authorization Through the People

The notion of people and community as a source of political authority is quite visible in the long history of Christian political thought. It was no novelty of the contract and natural rights theorists of the seventeenth and eighteenth centuries. To trace the origins and usages of that notion would be excessive for our purposes. Suffice it to say that the idea of authority from the community was very prominent throughout the Middle Ages, and played a role in the papal-imperial struggles, in the election of kings, and in the political efficacy of custom and tradition. There are notions of community compact as source of royal authority in the Huguenot tract "Vindiciae Contra Tyrannos" (1579), in *Of the Laws of Ecclesiastical Polity* by the Anglican Richard Hooker (1554–1600), and in *The Laws and God the Lawgiver* by the Jesuit Francisco Suarez (1548–1617). Unless John Wesley were oblivious to this history, he could not have supposed that the idea of authorization of government by the people was an invention of John Locke brought to prominence by English and American radicals of the late eighteenth century.

Of course, writers in this history were aware of the tension between God and people as sources of political authority. As Christian writers, they worked in the tradition of Romans 13, and never doubted the primacy of God as Author. However, different writers dealt with the tension in different ways. Some treated authority from the people as antithetical to the divine source, and denied the former, whereas others sought to reconcile the two. The reconciliation always took the form of arguing that God was the original source of authority, but gave authority to the people who then would either transfer it to the rulers or delegate it to them. In the first case, the people would cease to have authority because the ruler now had it. In the second, the people would retain authority ultimately because the ruler was not the recipient of transferred authority, but one called to participate in their authority and act on their behalf. In either case, however, the authority went from God by way of the people to the ruler; it did not go to the ruler without that mediation.

When we place John Wesley in this history, he falls in the camp of those who argue the unmediated transfer of authority from God to those who rule. This placement is not as comfortable as he might suppose, because in his century it associated him with the Jacobites, who held views on the superiority of the monarch to Parliament and law that were contradictory to his own. Also, it was not a necessary stance for him to claim, for two reasons. One was that he could have bought into the theological alternative I have just sketched, and allowed that authority came to the rulers through the people without denying that it originated with God. The other was that he could have recognized the community sources of some of the nontheological elements fundamental to his thinking on political authority. Wesley saw authority vested in the ancient constitution, in Parliament (not in the king only), in the courts, in prescriptive rights, in common law and constraining traditions. What he apparently did not recognize was that these institutions and traditions were organic elements of authorization arising from the interactions of the English people over centuries of political history. The people authorized power through these social creations. Wesley accepted and honored these institutions and traditions, and by implication the popular and communal sources of their authority. Had he acknowledged these sources and connected them with the theological alternative I described, he would have remained true to both his constitutionalism and his commitment to God as origin. He also would have confirmed the organic historical sense he shows elsewhere, the sense of how values come to expression through long-term and interweaving development, and not insisted in a wooden fashion to know precisely the occasion and moment when the people as a whole gave their consent.

Richard Hooker's Social Compact

Almost two centuries before John Wesley attacked the concept of the social compact, the great Anglican theologian Richard Hooker wrote in support of it. For that reason, John Locke, midway between the two, would refer to him as "the learned and judicious Hooker." Hooker acknowledged that some rulers held office by direct divine appointment, and therefore exercised power by divine right. Others, however, presumably including those in England, received their power from the people. The origin of government, in that case, was in a common agreement of the multitude to remove themselves from the inconveniences of a nongovernmental condition by creating the mechanisms of government and ceding power to governors. "To take away such mutual grievances, injuries, and wrongs, there was no way, but only by growing unto composition and agreement amongst themselves, by ordaining some kind of government public, and by yielding themselves subject thereunto, that unto whom they granted authority to rule and govern, by them the peace, tranquillity, and happy estate of the rest might be procured."[33] Fathers have supreme power over their families, he observed, "Howbeit over a whole grand multitude having no such dependency on anyone, and consisting of so many families, as every politic society in the world doth, impossible it is that any should have complete lawful power but by consent of men, or immediate appointment of God."[34] What was true of government as such, Hooker claimed to be true also of law: "The lawful power of making laws to command whole politic societies of men belongeth so properly unto the same entire societies, that for any Prince or potentate of what kind soever on earth to exercise the same of himself and not either by express commission immediately and personally received from God, or else by authority derived at the first from their consent upon whose persons they impose laws, it is no better than mere tyranny. Laws they are not therefore which public approbation hath not made so."[35]

Hooker does not require that consent be given individually; it can be communicated through representatives of the people. "But approbation not only they give who personally declare their assent by voice sign or act, but also when others do it in their names by right originally at the least derived from them. As in parliaments, councils, and the like assemblies, although we be not personally ourselves present, notwithstanding our assent is by reason of others agents there in our behalf."[36] Furthermore, the consent once given by an earlier generation of the people is binding subsequently on succeeding generations. "And to be commanded we do consent, when that society whereof we are part hath at any time before consented, without revoking the same after by the like universal agreement. Wherefore as any man's deed past is good as long as himself continueth: so the act of a public society of men done five hundred years since standeth as theirs, who presently are of the same societies, because corporations are immortal: we were then alive in our predecessors, and they in their successors do live still. Laws therefore human of what kind soever are available by consent."[37]

This last quotation manifests Hooker's profound belief in the organic character of the political community—for England, specifically in the union of crown, church, and people. Wesley held this belief, also. Moreover, Hooker's statement that "we were then alive in our predecessors" resonates with Wesley's explanation of how later human generations came to be involved in the original sin of Adam.[38] Therefore, Wesley could have accepted and supported the same representational and historical concepts that allowed Hooker to provide the connections in his theory of consent. He chose instead to adopt a more individualistic and literal approach to questions of consent and transmission of power. Obviously he did so because the Lockean advocates were basing their arguments on individual natural rights, and Wesley attempted to refute them on their own terms. In doing so, however, he turned his back on his own rich tradition in political thought.

Hooker's consent argument was not theological, strictly speaking. It was an inference from human necessity, by contrast with Locke's derivation of authority from individual human right. However, Hooker took the precaution to draw the consent argument into a theological context. Like Wesley, he never doubted that God was the one true and ultimate source of political authority, his brief for consent of the people notwithstanding. Like other Christian writers before and since, Hooker tried to reconcile the two sources by allowing that human beings confer authority on the rulers in a proximate sense with the proviso that God ultimately must confirm their authorization. "So God doth ratify the works of that Sovereign authority which Kings have received by men."[39] In this manner Hooker stayed with the teaching of Romans 13—that governing authorities are ordained by God—while acknowledging the reality of the human sources of authority.

There are serious problems with this argument, among them the implication that God must endow with authority whomever the people choose as rulers. But that is no worse than Wesley's apparent belief that God anoints the supreme authority, whatever its moral quality or the derivation of its dominance. For Hooker, as for others, this device allowed him to fit into the long and respected Christian tradition described in the previous section. God and people need not be set in opposition as sources of political authority. God is primary, to be sure, but the people play a significant and at times necessary role in the process of authorization.

We cannot attempt here a point-by-point comparison of Hooker and Wesley on the question of political authority. However, they agree in so many ways—the organic understanding of the British community, the subordination of the king to law, the ultimate divine ordination of government—as to allow the supposition that Wesley could have been comfortable with Hooker's formulation of the consent issue were it not for his political stance of resisting the next and more democratic stage of articulation of English society. It was that political stance, not the theological necessity of excluding the people from the authorization process in deference to the Almighty, that stood in the way of his accepting Hooker's formulation—assuming he was aware of it.

The Political Image

Among the paths Wesley did not take to develop his thinking on political authority, surely the most important is that of the political image. The political image is one of the three modes of the human imaging of God that Wesley identified, the other two being the natural and the moral images. Wesley was preoccupied with the moral image, which consisted in the reflection of divine love. Its loss and recovery were at the center of his theology and his evangelistic mission. He showed little interest in the other two images, and did not explain their meaning fully or draw their implications for the Christian life. That is regrettable in both cases, but especially so, for our present purposes, in the case of the political image. I shall devote the final chapter of the book to expounding this point and drawing its implications, and therefore shall not do so here. It will suffice for the present to say that the political image, as Wesley defines it briefly, is the governance of the world given by God to humankind as God's agent. It includes self-governance, along with dominion over the "lower creatures." The political image is political responsibility assigned to the whole of humankind. It is not hierarchical, it does not favor a political class against the rest of the people, it is antithetical to the concept of sovereignty as used by Wesley. In other words, it is a concept of political authority drawn from Wesley's own theology that stands his publicized understanding of political authority on its head. Had he taken his own central theology of the image of God with full seriousness, he could not have continued with a concept that excluded the people from political responsibility and the process of political authorization.

CONCLUSION: CONFLICT AND TRANSFORMATION

Everything that John Wesley wrote on the subject of political authority aimed at defending the constitutional order of England in the latter part of the eighteenth century. That defense involved the subordination of power, including royal power, to law and to institutional restraints. It involved also the exclusion of the people both from political participation and from the process of authorizing power. Wesley supported this defense of the constitutional order with a general theory of political authority that made no inherent provision for the kinds of limitations on power that he prized so highly in English constitutionalism. Furthermore, he confirmed this general theory with biblical texts that derived authority from God as transcendent first person of the Trinity, but did not involve the immanent deliverance and redemptive power of the second and third persons. One result of this particular combination was Wesley's inability to provide a theological rationale for the structural limitations on power that are of the nature of constitutionalism. Another result was the irrelevance to his politics of his evangelical theology.

The resolution of these problems in John Wesley's political thought requires a transformation in his theological approach to politics from one that works primarily with the first person of the Trinity to one that is fully trinitarian. I have suggested that this can be done within Wesley's theology by developing the meaning of the *political image of God*. That would enable—and indeed would demand—a change in the summary formula for a Wesleyan understanding of political authority to read: *from God through the people*. This theological transformation in turn would require fundamental revisions in his theory of supreme power and sovereignty.

CHAPTER EIGHT

POLITICAL AUTHORITY III
POLITICAL OBLIGATION

One could write the history of Christian political thought in large measure as a survey of the uses of Paul's admonition in Romans 13: "Let every soul be subject unto the higher powers. For there is no power but of God: the powers that be are ordained of God." This text is at least as prominent in that history as the Tribute Passage: "Render to Caesar the things that are Caesar's, and to God the things that are God's."[1] Each at times is used as a commentary on or reinforcement of the other. However, the Romans text, despite some controversies over exegesis and interpretation, is more concrete and explicit than the synoptic text. It addresses the relationships of governors and governed with directives that appear as unmistakable as they are restrictive:

> Whosoever therefore resisteth the power, resisteth the ordinance of God: and they that resist shall receive to themselves damnation. For rulers are not a terror to good works, but to the evil. Wilt thou then not be afraid of the power? do that which is good, and thou shalt have praise of the same: For he is the minister of God to thee for good. But if thou do that which is evil, be afraid; for he beareth not the sword in vain: for he is the minister of God, a revenger to execute wrath upon him that doeth evil. Wherefore ye must needs be subject, not only for wrath, but also for conscience sake. For this cause pay ye tribute also: for they are God's ministers, attending continually upon this very thing. Render therefore to all their dues: tribute to whom tribute is due; custom to whom custom; fear to whom fear; honour to whom honour. (Romans 13:2-7)[2]

The commanding style of the admonitions in this text, Paul's authority in the church, and the critical interaction of Christians with imperial and regal power across the centuries made it fundamental to discussions of Christian political responsibility, at least until the rise of European democracies and the accompanying changes in attitudes toward authority and obedience.

The content of this passage from Romans supports the formation of Christian attitudes on two major related issues. One is the authority by which governments exercise their power—the concern of the preceding chapter. The other is the ground and limits of political obligation—the concern of the present chapter. For both cases the passage imposes a high view of the civil authorities. They receive their authority from God; they are ministers of God; they act in God's place and on God's behalf; they should be feared and honored as one would fear and honor God. The implications are clear, and they are drawn: one must obey them as one would obey God, and one must not resist them. This attitude of submissiveness to the authorities is a requirement of conscience, and not mere prudential survival behavior.

However, if one writes the history of Christian political thought as the history of the usage of Romans 13, one must include in that history its companion verse, Acts 5:29: "We ought to obey God rather than men." In the New Testament the two passages have nothing to do with each other. Nevertheless, in the history of the church's relationship with political powers, the second passage was employed to limit the apparent absoluteness of the first. Christians must be in subjection to the civil authorities, for those authorities are ministers of God and are acting in the place of God. However, if the civil authorities—who despite their divine ordination remain sinful and errant human beings—require something contrary to the command of God, Christians must obey God directly and not the seconded command of God's political agents. For centuries, this formula was understood to mean that the rule requiring obedience was the norm for political behavior, but that occasions might arise for justifiable and necessary exceptions. In those exceptional cases Christians should not resist, and in particular, they should not take up arms against the Lord's anointed. Rather, they simply should decline to obey, and should take the consequences of disobedience—however drastic they might be.

By John Wesley's time the long and broad Christian tradition had explored further modifications of the formula, including allowable tyrannicide and the disciplining of kings by so-called "lesser magistrates." In Wesley's immediate historical stream, however, the supporters of royal authority in cooperation with leaders of the church had focused political morality on the older, more restrictive rule of passive obedience. John Wesley's Tory tradition embodied the substance of the obedience ethic in a form hardened by political struggle. In that tradition the king was set above the law because he was the source of the law. He was set above Parliament and all lesser magistrates, also, because they were his delegates and received their authority from him. The monarch reached this eminence by indefeasible hereditary divine right of succession to the throne. Therefore the only proper posture before this exalted personage, his laws and his decrees, was that of passive obedience and nonresistance. Both of the political Homilies enforced the rule with warnings of uncontrolled public disorder certain to result from disobedience to governors, and the reminder that disobedience to God's lieutenants placed one's soul in peril of hell's fire. Although the Homily of 1547 included the Acts 5:29 exception, the Homily of 1570 pointedly did not. Popular manuals of Christian conduct, perhaps most prominent among them *The Whole Duty of Man*, taught Romans 13 as the primary rule with the Acts 5:29 exception in a subordinate role.[3]

John Wesley's mother, Susanna, embraced this teaching in pious good conscience and without reservation. His father, Samuel, embraced most of it, but not all. John himself was cast in this Tory mold. He was fully confident of the rightness of Paul's text and of the religious confirmation of political order drawn from it by the Tories. Writing to Walter Churchey on 25 June 1777, he said, "It is my religion which obliges me 'to put men in mind to be subject to principalities and powers.' Loyalty is with me an essential branch of religion, and which I am sorry any Methodist should forget. There is the closest connexion, therefore, between my religious and my political conduct; the selfsame authority enjoining me to 'fear God,' and to 'honour the King.' "[4] Years earlier he had written of the Methodists that, "they have no conception of *piety* without *loyalty;* knowing 'the powers that be are ordained of God.' "[5] Wesley also shared the high view of magistracy derived from the Romans text, explored through centuries of Christian inquiry into authority and obedience, and politicized formally in the Homilies of the sixteenth century. Magistrates for him were ministers of God, not mere political officials. He expected them to imitate God in the conduct of office, and expected his Methodists—and all other persons—to give them the deference and respect due God's representatives. Obedience was a fundamental virtue—in political contexts as in all other contexts in which authority was structured by role and office. Priests of the Church of England were required to read the Homilies to their congregations, in order to assist the inculcation of obedience and encourage its practice. The Anglican priest John Wesley read them to his congregations. When late in life he wrote to Lords Dartmouth and North that he was "a High Churchman, the son of an High Churchman, bred up from my childhood in the highest notions of passive obedience and non-resistance," he was describing accurately and faithfully his religious-political formation.[6]

On the other hand, our political portrait of John Wesley to this point is that of a transitional figure in the context of eighteenth-century British politics, who used Tory rhetoric in support of a Whig constitution that owed its existence to the rejection of monarchical absolutism and indefeasible hereditary right. In this transitional role, he held to his early formation in significant ways, often with public representation of it, while modifying, if not simply changing, the basis of his action. He did that with respect to both ecclesiastical and political obligation.[7] Staying within the structures, honoring the relationships, teaching and requiring the rule concerning obedience to those set in authority over us, he nonetheless reshaped authority relationships from passive to active, and at times moved the burden of proof from the one receiving the orders to the one giving them.

With these moves Wesley departed from the clarity and coherence of traditional passive obedience, and introduced ambiguity and conflict. He did not simply adjust the traditional political ethic—he changed it—and in changing it invited more complexity into the process of moral reasoning. How and why did this happen? Did he ultimately provide some recognizable shape for his resulting ethic of obligation? To pursue these questions we shall distinguish (without finally separating) the changes in the ethic that emerge in ecclesiastical contexts from those that emerge in political contexts. Having done that, we shall consider two forms of intervention—political criticism and political activism—that involve some degree of departure from the traditional norms.

REVERSING THE PRIORITY OF TEXTS

One can see the basic pattern of Wesley's ethic of obligation in his 1755 paper titled "Ought We to Separate from the Church of England?" There he asked, "Ought we, lastly, to renounce all submission to the governors and laws of the Church?" He answered, "It is not plain to us that it is either expedient or lawful, seeing the rubrics are laws confirmed by Parliament, and the bishops are constituted (in some measure) governors by the same authority. Therefore we hold ourselves obliged in things indifferent to submit to both, and that by virtue of God's command: 'Submit yourself to every ordinance of man for the Lord's sake.' "[8] Previously in the same paper Wesley had written, "But we dare not so submit to those governors or those laws as to omit (1) preaching of the gospel in all places; (2) using sometimes extemporary prayer; (3) assisting those which desire to forward each others' salvation; (4) encouraging others to do the same, though they are not episcopally ordained."[9]

The duties of obedience to civil and ecclesiastical officials and of submission to "every ordinance of man" remain in force. Wesley and his Methodists will continue to honor these authorities and to submit to them. However, in this declaration Wesley has made significant changes in the traditional ethic of obedience. First, he has reduced the scope of obedience to "things indifferent." The conservative tradition of Romans 13 insisted on obedience to governing authorities in all things—presumably including things not indifferent—except where what was commanded required the violation of a clear command of God. The reference to "things indifferent" reflects seventeenth-century (and later) conflicts over religious liberty in England, not the intent of the longer tradition. Wesley explains the application of this concept in his discussion of obedience to pastors:

Now the things which they enjoin must be either enjoined of God, or forbidden by him, or indifferent. In things forbidden of God we dare not obey them; for we are to obey God rather than man. In things enjoined of God we do not properly obey them, but our common Father. Therefore if we are to obey them at all it must be in things indifferent. The sum is: it is the duty of every private Christian to obey his spiritual pastor, by either doing or leaving undone things of an indifferent nature—anything that is in no way determined in the Word of God.[10]

But who identifies and interprets the pertinent texts from Scripture that disclose what is required by God and what is forbidden? Wesley was not willing to concede that role unqualifiedly to the ruling authorities, either ecclesiastical or civil. Certainly he trusted his own judgment to a large extent, although that trust was based in part on his assumption that the meaning and relevance of Scripture were plain, not obscure. Ultimately, however, the responsibility rests with the individual conscience.[11] That resolution opens a considerable range of possibility for determining whether what is commanded by the authorities is a matter of "things indifferent." At the same time it reduces the range of what rightly can be required or forbidden by those authorities.

Second, and of much greater consequence, Wesley has radicalized the notion of obedience to God, giving it immediacy in consciousness by contrast with the intermediate character of the rule of obedience to governing authorities and their laws. "We must obey God rather than men" becomes the primary rule, supplanting the primacy of "Be subject to the governing authorities." No longer is it used mainly as the rare occasion for making an exception to the rule. Granted, the authorities are ministers of God, but their authority is secondary and derivative whereas the authority of God is primary and original. Allowing the will to be directed in faith toward God at all times, relativizes all relationships, rules, and requirements. However, it does not dismiss them. Rather, this theocentric context of all action allows the obedient person to function routinely within authoritative structures or systems of relationships, thereby honoring the rule of obedience to governing authorities, but with an enhanced sense of their secondary and derivative character. In this framework for understanding moral responsibility, one is not simply in a passive stance before divinely ordained rulers, hoping not to hear wicked and blasphemous commands. One is in an active stance before God, following the divine command in every thought and motion, and monitoring the requirements of honored authorities in the light of the primacy and immediacy of answerability to God. Active obedience to God, not passive obedience to human rulers, is the governing concept.

Moreover, obedience to God discloses Wesley's own calling and equips it with a kind of morally protective shield against all efforts to restrain it in the name of obedience to rulers and established rules. In the passage quoted above from "Ought We to Separate from the Church of England?" Wesley excludes from required submission the preaching of the gospel in all places, the use of extemporary prayer, mutual assistance among those desiring salvation, and the use of unordained persons. These are not examples of "things indifferent." They are fundamental elements of his evangelistic mission. There is nothing indifferent about the proclamation of God's forgiving grace, nor are the means necessary to rescue souls from perdition to be justified as occasional exceptions to the governing rule. God's call is the primary delineator and determinant of moral responsibility. All other claims and claimants, especially those requiring passive obedience, must stand aside for passionate activity in the service of God.

In a letter of 10 April 1761 to (presumably) the Earl of Dartmouth, Wesley confirms this transformation of the ethic of obedience:

> Some years since, two or three clergymen of the Church of England, who were above measure zealous for all her rules and orders, were convinced that religion is not an external thing, but "righteousness and peace and joy in the Holy Ghost," and that this righteousness and peace and joy are given only to those who are justified by faith. As soon as they were convinced of these great truths, they preached them; and multitudes flocked to hear. For these reasons, and no others, real or pretended (for as yet they were strictly regular), because they preached such doctrine, and because multitudes followed them, they were forbid to preach in the churches. Not daring to be silent, they preached elsewhere, in a school, by a river-side, or upon a mountain; and more and more sinners forsook their sins and were filled with peace and joy in believing.[12]

Radical reorientation of obedience to God issues in a move from externals in religion to inwardness, which in itself demotes (without necessarily discarding) the authority of rulers and rules. Moreover, the discovery of the inner power of faith compels the young priests to proclaim this liberating experience to others. Such proclamation evokes opposition from those who stand guard over the externals—over rules, procedures, and structures. When the priests become irregular by reason of persisting in their evangelistic practices, or at least are considered irregular by the authorities in church and state, obedience to God becomes the grounds for justifying resistance to orders to cease and desist from these practices and conform themselves once again to established rules. Preaching of justification by the Wesleys and their associates is obedience to God. It is now their calling, the center of their lives, far more compelling to them than the rules and orders of the church of which they are priests.

Wesley continues:

> But at the same time huge offence was taken at their "gathering congregations" in so irregular a manner; and it was asked—(1) "Do you judge that the Church with the authority of the State has power to enact laws for her own government?" I answer: If a dispensation of the gospel is committed to me, no Church has power to enjoin me silence. Neither has the State; though it may abuse its power and enact laws whereby I suffer for preaching the gospel. (2) "Do you judge it your duty to submit to the laws of the Church and State as far as they are consistent with a good conscience?" I do. But "woe is me if I preach not the gospel": this is not consistent with a good conscience.[13]

Wesley is reminded by the questioner that the church's legislative power is backed by the authority of the state. That fact places the state and its own divine ordination behind the church's legal power to compel behavior and punish disobedience. Therefore, it places the parson who is irregular in ecclesiastical matters in disobedience to both civil and church authorities, as well as under the sanction of Romans 13. No matter. Neither the church nor the state has legitimate authority to silence his preaching. He will continue to fulfill his calling, and will take the consequences of his disobedience.

On one occasion Wesley canceled his plan to preach in a man's house, because the mayor of the town (Camelford) threatened to prosecute the man if he did so. Wesley did not abandon the preaching engagement, however; he simply preached in someone else's house.[14] In Roughlee, a magistrate insisted that he not come to that town again. "I told you," Wesley replied, "I would sooner cut off my hand than make any such promise." Subsequently, Wesley agreed not to preach at Roughlee *at this time*—an apparent compromise.[15] Neither in these cases nor in others, however, did he acknowledge the right of the civil authority to disallow his preaching. Wesley's change of preaching plan or venue reflected some prudential consideration, such as avoiding the prosecution of his friend or providing occasion for mob riots. If he chose to disregard such considerations, he went ahead and preached despite the disapproval of the magistrates. In Hammond's Marsh, for example, the mayor refused permission for him to preach, fearing incitement of the mobs. "He [the mayor] answered plain, '*I will have no more preaching;* and if Mr. Wesley attempts to preach, *I am prepared* for him.' " Wesley then wrote in his journal, "I began preaching in our own house soon after five." The mayor then ordered the town drummers and sergeants to drum him out of town. "They continued drumming," Wesley wrote, "and I continued preaching, till I had finished my discourse."[16]

Wesley had not always been so resolute. In July 1743, the mayor of Newcastle-upon-Tyne sent him a note informing him that he "discharges you from preaching at the Sand Hill any more" (because of the tumult Wesley allegedly raised the previous Sunday). On 12 July, Wesley replied, "I reverence all magistrates as the ministers of God. Therefore at the Sand Hill I will preach no more. This is my answer to you as a magistrate."[17] Contrast his response to this "discharge from preaching" with one in Shaftesbury in 1750, as well as with the aforementioned incidents in Camelford (1747) and Roughlee (1748). When a constable of Shaftesbury came and said to him, "Sir, the mayor discharges you from preaching in this borough any more," Wesley replied, "While King George gives me leave to preach, I shall not ask leave of the Mayor of Shaftesbury."[18] Was the Newcastle incident an isolated one, or did Wesley's attitude toward obedience to authorities undergo a significant change in a few short years? One probably cannot be sure of the answer. What is clear, however, is that the response to the mayor of Newcastle observed the principles of passive obedience and nonresistance, whereas the others did not. The other responses placed obedience to God above obedience to magistrates as ministers of God. In terms of guidance from scriptural texts, they placed "We must obey God rather than men" above "Be subject to the governing authorities." Nevertheless, the persistence of some degree of deference to authorities, even in these refusals, manifests Wesley's continuing respect for civil authorities and his intention, where possible, to be conciliatory and to avoid disorder. He had not dismissed the rule of obedience to governors; he had simply displaced its primacy in favor of the primacy of obedience to God.

Wesley did not see his refusal to obey these magistrates as defiance of the law. To the contrary, he held his right to preach to be guaranteed by law and by royal authority. In answering the mayor of Shaftesbury, he appealed to a temporal authority higher than that of the mayor, that is, to King George II. On other occasions, he argued the legal permissibility of his actions. Nevertheless, he did not understand his commission to preach to rest ultimately on or require legal or official authorization. It was given to him by God as a commandment, not by monarchs and legislators as a civil right. The clear inference from his letter to Dartmouth is that obedience to God would require disobedience to law, magistrate, or king, should that become necessary in order to fulfill the divine commission to proclaim the gospel of God's saving grace. Nor need one rely on inference. In the letter, he stated explicitly, "(i) If there is a law that a minister of Christ who is not suffered to preach the gospel in the church should not preach it elsewhere, I do judge that law to be absolutely sinful. (ii) If that law forbids Christian people to hear the gospel of Christ out of their parish church when they cannot hear it therein, I judge it would be sinful for them to obey it."[19] This statement is more than a justification of disobedience; it is a critique and negation of particular laws in the name of the gospel. In this regard, passive obedience and nonresistance have been left far behind.

Wesley recognized the subversive implications of this stance, and justified them in principle. In the same letter to Dartmouth he acknowledges the charge of subversion, but denies its accuracy. Wesley and his preachers recognize the need for an established civil and ecclesiastical order, but they are subverting neither the one nor the other. "This preaching is not subversive of any good order whatever. It is only subversive of that vile abuse of the good order of our Church whereby men who neither preach nor live the gospel are suffered publicly to overturn it from the foundation, and in the room of it to palm upon their congregations a wretched mixture of dead form and maimed morality."[20] Nevertheless, he makes some moves in the letter that subvert the ethic of passive obedience, if not the order itself. First, in replying to the charge that they are violating the constitution of the church, he distinguishes between the doctrine of the church and its rules of external order. The doctrine is the heart of the constitution; the rules are simply replaceable parts of the structure. Wesley and his colleagues defend the doctrine; they will replace the parts of the structure should those parts become rotten or otherwise unserviceable. Second, the urgent necessity of rescuing souls from destruction overrides the requirement of exercising religious ministry through approved means and channels. They intend and hope to maintain regularity of church law and practice, but if forced to become irregular to answer the call of God to preach the gospel, they will do so. Third, in an extreme case of falsity of doctrine at the center of the civil and eccelesiastical order, they will act so as to subvert that order in order to speak the truth of God.

This third point manifests the extreme to which Wesley was willing to go in his revision of political obligation and politically supported religious obligation. He appeals to the example of Martin Luther:

Suppose one had asked a German nobleman to hear Martin Luther preach; might not his priest have said (without debating whether he preached the truth or not): "My lord, in every nation there must be some settled order of government, ecclesiastical and civil. There is an ecclesiastical order established in Germany. You are born under this Establishment. Your ancestors supported it, and your very rank and station constitute you a formal and eminent guardian of it. How, then, can it consist with the duty arising from all these to give encouragement, countenance, and support to principles and practices that are a direct renunciation of the established constitution?" Had the force of this reasoning been allowed, what had become of the Reformation? Yet it was right; though it really was a subversion of the whole ecclesiastical constitution with regard to doctrine as well as discipline. Whereas this is no such thing.[21]

Wesley is making a case for justifiable subversion of the civil and ecclesiastical order. He denies that his own work is subversive of the English establishment, but he affirms Luther's subversive Reformation. Obviously, this is not an ethic of passive obedience. It is active obedience to God, reversing the priority of the Scripture texts in the traditional formulation, and subordinating rules and offices to evangelistic ministry.

AUTHORITY, RIGHTS, AND THE ENGLISH LEGAL TRADITION

These revisions of Wesley's inherited ethic of obedience to governing authorities involve political as well as ecclesiastical obligation, but they arise in relation to his evangelistic ministry. They pertain to his concerns for preaching, the reform of the church, the defense of doctrine. Although at times Wesley argues the legal correctness of his activities, his principal appeal for justification is to the command of God. Does he also set aside or revise the ethic of passive obedience and nonresistance with regard to matters that are not evangelistic and churchly, strictly speaking—specifically matters having to do with individual rights and public policy? If so, does he appeal for justification to nontheological norms, such as rights claims and the law (by contrast with his theological appeal to obedience to God)? Does passive obedience effectively come to an end as a controlling political ethic?

There is substantial evidence that throughout his life Wesley honored and respected the English legal tradition, and called upon it to support his own rights and liberties.[22] The importance of this is, first of all, that the legal tradition represented a line and locus of authority with its own historical development. It was supported by scriptural arguments for obedience, but was not dependent on them originally or inherently. The importance, secondly, was that the law stood between the citizen and the ruler or magistrate, blocking the unmediated authority of commands, and allowing the citizen to say, "We must obey the law rather than the magistrates," instead of relying always on, "We must obey God rather than men." The law could be used justifiably against abusive or recalcitrant magistrates, without offending against their office as "ministers of God."

From early on Wesley's dealings with magistrates worked more directly with the legal tradition than with the tradition of Romans 13, even though the scriptural admonitions always conditioned his view of magistracy. Wesley, as we know, was the target of legal actions in Savannah resulting from his involvement with Sophia Hopkey, who married Mr. Williamson apparently to spite Wesley. Colonel William Stephens was deputized by the Trustees of Georgia to report on Wesley and other matters pertinent to the colony. In his journal of October 1737, he recorded that Wesley allegedly had teamed up with a Mr. Bradley—also under accusation—to harass the court.

> Before my coming, [Bradley] had bid open defiance to the court, and on several occasions, at other times, Mr. Wesley and he, and some others, who were closely linked in opposing the Magistrates in the Execution of Justice, used to come into the Court in a menacing manner, crying out, Liberty, calling to the people to remember they were Englishmen, etc. and that Mr. Wesley was generally the principal Speaker, to harangue the people though he had no sort of business or any call there; insomuch, that they had been divers times apprehensive of being mobbed and turned off the Bench.[23]

If Stephens's report is reliable, it shows a kind and degree of activism by Wesley not recorded previously or subsequently. Obviously, it is not passive obedience. More to the point of our present inquiry, it shows that Wesley's awareness of English liberties was sharp and long-standing, and that his willingness to insist on his rights and to challenge magistrates with the law was present at a relatively early age and in the presence of contrary civil authority. They were not contingent on or derivative from any supposed change in political sympathies, or any waning of the ethic of passive obedience. Parenthetically, however, one must observe that it is difficult to know what to make of Stephens's report. At least part of it is based on hearsay a year old, although some of it represents his own observations. Stephens is attempting to be fair, but one has the sense of some bias in reportage and interpretation that works to Wesley's disadvantage and to the favor of William Causton, Sophie's uncle and guardian.[24]

If we turn to Wesley's own account, we do not find such aggressive and disruptive rights advocacy. Nevertheless, Wesley is not passive; he stands his ground and defends his actions. He denies the right of court officials to interrogate him on his refusal of communion to Mrs. Sophia Hopkey Williamson, on the grounds that it is an ecclesiastical matter and outside their jurisdiction.[25] He appears at court repeatedly when required to do so, but refuses to post bail.[26] Ultimately, of course, he flees the colony and returns to England in order to avoid a prosecutorial process that he believes is rigged against him.[27] Clearly this is a man with a strong sense of his rights as an Englishman, and a sturdy unwillingness to allow the magistrates, though ministers of God through their office, to infringe on those rights. His response to them definitely is not passive obedience in the literal sense. However, there is nothing in Wesley's own account to support the claim that he was the leader and "principal speaker" of an unruly mob that burst into the courtroom and disrupted the proceedings. Moreover, contrary to Stephens's claim, he did have business in the court.

Stephens reported also that "Mr. Wesley preached on.... Is it lawful to give tribute unto Caesar or not? from whence he discoursed largely on the duties of Magistrates in their several subordinate Ranks and Degrees, and the Obedience due from the People; setting forth how far it was, nevertheless, consistent with Christian Liberty, for People to insist on their Rights, when they found themselves oppressed by inferior Magistrates exercising discretionary Authority, which exceeded their Commission."[28] It was appropriate, of course, for Wesley as a priest to preach on this text, and to admonish both magistrates and people on their responsibilities. Given the timing, however, and the relative absence of other evidence that he preached sermons with political content, one must wonder whether he was pleading from the pulpit a case that he believed himself unlikely to win in court.

Unfortunately the sermon itself does not survive, nor does Wesley ever refer to it.

The comment about the consistency of Christian liberty with demanding one's own rights when oppressed by "inferior magistrates" (i.e., lower-level officials) does not imply sheer defiance of authorities, once Wesley has added the qualifiers of "discretionary Authority" and "which exceeded their Commission." However, it is not what one expects of a practitioner of passive obedience, and if reported correctly, may have been introduced by him to support his own activism. Possibly it was cited by Stephens as a contradiction to the preaching on obedience, and in support of his account of Wesley's leading the mob. If Wesley in truth said that, it would provide an important insight into his political understanding even if the reports of involvement with mob and disruption were false. Unfortunately, Wesley does not corroborate this comment in his own words, and it is not confirmed by others in the same context. In a letter to his mother of 13 January 1735, he mentions six meanings of liberty—none of which is political.[29]

However, the comment does connect with his response to mob riots against the Methodists in England in the 1740s. When the rights of the Methodists to religious practice and proclamation and to security of their persons and property were violated repeatedly, Wesley hesitated at first to seek the protection of the law, his hesitation prompted by both legal ignorance and moral reservations. Soon, however, he began to move with increasing resolution to use the law as a means of both defense and deterrence. On 20 June 1743, he wrote in his journal:

> Although I knew all that had been done here was contrary to law as it was to justice and mercy, yet I knew not how to advise the poor sufferers or procure them any redress. I was then little acquainted with the English course of law, having long had scruples concerning it. But, as many of these were now removed, I thought it best to inquire whether there could be any help from the laws of the land. I therefore rode over to Counsellor Littleton at Tamworth, who assured us we might have an easy remedy if we resolutely prosecuted, in the manner the law directed, those rebels against God and the king.[30]

Wesley does not say what the scruples were, or why they were removed. Nor does he seem to remember an earlier occasion when he appointed members of the congregation to seize a mob leader by force, bring him to the constable, and then accompany the constable while he delivered the man to the justice of the peace.[31] As time moved on, however, he used the law more frequently and readily for protective purposes.[32] He seems to have become quite knowledgeable concerning how that was to be done, what one could expect from it, and how one could use threats of fines and damage suits as deterrents.[33] If the perpetrators were themselves civil officials of some sort, that did not shield them from his legal actions or threats of action. In August 1748 he offered this warning to James Hargrove, Constable at Barrowford: "Only one piece of advice permit me to give. Do not consult herein with some petty attorney (who will certainly say your cause is good), but with some able barrister-at-law. This is the course I take. The counsel to whom I applied on this very Act of Parliament . . . were Counsellor Glanville, a barrister of Gray's Inn, and Sir Dudley Ryder, the King's Attorney-General. I am your real friend."[34] On 9 July 1766 he wrote to Francis Wanley, Dean of Ripon, and a magistrate who refused to administer justice to the Methodists: "I well know the advantage these laws give us in the present case: I say us, because I make the case my own, as I think it my bounden duty to do. I have had many suits in the King's Bench, and (blessed be God) I never lost one yet. But I would far rather put an amicable end to any dispute when it can be done."[35]

Whether Stephens's report to the Trustees is accurate or not, there nonetheless is evidence that John Wesley was a rights-conscious person, and to some extent a rights-active person, even during the years when he was supposed to be governed firmly by the principles of passive obedience and nonresistance. The further evidence is that his awakened consciousness and sporadic activity grew into a deliberate and legally informed method of action as the years moved on. That point is of signal importance for understanding his attitude toward political authority and obligation. His decentralizing of Romans 13 resulted not primarily from his endorsement of limited monarchy, important though that was to him, but from his attitude toward law. For Wesley, the law was the embodiment of

English liberties and their protector. The authority of the law was superior to the authority of public officials. On more than one occasion he asserted that the mere will of the king was not to be obeyed. "The King of England . . . is a sovereign prince; yet he has not power to bid me do the least thing unless the law of the land requires me so to do; for he has no power but to execute the law."[36] He said the same with regard to the will of bishops.[37] Therefore he felt free to disobey officials and even to bring them to court when he was convinced that he was acting in accordance with law, and the magistrates were not. He continued to regard them as "ministers of God," but his actions showed that he would not obey them as he obeyed God, but only as servants of God acting in accord with and enforcing the law. He would not be passively obedient when he could appeal to the guarantees and protection of authoritative law.

According to Norman Sykes, "the theory of the supremacy of the law to the king was of the essence of whig doctrine."[38] Wesley's attitude toward law and authority therefore connected him with a prevailing Whiggish attitude, and distanced him from the divine right tradition. Although one might claim, as Wesley certainly did, that the law also was supported by divine authority,[39] obedience to the regularity and continuity of law was of a different order from obedience to the variable and often unpredictable will of persons. Moreover, the social authority of the law was in its historicity and its emergence from societal values and interactions, that is, from the English people in their organic relatedness over time. The authority of rulers by divine right rested in the religious claim that God placed them above both law and people, and secured their position with the indefeasibility of that right delivered through biological succession. Wesley's elevating of the law above the will of persons in authority made it clear that in matters of rights and liberties he was operating within the legal tradition and not the tradition of passive obedience and nonresistance.

DEFENDING THE HOUSING OF LIBERTY

In the context of this analysis, Wesley's excursions into public conflicts in the 1760s and 1770s may appear to involve regression to an ethic of passive obedience. During those years he preached frequently on "Render to Caesar the things that are Caesar's," and "Be subject to the governing authorities." In doing so he attempted to enforce obedience to crown and governmental policy by using scriptural authority to back up arguments of a political and pragmatic nature. Evidently some of his contemporaries interpreted his interventions in regressive terms. Some of them, as we have seen, accused him of bringing back the old themes of Jacobitism. Many students of Methodist history also have pictured Wesley as a hard-line Tory and monarchist in political matters.

Hynson, by contrast, has argued that in this period Wesley's focused interest was in English liberties, and that his rhetoric of passive obedience and nonresistance essentially was a remnant of earlier commitments. He writes:

> By his acceptance of a limited monarchy, Wesley had cut the ground from under the notions of passive obedience and nonresistance. These ingrained biases did not disappear in Wesley's thoughts, although logically they had no support. Given the full range of his thoughts in the political tracts of 1768–82, these doctrines were vestigial. Wesley's reference to being "bred up from my childhood in the highest notions of passive obedience and non-resistance," should, therefore, be considered historical biography, not current (1775) conviction. Certainly, some of Wesley's utterances during the revolutionary period sound very much like the convictions of his younger years. The difference is that in 1775 the monarchy was viewed in instrumental terms, the liberties of Englishmen then primary.[40]

There is much to commend in this set of conclusions. Wesley's commitment to liberty was fully visible by the year indicated. He is on record as having supported several cases of agitation for liberties and justice, which he could not have done had passive obedience remained the primary norm. Early in the American controversy, Wesley expressed sympathy for the colonists, who—in his perception—were agitating for guarantees of their rights as English people. In "Thoughts upon Slavery" he justified attempted escapes by slaves as "the most natural act of 'running away' from intolerable tyranny."[41] In "Observations on Liberty" he defended the resistance of the Dutch United Provinces against Catholic

Spain, arguing that they were *"provoked by the violation of their charters!* yea, by the total subversion both of their religious and civil liberties; the taking away their goods, imprisoning their persons, and shedding their blood like water, without the least colour of right, yea, without the very form of law."[42] Also, he commended a mob of Sligo in Ireland for seizing a shipload of corn and selling it in the public market for the "common price." The merchants who owned the corn were hoarding it to corner the market and escalate their profits.[43] None of these approvals would have passed muster under strict application of the principles of passive obedience and nonresistance.

Having acknowledged Wesley's commitment to liberty, however, one must acknowledge also that it was limited by his perception of challenges to the housing of liberty. Wesley was committed primarily to historically developed, socially embedded liberties— "the liberties of Englishmen," to use Hynson's well-chosen words—not to abstract or unbridled liberty. When the supportive matrix of liberty—the constitution, the monarchy, the integrity of the empire—was threatened, he intervened to protect it. In those circumstances he set up a conservative stance in which he opposed the more radical advocates of liberty, especially those who challenged constitution and empire with an appeal based not in historic law, but in a naturalistic, individualistic philosophy: Wilkes and the English radicals, and the "Sons of Liberty" and other proponents of American independence.

When one considers Wesley's major interventions into public conflicts, what one sees is recognition of the nature of efficacious liberty as *ordered* liberty, and of the necessity to maintain the *order of liberty.* Advocacy of particular liberties against their denial is of great importance; maintenance of the systemic housing of liberty is of greater importance. In the light of this understanding, Wesley's conservatism represents the broadening of his long-standing commitment to rights and liberties to include support for the conditions of their maintenance, the efficacy of their protective and enabling legal tradition, and the means of their continuance into the future. It is not regressive nor is it antiliberal. But neither is his advocacy of liberty simply liberal. It is organic, historical, communitarian—providing yet more evidence of the similarity between his political thinking and that of his younger and politically more sophisticated contemporary, Edmund Burke.

But what of the rhetoric of obedience drawn from Romans 13, the Tribute Passage, and other pertinent Scripture texts? Hynson argues that by the 1770s the tradition of passive obedience and nonresistance was "vestigial," that Wesley's citation of his formation in this tradition was "historical biography." Fundamentally, that is correct. This particular political ethic had ceased long ago to be the driver of Wesley's active political consciousness. Its place had been taken by English law and constitutionalism, with their permissions to challenge magistrates and others who offended against the rights and liberties embedded in them. In another sense, however, Wesley's attachment to the obedience ethic was not simply vestigial. He continued to believe in it as scriptural truth, apparently not recognizing that he had allowed it to be supplanted in practice. Acting from that belief, he reached for Scripture to use as a hammer to beat down the opposition, and as a rod of chastisement to correct politically wavering Christian believers. That tactic created the impression that he was operating mainly under the old ethic of passive obedience to monarchs, when in reality he was using the theologically derived ethic as an ideological weapon to support less restrictive legal and political arrangements with lines and canons of authority derived mainly from nontheological sources.

LIMITS TO POLITICAL SPEECH

One of the firm General Rules of Wesley's United Societies was the prohibition of "*uncharitable* or *unprofitable* conversation, particularly *speaking evil of magistrates or of ministers.*"[44] This ban on speaking evil of civil authorities might appear to be simply a particular inference from the even more general rule against speaking evil of anyone, especially since the rule in question is placed under the rubric of "uncharitable or unprofitable conversation." Wesley preached a sermon on "The Cure of Evil-Speaking," in which he argued that evil speaking was not to be equated with lying and slandering. Rather, it "is neither more nor less than speaking evil of an absent person; relating something evil which was really done or said by one that is not present when it is related."[45] That might suffice to cover evil speaking of civil authorities, who usually are not present when persons criticize them. The inference argument is strengthened by Luke Tyerman's report that "to the rule prohibiting 'uncharitable or unprofitable conversation,' there was added, in the fourth edition, published in 1744, 'especially speaking evil of ministers or those in authority,' words now changed for 'magistrates or ministers.' "[46]

If Tyerman's dating is correct, the application of the rule to persons in authority may have been prompted by the Jacobite threat to the Hanoverian regime.[47] For Wesley, however, the ban on speaking evil of public officials had more force than a mere inference from a more general rule, and was not reducible to a prudent political move. Its source was a direct and specific command of God. Writing in 1782 on whether Christian ministers should preach politics, Wesley asserted, "There is a plain command in the Bible, 'Thou shalt not speak evil of the ruler of thy people.' "[48] To criticize the civil authority is to disobey God. In Wesley's view, this text reinforced and was reinforced by the directives of Romans 13. Moreover, he made adherence to the rule a condition of religious fellowship. Responding in 1777 to a published personal attack by Rowland Hill, he declared, "I say I will have no fellowship with those who rail at their governors, (be they Calvinists or Arminians,) who speak all manner of evil of them in private, if not in public too."[49]

The citations from 1777 and 1782 show that Wesley insisted on this practice in the later years of his long life. Entries in the student diary of young Mr. Wesley reveal its power over him at an early age. On 5 November 1725, he records talking with Robin Griffiths about passive obedience, and engaging in what he called "evil speaking" of Walpole.[50] On 14 December of that year, he "talked against King George," but then resolved not to "detract against the King." On 17 January 1726, he talked with Henry Sherman about passive obedience, and "vindicated Sacheverell." Inasmuch as Henry Sacheverell was identified with a particularly militant commitment to passive obedience, young Wesley apparently was binding himself more tightly under a discipline restrictive of political speech against the governing authorities.

One could supply more citations to show that throughout his life Wesley thought of this restrictive rule as normative for political behavior. One also can supply citations to show that he did not always heed it himself. His acid comments on the Tudor and Stuart rulers, though justified, certainly fit the definition of "evil-speaking" given in his sermon on the topic. So also did some of his observations on magistrates who did not protect the Methodists from riotous mobs, or worse, stirred the mobs against them. And one must include in this catalog of infringements of the rule his sarcastic explanation as to why he did not direct his socially prophetic "Thoughts upon Slavery" to the members of Parliament: "So many things, which seem of greater importance, lie before them."[51] It is not likely that John Wesley saw himself as violating the prohibition in any of these instances. If there is any evidence that he sensed some risk of doing so, it would be in the strained language he employed at times to express his disapproval. Nevertheless, despite his binding of the rule on the United Societies, he did not simply repress his own inclinations toward what he considered appropriate political criticism. Evidently the rule did not comprehend all norms for political behavior.

Of significance also are other variations. One is that the function of the rule changed with time and circumstance. For the young Wesley, not yet politically involved, it was an instrument of personal discipline. He required himself to refrain from detracting "against the King." For the mature and prominent Wesley, it served at times as an instrument for disciplining other persons. As indicated above, he refused religious fellowship with those who "rail against their governors." In the short note of 1782, he both allowed and required the enforcement of the rule through "preaching politics" for the purposes of defending the king and his ministers against false attacks and protecting the people from misinformation. Another variation was to move beyond the simple, moralistic definition of evil speaking set forth in his sermon, to accuse critics of King George III and his ministers of slander, and to demand that they be threatened with legal penalties. His attacks on what he took to be false and wicked political speech were especially sharp and bitter in 1768 and again in 1772 in the context of the Wilkes agitation.[52] Yet another variation was to add prudential considerations to simple moral duty in restricting political speech. "It is always difficult and frequently impossible for private men to judge of the measures taken by men in public offices. We do not see many of the grounds which determine them to act in this or the contrary manner. Generally, therefore, it behoves us to be silent, as we may suppose they know their own business best."[53]

One can detect a transformation in ethical method in these changes. Early on, Wesley's approach to political ethics is deontological. That is, it is governed by rules, commands, duties—not by goals and consideration of consequences. As Wesley becomes a public personage and develops significant interests in political institutions and conflicts, he becomes attentive to goals and consequences. His simple restrictive rule for obedience and political speech no longer suffices to define his political ethic. However, he does not develop a coherent alternative method for making morally structured political decisions. Nor does he give up his rule restrictive of political speech. The rule now comes into play mainly as an instrument for requiring conformity to his political goals. It functions much less as a general principle of political obligation.

Key to these inadequacies of ethical method is the theological problem noted previously. Wesley's hierarchical—from the top down—concept of political authority does not provide theological grounding for any political motivation that arises from outside the hierarchical system. He could not have worked out a political ethic adequate to his changing modes of political involvement without engaging dimensions of his theology excluded by the hierarchical concept. Had he done that, he would have had to modify, if not abandon, the concept itself.

POLITICAL SELF-EXCLUSION AND INVOLVEMENT

Self-exclusion of Methodists—especially Methodist clergy—from political involvement had something of the nature of a rule of political obligation. In fact, in the decades following the death of Mr. Wesley, the English Methodist Conference formulated and enforced what they called the "No Politics Rule." This self-exclusion was a *prudential* rule in that it attempted to render

Methodists less vulnerable to attack by making them politically less visible and less threatening. It was a *vocational* rule for Methodist clergy and lay preachers in that it required them to hold fast to their missional and evangelistic calling, and not allow themselves to be diverted to other concerns. It was an *authority limiting* rule in that it restricted the making and executing of public policy—including efforts to influence policy development—to persons who actually held public office. Wesley formulated a rare and principled exception in his brief advisory, "How far Is It the Duty of a Christian Minister to Preach Politics?" (1782). There he insisted that his preachers should "preach politics" only to refute "evil speaking" against the king. "If you mean this by the term, it is the bounden duty of every Christian Minister to preach politics. It is our bounden duty to refute these vile aspersions, in public as well as in private." Having done so, they were to leave off political preaching as soon as possible, "For it is our main and constant business to 'preach Jesus Christ, and him crucified.' "[54] This exception authorized a form of political intervention, but restricted it to a specified minimum. Persons who went beyond that minimum were guilty of a serious violation of political obligation.

Notoriously, Wesley did not take his own advice. In English domestic conflicts and later in the American War of Independence, he became an aggressive partisan for the constitution and for government policy. His "Thoughts upon Slavery" allegedly was addressed only to the consciences of slavers and slave owners, but in fact it abetted the attack on the institution through its wide public distribution. Lynwood M. Holland and Ronald F. Howell add that "he condemned, for instance, the poor laws, the penal code, the dreadful prisons, slavery, smuggling, the toll-gate tax (as 'addling' the poor with an unreasonable burden), scandals of sinecures and pluralities in the Established Church, the 'tyrannical' English administration of Ireland, scheming local officials, and unethical lawyers who perverted the law to 'embezzle' the ignorant impoverished."[55] Wesley offered justifications for his interventions, but showed no awareness of having violated or infringed on his self-imposed rule. He was acting as a peacemaker, pouring water on the flames, defending king, constitution, and the unity of the empire, protecting liberty and public order, promoting justice and safeguarding rights. These are worthy motives, but in putting them forward in public discourse Wesley did not confront the rule of self-exclusion from politics. They attach to random interventions, and do not spring from a unified theory of social and political action. When one puts Wesley's principled opposition to political involvement together with his record of political activity, what one has is a set of political impulses with no coherent, guiding political ethic.

Political activity in the absence of a coherent political ethic risked violation of this principle of political obligation under charges of imposture and usurpation. Passive obedience protected the rights and dignity of magistrates. Unauthorized persons who engaged in politics were both transgressing the limits of defined authority and dishonoring the magistrates by implying that they were incapable of fulfilling their responsibilities or unwilling to do so. Wesley apparently was mindful of this problem on the one occasion when he did set forth a pattern of corporate action for the enforcement of law. On that occasion he developed guidelines for how clergy and concerned laypersons could intrude themselves justifiably into efforts usually reserved for public officials. In his sermon before the Society for the Reformation of Manners, on 30 January 1763, he argued that "men who did fear God and desire the happiness of their fellow-creatures have in every age found it needful to join together in order to oppose the works of darkness, to spread the knowledge of God their Saviour, and to promote his kingdom upon earth."[56] Wesley extended this general concept into an organized plan for enforcing laws against Sabbath violations, gambling, public swearing, and prostitution. He saw this effort as a necessary projection of the mission of the Church of England "to oppose the devil and all his works, and to wage war against the world and the flesh, his constant and faithful allies."[57] The Society for the Reformation of Manners was organized for the purpose of prosecuting this effort.

Perhaps the most noteworthy aspect of the Society's crusade was the care they took in gaining authorization for their activities, and proceeding in such manner as to activate and inform public officials in regard to their own law enforcement responsibilities, rather than simply circumventing them and attempting to do their work for them. At the outset they cleared their proposal with Sir John Fielding, unidentified as to office, but apparently a person of rank and prominence.

He approved of the design, and directed them how to carry it into execution. Following his advice:

> They first delivered petitions to the right honourable the Lord Mayor and the Court of Aldermen, to the Justices sitting at Hick's Hall, and those in Westminster Hall. And they received from all these honourable benches much encouragement to proceed. It was next judged proper to signify their design to many persons of eminent rank, and to the body of the clergy, as well as the ministers of other denominations . . . and they had the satisfaction to meet with a hearty consent and universal approbation from them. They then printed and dispersed, at their own expense, several thousand books of instruction to constables and other parish officers, explaining and enforcing their several duties. And to prevent as far as possible the necessity of proceeding to an actual execution of the laws, they likewise printed and dispersed . . . dissuasives from sabbath-breaking, extracts from Acts of Parliament against it, and notices to the offenders.[58]

The thrust of the Society's campaign was to prod public officials to do their job of enforcing the law, and to educate them to their responsibilities on the assumption that nonperformance implied ignorance. When their careful efforts were ignored by constables and other officials, they began informing directly on persons who were violating the laws. They kept detailed accounts of their activities. Wesley was able to report that between August 1757 and August 1762 they had "brought to justice" 10,588 violators. Needless to say, their efforts provoked much opposition and numerous lawsuits—one of which resulted in a massive fine of three hundred pounds, thereby putting the Society out of business.[59]

One may object to the narrow, moralistic focus of this effort, and to the fact that it was directed only to the enforcement of particular "blue laws" and not to issues of social justice and societal transformation. For our present purposes, however, the "crusade" is important as an instance of public engagement that went well beyond passivity, and yet did so with full respect for established public offices, their authority, and their responsibilities. In this sermon Wesley demonstrates capacity for sustained and ordered thinking about Christian responsibility that is not sufficiently manifest in either his warnings against political participation or his own numerous political interventions.

A REVIEW: RECONSTRUCTIONS IN POLITICAL OBLIGATION

Wesley's ethic of political obligation starts out with a rule-based commitment to passive obedience, and then undergoes significant changes as he emerges from quietude and obscurity and becomes an active public figure. His compelling sense of religious commitment led him to radicalize the concept of obedience to God, thereby reversing the priority of Romans 13 over Acts 5:29, and subordinating passivity before civil and ecclesiastical authorities to activity before God. His firm and intuitive engagement with the English legal and constitutional tradition of rights and liberties established the immediate and primary authority of that approach to public responsibility, and elevated it above the scripturally derived passivity of obedience. He managed the transition from passive obedience to public authorities to active use of the law, one should note, without substituting legal absolutism for religiously grounded political absolutism. He did not hesitate to declare "sinful" those laws that prohibited the preaching of the gospel, or to contrast with natural justice the laws imposing and supporting slavery. Wesley was a passionate supporter of liberty. Yet his awareness of the social construction of effective liberty and his respect for and investment in the legal tradition led him to oppose those appeals to liberty that in his view were excessive and thereby threatened its protective and nurturing matrix.

As these changes appeared in Wesley's practice, he did not necessarily recognize them as alterations of his fundamental political ethic, perhaps because he always remained respectful of authority and never doubted the scriptural confirmations. One could not imagine John Wesley putting the bumper sticker "Question Authority" on his carriage! The persistence of this framework of authority served the important purpose of confining tendencies toward excessive subjectivity when he shifted the ethical burden from rule conformity to responsibility of the individual conscience before God. His revision of his inherited political ethic, after all, required more discernment of the will of God, including interpretation of commands and decision between apparently competing commands, than did the simple formula of passive obedience with provision for the occasional exception. Wesley's retention of the framework of obedience helped prevent the discerning conscience from descending into "enthusiasm." Usually Wesley argued that his departures from established procedures were not arbitrary or eccentric or the result of personal whims, but were in accord with canon or civil law properly understood, or if not with those, then with clear commands of Scripture.[60] In political terms, however, his retention of this framework reflected his conviction that the alternative to absolutist authority was not antiauthoritarian individualism. It was liberty in a context of order, an organic constitutionalism that matched rights with duties and respect for the governed with respect for the governors.

Again in the case of political obligation one observes the secularization of Wesley's politics. The context of obligation emerges as organic constitutionalism and the legal ordering of liberty. This context establishes prominence in his thought and action without notable theological grounding. The theologically grounded politics of obligation and obedience is reduced almost to irrelevance, or at times to ideology—God and Scripture summoned for the purpose of enforcing conformity. The incongruity is a problem in theological method. Wesley's theological approaches to politics start from above—with God the Father. His law and constitutionalism draw much of their authority from below. Hierarchical theology and the actuality of Wesley's politics touch each other, but they do not interact to produce an integral theology of politics.

CHAPTER NINE

GOVERNMENT IN CONTEXT
THE NATURE AND PURPOSES OF POLITICAL INSTITUTIONS

Debates on public policy in the United States and other countries often work with implicit answers to the question of the nature and purpose of political institutions without ever arguing the question itself or establishing the ground on which the assertions are made. Which kinds of policies are appropriate for government action, and which are not? How broad should the policy concept of the public good be? To some persons it is clear that governments should have no purposes beyond providing for order and defense, especially the defense of private property. Others argue that government should "promote the general welfare," to use the phrase from the Preamble to the Constitution of the United States—that it should serve that welfare also in education, health, the arts, and other matters of public concern and benefit.

Christian writers across the centuries have entered this debate at the fundamental level, attempting to clarify the issues by pointing to alternative groundings, and providing understandings of state and government derived from Scripture and from theological construals of political reality. Although their starting points are varied, frequently they have drawn their arguments from theological anthropology, that is, from concepts of human nature shaped by theological reasoning, and have approached questions of the nature and purpose of government from its supposed origin in human nature either as created originally or in its sinful condition after the Fall of humankind. The United Methodist bishops' document *In Defense of Creation* combines both explanations by stating that "The powers of government are not only legitimate expressions of the creation's natural order of political community; they are necessary constraints upon human sinfulness."[1]

The questions for this chapter pertain to how John Wesley

viewed the nature and purpose of government, whether and in what ways he thought theologically about government, and whether he offered any significant contribution to Christian understanding of political institutions. At the outset, the prospects for confident and compelling answers to these questions seem dim. Wesley did not discuss the theoretical issues as such, wrote no treatise on state and government, did not comment on whether he thought political institutions originated in creation or in the Fall, and did not give a clear indication as to how one should think theologically about such matters—or indeed whether he considered such thinking important. If he was influenced directly or indirectly by the political Homilies of 1547 and 1570, he did not acknowledge it. He did not refer to the Homilies or cite them, and did not use modes of argumentation that resonate with them on this point. In chapter 6, I argued that he did not agree with the Homily of 1547—that governments generally and monarchs specifically were institutions of original creation—but more likely took the view of the Homily of 1570, that political institutions arose out of the fallen condition of humankind and in response to its raging disorder. However, he did not reflect openly and directly on these questions, and did not extend them systematically into a theory of government.

It is obvious that Wesley was interested far more in the source of governmental authority, and in pointing to God as the source, than he was in reflecting and commenting on the kinds of activities in which governments should or should not engage. Events of his time forced his attention to the former issue, but apparently not to the latter. That is why this book devotes three chapters to the problem of authority and only one to the nature and purposes of government, and examines the two topics in the order of priority that Wesley himself seems to have assigned to them.

Of additional significance is that John Wesley identified government with the supreme power prevailing in any society.[2] If government always is to be identified with supreme power, whatever that power may be and whatever it may attempt to do, there is nothing further to be said about the inherent nature and purposes of government. Supreme power will be what it will be, and will do what it will do, up to the limits of that power. Further generalizations from the nature of government are neither possible nor relevant. One can argue that divine ordination of supreme power directs government to perform certain tasks and to act in certain ways, but those are inferences from the intentions of God and not from government in its being as supreme power. So far as I know, John Wesley did not confront that problem. His interest in government as supreme power deriving its authority from God was to put an end to the argument that government derived authority from the people through their natural right to consent to be governed. He did not overtly connect this issue to those of the nature and purposes of government.

In the light of these problems, and in the absence of any obvious road into the analysis of Wesley's basic concepts of state and government, we shall begin our inquiry with what appear to be defining—if unreflective—statements by him of government's purposes. We shall ask about the theological meaning of those statements, whether they in fact *define* sufficiently to comprehend all functions Wesley assigns or allows to government, and whether they do so without embodying powerful contradictions. Subsequent to this inquiry by way of Wesley's "definitions," we shall analyze his pertinent writings using the standard creation-preservation typology. In the words of the United Methodist bishops' document quoted above, did Wesley believe that the "powers of government are . . . legitimate expressions of the creation's natural order of political community," or that fundamentally they are "necessary constraints upon human sinfulness"? That approach will allow for a more conceptual investigation, and will put Wesley into conversation and comparison with major figures in Christian history who represent the alternative orientations. It also may distort the results of inquiry, unless one is open to other theological possibilities.

One serious theological possibility is the concept of God as the foundation for theological thinking about politics. So much of John Wesley's ethics is governed by the notion of *imitation of God* that one should expect that ethical foundation to apply also to his thinking about the nature and purposes of the state. One can say in advance that Wesley never makes that application systematically and consistently. Nevertheless, there is enough of *imitatio dei* in some of his random comments on government to allow the possibility that it is the undisclosed principle of coherence in his political thinking. If that possibility can be established as a credible hypothesis, it opens the way to the recovery of the political image of God for a Wesleyan political language.

THE ENFORCEMENT OF MORALITY, THE MAINTENANCE OF TRUE RELIGION

On 10 November 1736, John Wesley wrote from Georgia to a Mr. Verelst, stating that "we have an advantage here which is not frequent in other places, that is, a magistracy not only regular in their own conduct, but desirous and watchful to suppress, as far as in them lies, whatever is openly ill in the conduct of others. I am obliged to you for the hint you give as [to] the regulating that too-prevailing neglect in the case of administering public oaths. Without doubt it should be done with all possible solemnity. For surely no hurry of business can excuse any want of reverence towards the God to whom all our business should be consecrated, since it is for his sake that we ought to undertake everything, as well as to perform everything as in his sight."[3] A few months later, on 4 March 1737, he wrote to the Trustees of Georgia, commending the public officials: "I can't but acknowledge the readiness of the magistrates here, Mr. Causton in particular, in assisting me, so far as pertains to their office, both to repress open vice and immorality, and to promote the glory of God by establishing peace and mutual goodwill among men. And I trust their labour hath not been quite in vain. Many ill practices seem to lose ground daily, and a general face of decency and order prevails, beyond what I have seen anywhere else in America."[4]

These two statements are as close as Wesley comes in his early years to defining the nature and purposes of government. Government is an enterprise consecrated to the glory of God for the advancement of moral behavior, the suppression of openly ill conduct, and the establishment of peace and mutual goodwill. It is a public undertaking in which magistrates cooperate with Anglican priests, for it is a common task in a holy calling for the governance of one community under God. In the second letter

Wesley is writing from the standpoint of the priest, and adds "so far as pertains to their office" to the participation of the magistrates. However, in the first letter he makes no such reservation, and the words and tenor of both letters together make clear that he is defining the office of magistrate even more than that of the priest.

These presumptive definitions may presuppose or imply the protective and punitive functions of government, especially the making and enforcing of laws against harmful and disruptive behavior, but Wesley does not give prominence to them. Instead he emphasizes the magistrates' responsibility to enforce morality—to coerce members of the community to exhibit at least external goodness, not simply to prevent or punish their threats to or assaults on others. This provision anticipates the activities described years later in his sermon on "The Reformation of Manners," in which he established a program for the enforcement of what today we would call "blue laws," including requiring observance of the Christian Sabbath.[5] Government is to engage in moral and (to some extent) religious policing—functions that go well beyond coercive application of the law to protect life, liberty, and property. Moreover, Wesley is charging government with the positive responsibility for establishing goodwill among the members—an educative and community-building function, involving constructive and cultural tasks not readily or appropriately symbolized by the sword.

Forty years after the letters to Mr. Verelst and the Georgia Trustees, Wesley restated his view of the purposes and functions of government in "A Calm Address to the Inhabitants of England." Referring to King George III, then under political assault, he asked, "Should we not remember him before God in prayer, that his throne may be established in righteousness? that he, and all which are in authority under him, may duly administer justice, to the punishment of wickedness and vice, and the maintenance of true religion and virtue?"[6] Wesley appropriately acknowledges the administration of justice to be the primary function of governors, and by adding the qualifying word "duly," implies strictness but also the virtues of fairness, evenhandedness, and mercy. He then goes on to identify the aim of such administration as "the punishment of wickedness and vice, and the maintenance of true religion and virtue." Wesley does not specify what he means by "wickedness and vice," but his attitudes across the years are sufficiently clear as to allow the inference of both immoral conduct and harmful and destructive behavior. Therefore, we are entitled to see consistency in his views of the purposes of government in this regard across a long span of time, and especially to take note of his persistent interest in the legal enforcement of morality and in governmental responsibility for education in virtue.

However, the inclusion of "maintenance of true religion" appears to expand his list of proper purposes of government. In fact, it does not, if we place his sentiments in a context not disclosed fully in the two early letters. In his "Ought We to Separate from the Church of England?" (1755), discussed in an earlier chapter, Wesley defended the role of Parliament in defining rubrics and appointing bishops, the regulating of divine worship by magistrates, and the intervention of King Edward VI whereby he "restored the scriptural worship of God . . . and . . . gave several rules for the more decent and orderly performance of it."[7] In the 1730s, as a young priest under appointment to the colony of Savannah, and as a willing supporter of the Erastian English establishment, he would not have thought differently about the "maintenance of true religion," and might have included it comfortably in his letters praising the magistrates for their cooperation. There is no reason to doubt, therefore, that Wesley believed government exercised religious functions and served religious purposes in direct as well as indirect ways.

Two observations are appropriate at this point. First, if Wesley intended these statement as definitions of governmental responsibilities, he left out some functions that he allowed or required in other circumstances, among them the support and protection of English liberties—especially religious liberty. That particular omission is more than a failure to be sufficiently inclusive. It is the neglect of a governmental responsibility not always compatible with repression of immoral behavior and maintenance of true religion. Second, Wesley offers no theological justification for identifying morality and religion as governmental responsibilities and for making them central to the governmental enterprise. He seems to assume that the theological grounds are self-evident. The notion of conducting public office to the glory of God may provide some clue to the direction of his thinking, but it does not necessarily imply moral education and enforcement and religious governance any more than the enforcement of law or the encouragement of a healthy and distributive economy. Are there theological grounds for his stance on these matters, and if so, on what terms are they defensible?

These two observations set the agenda for further examination of what at first glance seem to be defining statements. We shall address the second one first, because it relates both to the justification for government itself and to the identification of particular responsibilities.

A Calvinist Political Theology?

In the absence of explicit declarations and arguments, one can search for Wesley's theological reasoning by comparing him with major figures in the history of Christian thought who have expressed themselves more thoroughly and extensively on fundamental political questions. If one does that, the person who comes to mind most readily is John Calvin. Wesley's proclivity for assigning magistrates the task of policing personal and public morality recalls Calvin's participation in the tight and detailed regulation of Geneva's Christian Polity by the dual government of magistrates and pastors. (Wesley might not have been so militant and comprehensive as Calvin's Geneva in this regard, although his commitment to fulfilling the whole law of God and his zeal in "Reformation of Manners" make one wonder.) His idea of an educational and cultural function for government in eliciting and nurturing virtue also suggests Calvin, as does his requiring a role for public officials in maintaining true religion. Distinguishing Christ's spiritual rule of the inner kingdom from the external rule of secular government, Calvin wrote, "The end of secular government, however, while we remain in this world, is [1559:] to foster and protect the external worship of God, defend pure doctrine (FV: and religion) and the good condition of the Church, accommodate the way we live to [the requirements of] human society, [1536:] mould our conduct to civil justice, reconcile us to one another, and uphold and defend the common peace and tranquillity."[8] Calvin adds subsequently that civil order "prevents idolatries, sacrileges against the name of God, blasphemies against his truth, and other scandals to religion from emerging into the light of day and spreading (FV: being sown) among the people; it prevents disturbances of the public peace; it allows each to remain safe and unharmed in the enjoyment of what is his; it makes possible innocent contacts between people; [1539:] and it sees to the cultivation of upright conduct and decency. [1536:] In short, it upholds a public form of religion amongst Christians, and humanity amongst men."[9] The duties of magistrates extend to both tables of the Decalogue, that is, to divine worship and religion as well as to matters of temporal justice.[10]

One cannot cite comments from Wesley to cover every one of these points, but there is no clear evidence that he would disagree with any of them. It is clear that he shares Calvin's commitment to an activistic government whose proper tasks are not limited to protective and punitive functions prompted by the presence of sin in the world. Both Calvin and Wesley recognize with Luther the divine ordination of governmental power to protect the innocent and punish the lawbreakers, and to defend the national territory against its enemies, but both confer on government a role in disciplining society and personal and social behavior that goes well beyond Luther's central interest in government as God's means of preventing or stemming the chaos generated by original sin. Both want government to enforce morality and not law only, although neither makes a careful distinction between the two. Both want government to engage in the social formation of virtue and habits of civility. Both want government to maintain "true religion." Both see the enterprise of government as a means of giving glory to God, and not only as a means of dealing with needs and problems arising from human nature. One can make distinguishing comparisons too sharply and superficially, especially in the light of changes in the views of both Luther and Calvin over time, and Luther's own practical requirement of a religious role for government. However, Wesley, like Calvin, supports a view of government whose functions are not exhausted by the theological concept of *order of preservation* usually associated with Luther—or at least with Lutheran ways of thinking about state and government.

Nevertheless, the case is not conclusive for Wesley's fundamental dependence on Calvin in these matters. Wesley makes no reference to having derived his views on the nature and purposes of government from Calvin, does not cite Calvin on political questions, and offers no evidence of Calvinist theological method (or any evident method, for that matter) in arriving at his position. Those reservations are not decisive, of course. Wesley certainly was dependent on Calvin—indirectly if not directly—in distinguishing among ceremonial, judicial, and moral law in the Old Testament, and in formulating his own understanding of the three uses of the law—even though he didn't say so.[11] He may also have drawn from Calvin—without acknowledgment—his convictions that the government should enforce and encourage morality and maintain true religion.

The more serious reservations are substantive. To begin with there were fundamental differences between the two on the question of liberty. Calvin followed Luther in his unwillingness to allow the inference of political liberty from evangelical liberty.[12] Wesley also did not attempt to infer political liberty from evangelical liberty, but he was a stout defender of a range of liberties on other grounds. The differences were especially sharp with regard to religious liberty. Wesley was a stalwart champion of religious liberty, whereas Calvin offended against religious liberty in ways that Wesley never would have countenanced—especially Calvin's arrangement of the trial and execution of Michael Servetus on charges of heresy.[13] We shall note subsequently that Wesley's commitment to liberties of various sorts does not fit well with the repressive implications of his assignment of moral and religious functions to government. In terms of the present comparison, however, Wesley's commitment drew a sharp line between John Calvin and himself.

Even more pertinent to our present comparison is that, despite strong similarities, Wesley and Calvin have different understandings of Christian society. Both of them subscribe in effect to a concept of *corpus christianum*—a Christian society in which all or most persons are members of both church and state, and church and state in their administrative and executive presence are complementary and cooperative arms of the same society. For Wesley, this society exists already in the British community, or more exactly for some purposes, the *English* community. It is an integrated political society with components of crown, church, and people. Essentially it is a historical and cultural reality, with deeply embedded and pervasive theological symbols and components. For Calvin, however, the Christian society is an ideal to be achieved as a holy commonwealth under the kingship of Christ—the result of magistrates and ministers working together to reduce the body of citizens to the body of the elect of God, or at least to bring under Christian discipline those who do not rightly and willingly conform. In this context, Wesley's basic social sentiments are comprehensive and inclusive. They are manifest, among other ways, in that he was ecumenical and neither doctrinally nor confessionally exclusive in religious practice, and welcomed Quakers, Baptists, Catholics, Presbyterians, and others into Methodist meetings without requiring any change in religious affiliation. Calvin's social sentiments, by contrast, are reductionistic and exclusive. Their principles of inclusion and exclusion are the presumptive tests of election: regular attendance on the services of word and sacrament, adherence to true doctrine (as set forth in Calvin's *The Institutes of the Christian Religion*), and the morally upright life.

Of central importance for our purposes, Wesley's attitudes toward the relationships of church and state in the *corpus christianum* are Erastian, whereas Calvin's tend to be church-dominated. Wesley acknowledges readily that monarchs and other magistrates exercise jurisdiction over both church and state. Calvin allows significant attention by government to matters of religion, but only by public officials vetted by the church for correctness of doctrine and probity of conduct. Wesley's state controls Wesley's church—with Wesley's blessing. It is authorized under God to give laws to the church, make ecclesiastical appointments, and restore true doctrine.[14] Under Christ, the " 'king is the supreme governor of the Church of England.' "[15] Directly or indirectly, by contrast, Calvin's church controls Calvin's state.

The attempt to provide Wesley's political definitions with theological substance by throwing him into the arms of Calvinism finally is not convincing, despite important similarities and some evidence of influence. It seems far more likely that his position is peculiarly English—a cultural combination of Puritan moralism, perhaps inherited from his Dissenter ancestors, and the church-state notions of English Erastianism with their subordination of church to government. The former is related to Calvin, of course, although with an English historical development that affected its character and substance. The latter is a product of the interaction of the English monarch with the Pope on the one hand and English religious diversity on the other. It is not a result of Calvinist influence.[16] Puritan moralism, reinforced by Catholic and Anglican perfection, is demonstrably very strong in Wesley's thought and practice.[17] His indoctrination with the Erastianism of the English establishment is beyond dispute. This combination, and not Calvinist influence—I would propose—is the primary determinant of Wesley's opinions on the moral and religious functions of government.

The primary issue, however, is not whether Wesley was a political Calvinist, but whether his advocacy of moral and religious responsibilities for government represented a definite theological position and argument. What this comparative analysis has shown is that Wesley's views reflected the British community and establishment, and were not supported by any evident or apparent line of theological reasoning. It is true that he recognized Christ as the supreme lawgiver over the church in this hierarchical scheme, but he did so apparently to legitimate the law-giving function of monarch and magistrates with regard to the church, not to provide a substantive theological rationale for the relationship. No noticeable christological content derives from the subordination of civil lawgivers to Christ.

The conclusions one must draw are that John Wesley clearly believed it was the proper role of government to repress immoral behavior and to maintain true doctrine, but that his convictions in this regard depended on the historical contingency of the British community and the English establishment. They revealed no theological grounds for inclusion in a general theory of church-state relations or for a theologically derived understanding of the nature and purposes of government.

But Are These Statements Definitions?

The other question to put to Wesley's random words on the moral and religious responsibilities of government is whether one should treat them as intended definitive and exclusive renderings of magisterial and governmental responsibility, or only as a selection from a larger picture, perhaps reflective of a momentary agenda. The statements are consistent across the years, but they do not comprehend everything Wesley allowed to or required of the workings of governments. The documents quoted—especially the Georgia letters—give only scant attention to "order of preservation" functions, and that mainly by implication, by contrast with the prominence Wesley gave them elsewhere. Even more doubtful is the case for inclusion of Wesley's advocacy of government intervention into the workings of the market system on behalf of the poor, hungry, and unemployed—the argument of "Thoughts on the Present Scarcity of Provisions," to be considered later. The definitions, so called, do not exclude such intervention, but neither do they include or even seem to suggest it.

Most problematical, however, is Wesley's failure to draw these particular statements of governmental purpose into conversation with his profound commitment to liberty, and especially to religious liberty. In numerous tracts and sermons Wesley made abundantly clear that the protection of English liberties is a fundamental responsibility of government, that governments should be judged by this criterion, and that George II and George III should be praised and supported by the English people because they fulfilled this responsibility with such dedication. Two of Wesley's major political essays—"Thoughts upon Liberty" and "Some Observations on Liberty"—defend king, constitution, and British community on the grounds that they are bulwarks of liberty, guardians of the greatest degree and kind of liberty enjoyed anywhere in the world, perhaps ever! Other writings of Wesley do the same. Yet there is no mention of English liberties or other liberties in the two letters from Georgia of 1737, where he commends the readiness of magistrates in one case to "suppress as far as in them lies whatever is openly ill in the conduct of others," and in the other "to repress both vice and immorality." Nor is there any in the passage cited from "A Calm Address to the Inhabitants of England," praying that the king "may duly administer justice, to the punishment of wickedness and vice, and the maintenance of true religion and virtue," despite the fact that Wesley celebrates English liberty in the same document.

One might suppose that the defense of liberty simply could be subsumed under the protective functions of government, which I have agreed are at least implied, if not actually stated, in Wesley's formulations. The problem, however, is not that mention of liberty is omitted—possibly unintentionally. Rather, it is that the liberties Wesley advocates are at least in tension if not in conflict with the central proposals of these documents—that governments exist to repress immorality and maintain true religion. That is true especially with regard to religious liberty, which Wesley considered a natural right, grounded in creation and structured in the relationship of the human conscience to God. How could Wesley both declare religious liberty to be a fundamental fact of divine intention in creation, and assign to government the task of maintaining true religion—knowing, as he certainly did, that religious conscience often would rebel against governmental definitions of truth and the enforcement of those definitions?

Surprisingly, Wesley did not reflect on his own Methodist experience as a means of testing his statements about the religious responsibilities of government. He and the Methodists were attacked and hounded by officials of both church and state, who accused them of, among other things, teaching false doctrine and destabilizing the religious-political establishment. The "maintenance of true religion," in their view, required the suppression of the Methodists! His experience as the leader of what was perceived to be and turned out to be a sectarian movement, should have warned him against any view of governmental functions that included the establishment and maintenance of religious uniformity. However, there is no evidence of systematic engagement on his part with these apparent contradictions. His closest approach to doing so is his allowance of obedience to authorities only in "things indifferent," while retaining the necessity of proclaiming the central truths of the Christian faith even against the orders of the authorities. Even in that case, however, he does not appear to think through the problem of limiting the religious role of government to "things indifferent," despite awarding it responsibility for maintaining true religion, and also reserving to himself the prerogativ of deciding which things are indifferent and which are not. Moreover, he was willing under those circumstances to risk subverting the whole order of church and state to pursue his religious vocation as he understood it, and not simply as defined by government and church in relation to the "maintenance of true religion."[18]

That Wesley should fail to face these contradictions and resolve them indeed is surprising in view of his personal experience and his painful awareness of offenses both sporadic and systemic by English governments against the religious liberty of Dissenters and others not visibly aligned with the Church of England. However, it was characteristic of him to embrace such contradictions without attempting to work them out. Earlier I noted Wesley's tendency to hold simultaneously and knowingly a church-type and a sect-type view of religious organization and community without attempting to reconcile them. I noted also his failure to draw the implications for church-state relationships of his frequent and severe criticisms of the Constantinian settlement with the Church of Rome. It was quite like him, therefore, to retain "maintenance of true religion" as a requirement of government against the background of the English struggle to avoid having "true religion" maintained in England by a Catholic king, and to experience the religious perse-cution of the Methodists without asking whether it should be with-in the province of government to decide what is true and what not true in matters of religious faith and practice.

Apparently Wesley tended to accept the perpetuation of cultur-ally defined norms that he found basically or generally satisfacto-ry, and to treat exceptions to or conflicts with the norms as matters for correction or for pragmatic adaptation. That the government should have religious responsibilities is a norm not merely gener-ally acceptable; fundamentally, in his view, it is correct. If the monarch should be of the wrong faith, if the authorities should act at times against those who are proclaiming the true faith, those are problems of personnel and practice—not problems with the norms. It suffices in the one case to support the Protestant Hanoverians against the Catholic Stuarts, in the other case to encourage the authorities to understand the nature and limits of their legal responsibilities and to tell them the truth about the Methodists. When Wesley commends to government the maintenance of true religion in the face of these contradictions, he is displaying the uncritical retention of a cultural attitude that can be called to duty when it seems useful, and to which contradictions can be accommodated. He does not seem to be making a theologically serious statement about the religious functions of government.

The risk in reducing Wesley's statements to their transient cultural sources is that the same might be done with his commitments to liberty, embraced and commended as they were with the force of cultural authority. The burgeoning yet very old sentiments of English liberty were grounded in the ancient constitution; given a new political foundation and direction in the events of 1688–89; socialized through the organic character of the British community; and housed, protected, and explained in the mixed constitution of the eighteenth century. They were a profoundly *cultural* reality. We shall have occasion in the next chapter to examine Wesley's understandings of liberty, and to ask whether he offered any reasons to commend them beyond the reach of their social sources and settings. At minimum, however, one can state that by deriving *religious* liberty from the doctrine of creation, Wesley provided it with a serious theological foundation that he did not arrange for governmental moral and religious responsibilities. That being so, the provisions for human liberty, *at least in that form*, have a much better title to incorporation into an enduring Wesleyan understanding of the functions of government than the elements of government repression of immorality and maintenance of true relgion—even though Wesley included the latter without qualification in his own statements. A further point is that Wesley's liberties meshed with and were foundational to the advancing phase of articulation of British society. His advocacy of the repre ssion of immoral behavior and the maintenance—by government of true religion belonged to a form of historic articulation that was passing away.

The answer to the second question, then, is that these statements by Wesley were not formal and exclusive definitions of the purposes and functions of government. They did in fact include some affirmations of proper and expected governmental functions. They also omitted some, and they failed to acknowledge severe conflicts among Wesley's expectations. Essentially, they were routine and unreflective statements of what apparently was a generally accepted point of view. As such, they left much more to be said.

GOVERNMENT AND THE "ORDERS": A COMPARATIVE TYPOLOGY

That being so, we proceed to our second type of inquiry into Wesley's understanding of the nature and functions of government: whether he used or implied concepts of *order of creation* and *order of preservation* in his political thinking, and if so, what those concepts yielded with regard to the questions of this chapter.

The use of "orders" terminology is rooted in Martin Luther, but it has become the common property of anyone who attempts to distinguish the divine work of original creation from the divine work in instituting measures to counteract the disruptive effects of original and actual sin. Actually, the orders, so called, are three in number: *creation, preservation, redemption.* Karl Barth and Dietrich Bonhoeffer included government in the circle of redemption by making it instrumental to the work of Christ, drawing—in Barth's case, at least—on John Calvin's relating of Christology to politics.[19] However, most Christian writers who attempt a theological analysis of state and government work with the contrast of the first two orders. This choice commits them—usually intentionally—to propositions concerning the relationship of human nature to politics. In the first case, government is understood to be an integral element in the constitution of human nature as social. In the second, it is an organization of the forces of disruption against themselves, and appears in human experience only in response to the presence of sin. The differences in interpretation based on these concepts have important implications. Characteristically they imply relatively greater optimism or pessimism in expectations of government conduct and achievement, and also distinctions with reference to what is assigned or allowed to the workings of government.

Government as an "Order of Creation"

If John Wesley believed that government was a natural order of community, designed for and present in original creation, he did not say so—unless one takes his affirmation of the *political image of God* as a statement of that position. The principal difficulty with doing so is that having set forth this promising concept, Wesley walked off and left it, never employing it to explain and justify any of his public political comments. Despite this neglect on his part, we must examine his understanding of the political image in this phase of the research to ask whether it might have led him to an "order of creation" theology of political institutions had he chosen to follow that lead.

In his notes on Genesis 1:26-28, Wesley states that "God's image upon man consists . . . in his place of authority. Let us make man *in our image* and *let him have dominion.* As he has the government of the inferior creatures, he is as it were God's representative on earth. Yet his government of himself by the *freedom of his will,* has in it more of God's image, than his government of the creatures."[20] That certainly is a creational concept, because it establishes government fundamentally and irrevocably in the constitution of human nature. In that respect it recalls Thomas Aquinas, for whom government is a natural and necessary extension of human sociality, that is, of the being of the human as a social and political animal. Government, according to Aquinas, is a rational instrument for managing the complexity of society, including the division of labor, and directing the society toward the achievement of the common good. It is ingredient in human association from its beginning and does not arise initially in response to fallen nature, although given the presence of sin in the world, it is charged with maintaining peace and order as elements of the common good.

However, this comparison breaks down when one perceives that Aquinas and Wesley were not actually talking about the same thing. When Aquinas spoke of government he was referring to an *institution of society*—one operated by some of its members for the benefit of the whole society. When Wesley spoke of government in the political image passage, he was referring to the *vocation of humankind,* not to an instrument of societal leadership and control, and assuredly not one managed by some human beings but not others. The dominion Aquinas saw in creation is that of the leaders of political society over the other members. The dominion Wesley saw is the common stewardship of the rest of the created order by the entire human race. Aquinas justified this natural dominion (contra Augustine) by contrasting it with the unnatural dominion of slavery—arguing that the former dominion is for the good of those who are led, whereas the latter is for the good of the owner of the slaves.[21] Wesley explained it as a vicarious role whereby humankind represents God in the governing of the world. Doubtless one can infer from Wesley's "political image" something concerning the rightful purposes of political institutions, but *government as an institution of society* is not what he is talking about in this commentary. Therefore, one cannot use it to conclude that the "powers of government are . . . the legitimate expressions of creation's natural order of political community" in the same unmediated sense that one can for Thomas Aquinas.

Another problem with using Wesley's comment on the political image to establish a creational theology of government and its purposes is that the political image is not simply creational. Granted, it is a constitutive element of human nature as created by God, but it does not stand alone or function rightly alone. It is a relational component of the whole image of God, and it directs political vocation in proper fashion only when the whole image is intact. Specifically, it depends on the *moral image of God*, the mirroring of the love of God, to disclose and clarify its purposes and to keep it rightly ordered. Political imaging employs the instrument of rationality, as does Aquinas's government as dominion, but reason is not its sufficient guide. There is no right ordering of government as political imaging of God except that which is ordered by love for God. If love for God is not present, the ordering cannot be right, nor can the purposes of the institutions be fully clear to those who are running them. Given these further considerations, it is impossible to derive a Wesleyan theology of political institutions from creation alone, or from creation unmodified by the loss of the moral image of God.

These arguments suffice to show that John Wesley would not have produced anything similar to the Thomistic understanding of political institutions even if he had developed his political image concept into a fully operational political theology. The use of the political image concept requires its incorporation into a theology providing for the recovery of the moral image of God. It does not generate a theological understanding of political institutions out of creation alone.

Of course, this line of reasoning pertains to what might have been had Wesley developed his theological understanding of politics out of his *image of God* theology—which he did not do. If, however, we follow the method of sifting through his statements looking for what might resemble Thomistic or other natural theology foundations for political thinking, what do we find? There are two concepts reminiscent of Aquinas, if not linked with him historically, in statements by Wesley related more or less to politics. One is the notion of "public good" (stated variously by Wesley as "national good" or "benefit of empire"), which suggests Aquinas's "common good." The other is natural law. The latter, of course, is a fundamental category for Aquinas and others in the Thomistic tradition. Do they offer evidence of an "order of creation" understanding of political institutions?

Actually, surrogate terms for "common good" appear rarely in Wesley's writings. I have found only one use of the term "public good." It appears in his comment on Romans 13:6, where Paul explains why Christians should pay taxes to the authorities. Wesley wrote: *"Because they are ministers* (officers) *of God for* the public good. *This very thing*—the public good."[22] That is his most authoritative use of the concept—because he employs it to explain Scripture. It is also the vaguest. It has no content given or implied contextually beyond the statement earlier in the passage that the authority is "the servant of God to execute wrath on the wrongdoer" (13:4*b*). Otherwise it is open-ended. This open-endedness can be read as an advantage, however. It allows a wide range of consideration of what might constitute the public good in particular situations, and does not restrict the authorities to protection from and punishment of wicked behavior.

In "Free Thoughts on the Present State of Public Affairs," Wesley includes among the desirable qualities of Ministers of the Crown that they should be "men attached to no party, but simply pursuing the general good of the nation."[23] The use of "general good" here, sets it in contrast to partisan loyalties, which Wesley took to be destructive of the interests of the whole society. It is connected also by implication with the concept of virtual representation, that is, with the moral capacity of virtuous men of property to consider broad public interests in their legislative actions, and not subordinate them to the narrower interests of the districts from which they were elected. In "A Calm Address to Our American Colonies," Wesley, following Samuel Johnson, insisted that "the supreme power in England has a legal right of laying any tax upon them for any end beneficial to the whole empire."[24] The language of "beneficial to the whole empire" is counterpoised explicitly to the asserted parochial rights of the colonies to legislate for their own interests. Implicitly, it is a denial in part of what would emerge later in Catholic social thought as the principle of subsidiarity.[25] Also, the language reflects the contention of the document—and of other writings by Wesley that are not dependent on Johnson—that authority is lodged in the supreme power by divine ordination, not in colonial governments by consent of the governed exercising individual natural rights. Divine ordination commissions government to act for the public good. A consent theory of authorization commissions it to make public good instrumental to private good.

These last two examples of corporate-good terminology illustrate that the content emerges with application in particular situations. That is testimony both to the flexibility of the concept and to the concreteness of Wesley's political thinking. Further evidence of concreteness is that in these two instances, Wesley uses "national" and "empire" rather than "common" as terms of reference transcending individual and parochial good. Those terms refer to finely woven corporate realities, rich with symbolism, deep in historical memories. They are not merely associations of individuals, needing leadership to help them create the social conditions for pursuing and enjoying particular goods. These observations make clear that Wesley is working conceptually in the context of the organic British community, not in that of Aristotelian-Thomistic philosophy. To see the difference, one need only consider the more abstract and explicitly Thomistic language of Richard Hooker:

> The good which is proper unto each man belongeth to the common good of all as a part of the wholes . . . perfection. But yet these two are thinges different; for men by that which is proper are severed, united they are by that which is common. Wherfore besides that which moveth each man in particular to seeke his private, there must of necessitie in all publique societies be also a generall mover, directing unto the common good and framing every mans particu-

lar to it. The end whereunto all government was instituted was *bonum publicum*, the universall or common good.[26]

John Wesley very well may have agreed with this argument. It was his inclination, however, to think about such matters from within the political community and with respect to community conflicts, rather than to reflect abstractly on the rational requirements of human beings in a state of nature. The political community as he understood it existed, of course, in a fallen world, and not in the condition in which it came from the hand of God. *Public good* receives its content from the quality and actualities of human existence in that world, not from the myth or *logos* of creation.[27]

If John Wesley established a natural law basis for political society, one would expect to find it in his sermon, "The Original, Nature, Properties, and Use of the Law." There Wesley writes on the nature of the universal moral law of God, clearly a natural law concept, and expounds on three manifestations of it, which correspond to eternal, natural, and divine law in Aquinas. Wesley does not use those terms, and his terminology is more neo-Platonic than Thomistic, but the categories clearly are recognizable. The origin of the moral law he traces

> even beyond the foundation of the world to that period, unknown indeed to men, but doubtless enrolled in the annals of eternity, when "the morning stars" first "sang together," being newly called into existence. It pleased the great Creator to make these his first-born sons intelligent beings, that they might know him that created them. For this end he endued them with understanding, to discern truth from falsehood, good from evil; and as a necessary result of this, with liberty, a capacity of choosing the one and refusing the other. By this they were likewise enabled to offer him a free and willing service. . . . To employ all the faculties which he had given them, particularly their understanding and liberty, he gave them a law, a complete model of all truth, so far as was intelligible to a finite being, and of all good, so far as angelic minds were capable of embracing it.[28]

With the subsequent creation of humankind, God "gave to this free, intelligent creature the same law as to his first-born children— not wrote indeed upon tables of stone, or any corruptible substance, but engraven on his heart by the finger of God. . . . Such was the original of the law of God. With regard to man, it was coeval with his nature. But with regard to the elder sons of God, it shone in its full splendour 'or ever the mountains were brought forth, or the earth and the round world were made.' "[29]

Subsequently in the sermon, Wesley speaks of this law as

> an incorruptible picture of the high and holy One that inhabiteth eternity. It is he whom in his essence no man hath seen or can see, made visible to men and angels. It is the face of God unveiled; God manifested to his creatures as they are able to bear it; manifested to give and not to destroy life; that they may see God and live. It is the heart of God disclosed to man. Yea, in some sense we may apply to this law what the Apostle says of his Son—it is "the streaming forth" or outbeaming "of his glory, the express image of his person."[30]

Continuing his poetic portrayal, Wesley asks, "What is the law but divine virtue and wisdom assuming a visible form? What is it but the original ideas of truth and good, which were lodged in the uncreated mind from eternity, now drawn forth and clothed with such a vehicle as to appear even to human understanding?" The law of God is "supreme, unchangeable reason; it is unalterable rectitude; it is the everlasting fitness of all things that are or ever were created. . . . a copy of the eternal mind, a transcript of the divine nature; yea, it is the fairest offspring of the everlasting Father, the brightest efflux of his essential wisdom, the visible beauty of the Most High."[31]

Even without specifically Thomistic language, the categories of eternal and natural law are clear and unmistakable in these passages. Nothing can destroy the moral law, because it is, after all, nothing less than the mind of God. However, the *knowledge* of the moral law is impaired quite seriously with the entry of sin into the world. "But it was not long before man rebelled against God, and by breaking this glorious law wellnigh effaced it out of his heart; 'the eyes of his understanding' being *darkened* in the same measure as his soul was 'alienated from the life of God.' "[32] Thereafter the possibilities of knowing the moral law depended not on reason as a natural and native faculty of humankind, but on prevenient grace and divine law.

And yet God did not despise the work of his own hands; but being reconciled to man through the Son of his love, he in some measure re-inscribed the law on the heart of his dark, sinful creature. "He" again "showed thee, O man, what is good" (although not as in the beginning), "even to do justly, and to love mercy, and to walk humbly with thy God."

And this he showed not only to our first parents, but likewise to all their posterity, by "that true light which enlightens every man that cometh into the world." But notwithstanding this light, all flesh had in process of time "corrupted their way before him"; till he chose out of mankind a peculiar people, to whom he gave a more perfect knowledge of his law. And the heads of this, because they were slow of understanding, he wrote on two tables of stone; which he commanded the fathers to teach their children through all succeeding generations.

And thus it is that the law of God is now made known to them that know not God. They hear, with the hearing of the ear, the things that were written aforetime for our instruction. But this does not suffice. They cannot by this means comprehend the height and depth and length and breadth thereof. God alone can reveal this by his Spirit.[33]

This strange passage yearns for additional explanation, which Wesley does not give. God's reconciliation to humankind through Christ precedes the giving of the Ten Commandments to Moses, a reversal of historical events that may imply a cosmic reconciliation in the halls of eternity foreshadowing the visible crucifixion. As a result of this (apparently transhistorical) reconciliation, God performs an act of partial new creation in which the law once again is written on the hearts of humankind, or specifically on the hearts of the first parents, but not as clearly and fully as in the original creation. The benefits of this reinscription are extended to all subsequent human beings through the prevenient activity of enlightening grace. Once more, however, it does not produce the intended results. Humankind misbehaves badly again, whereupon the patient and persistent God sends them a law written on stones. This law now is the necessary means for reading the expectations of God, which God's children should have been able to read in their own hearts. Yet even this form of presenting the law does not provide for self-evident comprehension. One must be a believer, led by the Spirit of God, to grasp content and meaning in their fullness.

Our present purposes do not require fuller analysis of this argument. It is sufficient to recognize that this view of the effect of the Fall on the ability of human reason to understand the law, and of the will to follow reason's understanding, eliminates the possibility of establishing a basis for law—and therefore for government—in nature apart from grace, or in creation in its original condition as distinguished from its refractions in the fallen order. The eternal moral law remains. Even though it is "wellnigh effaced" from the human heart, it is sufficiently knowable to establish responsibility for failure to obey it. However, even the minimal knowledge of this law requires the assistance of prevenient grace. The fuller knowledge is disclosed only through divine law and the workings of the spirit of God.

One must keep these important qualifications in mind when attempting to make sense of Wesley's few statements about the *natural image of God*.[34] The natural image includes, among other elements, the capacity to think rationally. It is the locus of reason. The natural image is distorted and disordered by the Fall, but not lost altogether. Rational capabilities remain in the human being. One may be tempted to suppose that the retention of this capability invites wider possibilities for a creational ethic, including a political ethic and a more extensive use of natural law, than I have been willing to allow. However, although reason retains its capabilities for technical rationality, and to some extent for distinguishing between right and wrong, it has no real access to *truth in a fundamental sense*. The proper working of reason, the fully informed working of reason, depends on the *moral image of God*—the reflection of the love of God. That aspect of the image of God has been lost completely in the Fall. Reason recovers its access to the truth of God and its true knowledge of God's eternal and natural law only with the recovery of the moral image.[35] The implications of this relationship of the images come to expression in Wesley's insistence that real knowledge of the law of God comes only by way of the enablements of prevenient grace and the offering of divine positive, that is, not natural, law.

There is a further and highly important reason for discounting Wesley's sermon on law as a provider of a natural law basis for Wesley's political ethic: he makes no mention of *human* law in reflecting on the types of law. Aquinas discussed four types of law: eternal, natural, human, divine. Human law, which he divided into civil law and custom, was the instrument used by government to direct the political society in its pursuit of the common good. Government was required to embody the natural (moral) virtues— wisdom, temperance, courage, and justice—in this directive role, and in doing so, also to assist the members of the society to acquire and practice them. Wesley's discussion covers the categories of eternal, natural, and divine law, but makes no reference whatever to human law in any form. Therefore he does not explore the relationship of human law to the other forms, including natural law. Moreover, when later in the sermon he discusses the uses of law (an adaptation of Calvin's threefold uses), he says nothing about a political use of the law.[36] Not surprisingly, there is no discussion in the sermon of the origins of government in creation, or of its obligation to shape human law in accordance with natural law.

The absence of attention to human law when Wesley writes about law in created nature with theological interest and some degree of theoretical exploration is matched by the absence of theological or theoretical interest when he makes practical application of natural law concepts. In his influential tract titled "Thoughts upon Slavery," Wesley offers an evident natural law argument in setting human law in contrast to justice. He wrote:

> The grand plea is, "They are authorized by law." But can law, human law, change the nature of things? Can it turn darkness into light, or evil into good? By no means. Notwithstanding ten thousand laws, right is right, and wrong is wrong still. There must remain an essential difference between justice and injustice, cruelty and mercy. So that I still ask, Who can reconcile this treatment of the Negroes, first and last, with either mercy or justice?[37]

In the next few lines he demands to know where the justice is of "depriving them of liberty itself, to which an Angolan has the same natural right as an Englishman, and on which he sets as high a value?" He then declares, "I absolutely deny all slave-holding to be consistent with any degree of natural justice."[38] His contrast of human law with justice and his use of terms such as *natural right* and *natural justice* all are natural law usages in political and social discourse. Similarly, his frequent references to the "heathen morality" or "heathen honesty" of the Turks and Romans carry the implication of moral understanding usable for governing and for personal relationships even where absence of Christian faith prevents the ordering of such matters according to the "imitable perfections" of God. That is a kind of concession to natural law, even though a grudging one. To these items of evidence one should add his contention, based on the writings of the Huguenot Quaker . Anthony Benezet, that the African peoples had well-designed, competently directed, political and social institutions before the Christian Europeans arrived to enslave them.[39]

The criticisms of slavery show Wesley's inclination to use the natural law concepts as critical principles for the examination of human law and practice, but no inclination to formulate a political ethic of which natural law is a central ingredient. He simply uses them in straightforward fashion as rhetorical weapons, apparently assuming that his readers will understand them and acknowledge their moral authority. This usage reflects his practice of speaking in vernacular moral language and common-sense terms when he cannot assume the hearers' or readers' commitment to scriptural truth.[40] It does not reflect a carefully considered natural law ethic. In any event, this rare usage is a thin foundation on which to attempt to build a case for his derivation of political institutions from created nature—especially in view of his apparent lack of interest in making that case for either human law or government.

Whatever Wesley's exposure to Aristotle may have been in his Oxford student days, there is no evidence of his having been influenced by the Aristotelian tradition in political philosophy, including its prominent representations in Aquinas and Hooker. That, of course, is the main line of "order of creation" thinking. Given Wesley's organic view of the British community, he might have experimented with the Aristotelian concept of the *polis*—used centrally by Aquinas—but did not seem to be aware of it or of the language of *perfect society*. Wesley thought of the human being as person-in-society, but did not speak in Aristotelian-Thomistic terms of the "political and social animal." In fact the Aristotelian concept of "political animal" (*zoon politikon*), requiring as it does active participation in the life of political society for the fulfillment of rational humanity, is quite the opposite of Wesley's deliberate and principled exclusion from politics of anyone without authorization to serve in office. Wesley shows no dependence at all on Thomas Aquinas, and does not cite him. Despite superficial similarities—as I have shown—he does not use Thomistic language, and in important respects does not think like Thomas.

Had Wesley wanted to draw on a more proximate, English treatise with explicit dependence on Thomistic political philosophy, he need only have turned to Richard Hooker's *Of the Laws of Ecclesiastical Polity.* Hooker's opposition to Roman Catholic control of the Church of England did not stop him from employing Aquinas's concepts of natural law, political society, common good, and natural dominion to explain and justify English political arrangements.[41] However, Wesley shows no more interest in—or awareness of—Hooker in this regard than he did with respect to Hooker's views on contract theory and the popular sources of political authority.

We are closer to Wesley's understanding of natural law, and therefore to the theological foundations of government, if we work with his frequent comments on "ordinary heathen morality" rather than with a Thomistic understanding of natural law rationally available to human law apart from grace for the pursuit of justice and other moral virtues. Wesley seems to speak disparagingly of such morality. Indeed, he is respectful of it without accepting it as a proper norm for Christians. It represents an operation of reason guided by prevenient grace for the regulation of behavior in a sinful world, and without the enlightenment of divine, that is, scriptural, law. It presupposes the residual presence, dimly seen, of aspects of the created order in a fallen world, or put differently, the created order perceived however dimly with the beneficent assistance of divine grace. Wesley does not offer an opinion on how the Romans and "Turks" (Muslims generally) rule kingdoms in an orderly and civil manner without the assistance of specifically Christian knowledge. Nevertheless, his references to Roman morality and to what "even the Turks know" imply the workings of this grace-assisted reasoning rather than reason operating confidently apart from grace and in preparation for it. It is God's means for allowing governance in a world where the knowledge of the law is "wellnigh effaced." If it is natural law, it is law for human nature where sin is presupposed. However, that interpretation places Wesley much closer to the great Reformers—to Luther and Calvin—than to Thomas Aquinas in his understanding of natural law.

To conclude this inquiry, one can agree that there are creational elements in Wesley's thinking about politics and the purposes of the state, and yet deny that they add up to anything resembling a classical "order of creation" position. Neither the methodology nor much of the substance of that position is present in the literature. If John Wesley ever said something to the effect that "the powers of government are . . . legitimate expressions of creation's natural order of political community," he did not publish it. If he thought in those terms, he did not leave significant traceable clues in his numerous items of political commentary. Creational elements in his thinking, such as they are, always appear in contexts where they are reactive rather than foundational, where the reality they help clarify already has the character of the fallen order. Because of this particular contextual character, knowledge of God's original intention depends on divine grace, not on the workings of reason apart from grace. And the ability to make good on what one understands thusly depends on the guidance and enablement of the Spirit of God, not on the capability of a will not yet restored to the love of God. Insofar as one can detect in Wesley's political thinking a nature-grace relationship, consciously active or only implicit, it is manifest as original nature and reason in the context of forgiving and renewing grace, not as grace building on nature and completing it.

Government as an "Order of Preservation"

In the history of Christian political thought, the principal alternative to a creation-based interpretation of the nature and purposes of government is one based on response to the effects of sin. Original sin destroys the harmony of creation, and in doing so generates a flood of passions that produce disorder and propensities to egoism, violence, civil unrest, and war. God's answer to this radical disruption of God's Eden is the imposition of an order enforced by coercion, not by love and consent. The substantive nature of the order is not reason so much as it is sin turned against itself—force against chaos. The sword is its symbol and instrument. Its principal political value is order, which supersedes the other political values of liberty and justice. Justice is understood to be the enforcement of positive law, not the enactment into law and public policy of greater equality and liberty. Inasmuch as government appears in human experience initially as an institution to preserve humankind against the devastating effects of sin, the tendency of some representatives of this position is to limit the functions of government to those having to do with order, protection, and punishment, thereby excluding educational and welfare functions, among others. The *locus classicus* of this general position is Martin Luther's "On Secular Authority."[42] In Wesley's more immediate ecclesiastical tradition, it is the explanation for government given in the Homily of 1570 (which Wesley does not cite, however).

It is much easier to find evidence of the "order of preservation" view of the origin and purposes of government in Wesley's writings than of the "order of creation" view. Commenting on the indigenous peoples of North America, he wrote in his journal of 2 December 1737 that "they have no religion, no laws, civil government . . . everyone doth what is right in his own eyes."[43] He repeated this observation in his sermon on "The Imperfection of Human Knowledge."[44] On one occasion he stated that giving up the laws of the country was like breaking the dams—an attitude that recalls Luther's view of government as a "dike against sin."[45] Similarly, Wesley saw the king as the substantial presence of order in British society, as the main bulwark against the flood of anarchy and tyranny threatened by the "warm men" for liberty, and as the wall defending Methodists, Dissenters, and sectarians from mob violence and religious persecution.

When Wesley spoke directly of the tasks of rulers at various levels, as he did in his sermon on "The Great Assize," he emphasized protective responsibilities:

> "How beautiful are the feet" of those who are sent by the wise and gracious providence of God to execute justice on the earth, to defend the injured, and punish the wrongdoer! Are they not "the ministers of God to us for good," the grand supporters of public tranquillity, the patrons of innocence and virtue, the great security of all our

temporal blessings? . . . Ye truly honourable men, whom God and the King have commissioned in a lower degree to administer justice, may not ye be compared to those ministering spirits who will attend the Judge coming in the clouds? May you, like them, burn with love to God and man! . . . May ye remain the establishers of peace, the blessing and ornaments of your country, the protectors of a guilty land, the guardian angels of all that are round about you![46]

As means to execute these duties, Wesley believed that the sword was given by God to the state as an instrument of capital punishment, and that states should have military forces sufficient to protect their people and territory.[47]

Even without the support of a clearly stated natural law ethic, Wesley's commitment to the role of law in government, and to its strict and at times severe enforcement, is clear and unambiguous. In the earlier chapter on "Political Obligation" we took note of his deep and long-standing respect for the English legal tradition, and of his quick, persistent, and knowledgeable use of the law to protect his own interests and those of his friends and followers. Frequently in his journals he commends officials when they enforce laws against rioters attacking the Methodists, and even more frequently reprimands them when they fail to do so (or when the officials themselves are the instigators of the attacks). He did not accept the excuse that officials were powerless to act in the face of contrary public sentiment or unrest. In his view the law possessed inherent majesty as well as intimidating power, which people would respect when magistrates had sufficient courage and commitment to justice to enforce it. His journal entry of 20 April 1752 records that "I preached at Wrangle, where we expected some disturbance, but found none. The light punishment inflicted on the late rioters (though their expense was not great, as they submitted before the trial) has secured peace ever since. Such a mercy it is to execute the penalty of the law on those who will not regard its precepts! So many inconveniences to the innocent does it prevent, and so much sin in the guilty."[48] His entry on 27 March 1753 reports that the Mayor of Chester, "a man of courage as well as honesty, will suffer no riot of any kind, so that there is peace through all the city."[49] Wesley reported again on 28 March that when a mob gathered, the mayor threatened to come read the Act of Parliament against rioting to them. "But it needed not. After his mind was known, none was so hardy as to make a disturbance."[50]

More often than not, Wesley's references to the proper and expected functions of government pertain to enforcement of the law, maintenance of the peace, protection of the innocent, and punishment of the wicked. These functions are prompted by the presence of sin in the world, not by the corporate needs present in original creation. All these evidences of "preservation" motifs would seem to support the argument that Wesley explained political institutions as necessary derivations from and provisions for the fallen condition of humankind, or at least assumed that they were. However, that conclusion would be hasty and in some respects erroneous. In the first place, Wesley assigned or allowed to government other tasks not inherently or even primarily subsumed under "order of preservation" functions. They include economic intervention on behalf of the poor, encouragement and enforcement of morality, education to civility, and maintenance of true religion. These functions receive attention elsewhere in this chapter. Here we note that Wesley's acceptance of them—indeed, his enthusiasm for some of them—implies an understanding of government not reducible to that of an institution existing mainly, if not solely, to deal with the effects of sin and therefore limiting its functions to preservation and punishment.

In the second place, Wesley did not appoint order as the exclusive or even the dominant political value, which he probably would have done were he a kind of Lutheran scholastic, thinking of political institutions simply as divinely instituted means of preserving the world against chaos. Wesley feared chaos and had great appreciation for order in society, and for the ordering function and effectiveness of government. However, he supported political order with a particular quality, specifically, the kind that confirmed and protected individual liberties. The distinction is important, not only because of the affirmation of liberty, but also because of the feedback of liberty on the concept of order itself. A government committed to the protection of liberty must be influenced by that commitment in the concept of its own power. Power defending liberty is responsible power, not irresponsible force whose central purpose is to bridle and tame wild beasts.

Leon Hynson has argued with considerable persuasiveness that *liberty* was Wesley's primary political value, and that his criterion for the legitimation of particular forms of government, as well as for particular regimes, was the degree to which they served to protect and advance liberty.[51] I incline more to the view that he saw order and liberty as correlative and interdependent political values, and did not assign one priority over the other. Wesley's attempts to calm the raging passions of civil unrest and colonial rebellion served—as he saw it—the cause of liberty by protecting the institutions that embodied and thereby supported liberty. They served also to maintain a necessary civil order against the disruptive agitation of extremists for liberty.[52] Order and liberty together—an ordered liberty or a liberty-filled order—are fundamental political values. However, the main point for present purposes is not whether liberty or order is the primary political value, but that Wesley did not believe order to be the dominant political value, however much he may have treasured it. Therefore he did not see the maintenance of order as the defining or exclusive task of government. Liberties arising from nature and history suggest a political ethic broader than one that takes its cue solely or primarily from the disordering effects of sin.

Perhaps the strongest argument against a strict "order of preservation" interpretation of Wesley's understanding of government and its purposes is this one: although Wesley identified government with the supreme power existing in any society, he never argued that sin-generated disorder in society required the coercive efforts and institutions of a supreme power. Had he done so, had he imagined government from the starkly negative portrayals of fallen human nature of his sermon "Original Sin" and his long essay "The Doctrine of Original Sin, according to Scripture, Reason, and Experience,"[53] it seems likely he would have inferred and subscribed to something like Tudor or Stuart absolutism. Instead he simply accepted supreme power, discerned in it the reality of government, and declared it authorized by divine ordination. With that method, he opened the way in theory to accept supreme power in monarchical, aristocratic, or democratic form. In actual practice, he supported with great conviction and enthusiasm a constitutional government with limited power and with mutual limitation of the power of its branches. His support measured *that particular kind of government* against alternative forms—Stuart Catholic absolutism and Wilkite democracy. It was not a defense of government in the abstract against the chaos of no government at all.

One might argue to the contrary that Wesley's statement that "giving up the laws of one's country is like breaking the dams" clearly suggests a concept of government derived from a view of the radical effects of the Fall. Actually, it was a prediction made from the standpoint of existing political arrangements, and was intended to confirm and protect them. It was not an inference from sinful chaos to government. Notice that he speaks of giving up laws, not centralized coercive force answerable only to God—if to anyone. The context of imagination is lawful government under threat, not wildly destructive disorder crying out for regulation of whatever kind. Moreover, the laws of which he speaks are rules of reason and public acknowledgment developed through long historical experience, not positivistic commands of the moment requiring no further justification. Wesley's warning of chaos in this eventuality presupposes original sin as a present tendency in persons under the laws and administering the laws. It does not infer the rule of law from original sin.[54]

In the light of this observation one can—and indeed must—draw the conclusion that the understanding of human nature implicit in Wesley's view of government and law is not the same as the one explicit in his theology of salvation. Human nature in the latter context is thoroughly sinful; human beings therefore are incapable of contributing to their own salvation by their own will and merit. Human nature in the former context is ambiguous; human beings are capable of governing and capable of obeying the law, but the inclination to disobey and to turn government to their own selfish purposes is always present. This more Niebuhrian, less Lutheran, view of human nature allows to government more and different functions than those derived solely from a concept of *order of preservation*. It implies also—as I argued in an earlier chapter—that Allen Lamar Cooper clearly is wrong in claiming that Wesley derived a notion of political incompetence from his concept of original sin.[55]

There is no doubt that Wesley thought of preservation and protection as self-evident and irreducible responsibilities of government, and considered governments failures in their calling when they failed at those tasks—whatever else they might do. No truly Wesleyan theory of political institutions can omit or minimize the work of preservation and protection, or seek to discard the instruments of force that empower it. Nevertheless, a comprehensive analysis of Wesley's writings and comments on politics demonstrates clearly that he saw no simple linkage of political institutions with original sin as their source, and therefore drew no simple inference limiting the range of governmental responsibilities to dealing with the effects of sin. His decision to place the work of magistrates in the service of the public good implies a much more open concept. Certain of his other statements on the tasks and purposes of government confirm it.

Contextual Theology—Not Paradigmatic

Neither creation nor preservation appears as a dominant theological paradigm in John Wesley's thinking about the responsibilities of government, even though both play a role. Wesley does not deduce a theory of what governments are to do and not do from either concept. In Wesley's political thinking, theology works contextually. That is true at a more abstract level, where creation is encountered and perceived only in a context of human sinfulness, and sin always is limited and challenged by a context of grace. It is true also in the concreteness of politics. The appeal to natural law is a critique of existing law, not an effort to define a political ethic apart from faith. The political acknowledgment of original sin is as a persistent and permanent tendency of behavior even in organized and "civilized" societies, not as a reading of human nature that requires a corresponding theory of the state. This contextual engagement of theology fits in with what we know of Wesley's political style. He is a reactive thinker, a polemicist—not a systematic theorist. He tends to play the hand that is dealt him. Theology comes into play when issues arise that seem to require its presence. An advantage of this style is that it leaves the way open for government to address emergent public needs, and does not restrict it prematurely to dogmatically defined tasks. A disadvantage is that it does not disclose or clarify a dominant theological paradigm that moves effectively from one context to another.

A RANDOM CALL FOR ECONOMIC INTERVENTION

Wesley's tract from 1773 on "Thoughts on the Present Scarcity of Provisions" is a call for government intervention in the economy that offers no justification—from creation, Fall, or any other perspective—for an economic role for government, and suggests no need to do so.[56] In that tract Wesley offers a multicausal and systemic examination of widespread and dire conditions of hunger and unemployment, and proposes government policy to correct them. Persons are hungry because downsizing has created massive unemployment and because profit-oriented changes in the economy have reduced the supply of foodstuffs and thereby driven up the prices. Grain for bread is converted into distilled liquors; oats for breakfast cereal are fed to the horses of the wealthy; acreage formerly used to raise sheep now is devoted to raising horses for the French luxury export trade and for domestic luxury use; the enclosure of lands to form large estates has eliminated small farms and gardens, which fed whole families. To counteract these economic trends and restore employment and reduce food prices, Wesley suggests a number of measures—most of which involve interventionary government policy. He proposes prohibition of the making of distilled liquors,[57] the settling of hefty taxes on luxury horses (especially horses for export) and carriages, the elimination of other taxes that drive up prices on necessities, curbing luxury by law and example, reducing the national debt (by simply erasing half of it!), and the canceling of useless and unwarranted pensions.

Wesley does not seem to use any general economic theory to guide and support his analysis, but his implication is that a free market system allowed to run its course without societal and governmental restraints creates radically unequal distribution of goods and income, socially and humanly dysfunctional allocations of scarce resources, and therefore unemployment and hunger.[58] He neither proposes nor opposes a welfare system for such conditions. Instead, he argues for governmental policies to provide work by changing the allocations of the economic system. His tax proposals are targeted, not general. That is, he advocates increasing some taxes to encourage changes in investment, and decreasing others to make existing goods and resources available to more people. He says nothing about raising or lowering taxes as such as a means to restrain or encourage economic growth and productivity. It is noteworthy that Wesley does not attribute unemployment to laziness on the part of the unemployed, but rather to victimization of workers by the economic system. On other occasions he denounces the insistence of the well-to-do that persons are poor because they are lazy. His teaching on this point was either forgotten or rejected in the nineteenth century by some of the affluent Methodists in England and elsewhere, who accused the poor and unemployed of being the causes of their own distress.

We need not pause to inquire whether Wesley's analyses were correct or whether his proposals made economic sense. Surely one would like to hear more explanation of the suggestion to abolish half the national debt! For present purposes, the importance of the tract is its demonstration that Wesley did not limit the purposes of government to those of order and defense, but left the definition of purpose open to varying circumstances while assuming that the protective functions of government always were constant in principle. In this case he urged the government to use its legislative and taxing powers to address critical human needs through direct intervention in the economy. He offers no explicit theory of government, its responsibilities and limits. Specifically, he does not use the occasion to propose a general theory of government intervention, and certainly not of centralized government control of the economy. Nor does he address the problem in terms of "public good." People are unemployed, poor, and hungry. They need help. Obviously, the persons who profit from the system are not going to help them, nor will the miraculous workings of the market system deliver goods, services, and employment to the points where they are needed most. Therefore the government should come to the assistance of those who are placed in such dire straits by the efficient and apparently logical workings of the profit-oriented economic system. Wesley evidently sees no violation of a divine mandate for government in this proposal. To the contrary, one supposes he would discern a violation of divine mandate were the government simply to ignore the unemployed, the poor, the hungry; and an even greater violation were the government to place its power at the service of those who profit from the system.

John Wesley did not make comparable analyses and proposals in other tracts or sermons. One may be tempted, therefore, to dismiss it as a one-time (or "one-off," as the British say) comment with no serious implications for the responsibilities and limits of government. That surely would be a mistake. The sentiments of this tract reflect Wesley's deep and abiding concern for the poor, his suspicion of economic power, and his openness to the ranging concerns of government.[59] In no way does the tract contradict Wesley's conviction that government is in fundamental respects an *order of preservation*. It may imply an extension of the protective functions of government into the workings of the economic system and on behalf of those who do not have sufficient power to compete and to protect themselves against the most inhumane effects of market efficiency. That would be entirely consistent with the prophetic attitude toward government in the Old Testament. However, what is primary here is compassion, not protection. The essay shows that—for Wesley—the functions of government need not be inferred from either original creation or original sin, inasmuch as he neither appeals to nor implies either of those sources in this random call for economic intervention. Apparently the uses of government are adaptable, in his view, to a variety of human needs without requiring a formal or specific theological justification.

THEOLOGY, NOT ANTHROPOLOGY

The theological source of Wesley's call for government intervention in the economy on behalf of the poor, hungry, and unemployed ceases to be a mystery when we recall that a basic principle of his ethic is the imitation of God. "By Methodists," he wrote, "I mean a people who profess to pursue (in whatsoever measure they have attained) holiness of heart and life, inward and outward conformity in all things to the revealed will of God; who place religion in an uniform resemblance of the great Object of it; in a steady imitation of him they worship in all his imitable perfections; more particularly in justice, mercy, and truth, or universal love filling the heart and governing the life."[60] In the sermon on "The General Deliverance," after reviewing the suffering imposed on animal life by human sinfulness, Wesley suggests that these considerations "may encourage us to imitate him whose mercy is over all his works."[61] If *imitatio dei* is fundamental to Wesley's understanding of moral responsibility, it is not surprising that he should call on government to intervene with justice and mercy on behalf of those members of the society who have been stripped bare by the workings of the economic system. He does not need to inquire whether such intervention is suggested or legitimated by Creation or Fall, or even by the public good. He need ask only about the justice and mercy of God.

Is *imitation of God*, then, Wesley's fundamental political principle? Does one draw conclusions for the responsibilities of government by observing the nature and workings of God, rather than by inferring them from human nature in whatever condition? That prospect appears confirmed by his use of the *analogy of God* in his sermon the "The Great Assize." With judges and magistrates seated before him, Wesley asked:

> And does not every one of these represent not only an earthly prince, but the Judge of the earth. . . . O that all these "sons of the right hand of the Most High" may be holy as he is holy! Wise with the "wisdom that sitteth by his throne," like him who is the eternal wisdom of the Father! No respecter of persons, as he is none; but "rendering to every man according to his works": like him inflexibly, inexorably just, though pitiful and of tender mercy! So shall they be terrible indeed to them that do evil, as "not bearing the sword in vain." So shall the laws of our land have their full use and due honour, and the throne of our King be still "established in righteousness."[62]

A few lines later he shifts the focus of the analogy to the angels ("ministering spirits"); however, the content of the ethic is the same, because the angels are understood to be imitating the divine character and action. Public officials understand the nature of their duties and execute them rightly by observing and imitating God.[63]

The implication is clear: any *Wesleyan* theological thinking about the nature and purposes of government must take as its starting point God and the ways of God, not human nature whether as created or as fallen. This distinction, of course, is not a dichotomy. Christian political thought of whatever brand inevitably has to do with a Christian understanding of human nature. However, human nature is not an entity apart from God from which a theory of government can be inferred. If humankind indeed has a "nature," it is whatever reality is conferred by God in creation, distorted by sin, and renewed in redemption. That is the notion conveyed in Wesley's undeveloped concept of the *political image*. The human reality of *political image* is a vocation to imitate the governance of God. To know the meaning of governing is to know the ways of God's governing. To infer functions of political institutions from human nature is to infer them from human existence in the divine-human relationship.

If John Wesley indeed was thinking in those terms, it helps explain why he could assign or allow a variety of responsibilities to government without setting dogmatic limits. What government is expected to do can be as varied as the range of concern God has with the world. That is imprecise, of course, and it may leave kings and magistrates somewhat confused as to what they should do *as a matter of course* and without consulting divine oracles. Wesley left no doubt that what they should do as a matter of course was to administer justice, that is, to enforce the law. Enforcement of law is an *order of preservation* function. It is fundamental to Wesley's understanding of governmental responsibility. At times he argued the pragmatic necessity of this work. He noted, however, that God administers justice to the world (sometimes using the figure of Christ as judge). Public officials at all levels should imitate the divine practice, being strict in the administration of justice, but tempering it nonetheless with mercy. Nevertheless, using the model of God's governance, they are not restricted to this central function. Government should act also when there are public needs not reducible to law enforcement, and especially when there are needs that evoke the justice, compassion, and mercy of God. Those are the principles that derive from an understanding of God and God's ruling as sources of a theological understanding of government.

An obvious objection is that this concept is an advisory for Christian believers, not for just anyone who happens to be a public official. That is true, of course. It is why Wesley reverted often to speaking in natural law, logical, and common-sense terms, rather than quoting Scripture. However, if theological insight is true, one does not abandon it simply because it is not widely shared. One engages in public debate to illuminate political reality beyond what may be perceived routinely and perhaps consensually in natural law, logic, and common sense.

Unfortunately, as we know, John Wesley did not provide any model for thinking through political issues using this method. His participation in public debate, like his political thinking, was polemical, reactive, sporadic, and discontinuous. Doubtless he assumed that he was illuminating political reality beyond the usual norms and methods of political discourse, but he did not offer much by way of systematic inquiry into or illustration of the political meaning of imitating God. It would have been quite useful, for example, for him to have explained and defended the notion of the educational function of the state that is implicit in his letters from Georgia to Mr. Verelst and the Trustees. Is that function perhaps an imitation of the wholemaking work of God expressed in the more mature understandings of *shalom* and the Christian doctrine of reconciliation? If so, does imitating God's wholemaking work have wider implications for political responsibility and action?

Perhaps I have distorted the issue for Wesley by stating it in a form for teleological thinking, that is, as an inquiry into the purposes of government, whereas in politics Wesley basically was a contextual thinker. The inquiry into purposes and functions of political institutions may not be so important to someone who feels at home in the surrounding institutions and generally knows without reflecting on the matter what they are supposed to do. Wesley's political context was the organic British community, not the contractual society formed by John Locke's individuals living in a state of nature. Government for Wesley was a constitutive element of community, not an instrument of individual interests. The community is home to its members, a definer of identity, and also the guardian of political values. Government is instrumental, to be sure, and in particular to individual liberties, but the instrumentality is embedded in the community, its memories and symbols, and is not simply attached to particular values as means to an end.

Wesley's contextual method of political thinking is apparent also in his constitutionalism. The constitutional order Wesley admired and supported was a product of history, not an intellectual creation out of theological dogma. It emerged historically, as I showed earlier, as a representational alternative between absolutism and democracy. Wesley accepted it because it was given to him providentially, and because he perceived it to be righteous and just. He may have felt little need to open up some questions of purpose that did not seem to him to be live ones, or to look for theological reasons for functions of government, which seemed to him self-evidently to be settled and appropriate.

Nevertheless, he should have faced the issues of governmental purpose more directly, with more engagement between the central lines of his theology and his occasional flares of political commentary, and with more critical awareness of transient cultural elements in what he took to be certain truth. His society was fluid, not fixed. Issues of political theory were in contention. It was a time to draw together the scattered elements of his political thinking, and to provide a formulation with coherence and theological depth. It was a time to demonstrate both to Britain and to the Methodist movement the possibilities of understanding politics in terms of the imitation of God. Wesley exposed the lines of a theological method for political thinking that proceeded primarily from the understanding of God, not primarily from theological anthropology. However, he did not use it consistently and systematically in reflecting on the nature and purpose of political institutions. That task remains as a constructive one for Wesleyan theology.

One can say at minimum, however, that Wesley did not confer a restrictive notion of government on those who would follow him in the Methodist movement. Wesleyan theology, I have argued, cannot avoid the elements of order and defense in developing a constructive understanding of governmental responsibilities, but neither is it confined to those elements. In nontheological language, Wesley's concept of public good encourages and requires government's attention to other constant and significant needs and interests, as well as to previously unrecognized ones as they emerge in community experience and public consciousness. In theological language, Wesley's concept of the imitation of God—applied to government—requires of government sensitivities, energies, and commitments that mirror the divine compassion, justice, and mercy.

CHAPTER TEN

RIGHTS AND LIBERTIES

John Wesley was a fervent and unwavering defender of English liberties, but was he also an advocate of human rights? Writers on Wesley's politics in recent decades, led by Bernard Semmel and Leon Hynson, with more recent contributions by Theodore Jennings and Theodore Runyon, have argued the affirmative.[1] Semmel and Hynson contend that as Wesley matured politically and became more prominent nationally, he left behind his conservative formation in divine right thinking and passive obedience and became an advocate for liberal political values and virtues— using natural rights terminology as the approximation of what later would be termed "human rights." Semmel suggests furthermore that Wesley's theology prompted and confirmed this movement, and in doing so, encouraged him to adopt individualistic and contractarian concepts characteristic of the Enlightenment. He asked, "Could such views of universal redemption, free will, and tolerance fail to make a decided impact upon Wesley's political ideas, leading him, even as it had the Arminian Grotius, to the political theory of the Enlightenment—with its liberal individualism, its view of free contract, and of natural rights—which seemed so much a translation of Arminian theological doctrine?"[2]

All of the writers mentioned point to Wesley's vigorous arguments for religious liberty and against slavery; to his passionate concern for civil liberties of various kinds—security of life, person, and property, and freedom to speak and to publish; and to his refusal to accept the claim that racial differences correspond to differences in moral qualities and intellectual capabilities. The effect—and doubtless the intention—of their revision is to give John Wesley a different political portrait, rescuing him from the archconservative renderings of earlier Wesley scholars, bringing

303 ——

him closer to the democratic politics he resisted so strenuously, and making him more accessible to and usable for present and succeeding generations of persons in the Wesleyan movement. A further consequence—certainly intended by the writers—is the reaffirmation of human rights, recruiting Wesley as their champion.

There is no doubt that these writers are correct in arguing that the concept of natural rights (read later as *human* rights) played a role—and an important one—in Wesley's political thinking. Previous chapters of this book have confirmed that point by exploring Wesley's advocacy of rights and liberties, and noting occasions when he invoked justice and natural right to criticize slavery and religious repression. But was the role played by natural/human rights determinative of his political thinking? Was it fundamental, or was it secondary? Jennings contends that "for Wesley the question of human rights is the decisive norm for the development of a political ethic. It is this principle, rather than its specific application in terms of a constitutional monarchy, that is Wesley's lasting contribution to a Christian political ethic."[3] But if John Wesley was so committed to human or natural right as political fundament, why did he deny its application to political participation and to the authority of governments? Why did he accord primacy to the notions of divine ordination and government as supreme power? Why did he not follow the example of John Locke, and make natural right the foundation of a theory of government? These are not trivial or incidental questions. They pertain to the issue at the center of Wesley's political thinking, namely, political authority. Wesley clearly rejected the relevance of natural rights to political authority and participation, and placed any possible ownership of natural rights outside the political process. How, then, can natural or human rights be the "decisive norm" for his political ethic?

Central to the argument for John Wesley as a natural rights thinker is that he derived certain notions of rights and liberty from original nature as created by God. *Creation* and *nature* figure prominently in Wesley's political thinking, specifically and primarily with regard to liberty and rights. But they are not as prominent therein as *history* and *community*. The rights and liberties of which he is advocate and defender arise in history in most cases. They are anchored and interpreted in the customs and laws of the British community, and most notably in its constitutions—the ancient one and the arrangements of 1689. One does not grasp the meaning of rights and liberties for Wesley without perceiving that he views them in the mesh of institutions and traditions. Failing that perception, one risks translating his liberties into abstractions, his communitarian sentiments into contracts (as does Semmel), his social relatedness into C. B. MacPherson's "possessive individualism."[4] With that perception, however, one can see that Wesley's rights and liberties are of various kinds: traditional and prescriptive, inherited, concessions of government, legal, constitutional, and natural. The concept of *natural rights* has an honored place in the list, but it does not dominate his comprehensive view of rights and liberties, nor does it appear at the beginning of political and moral theory. It is one concept among several, and it comes into view when societal arrangements or the actions of the powerful abuse human beings—especially human beings in their relation to God—in truly fundamental ways. In those cases, as in Wesley's political ethic as a whole, it functions more as a critical concept than as a constructive one.

To these caveats concerning the role and primacy of natural right in Wesley's political ethics, one must add that *rights* are not separable from *duties* in his ethical thinking, and that when confronted with what he perceived to be chaos and political dissolution, he emphasized the *duty of obedience* over claims arising from natural rights philosophy. I shall have more to say about the relationship of duty to right later on. Here I mention it in order to challenge any claim or implication that *right* stands above or apart from *duty* as a principle of his political ethics.

One may conclude too readily that if the natural/human rights concept is not as central to his politics as we should like it to be, at least the discernible and predictable development of his thinking moves in that direction. Perhaps that is true to some extent, but fundamentally the issue is not one of inadequate development but of theological intractability. Wesley simply could not grow out of the concepts of supreme power and divine ordination that excluded natural rights from a role in political authorization and participation. He would have had to change his theological orientation to politics in order to overcome that exclusion. That is a problem we have seen in previous chapters, and one to which we must return in this one.

THE SOCIAL LOCATION OF LIBERTY

John Wesley began his tract "Thoughts upon Liberty" with these words: "All men in the world desire liberty; whoever breathes, breathes after this, and that by a kind of natural instinct antecedent to art or education. Yet at the same time all men of understanding acknowledge it as a rational instinct. For we feel this desire, not in opposition to, but in consequence of, our reason."[5] To "antecedent to art and education" he might have added, "and antecedent to sin as well." Liberty is a universal human desire arising out of rationality. It is elemental to human nature as created by God. Furthermore, it is more than simply a *desire*. Liberty is a functional necessity of being human and realizing one's true humanity. In his sermon "The General Deliverance," Wesley wrote: "He was, after the likeness of his Creator, endued with *understanding*, a capacity of apprehending whatever objects were brought before it, and of judging concerning them. He was endued with a *will*, exerting itself in various affections and passions; and, lastly, with *liberty*, or freedom of choice, without which all the rest would have been in vain, and he would have been no more capable of serving his Creator than a piece of earth or marble. He would have been as incapable of vice or virtue as any part of the inanimate creation. In these, in the power of self-motion, understanding, will, and liberty, the natural image of God consisted."[6] Liberty in the first case is an inherent psychological disposition. In the second, it is a theologically defined ingredient of the natural image of God, essential to recognizing and acting on the distinction between vice and virtue and to the human vocation of serving the Creator.

These are Wesley's constructions of the notion of natural liberty. Natural liberty with its power of free choice in turn is the basis of the argument for natural rights. There are problems, however:

natural liberty does not transfer directly from original creation into the concreteness of human existence either in its theological mode as freedom of the will or in its psychological mode as rational instinct. In neither case does it operate in experience simply as original natural endowment. Because of humankind's fall into sin, the original rational liberty of the image of God disappears into a will in bondage—a will incapable of doing anything pleasing to God. There is no "free will" for humankind as such in historical existence. The will that is free is the will released from bondage by the grace of God, not the will described mythically in the original structure of the image of God. John Wesley built his theology of grace on this fact. The distinction between Wesleyans and Calvinists is not that the former believe in natural liberty and the latter do not, but that Wesleyans believe that the prevenient, justifying, sanctifying grace of God opens the way to a recovery of lost liberty for all human beings, whereas the Calvinists believe that liberating grace is much more economical and selective in its elections. However, even Wesley did not believe in the persistence through time of the natural liberty of original creation, but rather in the possibility for liberty of the will in the context of grace.

Even without this qualification, it is not clear that *natural right* is a valid inference from *natural liberty* in the theological mode. The moral issue for the will in the natural image of God is not right, but responsibility. The liberty that is an element of the natural image works through the political image of God following the lead of the moral image. Its first order of business is obeying and loving God, not defining rights and claiming them.

More directly pertinent to the question of natural or human rights, Wesley does not allow the psychological disposition to liberty to operate as abstract rationality or rational instinct without qualification. Liberty for Wesley becomes meaningful, definable, and defensible when it has a specific social location. One can see the transition to that conclusion in the opening pages of "Thoughts upon Liberty." At the outset he seems to be speaking in praise and affirmation of liberty as such.

Was it not from this principle, that our British forefathers so violently opposed all foreign invaders; that Julius Caesar himself, with his victorious legions, could make so little impression upon them; that the Generals of the succeeding Emperors sustained so many losses from them; and that, when at length they were overpowered, they rather chose to lose all they had than their liberty; to retire into the Cambrian or Caledonian mountains, where, if they had nothing else, they might at least enjoy their native freedom?

Hence arose the vehement struggles of the Cambro-Britons through so many generations against the yoke, which the Saxons first, and afterwards the English, strove to impose upon them; hence the struggles of the English Barons against several of their Kings, lest they should lose the blessing they had received from their fore-fathers; yea, the Scottish nobles . . . would no more bear to be enslaved than the Romans. All these therefore, however differing from each other in a thousand other respects, agreed in testifying the desirableness of liberty, as one of the greatest blessings under the sun.[7]

When he brings the advocacy of liberty out of the heroic and leg-endary past and into his own time, he is more reserved—even to the point of being negative. He speaks of "the whole kingdom . . . panting for liberty," and mocks the association of liberty with "our great patriot," that is, John Wilkes—for whom he has intense dis-like. "Why is all this, but because of the inseparable connexion between Wilkes and liberty; liberty that came down, if not fell, from heaven; whom all England and the world worshippeth?"[8] Evidently there are aspects of liberty that John Wesley does not like. Therefore he turns to definitions of liberty to gain clarification. Does liberty include freedom to murder, steal, kidnap, rape; to assassinate rulers? Obviously not—these are rhetorical questions. Wesley is confident no sane person would allow such liberties, but would insist on a definition of liberty that is morally defensible. "What is that liberty, properly so called," he then asks, "which every wise and good man desires? It is either religious or civil."[9] The free rational instinct now settles into identifiable shapes, and only in these shapes is it allowable. For the next several pages he proceeds to provide definitions and explanations of these two liberties.

Where Wesley arrives in this transformation of the understand-ing of liberty is not where he started out. At the outset of the essay he was speaking of liberty mainly as self-determination without limit. His examples of expression of the desire for liberty involved resistance to alien domination and to the centralization of power in a particular country. When he comes to the point of defining liberty specifically as religious and civil liberty, he is talking about protections provided to individuals by the constitutional, governmental, and legal structure of a particular country. He retains the concept of self-determination, but with less choice and less vulnerability. Liberty now has a social location, and a definition to fit the location. Wesley's intention certainly is to defend liberty as he has defined it. His intention also, if not primarily, is to defend the structure and substance of its social location. The notion of liberty set forth at the beginning of the essay fits well with a concept of natural right. The notion of particular liberties in a social location carries the implication of positive or historically emergent rights. Given Wesley's understanding of particular liberties existing in and requiring a social location, one must ask whether there is any further place in his thinking for natural rights.

Gospel or spiritual liberty is the freedom to love God and neighbor, granted to those who emerge from the fallen condition of humankind by divine grace. It is celebrated in the words of Charles Wesley's great hymn: "He breaks the power of canceled sin, he sets the prisoner free." However, the parallel between the natural liberty of the image of God and the natural, rational instinct of liberty does not mean that the social location of liberty is a fallen condition comparable to the sinful state of the will in bondage. *Social location* is not the result of a fall; it is the normal condition of human nature. In that sense, it manifests the order of creation. However, the fact that liberties must be defined and protected in social locations testifies to the presence of sin. It would seem, therefore, that these liberties are never purely natural. They are never simply *order of creation*. In every case they are experienced and valued as *order of preservation*. Inevitably their function—and to a large extent their reality—must be understood from the interior of historical experience and not from some prehistorical or extrahistorical concept of what is natural or creational. Even if one finds some uses of the concept of natural right in Wesley's political and social rhetoric— and the uses are there—one still must attend to their meaning and function in a social location.

RIGHTS AND THE POLITICAL PROCESS

The Political Exclusion of Natural Rights

The clearest evidence that John Wesley was not a consistent human rights or natural rights thinker is that he rejected the concept of political rights based on individual natural rights and did not include political rights in any listing of civil liberties. In political society, according to Wesley, the concept of *right* belongs in essence to the supreme power, not to the members of the society. The supreme power has the right to tax the people, to legislate generally, to dispose of life, liberty, and property—without the consent of the people. The people have no right at all to be represented in the deliberations and decisions of the government, and no inherent right to vote in the election of those who deliberate and decide. Moreover, they have no right to be free of the command and control of government, that is, no right to independence. However, they do have a clear *duty* to obey those who—under God—are set in authority over them.

This assignment of rights to the government and therefore not to the people has several justifications (which I shall summarize, for the most part, because they have been discussed in other chapters). First, it derives from the nature of supreme power as sovereign authority. The right to decide and command, to tax and to legislate, is inherent in the nature of sovereignty, which is indivisible. Assignment of political rights to the people denies the nature of sovereignty and thereby undermines the authority of the government. Second, the supreme and sovereign power is ordained of God to exercise whatever power it has. Its authority descends from above in hierarchical fashion; it does not rise up from below. There is no defensible claim to authorization of government by individual right of consent or popular consent. Third, political society differs in fundamental respects from an alleged presocial "state of nature." Whatever may be said for natural rights in a presocial condition, the same arguments do not apply to rights in political society.

This third justification requires further explanation. In a notable and sometimes misunderstood passage in "A Calm Address to Our American Colonies," Wesley (and before him Samuel Johnson) concedes that there may be such things as rights in a state of nature, but then argues against their relevance to the issue of representation for the purpose of taxation.

> But you say, you "are entitled to life, liberty, and property by nature; and that you have never ceded to any sovereign power the right to dispose of these without your consent." While you speak as naked sons of nature, this is certainly true. But you presently declare, "Our ancestors, at the time they settled these colonies, were entitled to all the rights of natural-born subjects within the realm of England." This likewise is true; but when this is granted, the boast of original rights is at an end. You are no longer in a state of nature, but sink down into colonists, governed by a charter. If your ancestors were subjects, they acknowledged a Sovereign; if they had a right to English privileges, they were accountable to English laws, and had ceded to the King and Parliament the power of disposing, without their consent, of both their lives, liberties, and properties. And did the Parliament cede to them a dispensation from the obedience which they owe as natural subjects? or any degree of independence, not enjoyed by other Englishmen?[10]

The location changes, and with it the concept of rights. In a pre-social condition ("naked sons of nature")—which, in Wesley's view, never existed—one can speak of natural rights. Also, one can claim rightly, *in that condition only*, that one never has ceded such rights to any sovereign. However, in the context of English political society, one must speak not of natural rights but of the "rights of natural-born subjects." These are not the same rights, although they may sound the same if the passage is not read carefully. They are rights of the people of England, not rights of human beings as such. They presuppose a history of the development and acquisition of such rights in the context of the ethos of English society. Essentially, they are Edmund Burke's *Rights of Englishmen*, not Thomas Paine's *Rights of Man*. One is born to the rights as a member of this society and not another. One does not own them in the divinely crafted ontology of one's human being.[11]

Moreover, these rights of the English presuppose the preexistence of government and a relationship to government. The government acknowledges and protects the "rights of natural-born subjects"; it is not answerable to any alleged natural rights of the subjects. To Johnson and Wesley the explanation is plain: the mere fact of existence in a political society, and of the acceptance of English rights, implies that one has ceded to the supreme power—directly or indirectly, explicitly or tacitly—the rights that one claims to have had in the natural, presocial condition. Whatever rights one may claim now are defined, allowed, and protected within this societal context. They are not deduced from human nature. The "natural-born subjects" have a duty of obedience to the government that protects the rights, but not natural rights claims against the government.

The colonists also put forward *ancestral* or *inherited* rights as the basis for their asserted rights to organize their own colonial governments, elect their own representatives, pass their own laws, assess their own taxes, and to do this independently of the control of the British Parliament. Wesley accepts the notion of ancestral rights, but denies that they offer the entitlements claimed by the colonists. In the first place, most of the "ancestors" did not have the right to vote. Voting is not an inherent right of all Englishmen; it is the privilege of a few. Obviously, therefore, it does not establish a natural right against the sovereignty of the British government. Moreover, Wesley insists, the colonial ancestors made their rights of no effect by emigrating to America, where they could not exercise them effectively in relation to British institutions and "within the realm of England." What the colonists have now are *conferred* rights, which they received through a charter granted them by king and Parliament. These are real and comfortable rights, Wesley insists, and they support abundant and important liberties. However, the charter of the colony is their source, guarantee, and limit. There is no other form of entitlement, especially no appeal to nature. Acceptance of the charter and its benefits implies and requires acceptance of the sovereignty of the British government, and acknowledgment of the duty to obey it. To summarize: the colonists "do inherit all the privileges which their ancestors had; but they can inherit no more. . . . You are the descendants of men who either had no votes, or resigned them by emigration. You have therefore exactly what your ancestors left you; not a vote in making laws, nor in choosing legislators; but the happiness of being protected by laws, and the duty of obeying them."[12] The colonies "have certainly a right to all the privileges granted them by royal charters; provided those privileges be consistent with the British constitution."[13] However, the "right to the privileges" is not a natural right. It is a concession of the government, a matter of governmental self-limitation—not an inherent or external claim against it.

Political Rights as Positive Rights

Under the terms of Wesley's argument, all rights in society that pertain to political authority are positive rights of some sort, not natural rights. By *positive*, in this case I mean rights that emerge in time and not from eternity, and that are traceable to historical conflicts and decisions, not to the designs of God or nature. They are rights of Englishmen, ancestral or inherited rights, rights conferred through charter. They are not *human rights*. Such rights have the quality and substance of history and society, not of metaphysics and ontology. They are *posited*, not *discovered*.

In Wesley's treatment of positive rights, moreover, there is a notable difference among kinds of rights. This difference raises a question of consistency in his argument concerning the authority of government: there are rights conferred by the government, and there are rights of Englishmen and ancestral rights that are not conferred by government. The two types of rights are morally and legally different. The former are acts of government with no supporting historical memory and no institutional embodiment prior to their enactment and conferral. They reinforce the authority of government, because an action of government is their only source. By implication, what the government gives, the government can take away. The latter are elements in the ancient constitution—a social and moral reality often assumed or implied by Wesley but never mentioned by him in explicit terms. Even without being designated *natural* or *human*, these powerful historic rights establish claims against the supreme power, and by implication qualify its sovereignty. The government cannot take them away rightly, because it did not give them.

The possibility of limitations to supreme power, manifest in this distinction between types of rights, is reinforced by Wesley's statement that the provisions of the charter granted to the colonists must be in accord with the British constitution. Implied in the statement is the superiority of constitution to government. The government is not entitled to grant privileges by way of charter if the privileges are not constitutional. Which constitution did Wesley have in mind—the ancient constitution, or that of 1689? Usually he meant the latter when speaking of rights and liberties, although at times he implied the former without actually naming it. In this case, he probably is thinking of both without making a distinction, but at minimum his criterion of constitutionality includes the ancient constitution because of the reference to ancestral rights. However, the fundamental issue here is not the identification of the particular constitution, but that the government is subordinate to the constitution. Apparently the constitution is *supreme power,* not the government. If so, that would mean that *rights of Englishmen* or *inherited rights* are limits to the power of government if they are embodied in the unwritten constitution, even though they are not natural or human rights.

Nevertheless, Wesley is clear that there is no natural right (i.e., no *human* right) to participate in government, or to make exceptions to the rule of obedience to government. The protective rights in political society are positive rights, not natural rights. One might detect some emergent exception to this position in the arguments he makes in "Thoughts Concerning the Origin of Power," where he asks why women, youth, and unpropertied persons should not be entitled to give consent to government if the criterion of participation is a natural right ingredient in human nature.[14] Doubtless these arguments imply commitments to equality that in principle were at odds with the class differentiations and gender-discriminatory practices of eighteenth-century English society, and reflect Wesley's application of "parity of reason" to expose irrational arguments governing political practice, but they are not arguments for natural rights to political consent and participation. Wesley's intention certainly was not to invoke the logic of natural right to consent and participation in order to expand the electorate and universalize it. Rather, it was to demonstrate the hypocrisy and self-contradictory character of the arguments of the proponents of a political theory grounded in natural rights. By no stretch of the desire for a more liberal Wesley can one turn this *reductio ad absurdum* into a Wesleyan argument for nature-based political rights.

DUTY, LAW, AND LIBERTY

John Wesley's deliberate and vigorous exclusion of natural rights from the political process is not the only barrier to portraying him as a human rights thinker. Another barrier is that the basic principle of his political ethic is duty, not individual rights. Wesley's political-moral doctrine begins with the notion of existent supreme power, which, by reason of its supremacy in the political society, receives divine ordination to exercise the power under God. This notion of divine ordination entails the duty of subjects to obey those who are set in authority over them, with the understanding that they are obeying persons who stand in the place of God. It does not stipulate certain rights as limits to or claims upon the government as supreme power. To the contrary, the supreme power has "the power over life and death, and consequently over our liberty and property, and all things of an inferior nature."[15] The duty of obedience is binding, therefore, in absolute monarchies, as well as in societies with constitutional governments that protect the liberties of the people with legal guarantees. By constructing his political ethic on this foundation, Wesley follows—without naming—the Homily of 1570, which makes obedience the fundamental political virtue. To the provisions of this Homily, Wesley adds the historic exception: "We must obey God rather than men." Otherwise, he does not change the foundation. Specifically, he does not change it to a foundation in individual rights. Had he done so, he could not have objected to John Locke's contention that governments exist to protect the rights of the members of the political society, receive their authority by consent of the members, and may be changed by them should they fail to provide that protection.

How, then, can there be liberty, if duty and not right is the foundation of the political ethic? Wesley's answer is that liberty requires a constitution and an authoritative legal order. A constitution (I interpolate) is either a form of supreme power that embodies and guarantees liberties, or a limit to government as supreme power with specific reference to the rights and liberties of the subjects. In either case it is a structural arrangement within the society that names the liberties and provides the protective housing for them. I have mentioned several times that Wesley frequently trumpeted the Whiggish slogan, "English liberties began with the Revolution." Obviously, he did not mean that there was no concept of liberty in England until 1689, or even that the historic tradition of English liberties amounted to nothing until then.[16] His point, rather, was that the constitution of 1689 as supreme power established the liberties in law and guaranteed them firmly, whereas Tudor and Stuart absolutism as supreme power tended to ignore or suppress them. That conviction powered the support Wesley gave to the Hanoverian limited monarchy and the British constitution throughout his long life.

The duty of obedience was the same in both cases. However, the difference was that obedience rendered to the absolutists did not translate into the benefits of liberty, whereas obedience to the constitutional government established in 1689 not only secured liberty, but enhanced the ability of the government to protect it. Liberty, or freedom, according to Wesley, was life under the law and in respect of the law. Without the law there was no liberty. Responding to claims to a natural right to independence, Wesley wrote: "Whoever is born in England, France, or Holland, is subject to their respective Governors; and 'must needs be subject to the power, as to the ordinance of God, not only for wrath, but for conscience' sake.' He has no right at all to be independent, or governed only by himself; but is in duty bound to be governed by the powers that be, according to the laws of the country. And he that is thus governed, not by himself, but the laws, is, in the general sense of mankind, a free man."[17] True liberty is ordered liberty. Freedom is freedom only under the law.

What we have here is a practical political observation, not some pre-Hegelian notion of the immanence of God in the positive laws. Wesley is not arguing that one becomes free through affirming the law as the historical manifestation of divine reason. Freedom for Wesley is a natural, rational instinct, but it takes concrete form only in a legally structured setting. Apart from that setting it is either licentious behavior with no restraint, or complete vulnerability to the predatory behavior of others. Freedom depends on law. The laws, therefore, must be obeyed for the sake of freedom. Of course, the laws must be obeyed primarily because they are *laws*, issued and enforced by divinely authorized supreme power. Duty remains the governing moral consideration. However, when arguing publicly with persons who seemed to him to give primacy to liberty as the overriding political value, and to liberty as an abstract concept, Wesley found it necessary to emphasize the practical importance of the duty of obedience to the conditions of liberty.

In this constitutional scheme *everyone* is subordinate to the law, and is bound in duty to obey it. That provision applies to kings and all others in authority—those for whom the *Book of Common Prayer* invokes divine guidance. As we have seen over and again, Wesley believed that the mere will of the king carried no legal or moral authority. Whatever the king willed must be by way of execution of a law of Parliament. Similarly, the magistrates charged with enforcing the law are governed themselves by the laws they enforce. They have the same duty of obedience as other subjects, except that the weight of their responsibility is increased by the majesty of their office. This legal system, grounded in the constitution of limited and balanced government, and from which no one is exempt, is the definer and guarantor of English liberties. Wesley's commitment to liberty in that context explains why he opposed with such vigor, and at times ferocity, the agitations for liberty and natural rights that seemed to him to weaken the supporting system. Against the Americans and their crusade for independence he wrote, "Here is *slavery*, real slavery indeed, most properly so called. For the regular, legal, constitutional form of government is no more. Here is real, not imaginary, bondage; not the shadow of English liberty is left."[18] The rights and liberties that really deliver freedom and entitlement to the people are the ones embodied in law and constitution, not the abstract and extrasocial concepts of right and liberty. To enjoy the liberties, one must accept and perform the duty to obey.

THE INTRASOCIETY REALITY AND ROLE OF NATURAL RIGHTS

Having listed and examined the reasons why John Wesley declined and opposed the natural or human rights tradition, I now must acknowledge the several occasions on—and various contexts in—which he employed explicit natural rights language, and in doing so created a place for natural rights in his political ethics. The principal contexts were three: his opposition to slavery, his defense of religious liberty, and his assertion of the natural rights of nations and some ethnic groups. There were a few other occasions when Wesley appealed to natural rights, or perhaps implied natural rights concepts, but these usages are at times obscure and in any case are undeveloped. For example, he believed in the natural rights of women based on their equal rationality with men, but allowed the application of this belief to be muted or deflected. The three principal contexts leave no doubt that he thought in natural rights terms, at least in those situations. Of special importance is that he understood these natural rights to apply to conditions *within society*. That distinguishes them from political rights of consent and self-governance in a presocial state of nature. As we have seen, Wesley conceded the reality of such rights, but his concession was an irrelevancy because he did not really believe that a presocial state ever existed (except, perhaps, as the prevailing condition of international society). In the cases now before us, he understands natural rights to constitute authoritative limits to power and law.

Slavery and "The Right to Liberty"

Wesley encounters the problem of slavery in two contexts. The first is that of the enslavement of Africans for sale and service in the New World. The second is the dispute over a natural right to representation, especially with reference to the conflict with the American colonies. In both of them he makes prominent use of the concept of a natural right to liberty. In his celebrated "Thoughts upon Slavery" (1774)[19] Wesley defines slavery as "domestic slavery, or that of a servant to a master," and—quoting Mr. Hargreave's *Plea for Somerset the Negro*—distinguishes it from "that mild, domestic service which obtains in our country."[20]

> Slavery imports an obligation of perpetual service, an obligation which only the consent of the master can dissolve. Neither in some countries can the master himself dissolve it, without the consent of Judges appointed by the law. It generally gives the master an arbitrary power of any correction, not affecting life or limb. Sometimes

—— 318 ——

even these are exposed to his will, or protected only by a fine, or some slight punishment, too inconsiderable to restrain a master of an harsh temper. It creates an incapacity of acquiring anything, except for the master's benefit. It allows the master to alienate the slave, in the same manner as his cows and horses. Lastly, it descends in its full extent from parent to child, even to the last generation.[21]

Slavery defined in this manner is the total ownership and control of one human being by another. It is reminiscent of Aristotle's concept of the slave as a "living tool." Wesley demolishes the justification for this arrangement, first, by declaring it a flagrant violation of "liberty itself, to which an Angolan has the same natural right as an Englishman,"[22] and then refuting the arguments for a supposed right to enslave.

For the latter purpose he draws at the outset on the eminent jurist, Judge Blackstone. Blackstone argued against slavery on three points. First, he denied the right to enslave prisoners taken as captives in war. The laws of nations allow the right to kill the enemy as a matter of self-defense, but taking the enemy captive terminates the relevance of that right because his captivity eliminates the threat. " 'War . . . gives us no right over prisoners, but to hinder their hurting us by confining them. Much less can it give a right to torture, or kill, or even to enslave an enemy when the war is over. Since therefore the right of making our prisoners slaves, depends on a supposed right of slaughter, that foundation failing, the consequence which is drawn from it must fail likewise.' "[23] Second, no one rightly can enter a contract to enslave himself, because the value received by enslavement is in no way equivalent to the liberty that is given away. Blackstone allows for indentured servitude, which has contractual limits, but not for slavery, which has no limits. Third, there is no right to enslave those who are born into slavery, because any such right is dependent on the validity of the first two arguments. But those arguments have been shown to be invalid. Therefore there is no justification for enslaving the children of slaves.[24] It is curious that Blackstone did not decide against the enslavement of children of slaves simply on grounds of the natural right to liberty, and that Wesley did not prompt him on the matter.

Wesley continues with several refutations of the alleged necessity of slavery, and then concludes with this summary—addressed to a man whose plea was that he did not buy Negroes, but only retained those inherited from his father: "Had your father, have you, has any man living, a right to use another as a slave? It cannot be, even setting Revelation aside. It cannot be that either war, or contract, can give any man such a property in another as he has in his sheep and oxen. Much less is it possible, that any child of man should ever be born a slave. Liberty is the right of every human creature, as soon as he breathes the vital air; and no human law can deprive him of that right which he derives from the law of nature."[25] These last two sentences state the natural right argument against enslaving the children of slaves, which Blackstone failed to make, and which Wesley failed to add to his citation of Blackstone.

Apparently Wesley sees this natural right to liberty as justifying active resistance to the condition on the part of the slave. He speaks of rebellion as "asserting their native liberty, which they have as much right to as the air they breathe."[26] He refers with obvious approval to "the most natural act of 'running away' from intolerable tyranny."[27] However, he does not challenge the master-servant relationship where it does not involve slavery (according to this definition), nor does he extend the natural right to liberty to any other entitlement. Essentially this right is limited to freedom from total ownership and control. Nevertheless, it is a natural right that has normative force *within society*, as least as a critical principle. Years later he moved on to urge the abolition of the slave system, eventually supporting members of Parliament engaged in the proposing of abolitionary legislation.[28]

The second context in which Wesley asserts a natural right of liberty over against slavery is that of the conflict between England and the American colonies. The colonists argued that being subject to laws made by the English government without being represented was tantamount to slavery. Of course, Wesley denied that it was any such thing. As we know by now, he rejected the idea of a right to representation. Government, in his view, was no less authoritative and no less responsible simply because the people governed were not represented. The authority to govern and make laws came from God, not the people. Moreover, he scoffed at the claim that the colonists were slaves because they had no say in the making of laws that governed them. The practical reality of slavery was the condition of the Africans owned by the colonists, not the condition of the colonists themselves. The colonists would experience the reality of slavery in the absence of constitutional and legal provisions protecting a person's enjoyment of life, liberty, and property—not simply in the absence of representation. Wesley offers a definition of slavery appropriate to the terms of conflict: "Slavery is a state wherein neither a man's goods, nor liberty, nor life, are at his own disposal. Such is the state of a thousand, of ten thousand, Negroes in the American colonies. And are their masters in the same state with them?"[29] The laws of England protect the life, liberty, and goods of the colonists. In doing so, they confirm their natural right to liberty. The laws do not offer the same protection to enslaved Africans. By failing to do so, they deny their natural right to liberty. That protection, not the presence or absence of representation, determines the difference between slavery and freedom.

In the first context, slavery is a matter of one's being owned and totally controlled by someone else within a system that confirms and legalizes the relationship. In the second, it is a matter of total absence of protection, which may lead to a situation of the first kind—at least with respect to total control. In both instances, the natural right to liberty appears to be a negative right. That is clear in the first case in that the natural right to liberty is the right not to be owned and controlled. It is the right to be released from an unjust system of bondage. There the natural right claim is used within the system itself to criticize the system, reveal the injustice of its laws, establish the claim to individual freedom, change the laws, and even destroy the slave system itself. It is not used to lay claim to the fruits of distributive justice. The negative character of the right to liberty is clear in the second case, also, insofar as it pertains to the right to be left alone and without threat to one's person or belongings. In the second context, however, the natural right to liberty presupposes a system of legal and political protection. In the particular situation addressed by Wesley, such a system exists, and the natural right claim functions within the existing situation not to change or destroy it, but to affirm and strengthen it by requiring obedience to it. The process of doing so requires the refutation of other natural rights claims that threaten the protective system, and, in Wesley's view, open the way to slavery. The question here is whether the right to liberty is also the right to the kind of governmental and legal structure that protects the particular liberties. That is, does it go beyond the negative right to personal freedom and noninterference, and become a positive entitlement to a particular kind of legal and political system? Wesley does not say so, because his immediate purpose is to preserve an existing governmental system, not to call one into existence. However, that inference may be implied in his argument. Nevertheless, Wesley never means to say that any such right to a system protective of liberty must be guaranteed by political rights of consent and representation.

The first usage of natural right in a context of slavery tends to be anarchic, unless it is complemented by the second. It withdraws persons from an unjust system, and intends the destruction of the system, but does not *simply as natural right,* in those conditions, propose a different system. The second usage is inherently more political in character. It defines in broad outline the type of system needed to establish and maintain liberty and thereby to repel slavery. Wesley employed both usages, but without making the connection between the two to infer a notion of a type of free society derived from natural right.

Religious Liberty, or the Rights of Conscience

John Wesley argued consistently that liberties essentially were of two types: religious and civil. The former he spoke of regularly as a *natural right.* His most complete and best-known statement on religious liberty—or somewhat more broadly *right of conscience*—is set forth in his "Thoughts upon Liberty." There he asked:

> What is that liberty, properly so called, which every wise and good man desires? It is either religious or civil. Religious liberty is a liberty to choose our own religion, to worship God according to our own conscience, according to the best light we have. Every man living, as a man, has a right to this, as he is a rational creature. The Creator gave him this right when he endowed him with understanding. And every man must judge for himself, because every man must give an account of himself to God. Consequently, this is an indefeasible right; it is inseparable from humanity. And God did never give authority to any man, or any number of men, to deprive any child of man thereof, under any colour or pretence whatever. What an amaz-

ing thing is it, then, that the governing part of almost every nation under heaven should have taken upon them, in all ages, to rob all under their power of this liberty! yea, should take upon them, at this day, so to do; to force rational creatures into their own religion![30]

This statement is an unambiguous declaration of natural right. Religious liberty is grounded in human nature, in original human nature as created by God, in human reason, and in the God-given power of contrary choice that is the necessary accompaniment of reasoning. Because rationality is integral to human nature, the right is indefeasible. That is, it cannot be taken away justifiably for any reason. Because rationality is inherent in all human beings, the right is universal. This right excludes governmental and other forms of power from coercing conscience and from dictating and punishing religious practice. No government anywhere of whatever persuasion, power, or majesty is entitled to infringe on it.

John Wesley certainly set a high value on rational freedom and its legal protection, but what makes religious liberty a natural *right* for him is not the sanctity of rational freedom itself but what it implies for a person's relationship to God. The former is instrumental to the latter. "Religious liberty is a liberty to choose our own religion, to worship God . . . according to the best light we have." Wesley does not mean to suggest that choosing one's religion is a matter of indifference—of going down the cafeteria line until we find something we like, or perhaps choosing nothing at all. It is not a liberal "freedom of choice" plan. Rather, it is a responsibility of ultimate seriousness in which everyone must give an account of himself or herself to God. No one else can fulfill that grave responsibility for another, and no one should attempt or be allowed to do so. Coercing another person's religious belief is more than the violation of a right; it is a usurpation of the responsibility for one's eternal destiny. In his "Earnest Appeal to Men of Reason and Religion" (1744), he wrote:

Yet again: are we to be guided by our *own* conscience or by that of other men? You surely will not say that any man's conscience can preclude mine. You, at least, will not plead for robbing us of what you so strongly claim for yourselves: I mean, the right of private judgment, which is indeed inalienable from reasonable creatures.

You well know that unless we faithfully follow the dictates of our own mind we cannot have "a conscience void of offence toward God and toward man."[31]

It is for this reason—much more than to avoid violating the conditions of human rationality—that no person, no religious group, and certainly no government should ever override a human being's religious liberty.

One must have that clarification in mind when interpreting Wesley's grounding of the natural right to religious liberty in human rationality. The true location of the right is in the divine-human relationship, not in human reason apart from God. That conclusion follows necessarily not only from what Wesley says about accountability to God, but also from his placement of rationality and freedom of choice in the *natural image of God*. Its placement there establishes human *capability for God*.[32] This capability can be exercised rightly only through the *political image* of God and with the true guidance of the *moral image* of God. To speak of this natural right as being an aspect of Wesley's doctrine of Creation is correct up to a point, but the creational context does not suffice to give the concept its full meaning and power. The moral image of God, one should remember, is complementary to created human nature, but is not itself an element of Creation. The ultimate context of the natural right to religious liberty, therefore, is not God's Creation alone, but the whole work of God as it comes to expression in the Holy Trinity. In the final analysis, Wesley's natural right to religious liberty is more trinitarian than creational in its theological meaning. As we shall see subsequently, this particular perspective on the natural right to religious liberty has significant bearing on the question of political rights.

Of course, Wesley's inferring of this natural right from the power of choice accompanying rationality is essential to his case for it. The intention, surely, is to make a compelling case for religious liberty, even to persons who may not be as seriously interested in accountability to God. However, by establishing the divine-human relationship of accountability as the ultimate context of religious liberty, he underscores for believers the importance of sustaining a constitutional order that protects it.

The right to religious liberty has a *public character*—in several ways. First, it is a right to practice the religion publicly, not merely a right to religious belief as an interior matter. On the occasion of their political disagreement, Susanna Wesley petitioned her husband Samuel to allow her "little liberty of conscience" as a personal conviction. However, her son John Wesley's concern was with freedom of religious practice, and not only with internal freedom of thought. Second, religious liberty is public in that it is confirmed by law. On 9 July 1766, Wesley wrote to Francis Wanley, Dean of Ripon, and a magistrate who refused justice to the Methodists, reminding him of "liberty of conscience—that liberty which every man may claim as his right by the law of God and nature, and to which every Englishman in particular has a right by the laws of his country."[33] To an officer in Lowestoft, he wrote, "I am informed by some of my friends in Lowestoft that they have been frequently disturbed at their public worship by some officers quartered in the town. Before I use any other method, I beg of you, sir, who can do it with a word, to prevent our being thus insulted any more. We are men; we are Englishmen: as such we have a natural and a legal right to liberty of conscience."[34] The laws of England protect the natural rights of English people to religious liberty.

Third, religious liberty is public in that it allows or requires public criticism of public persons and institutions when they offend against it. Wesley openly and in print criticized the Tudor and Stuart monarchs for their abuses of religious freedom. In "Thoughts upon Liberty" he wrote with regard to religious coercion and persecution:

> It would not be altogether so astonishing, if this were the manner of American savages. But what shall we say, if numberless instances of it have occurred, in the politest nations of Europe? Have no instances of the kind been seen in Britain? Have not England and Scotland seen the horrid fires? Have not the flames burning the flesh of heretics shone in London as well as Paris and Lisbon? Have we forgot the days of good Queen Mary? No; they will be in everlasting remembrance. And although burning was out of fashion in Queen Elizabeth's days, yet hanging, even for religion, was not. It is true, her successor did not go quite so far. But did even King James allow liberty of conscience? By no means. During his whole reign, what liberty had the Puritans? What liberty had they in the following reign? If they were not persecuted unto death . . . yet were they not

continually harassed by prosecutions in the Bishops' Courts, or Star-Chamber? by fines upon fines, frequently reducing them to deepest poverty? and by imprisonment for months, yea, for years, together, till many of them, escaping with the skin of their teeth, left their country and friends, fled to seek their bread in the wilds of America? "However, we may suppose all this was at an end under the merry Monarch, King Charles the Second." Was it indeed? Where have they lived who suppose this?[35]

To document his charge against Charles II, Wesley follows with a vigorous critique of two acts of Parliament during his reign: the Act of Uniformity (1662), and the Act Against Conventicles (1662, revised 1670).[36] The former required all clergy and teachers to subscribe without reservation to the *Book of Common Prayer*. Failing such assent, they would be deprived of their benefices and not allowed to continue with their vocations. More than two thousand clergy were forced to resign their livings for noncompliance. Wesley commented:

> So, by this glorious Act, thousands of men, guilty of no crime, nothing contrary either to justice, mercy, or truth, were stripped of all they had, of their houses, lands, revenues, and driven to seek where they could, or beg, their bread. For what? Because they did not dare to worship God according to other men's consciences! So they and their families were, at one stroke, turned out of house and home, and reduced to little less than beggary, for no other fault, real or pretended, but because they could not assent and consent to that manner of worship which their worthy governors prescribed![37]

Two of the men who suffered in this purge of Nonconformity were John Wesley's great-grandfather, Bartholomew Wesley, and his grandfather, also named John Wesley.[38] Both men were forced out of their pulpits as a result of this act.

The latter act—Against Conventicles—prohibited unauthorized, non-Church of England gatherings for worship of more than five persons not members of the same family. Wesley understood this act to punish those who "continued to worship God according to their own conscience" after the punitive application to them of the Act of Uniformity. Persons who did so "were first robbed of their substance, and, if they persisted, of their liberty; often of their lives also. For this crime, under this 'our most religious and gracious King,' (what were they who publicly told God he was such?) Englishmen were not only spoiled of their goods, but denied even the use of the free air, yea, and the light of the sun, being thrust by hundreds into dark and loathsome prisons!"[39]

The Act Against Conventicles proved to be a useful weapon against the Methodists, even late in the eighteenth century. The Act of Toleration (1689) had granted some relief to Nonconformists, allowing them to have their own places of worship, preachers, and teachers. The Methodists claimed to be members of the Church of England, however, and not Nonconformists. Therefore the permissions of the Act of Toleration did not apply to them, and they were prosecuted as lawbreakers when they engaged in their usual religious activity. As late as 1790 Wesley found it necessary to complain to William Wilberforce (as a member of Parliament) about the ways in which the interplay of parliamentary acts pertaining to religion were used to attempt to destroy the Methodist movement.

Last month a few people met together in Lincolnshire to pray and praise God in a friend's house. There was no preaching at all. Two neighbouring Justices fined the man of the house twenty pounds. I suppose he was not worth twenty shillings. Upon this his household goods were distrained and sold to pay the fine. He appealed to the Quarter Sessions; but all the Justices averred the Methodists could have no relief from the Act of Toleration because they went to church, and that so long as they did so the Conventicle Act should be executed upon them.

Last Sunday, when one of our preachers was beginning to speak to a quiet congregation, a neighbouring Justice sent a constable to seize him, though he was licensed, and would not release him till he had paid twenty pounds, telling him his license was good for nothing because he was a Churchman.

Now, sir, what can the Methodists do? They are liable to be ruined by the Conventicle Act, and they have no relief from the Act of Toleration! If this is not oppression, what is? Where, then, is English liberty? the liberty of Christians? yea, of every rational creature, who as such has a right to worship God according to his own conscience?[40]

Wesley concludes the letter with reflections on the imprudence of driving away thousands of loyal subjects, and a request to the member to "speak a word to Mr. Pitt on that head." Implicitly, he was requesting that legislation pertaining to religious practice be changed fundamentally to make it reflective of the natural right to religious liberty. This form of public action is modest indeed, but Wesley's appeal indicates that he saw no need simply to be silent when suffering abuse of a basic natural right.

The fact that religious liberty is public in character means that it is a natural right *within society*. It is not simply antecedent to social existence. It is confirmed by positive rights in constitution and law, but unlike the alleged natural right of consent, it is not replaced or superseded by them. The same right is guaranteed also to all human beings by the laws of God and nature. That is to say, this legal right of the English derives ultimately from God and human nature, not from the legal code and traditions of a particular country. As a protected right it is a positive right, but it is a positive right because it is a natural right. It becomes public in constitution, code, and tradition, but its authority as *right* precedes such institutionalization. In this respect, Wesley's affirmation of religious liberty puts him undeniably within the natural or human rights tradition—at least on this point.

Wesley's affirmation of the rights of conscience was a firmly held principle of his entire public career, not an awakening or a conversion late in life. The citation from "An Earnest Appeal to Men of Reason and Religion" of a right of private judgment inalienable from reasonable creatures shows that he was declaring himself publicly in such terms at least as early as 1744. Earlier citations suggest more commonly the rights of English people or the law of God (Scripture) as reasons for disallowing interference with religious belief and practice; however, Wesley combined nature, God, and English law so frequently in validating claims to rights that there is no reason to suppose a concept of religious liberty *as natural right* broke suddenly into his conscience. Moreover, his advocacy of this right cannot be explained and perhaps dismissed as merely a prudential maneuver to protect threatened and persecuted Methodists. Attacks on the Methodists certainly provided most of the occasions for his invoking this protection, but not all. The context of the tract "Thoughts upon Liberty" was the domestic agitation that Wesley perceived as an attack on king, monarchy, and constitution. Furthermore, his reference in his sermon on "The Catholic Spirit" to "the right of private judgment on which that whole Reformation stands" shows that he links that right to the Protestant if not the entire Christian experience, and not only to the Methodist experience.[41]

John Wesley belongs firmly and neither marginally nor accidentally in the natural rights tradition as it pertains to religious liberty. On the basis of the evidence, one must agree with that conclusion. Yet one must hedge the conclusion with these observations. First, Wesley's orientation to this right was from concern over individual responsibility to God, not from an interest in abstract rights of rationality. The nature of political and social combat in the eighteenth century pressed him to adopt language at times more characteristic of secular thinkers, but his concerns were not necessarily their concerns. Second, it will not do to think of Wesley as only or even primarily a natural rights thinker even on this important issue. As I have argued, he did not separate the natural right to religious liberty, grounded in divine Creation or vocation, from the English constitutional and legal tradition of rights and liberties. It distorts Wesley's approach to rights considerations to lift his natural rights usages out of this more integral and communitarian approach to political ethics. Nor is it clear that doing so serves our contemporary commitments to human rights.

Third, and this follows on what has just been said, the appeal to religious liberty as natural right *functions as a critical principle within an established order of law and government.* It is a negative concept directing the various forms and loci of power in society to leave people alone to pursue religious callings and commitments in their own way. It implies no pretensions to religious or political power, and it proposes no transformation of the religious order of society. Specifically, Wesley does not challenge the English religious establishment in the name of religious liberty. He is content to allow that establishment its own existence and self-justification, and to adhere to it as a (relatively) dutiful priest, while demanding that it not infringe the rights of those who think and worship differently. He does not call for reformation or abolition of the religious order in the name of religious liberty, nor does he use the natural right to encourage sectarian separation. The right to religious liberty serves as *order of preservation* for divergent religious thought and practice, not as a constructive principle for religious-social reconstitution. In that respect it is representative of most of John Wesley's thinking on rights and liberties.

The Roman Catholic Exception

Having said all that about Wesley's vigorous support for religious liberty as natural right, one cannot rightly pass by without reporting the one occasion when he constricted religious liberty almost to the point of forcing it into the realm of conscience alone. I refer to his late-in-life objection to removing legal restrictions on Roman Catholics. Beginning in the years following the Reformation in England, Catholics had been subject to a number of legal measures designed to reduce their influence on English public life. The measures included severe restrictions on landowning, including inheriting land from Protestants, and prohibitions of voting, holding seats in Parliament, receiving university degrees, and holding offices in the universities. These measures were codified between 1695 and 1727 in a series of laws known as the Penal Code. Some of the laws, although not all, were repealed or eased by the Catholic Relief Act of 1778. The passage of this act provided the occasion for riots protesting the relief granted to Catholics. Lord George Gordon, the alleged instigator of the riots, was imprisoned for libel, accused of high treason, and subsequently released.

Wesley opposed the relief act, and responded critically to it in a public letter in January 1780.[42] He responded to published criticisms of this letter by Father O'Leary, an Irish priest, in two further public letters in March 1780 that expanded his argument.[43] In December, at Lord Gordon's request, and with permission gained through Lord Stormont, Wesley visited Gordon in the Tower, discussed popery and religion with him, and found him to be a person well acquainted with the Bible.[44] When Wesley saw the grand jury indictment against Gordon later that month he pronounced it a "shocking insult upon truth and common sense!"[45]

Wesley's position in these letters is summed up in the words, "I insist upon it that no Government not Roman Catholic ought to tolerate men of the Roman Catholic persuasion."[46] What exactly he meant by *no toleration* is not entirely clear. At minimum, he meant that the Catholic Relief Act should not have been passed by Parliament, and that the previous restrictions on Catholics should have remained in force. Actually, he sounded more extreme than that. To the response that the act neither tolerates nor encourages Roman Catholics, he replied that the Catholics certainly understood it to imply toleration. "And does it not already (let alone what it *may* do by-and-by) *encourage* them to preach openly, to build chapels (at Bath and elsewhere), to raise seminaries, and to make numerous converts day by day, to their intolerant, persecuting principles?"[47] This anxious and aggressive language seems to imply that Wesley thought Catholicism in non-Catholic countries should be *suppressed.* He does not mean that, but he should not have been surprised that others took that to be his meaning. Essentially, what he seems to have wanted was a return to *status quo ante* and the avoidance of any measures that might allow the Catholics to increase in strength.

Wesley's reasoning in this matter was that Roman Catholics owed primary spiritual obedience to a foreign power, the Pope in Rome, and because of the nature and implications of that obedience could not honestly swear allegiance to the British government and constitution. Wesley reiterated again and again the decree of the Council of Constance that "no faith is to be kept with heretics." He observed that no subsequent public council ever had repealed this decree, and that therefore it remained in force as a Roman Catholic maxim. "But as long as it is so, nothing can be more plain than that the members of that Church can give no reasonable security to any Government of their allegiance or peaceable behaviour. Therefore they ought not to be tolerated by any Government, Protestant, Mahometan, or Pagan."[48] Oaths to governments taken by individual Catholics were not to be trusted, because the Pope claimed the power to dispense with oaths, and also to "pardon rebellions, high treasons, and all other sins whatsoever." Moreover, this power belonged to priests as well.

The issue here is not Catholic doctrine *as such.* To be sure, Wesley "detested" central aspects of Catholic doctrine: papal supremacy, transubstantiation, the role of good works in salvation, among others.[49] Yet he was an avid reader of Catholic writings on perfection and mysticism, and claimed to have learned much from them. His celebrated "Letter to a Roman Catholic" of 18 July 1749 acknowledged that both Catholics and Protestants served the same Christ, and it sought to delineate lines of Christian doctrine to which—he hoped—they subscribed in common.[50] The issue, rather, was that of the consequences that follow from a particular doctrine and their implications for public order, and the liberties of other persons. For Wesley, it was a simple matter of logic. Roman Catholics hold—and must hold—this belief about the spiritual power of the Pope. As long as they believe it, that is, as long as they are Roman Catholics, they pose an implicit threat to the liberties of other members of the society and should not be allowed to have public influence in Britain. He took that to be an obvious and straightforward deduction allowing no other possible conclusion. As a result, he wrote his letter of 12 January 1780 not as an attack on Catholics or Catholicism or Catholic doctrine, but "to preserve our happy constitution." Catholics with public influence will subvert the constitution and destroy the liberties that depend upon its strength and continuity. Therefore the paths to such influence must be denied them. It is an argument known to anyone familiar with the rhetoric of presidential elections in the United States in 1928 and 1960.

Neither was the issue simply one of individual peculiarity or bigotry. One may charge Wesley with bigotry against Roman Catholics and Catholicism, but his attitude is at least ambivalent and not simply negative.[51] His friendship with Catholics, his general openness to them, the presence of some Catholics in his meetings, and his willingness to learn from Catholic texts should allay that charge somewhat—although without dismissing it entirely. Moreover, his sentiments were not merely a matter of personal disposition, although doubtless they were influenced by his association in Georgia with a group of refugees "expelled from Germany by the Archbishop of Saltzburg."[52] He lived in an atmosphere that generated suspicion toward Catholicism and Catholics, and he shared that suspicion.[53] The grounds for suspicion also had some historical basis. Many of the restrictions on Roman Catholics were made into law in response to Catholic rebellions and plots of the sixteenth century and later. Wesley and others kept alive the remembrance of Catholic Queen Mary I and her "horrid fires." The intrigues within the seventeenth-century House of Stuart to return the Church of England to Rome were not forgotten, especially in view of the persistent efforts of eighteenth-century Jacobites to restore the Stuarts to the throne, and that most Catholics in England supported those efforts. Nor were Wesley's concerns about the tentativity of oaths without some merit. Basil Williams wrote, "The Pretender had found considerable support in 1715 from papist families, and the suspicion that the papists had designs not only against the dynasty but also against the establishment seemed in some measure confirmed by Stanhope's and Cragg's negotiations with them in 1719; for though representatives of the chief catholic families, Stonors, Blounts, and Howards, were quite ready to sign a binding promise of allegiance to George I, the ultramontane element obstinately refused to retract the claim set up by Sixtus V in Elizabeth's reign, that a pope had power to release the subjects of an heretic monarch from any promise of fealty."[54]

One might argue that by the end of the eighteenth century such concerns should have been laid to rest, but fears and suspicions do not die easily. Full Roman Catholic emancipation in England was not established in law until the latter part of the nineteenth century, and even today no Roman Catholic may ascend the throne.

John Wesley committed himself so passionately to the rights of conscience as to turn respect for the conscience of others into a prime Methodist virtue. In his "Advice to the People Called Methodists" he admonished his followers to "Condemn no man for not thinking as you think. Let everyone enjoy the full and free liberty of thinking for himself. Let every man use his own judgment, since every man must give an account of himself to God. Abhor every approach, in any kind or degree, to the spirit of *persecution*. If you cannot *reason* or *persuade* a man into the truth, never attempt to *force* him into it. If love will not compel him to come in, leave him to God, the Judge of all."[55] In the light of that declaration, reiterated in other places, it seems clear that Wesley did not consider these restrictions on Roman Catholics to be occasions of persecution or of coercion of conscience.[56] He makes that plain in his last public letter responding to Father O'Leary:

> Would I, then, wish the Roman Catholics to be persecuted? I never said or hinted any such thing. I abhor the thought; it is foreign to all I have preached and wrote for these fifty years. But I would wish the Romanists in England (I had no others in view) to be treated still with the same lenity that they have been these sixty years; to be allowed both civil and religious liberty, but not permitted to undermine ours. I wish them to stand just as they did before the late Act was passed; not to be persecuted or hurt themselves; but gently restrained from hurting their neighbours.[57]

In Wesley's view, the restrictions in force before the passing of the Catholic Relief Act did not equate with persecution, nor did they diminish religious liberty as a constitutional or natural right. He defended their full English and natural liberty to relate themselves to God according to the best light of their reason and conscience. No one should attempt to force them to do otherwise. The implication of this view, however, is that liberty of conscience is limited to the *right to believe.* It is internal liberty only, and if it is accorded some external allowance, that allowance is greatly circumscribed. Or at least that is what he appears to think when facing the issue of Roman Catholic influence. Religious liberty according to this understanding does not have the *public character* that is its property when exercised by Wesley and the Methodists. The more public Roman Catholic religious liberty becomes, the more it is perceived as a threat to the constitutional housing of religious and civil liberties. The effective scope of the natural right therefore is reduced by these practical and political considerations.

The Natural Rights of Nations

Wesley wrote that "Every nation . . . has a natural liberty to enjoy their own laws, and their own religions . . . we have no right to deprive them of this liberty."[58] Here also he is using natural rights language, and appears to be doing so with reference to political rights, among others. In this case, however, he is referring to rights of nations, not of individual persons, and to the reality of those rights in a *prepolitical* condition—that of international society, where there is no *polis* to provide the context of positive rights and give institutional structure to the duty of obedience. At one level, this natural liberty of nations implies a rejection of right of conquest:—"The Hollanders were not colonies from Spain, but an independent people, who had the same right to govern Spain, as the Spaniards to govern Holland."[59] At another level, it implies the persistence of the natural liberties even when one nation has come under the domination of another: "What if we had conquered France, ought we not still to have allowed them their own laws and religion? Yea, if the Russians had conquered Constantinople, or the whole Ottoman empire, ought they not to have allowed all they conquered, both their own religion and their own laws; nay, and to have given them, not a precarious toleration, but a legal security for both?"[60] These are natural rights claims of high significance.

Following his usual practice, Wesley does not explore the theoretical issues and problems involved in this statement. It would be useful, for example, to have his reflection on the possible differences between group rights and individual rights, and between groups and individuals in a state of nature. Wesley dismisses the notion of a historically real presocietal existence for individual rights-bearers, but implies without stating that "state of nature" is the normal condition of nations in relation to other nations. Most notably, however, he fails to offer reasons for the persistence of natural liberties when one nation comes under the dominance of another. In that case, the two nations presumably no longer are in a presocial condition vis-à-vis each other. One of them has established an inclusive society and has become the supreme power— authorized by God to dispose of life, liberty, and property. The transition should put an end to natural rights claims, including the right to independence, and replace them with rights of subjects. Nevertheless, Wesley insists that subordinated nations retain natural liberty to have their own religion and *to enjoy their own laws.* That he should argue for a natural liberty of religious preference and exercise is not surprising, given his convictions concerning the natural right of conscience. On that point, the rights of groups simply reflect the rights of individuals. However, that he should argue for a natural liberty of legislation suggests a fundamental conflict with his basic political theory. In that theory, the supreme power has sovereignty, and the concept of sovereignty rejects the notion of any other legislative authority, including any based on natural rights claims against the sovereign power.

Particular nations evidently retain natural political rights when they come under sovereign authority, whereas individual natural rights-bearers do not. Conquered peoples even retain a right to independence, whereas subjects of a particular government have no such right. Wesley apparently never supposed that the United Provinces of the Netherlands lost their right to independence—and other natural rights—when they came under the domination of Catholic Spain, even though Spain clearly was the supreme power. Against that background he justified their rebellion when Spain brutally and systematically violated both their fundamental rights and their chartered liberties. Similarly, he justified the struggle of the Corsicans against the Genoese, and the allied states of Italy against the Romans.[61] (To my knowledge, Wesley did not make the same case for the independence of Scotland, Wales, and Ireland from England, even though he remarked on several occasions that the Irish were treated badly by the English, and even though those countries were subjects of natural rights as nations in the same manner and degree as the Dutch, the Corsicans, and the Italian city-state dwellers. To the contrary, in his reply to Richard Price in "Some Observations on Liberty," he seems to defend the English claims to Scotland and Ireland, although without arguing the case directly.)[62]

One can only speculate as to the reasons for this distinction between the natural rights of national groups and individual persons. It is not the difference between voluntary and involuntary submission, because Wesley never supposed that individual submission to supreme power necessarily was voluntary. Almost certainly it has much to do with his sense of the corporate reality of nations and peoples as distinguished from the corporate dependence of individuals. That is, he thought of England and other nations as integral bodies, autonomous, self-reliant, largely or at least ideally self-sufficient—roughly, perhaps, on the model of Aristotle's *perfect society* (a concept he did not use)—whereas he thought of individual persons as socially embedded and mutually dependent. In political terms, individual persons were dependent for their protection on the laws of their country and the benevolence of their governments, whereas nations essentially were dependent on their own power. Whatever the explanation, it was clear to him that nations as such had natural rights of a political character that he could not concede to individual persons as such.

The Equality and Natural Right of Women

In his sermon "On Visiting the Sick" Wesley offers a reflection on the equality and natural right of women that is remarkable not only for its content but also for the rarity of this kind of statement in his published works. In response to the question, "By whom is this duty [visiting the sick] to be performed?" he answers, "by all that desire to 'inherit the kingdom' of their Father. . . . It is equally incumbent on young and old, rich and poor, men and women, according to their ability."[63] Apparently the inclusion of women in the duty of visiting the sick meets some (surprising) resistance, because Wesley feels moved to argue the point.

> "But may not *women* as well as men bear a part in this honourable service?" Undoubtedly they may; nay, they ought—it is meet, right, and their bounden duty. Herein there is no difference: "there is neither male nor female in Christ Jesus." Indeed it has long passed for a maxim with many that "women are only to be seen, not heard." And accordingly many of them are brought up in such a manner as if they were only designed for agreeable playthings! But is this doing honour to the sex? Or is it a real kindness to them? No; it is the deepest unkindness; it is horrid cruelty; it is mere Turkish barbarity. And I know not how any woman of sense and spirit can submit to it. Let all you that have it in your power assert the right which the God of nature has given you. Yield not to that vile bondage any longer. You, as well as men, are rational creatures. You, like them, were made in the image of God: you are equally candidates for immortality. You too are called of God, as you have time, to "do good unto all men." Be "not disobedient to the heavenly calling." Whenever you have opportunity, do all the good you can, particularly to your poor sick neighbour. And every one of *you* likewise "shall receive your own reward according to your own labour."[64]

These words begin as a refutation to some real or supposed objection to women visiting the sick, and end up as a powerful liberationist statement. Not only does Wesley establish the grounds for women's equality with men, he summons them to stand up and claim and demand that equality! At the outset, the argument for equality uses the Pauline words about the oneness of women and men in Christ. Then it moves to a declaration of natural right based on the notion that women are rational creatures no less than men. Human rationality is the basis of natural right, and women and men are not differentiated as to the basic faculty of capacity for reasoning. The argument is not rationalistic, however. Reason is an element of the natural image of God. Women, like men, were created in the divine image, and are coequal in that imaging. Moreover, the harsh comparison with "Turkish barbarity" seems to imply that the equality of women is an essential tenet of Christianity that distinguishes it from Islam.

This Wesleyan case for women's equality based on natural right is rare but not isolated. Wesley made essentially the same argument (excepting the Pauline language) in "Thoughts concerning the Origin of Power." In that instance, however, he employed it as part of a *reductio ad absurdum* against the consent basis of political authority. In this instance, he uses the natural right argument to certify and empower women for a type of ministry. That usage, one regrets to note, indeed was rare for Wesley. Wesley involved women widely and often prominently in the Methodist movement. They prayed, exhorted, visited, provided funds as well as the ordinary but essential support services, and organized classes. Some were appointed to head educational or charitable institutions, and some "traveled the connection."[65] The roles Mr. Wesley opened to women often were closed to them in other contemporary religious settings. Nevertheless, Wesley did not open these roles to women and make these appointments by reason of his recognition of *their natural right to equality*. He did so because he found them to be highly useful in carrying forward the work of God. The evidence of the fruits of their ministry was to him evidence of the presence and blessing of the Holy Spirit. It was for that reason, and not because of women's rights claims, that Wesley saw to it that women were prominently and widely employed in the Methodist movement. Other persons might deny the rights claims, but they could not rightly deny their effectiveness and their piety.

That analysis holds true especially with regard to the question of allowing women to preach. Wesley fundamentally was opposed to the practice. The Scripture—in 1 Corinthians 14:34-35 and 1 Timothy 2:11-12—was clear: women were not to speak in church as preachers or teachers or to have authority over men. In the dynamics of the expanding movement, however, gifted women moved beyond these limits, and often were drawn beyond the limits by Methodist congregations eager to hear them pray, testify, exhort—and preach! Wesley could not ignore these evidences of spiritual grace and effectiveness, and elected not to do so. Perhaps he remembered the amazing success of Susanna Wesley's kitchen prayer meetings when Samuel was away from Epworth. On the one hand, he could not bring himself to abandon what he saw to be a clear rule of Scripture. On the other, however, he found ways to discover ever-widening "exceptions" to the rule.

An exploration of this development is beyond the scope of our concern here. The point for our purposes is that Wesley opened the way to wider possibilities for women in ministry by making exceptions to an exclusive rule, not by recognizing and affirming a woman's right to preach. He might have used the same argument here as he did in the case of visiting the sick, but he could not, because of his view of the authority of Scripture and the—to him—self-evident meaning of the Pauline strictures. On the other hand, he could not turn his back on the undeniable evidence that God was blessing the ministry of these women. Therefore, he began to wedge open the future with "exceptions," including an "extraordinary call," but not with an appeal to women's natural rights.

The statement in "On Visiting the Sick" and the one in "The Origin of Power" make clear that John Wesley held a belief in women's equality and natural right based on inferences from human rationality and creation in the image of God. His sermon couples the Pauline argument concerning oneness in Christ with the rational argument. However, the absence of his use of the natural rights argument in the controversies over women's preaching, and his unwillingness to extend natural right into the realm of political authorization show that natural right was not a norm ultimately decisive for his judgment. That role belonged to the word of Scripture. Wesley could find ways to make the scriptural rules more flexible, but the appeal to natural rights was not one of those ways.

ARE CIVIL LIBERTIES "NATURAL RIGHTS"?

As noted above, John Wesley specifies the concept of liberty to two types: religious and civil. We have seen that he argues strongly for religious liberty, or the rights of conscience, as a natural right. He argues strongly for civil liberties, also, but does not use the term *natural right* in his rhetoric of advocacy. "Civil liberty," he writes,

> is a liberty to dispose of our lives, persons, and fortunes, according to our own choice, and the laws of our country. I add, *according to the laws of our country:* For, although, if we violate these, we are liable to fines, imprisonment, or death; yet if, in other cases, we enjoy our life, liberty, and goods, undisturbed, we are free, to all reasonable intents and purposes.[66]

The concept of civil liberty, in this rendering, refers to legal rights— to legally defined, protected, and limited freedoms within a particular society. Apart from the legal system, the civil liberties are mere abstractions. Within the legal system, they imply corresponding duties, especially the duty to obey the law and the civil authorities. Civil liberty allows one to live, move about, and enjoy what is one's own without the threat or reality of legally unjustifiable punishment, interference, or expropriation. It is a matter of legal or constitutional right, but not inherently of natural right.[67]

Of course, there may be a concept of natural right underlying one or all of the named civil liberties that creates a moral demand for its recognition in law. In his "Calm Address to Our American Colonies," Wesley concedes (at least for the sake of argument) the reality of natural rights to life, liberty, and property *in a presocial state of nature*, but quickly rescinds their applicability within civil society.[68] Is there perhaps a residual trace of these natural rights in Wesley's thinking about civil liberties?

Life. Wesley seems to resist speaking of a *natural right to life*, a notion that might allow to a person full right over its disposal. "It is allowed, no man can dispose of another life but by his own consent. I add, No, nor with his consent; for no man has a right to dispose of his own life. The Creator of man has the sole right to take the life which he gave."[69] Life is a gift of God, not a natural endowment constituting entitlement. The state may be authorized to take life, however, by reason of the responsibilities assigned to it through divine ordination. The procedures for and limitations to this authority are set forth in the constitution and legal codes of the society. These institutions establish legal rights to liberty. When one demands protection of one's life as a civil liberty, or when one demands a fair trial, one is demanding a positive, legal right. If Wesley means more than that, he does not say so.

Liberty. Liberty, of course, is the inclusive term Wesley uses for human freedom. As one item under the heading of "civil liberties," however, it refers to particular freedoms one has as guaranteed by law. These would include security of person, the right to assemble peacefully, procedural justice, redress of grievances—precisely the liberties often denied to Methodists when attacked by mobs instigated by magistrates and priests, and when charged before the same instigator-magistrates. Essentially these are "freedom from" examples of liberties. However, he means to include also more activistic liberties such as freedom of speech and press. In "A Calm Address to the Inhabitants of England" (1777), he condemned the American colonists for allegedly abolishing such protections, and boasted that in England "Every man says what he will, writes what he will, prints what he will."[70] On the other hand, his call for legislation to prohibit and punish what he considered mendacious and inflammatory speech and publication shows that he felt a need for limits to such active liberties that were not necessary when one was claiming only the liberty to be treated decently and legally, and otherwise to be left alone.[71] The extension of thought into the public arena through speech and publication risked interfering with the rights and liberties of other persons, whereas simply exercising the liberty to mind one's own business did not. Perhaps of greater ultimate importance, in Wesley's view, it risked undermining the political and legal system that established and protected the rights and liberties.

One might argue that a concept of natural right tells us why these liberties ought to be established as legal rights. However, Wesley himself does not make that argument. In a conflict where his opponents were asserting *natural* right against the constitutional system, Wesley thought it important to affirm existing *legal* right in its defense. There is some irony in that Wesley could insist stoutly that the English legal and constitutional establishment provided the best protection for religious and civil liberties of any country in the world, while finding it necessary often to protest the violation of such liberties in the case of persecution of the Methodists. Doubtless Wesley would respond that the problem lay with the persons charged with enforcing the laws, not with the laws themselves. As he remarked often, English liberties had never been so secure since the emplacement of the constitutional arrangements of 1689. That, of course, is an argument for legal and constitutional guarantees, not for natural rights. On the other hand, it does not necessarily exclude a concept of natural rights.

Property. Wesley certainly believed in property rights as a legal matter, but never, to my knowledge, did he speak of property as a *natural right*—except for the presocial possibility acknowledged in the "Calm Address." If ever he did so, he did not give any extended explanation of why he thought a natural right to property was the foundation of a legal right. The theological context for understanding Wesley on property is stewardship, not natural right. Property—like life, time, intellect—is a gift of God to be used in the service of God and for the blessing of God's people, especially for the poor. It is not a commodity reserved for one's own personal use, profit, and enjoyment.[72] That theological perspective placed Wesley's view of property in direct opposition to the views of those who claimed that a natural right to ownership of property gave one full and absolute jurisdiction over it. Keeping to his theological perspective, one can conclude that Wesley recognized no natural right to private property in any exclusive sense. It does not follow, however, that he recognized no *legal* right to private property within the context of the civil community. Subject to the laws of the society, one is entitled to use and enjoy one's property as one sees fit. The doctrine of stewardship means that a Christian should commit without reservation to using his or her privately owned property in the service of God. This doctrine is inconsistent with the particular notion of a natural right to property that provided important philosophical support to emergent industrial and commercial capitalism. It is not inconsistent with the notion of a legal right to property as a civil liberty.

Early in the life of the Methodist movement, Wesley advocated with some regularity a mild form of communism or mutual support as a goal for the community of Methodist Christians.[73] This advocacy took as its model and scriptural mandate the communal sharing portrayed in the book of Acts. It involved supporting the community and its needs with the proceeds from employment, commerce, and property sales, although not—apparently—a collective ownership of property or a commune type of productive enterprise. Wesley's adopting and promoting of this plan presumably reflects his thinking of Methodism as a tightly integrated, loving community of Christians within the larger society, rather than a religious society composed of individuals with common beliefs. Subsequently he appears to have surrendered this goal, and accommodated himself to a less ideal, less communal attitude toward both Christian ownership and Methodist membership. This early proposal and its later revision or reversal are movements within his theological ethic of stewardship. They have no direct bearing on his attitude toward property ownership as a civil liberty protected by law. Communally owned property would require such legal protection no less than individually owned property. If Wesley believed in a natural right to property, that would have been no barrier to this communal proposal. The surrender of property in its various forms to the community was understood to be a voluntary action reflecting a belief in God as the true owner of all things. It would not have been forcible expropriation.[74]

One should not confuse Wesley's defense of a civil liberty to own, control, and use property with intent to defend the property system itself. Wesley definitely believed in the civil liberties, including this one, but in the essays in which he wrote of them his central concern was to defend the constitutional system. His principal argument against the "warm men for liberty," as he called them, was that their harangues about natural rights, independence, and deprivations of liberty were subverting the system that protected the very liberties of which they saw themselves deprived. That he should defend property rights was incidental to his main purpose, namely, the safeguarding of the housing of all rights and liberties. On the other hand, one cannot overlook that in the minds of most of the persons who ran the political establishment, its central purpose was the protection of the property system. Wesley did not seem to share their aim, but in this context his advocacy of liberty and constitution supported it. His ethic for property in a societal or national context was one of giving and sharing grounded in a theological concept of divine ownership of everything. It was not one of dismantling the property system and replacing it with one more egalitarian in its concept, structure, and distributions. Nevertheless, had he believed in a natural right to property *as that doctrine was argued in his time,* he would have had to commit himself openly to a defense of the property system as such.

LIBERTY AND (HUMAN/NATURAL) RIGHTS: ASSESSING THE EVIDENCE

Nature and History

In John Wesley's thought on rights and liberties, nature is integrated with history, but in such a way that historical thinking predominates and natural rights thinking is relegated to a secondary and complementary position. Constitution, custom, and tradition are central in his thought. True liberty always coexists with law, and does not stand apart as an abstraction. Duties are correlative with rights, and the enjoyment of liberty implies the moral, religious, and practical necessity to obey the law and the magistrates who administer it—and to defend the constitution. Liberty is a rational instinct, but it takes permissible and authoritative shape in history as religious and civil liberty. This orientation to rights and liberties is concrete, contextual, historical, organic, and communitarian. It is neither naturalistic nor rationalistic.

Wesley is most explicit in subordinating nature to history in "A Calm Address to Our American Colonies." There he admits to human possession of natural rights to life, liberty, and property in a presocietal state of nature, but then nullifies the admission by (a) denying that such a state ever existed and (b) arguing that such natural rights were surrendered with entrance into society. He *excludes* nature from history; he does not merely *subordinate* it. His principal purpose, of course, is to exclude entirely from the processes of political authorization and participation any supposed natural rights of individuals to consent to being governed and to demand representation. The only political rights he recognizes other than those conferred by divine authority are those that are the patrimony of the English people or the concessions of their God-ordained government.

In "A Calm Address" Wesley is following Samuel Johnson, but he restates essentially the same argument in other documents. He thought of most rights as emergent in history, not derived from nature—and of most liberties as achievements in the history of the English people. Their authority came from custom and constitution, not from correspondence with nature. His frequent use of the Whigs' slogan "English liberties began at the Revolution" is the mark of a staunch defender of rights and liberties in their historic form as English liberties embodied in law and custom and confirmed by the constitution. It is not the mark of a person given to thinking primarily in terms of abstractions such as "human" or "natural" rights.

Up to this point, one sees Wesley employing the concept of natural right—grudgingly—as a presocial myth, not as a norm within society. However, he does use natural rights arguments, and in a societal context. When he does so, it is as a critical principle, most notably in his attack on slavery, or as a logical weapon for polemics, specifically in his insistence that women as rational creatures are by nature equal with men. In the case of religious liberty, he appeals to natural right both as a critical principle and as a form of protection with normative priority over other claims. With religious liberty, however, the line between nature and history becomes indistinct. The appeal to a natural right of conscience before God becomes a legal protection enforced by a king (George II) who will not tolerate persecution for reasons of religion.

What Wesley does not do is formulate the appeal to natural rights into a consistent method for moral and social decision making. He reaches for natural right when historical norms do not provide adequate protection for civil and religious liberties. Nor does he employ natural right as a normative basis for theoretical construction of social and political institutions. He does not invent a theory of society and government out of a doctrine of individual natural right, as does John Locke. And he does not rearrange the English religious establishment with right of conscience as organizing principle. In both cases he accepts what is given historically, and uses the natural rights appeal for corrections and adaptations.

Furthermore, in Wesley's rights thinking, nature is subordinate not only to history but also to Scripture. In his approach to decision making, a text from Scripture always trumped a principle grounded in nature or reason. Scriptural teaching concerning the divine ordination of governing power was the primary basis for his excluding the natural right to consent from political authority and representation. Scripture texts also required him to resist the preaching role of women, instead of arguing for "a woman's right to preach" based on a natural equality with men that made a woman equally authorized to visit the sick. Scripture at some points supported or at least tolerated slavery, which may have been the reason why he chose to "set Scripture out of the question" in order to attack slavery with the weaponry of natural right. He believed the polity of the Church of England to be in accord with Scripture, and therefore not open to reconstruction on other grounds. If Wesley accorded primacy to Scripture, which he did, he could not allow comparable authority to inferences and rulings from nature and reason.

Wesley does owe something to the rationalistic tradition of natural rights that emerged in and with the Enlightenment, but he owes more to an older English tradition of historical and organic thinking that he shared with Hooker and Burke. If he is going to be claimed for the cause of human rights, it must be with recognition of his primary rootage in that historical approach. Rights concepts associated with the Enlightenment exercised more limited influence.

Wesleyan Liberty and "Possessive Individualism"

The value of a natural rights claim is that it invokes an authoritative principle of criticism superior to the customs and laws of the community. The attendant risk is that it emerges as an individualistic expectation within a set of social relationships thought to be constructed contractually or accidentally out of individual interests. That risk leads it into what C. B. MacPherson has described as the liberal tradition of "possessive individualism." "The basic assumptions of possessive individualism," MacPherson wrote, are "that man is free and human by virtue of his sole proprietorship of his own person, and that human society is essentially a series of market relations."[75] Rights emerge from ownership of one's own person, and therefore are intensely individualistic, diminishing the (historically) corresponding notion of duty. Social institutions arise by way of contracts to protect and advance the rights and interests of the contracting persons. The system of market relations implies that there is no essential connection or interdependence between or among human beings. MacPherson sees possessive individualism as the central theme of liberal social theory, and also its central fault. Among other things, it makes it difficult for the liberal concept of rights to deal adequately with the problem of political obligation.

John Wesley's understanding of natural right, when anchored only in human reason, runs that risk—a tendency encouraged by his evangelistic mission of individual conversion. However, other elements in his thinking dispose toward a different result. One is the historical bent to which I have given so much emphasis. The history of rights is the history of a community working out the conditions of common existence and mutual relationship, and developing significant organic interdependence across the centuries. It is not the history of contracts among disconnected individuals, each responsible only for his or her own welfare. Individuals, in Wesley's view, do not create major social institutions to protect their rights and serve their interests; they meet these preexisting institutions when they are born, and discover that they embody and give authority to the rights and liberties of individuals.

Wesley's theological doctrine of stewardship is another element. His profound belief was that human beings belong to God, not to themselves. In his sermon "The Use of Money" (1760), he insisted that "As you yourself are not your own, but his, such is likewise all that you enjoy. Such is your soul, and your body—not your own, but God's. And so is your substance in particular."[76] If rights arise from ownership, surely they arise from God's ownership and not from one's ownership of oneself. The obligations correlative to rights are those established by divine will and in divine love, not those arising through contracts in the free market. Relationships among human beings fundamentally are those among sisters and brothers who are children of the one God, not those of entrepreneurial atoms interacting in the anonymity of a mechanistic market.

Wesley's historical and organic social thinking on the one hand, and his theology of stewardship on the other, put him into a different rights tradition from that of possessive individualism. It is more conservative than the liberal tradition, if one understands by that term something like the historical conservatism of Edmund Burke, and not the quasi-libertarian form of possessive individualism that has adopted the label of conservatism in our contemporary political struggles. Probably we should call it *communitarian*, if that term could be sociologically descriptive, and not simply another party label. It is *liberal*, however, in its affirmation of rights and liberties.

The friends of Wesley who also are friends of human rights must be careful to interpret Wesley in this more historical and organic tradition, and not lead him into the highly problematical one of possessive individualism. That is the danger of celebrating his affirmation of liberties without seeing them as he did in historical context. That is the danger also of attempting to explain his alleged latter-day liberalism in terms of the impact on his political thinking of his evangelical theology. The influence on his developing political ideas of his stress on the universal availability of salvation and the personal responsibility for accepting it is not as demonstrable as is sometimes supposed.[77] However, the effect of claiming such influence is to construe Wesley's thought on rights and liberties as individualistic and contractarian, with consequent implications for his constitutionalism.[78] That surely is an incorrect reading of his views. Unfortunately, Wesley's evangelical mission encourages this result, because its stress is much more on individual conversion than on societal transformation.[79] His theology supports the mission by focusing on the recovery of the *moral* image of God rather than the *whole* image of God, and especially by ignoring the *political* image of God. Yet the proper political context for understanding the developments in Wesley's concept of rights and liberties is the historic constitutional tradition leading from 1689: "English liberties began with the Revolution." The proper theological context for protecting his views from possessive individualism is the whole image of God, and in particular, the political image. It is not his missional theology of evangelism taken by itself.

"Generations" of Rights

Later political consciousness has come to regard Wesley's *civil liberties* as *human rights*. Why not assume that he anticipated the later developments, but simply used a different terminology? The question is appropriate. Wesley's "civil liberties"—life, liberty, property, freedom to speak, write, and publish—were liberal "natural rights" even in the eighteenth century, and subsequently have entered the canon of human rights. Recent rights literature has termed these early liberal rights "first generation rights," distinguishing them from the "second generation" of social and economic rights and the "third generation" of rights pertaining to group solidarity.[80] Wesley clearly is "first generation" in his thinking about rights and liberties. In that sense he may be said to belong in the human rights tradition and to have anticipated later human rights consciousness—except for the important exception of rights to political authorization and participation. However, his rights and liberties essentially are negative protections and immunities, not entitlements to social benefits. He does not enter the "second generation" of social and economic rights. His concern for the poor and powerless in society was profound and unrelenting, even to the point of calling for pertinent changes in government economic and tax policies in "Thoughts on the Present Scarcity of Provisions,"[81] but he did not establish his concerns as entitlements and argue for policy changes on the basis of rights. If he related to the "third generation" of rights, it was only in claiming that national groups had a natural right to their own religion and laws. Wesleyan preachers in nineteenth-century England would do double duty as labor organizers, and would campaign for rights to education, adequate working conditions and wages, and health care, among others. In their commitments and their sensitivities they were true heirs of John Wesley, but not in their corresponding rights language. Insofar as the second and third generations are included in what contemporary Wesley scholars mean by human rights, Wesley's own rights concepts do not anticipate them.

Political Rights and the Political Image

The principal barrier to including John Wesley in the ranks of natural or human rights thinkers is his repudiation of individual political rights other than those emergent in history or conferred by governments—neither of which are the property of all persons equally. Wesley's resistance to political rights as rights of all individual persons derives from his conviction that government is the supreme power in the land, and that as supreme power it receives its authority directly from God and not from the people. There can be no inclusion of all persons in political authorization and participation without a basic change in that political-theological doctrine. Absent that change, the celebration of Wesley as human rights champion lacks credibility, however impressive his rights record may be otherwise.

Wesley modifies the absoluteness of supreme power in two important ways. One is with the concept of a constitution, historically developed, that embodies and protects the people's liberties and arranges limits to governing power. The other is with the concept of freedom of conscience or religious liberty as natural right. "And God did never give authority to any man, or number of men, to deprive any child of man thereof, under any colour or pretence whatever. What an amazing thing is it, then, that the governing part of almost every nation under heaven should have taken upon them, in all ages, to rob all under their power of this liberty!"[82] Divine ordination of supreme power does not confer authority without limits. Even if freedom of religious conscience is the only limit of this kind, it is of inestimable significance in relativizing absolute power. Nevertheless, the right to religious liberty, even though universally valid, is not likely to bind government in the absence of an efficacious constitution. On the other hand, a constitution, however hallowed and heeded, is authoritative only within a given country; therefore, it is not a limit to supreme power as such. Both the institution and the universal require each other in order to bind divinely ordained supreme power to the recognition of rights and liberties.

However, neither of these modifications of supreme power gets to the heart of the matter, which is the doctrine of supreme power itself. As long as that remains in place, at least in Wesley's definition of it, there can be no universally valid human right to political authorization and participation—and, of course, no right to representation. The concept of supreme power, receiving its authorization exclusively from divine ordination, is an inner theological limit preventing Wesleyan theology from developing the amplitude and richness of a human rights political ethic. Removal of the limit requires a theological transformation, not simply an adjustment of political attitudes. The good news is that the same Wesleyan theology has the promise of self-correction in this regard. In previous chapters I have pointed to Wesley's neglect of the political image of God, which is elemental to the whole image of God, and to the restrictions that neglect imposes on his political thinking. It is abundantly clear that the concept of the political image as human vocation for the governance of the world under God cannot allow the exclusion of the people from political authorization and participation. Recovery of the political image for Wesley's theology restores universal human political responsibility. It is therefore essential to the further development of a Wesleyan understanding of human rights. Whether that allows for or requires another category of human rights called "political rights" is a matter for further inquiry. Self-evidently, the denial of the fulfillment of this political vocation is a denial of something fundamental to human nature. Moreover, it is a violation of the natural right to religious liberty, understood in the fullness of its meaning.

John Wesley does not have a theologically integrated understanding of rights and liberties. That is evident in his explanation of liberty with reference to a rational instinct and of natural right with reference to the natural image of God only, and in the risks of individualism that this explanation entails. An understanding genuinely integrated *on the terms of his own theology* would involve liberty and natural right in the whole image of God, and especially the political image. This lack of integration is confirmed by his comment concerning *superadding* "to Christian liberty, liberty from sin, true civil liberty; a liberty from oppression of every kind."[83] The comment seems offhand in any event, because one would expect Christian liberty to be superadded to civil liberty, rather than vice versa. But the main point is that reference to a superadded liberty implies a failure to involve the whole image of God.

That failure makes his effort less than a fully articulated Wesleyan theology. Full articulation comes only with the incorporation into Wesley's understanding of rights and liberties of his concept of the political image of God. With that incorporation comes a fundamental change in his orientation toward political authority, and therefore toward political rights. Without it, he remains only partially committed to the notion of natural or human rights.

As to the question with which this chapter began, John Wesley is a constitutional and historical thinker about rights and liberties before he is a natural or human rights thinker. The latter elements are present in his rights consciousness, but their rise to greater prominence awaits both the encouragement of historical developments and the transformation of Wesleyan theology arising out of fuller and more serious attention to the whole image of God.

CHAPTER ELEVEN

WAR AND PEACEMAKING

John Wesley loved peace and hated war. He urged peaceful ways and attitudes upon his followers, and saw himself as a peacemaker—above all in the American war. Wesley was also an English patriot—one who believed the British government should defend the empire against foreign enemies and internal dissolution, and discharge its international as well as domestic responsibilities with force of arms, if necessary. For Wesley, that combination was not a contradiction. In his view, preservation of the peace is the first duty of Christians and governments, as is peacemaking in times of conflict. However, when peace breaks down and war is the issue, governments are authorized and required by divine ordination to use force to protect their people and territory, and to safeguard the innocent and restrain and punish the wicked. Justifiable military action is limited to defensive responses to military attacks by others. Nevertheless, under appropriate qualifying conditions, armed response is a moral obligation of governments. Obedience to governments making such responses is a religious obligation of subjects or citizens. The end of war should be a return to peace—a peace of reconciliation, not of domination.

Although Wesley did not use the terminology, his normative attitude toward war and responsibility can be categorized as a form of the *just war ethic*.[1] He was a peacemaker, but not a *pacifist*. One can argue whether he was right or wrong to adopt that position as the outcome of theologically grounded moral reasoning, but that is where he stood. The *just war* stance alone is *Wesleyan* in the historical sense. The larger problem is that his writings on war show no real evidence of theologically grounded moral reasoning in arriving at the position. He seems to have been there from the beginning, and to have taken it for granted—more or less—thereafter.

There are few signs of serious wrestling with the possibility of a conflict between Christian love and killing of the neighbor in war, or between loyalty to the state with its power and to a messiah who renounces power and goes to the cross. There are no significant traces of reflecting at length and in depth on moral issues pertaining to resort to war and the conduct of war. Wesley's orientation to war and responsibility is sensitive and compassionate, and it rests on religious convictions, but it does not appear to have emerged from sustained and agonized spiritual and intellectual probing of fundamental issues.

Wesley's apparent indifference to these vital questions is all the more puzzling, because persons close to him in the movement took them with great seriousness. John Nelson, one of Wesley's preachers, resisted impressment into military service on explicit pacifist grounds. "When brought before the court, John Nelson refused to serve: 'I shall not fight; for I cannot bow my knee before the Lord to pray for a man, and get up and kill him when I have done. I know God both hears me speak and sees me act; and I shall expect the lot of a hypocrite, if any actions contradict my prayers.' When a uniform was forced on him, he responded: 'Why do you gird me with these warlike habiliments? For I am a man averse to war, and shall not fight, but under the Prince of Peace, the Captain of my salvation; and the weapons He gives me are not carnal like these.' "[2] In contrast, John Fletcher—Wesley's designated successor—wrote *The Bible and the Sword* to defend British military action against the Americans.[3] Fletcher proclaimed that "we are neither ashamed nor afraid to spread the justice of our cause before the Lord of hosts, and to implore his blessing upon the army going to America, to enforce gracious offers of mercy, and reasonable terms of reconciliation."[4] He contended that praying and using the sword are compatible ordinances, vindicated the king's proclamation of a general fast (which Wesley credited with turning the war in favor of the British), and warned against neglecting "the religious means of success."[5] Fletcher's position formally should be designated as *just war ethic,* but it borders on the *crusade* because of his combination of religious passion with political aims and his advocacy of religious means to reinforce the efficacy of military means. It is held back from that extreme by his emphasis on mercy and reconciliation.

These two persons close to Wesley adopted starkly opposed positions with regard to war—and claimed Christian authorization for them—with no record of comment from their leader. So far as we know, he did not commend or reprove either one. The absence of response on Wesley's part may indicate that he considered attitudes toward war to be among "things indifferent"—that is, opinions on which Christians may differ in good faith, but which are not to be listed among the dogmatic essentials of the Christian faith. Or it may offer additional circumstantial evidence that he did not worry over these issues to the extent that they did.

Wesley's lack of sustained, reflective attention to these challenges to faith and moral conduct is manifest also in that nowhere in his vast literary corpus does he offer a definitive statement of a Christian ethic for war. There is no single tract by John Wesley establishing a doctrinally authoritative *Wesleyan* attitude toward war and Christian responsibility. Martin Luther wrote "Whether Soldiers, Too, Can Be Saved" as a pastoral and theological advisory on the permissibility and limits of war making by Christians. In that tract, Luther used his well-known *two governments (zwei Regimente)* or *two kingdoms* concept of divine governance to establish the responsibility of the state for maintaining peace even with the sword, and of Christians for sharing in this "strange work of love." His reasoning employed the just—or justified—war ethic, with some use of categories recognizable as just cause, just intention, competent authority, and last resort, although without much attention to the morality of the means of war. John Wesley wrote a much shorter tract titled "Advice to a Soldier."[6] It contains absolutely nothing on the morality of war or of the pros and cons of Christian participation. Characteristically, it is a salvation tract reminding the soldier of the imminence and eventual certainty of death and admonishing him to get his soul right with God before the event. In that respect, it is not different from Wesley's "A Word to a Condemned Malefactor."[7] Anyone who reads it expecting a single tract devoted to the problem of war is certain to be disappointed.[8] There is no primer on war from John for the Wesleyans comparable to the one Martin left to the Lutherans.[9] It is not surprising that war as a problem for Christian thought and moral practice is not an area to which John Wesley made any significant theoretical contribution.[10]

Why Wesley should have neglected engaging fundamental religious and ethical questions concerning war is a matter for speculation, not for the presentation of hard evidence. He had no direct personal experience of war other than sharing in waiting for the anticipated (but not forthcoming) Jacobite attack on Newcastle in the '45 rebellion, or for threatened French invasions during the Seven Years' War. Fundamental issues were not raised for him with the immediacy and compulsion he would have known had press-gangs succeeded in forcing him into military service, or had he suffered personally the devastation of his country by military combat. England was involved in wars throughout most of his lifetime, but what notice he took of them was desultory and uneven. He was attentive of necessity to the '45, and strongly so to the American War of Independence. However, his journal never mentions by name the War of the Austrian Succession (1740–48), the War of Jenkins' Ear (1739–48), or the Seven Years' War (1756–63), although England was a major participant in all of them, and although he lists numerous occasions of preaching to soldiers during those years. He makes several references to the threat of a French invasion during the Seven Years' War, especially when visiting Ireland in 1756,[11] but never discusses the general course of the war. His literary record makes clear that he focused primarily on his evangelistic work, and glimpsed the wars of England mainly with peripheral vision—at least until the onset of the colonial rebellion.

Apparently there was nothing in the nature of the wars of Wesley's time that provoked his opposition to the policy of the British government, and thereby produced a conflict of conscience. During the '45 rebellion he supported Protestant George II and the House of Hanover against Catholic Bonnie Prince Charlie and the House of Stuart.[12] He prayed not only for the soul and temporal welfare of King George, but also for his protection from and success against his enemies. He offered his own services as a clergyman to the cause, if only for the purpose of improving the morals of the soldiers. His oft-quoted commentary on the irrationality of war—in "The Doctrine of Original Sin"—certainly implies criticism of English and French war aims on the continent during the Seven Years' War.[13] However, earlier in the same war—in 1756—he proposed to raise a troop of two hundred volunteers, to be armed by the government and to serve locally to help repel any such invasion.[14] Insofar as he saw the war as defensive, he supported it. Moreover, when he scolded the American colonial leaders for failing to consider the cost to England of protecting the colonies during the French and Indian War (the American phase of the Seven Years' War), he clearly was affirming the action of the British government.

Wesley offers far more commentary on the colonial American War of Independence than on the other English wars of his time. His response to that war was analyzed in depth in chapter 5 and need not be reviewed in detail here. The essential elements of his response were that he showed sympathy to the colonists early in the conflict, when he understood them to be seeking nothing more than redress of grievances as English people, but turned against them when he discerned their goal to be independence from England. Thereafter he supported the British government's use of military force to attempt to crush the rebellion. Also, he saw himself as a peacemaker, attempting to pour water and not oil on the flames, but emerged as a strong patriot for England and a partisan for the cause of the integrity of the empire and the authority of the constitution. The early possibilities for serious and sustained criticism of government war policy vanished with his changing perception of the struggle.

In the absence of a religious or moral challenge to *war as such*, Wesley supported the government's involvement in the wars of his time because he saw no grounds in particular cases for conscientious objection. Despite his numerous depictions of the horrors of war, he did not raise fundamental objections to the use of military force as instrument of national policy. Military force, as he understood it, was an inherent instrument of sovereign authority under God. It was not to be challenged in principle. His reading of the events of the colonial war led him to conclude that the Americans were wicked and immoral in their conduct of the war, but that the British forces were honorable. The latter provided him with no serious problems of conscience.

THEOLOGICAL PERSPECTIVES ON WAR

Wesley's inattention to a systematic study of war in the light of Christian faith does not mean that he made a clean separation between war and theological interpretation. At two points in particular his thinking about the problem was heavily—although not entirely—theological. One was the relationship between war and sin. The other was the role of divine providence in war.

War and Sin

Original Sin and the Sources of War

Why do wars occur? The question pertains to the fundamental sources of war—to why there is war in the world—and not primarily to the reasons or motives that lead to particular wars. In *Man, the State, and War*, Kenneth N. Waltz offers a useful typology of responses to this question.[15] Wars are to be understood from human nature—as a predictable fruit of original sin, in the language of theologians, or of collective egoism and insecurity in the language of secular political realists; or from the nature of political systems, the usual supposition being that autocratic systems are more prone to war than democratic ones; or from the nature of international relations—the absence of a world government to protect weaker states from stronger ones and peaceful states from predatory ones, or the instability of an ungoverned international system that regulates the international conduct of states through balances, alignments, and realignments. Some combination of the three may be more useful than single-factor explanations in detecting predispositions to international conflict, but usually one type of interpretation predominates over others in writings of particular thinkers on the problem of war.

When John Wesley's views on war are analyzed with the use of this typology, he appears predictably in the first of the three types. War derives from human nature, not from mistakes stumbling on original goodness, but from the derangement of human faculties and inclinations provoked by primal sin.

> From whence comes that complication of all the miseries incident to human nature,—war? Is it not from the tempers "which war in the

soul?" When nation rises up against nation, and kingdom against kingdom, does it not necessarily imply pride, ambition, coveting what is another's; or envy, or malice, or revenge, on one side, if not on both? Still, then, sin is the baleful source of affliction; and consequently, the flood of miseries which covers the face of the earth,— which overwhelms not only single persons, but whole families, towns, cities, kingdoms,—is a demonstrative proof of the overflowing of ungodliness in every nation under heaven.[16]

If the language is not plain enough, the fact that this observation terminates a major section of his *The Doctrine of Original Sin* makes clear that he is referring to fundamental disruption and corruption of human nature, and not only to particular sins that lead to war. It is a classical Christian answer, one given by many previous and subsequent theological writers in the course of Christian history. Sin destroys the primal peace with God, and plunges humankind into all sorts of miseries, the chief of which is war. Wesley makes the point again in the course of the conflict of Britain with her American colonies. It is not enough to look at particular "authors of the present evil; look in this glass, and see the ugly monster, universal sin, that subtle, unsuspected serpent that has inflamed our blood, and brought on the malignant fever of contention on our body. Here gaze, till its loathsome and hideous deformity makes you loathe her. Then you will not marvel, that when the divine restraint is withheld, we are capable of anything; even that which is the most likely to end in our present and eternal ruin!"[17] Indeed, Wesley does not simply *explain* war in terms of original sin; he uses it as *evidence* of original sin, and confirms the argument with examples of trivial and irrational justifications given for war making.[18]

As Waltz and others have pointed out, such an explanation may be useful for suggesting a general tendency of human behavior, but it does not give a sufficient account of *war as a social institution*. War is more than murder, theft, and rape on a grand scale. It is the most disruptive and destructive form of human conflict, the one that maximizes the effects of force by pitting the resources and energies of the largest social units against each other and enhancing them with technologies developed in the course of combat for more and more effective killing power. War weakens moral restraints on human aggressiveness and self-interest often to the point of dissolution, displacing habits of humanitarian sentiment with tribal or national loyalties and erecting negative stereotypes in place of the individual reality of persons created in the image of God. Most significantly, governments—with divinely ordained authority—command the ordering of all resources, and especially human resources, to serve the ends of the state in the violent prosecution of its political objectives. The notion of original sin may account for tendencies toward egoism and aggressiveness and their persistence through time, but it does not include within itself the concept of their translation into magnified and expanded forms.[19]

On the other hand, one can point to the institutionalization of reason and some degree of humane consideration in the form of diplomatic protocols and negotiations, international laws governing resort to war and the conduct of war, formalities of declaration, and the role of treaties and their morally and prudentially supporting principle of *pacta sunt servanda*.[20] These institutional forms might be considered *order of preservation* instruments for dealing with the effects of sin in a social context where there is no government to supervise and control all of the interacting parties. However, they also are rudiments of human community testifying that war is not merely the institutionalization of force, and that original sin is not the only operative aspect of human nature. A theological interpretation of war employing the concept of original sin does not suffice to convey war's institutional reality without the assistance of social scientific explanations. It does not even suffice as a theological interpretation if sin is the only dimension of human nature brought into consideration. Nevertheless, it is an empirically relevant hypothesis concerning the human reality underlying war, and therefore a persistent challenge to liberal and progressive hopes for the complete elimination of war as a human institution.

However much John Wesley, with his attribution of war to original sin, may have been representative of Waltz's first type, he did not leave the matter there. He also had some sense of the third type—that is, of the origination of wars out of instability in the international system, and therefore of explanations of war not reducible to theological interpretation. Specifically, he was conversant with and fairly confident in applying to interstate behavior the concept of balance of power. He identified the "balance of Europe" as a conceptual instrument of statesmanship when he asked whether the ordinary people of England understood it as well as did Mr. Pitt.[21] Late in life he recorded words of high praise for the king of Sweden's tract on the European balance of power.[22] Wesley's own use of the concept revealed his understanding of how Britain fit into the balancing system in relation to neighboring states, and how its domestic weakness or strength influenced the calculations of those states with respect to military action against it. The balance of power concept is implicit in his letter to Lords Dartmouth and North advising them against harsh measures toward the Americans. He argued that sending the British army to America would leave the home islands vulnerable to attacks by France and Spain, and in fact would invite them. It was the operative theoretical concept in his thinking later on, when he reversed his estimates along with his political commitments, arguing that France and Spain would not dare test British power, nor would Portugal enter the contest against Britain out of fear of undermining the balance protecting it from Spain.[23] It is evident that Wesley understood peace among nations to be an organization of power, with the implication that imbalances in the power arrangements, however produced, could destroy the peace. War can result from changes in the balance of power, not automatically, but as a result of calculations to be made by anyone who understands the system. One must note, however, that Wesley did not use the concept of balance of power in a broad and systematic way to analyze international politics. Essentially, he used it as a support for recommendations concerning stabilizing English society internally and concerning policies toward the American colonies. He did not use it to ask how other European countries might perceive British empire-building to be a threat to their own security and other interests, and then to use the results of that inquiry to challenge British foreign military and economic policies.

As to the second of Waltz's types, Wesley does not ask why some states are more prone to warlike behavior than others, and if so, what accounts for the difference. He insisted that monarchies—by which he meant limited monarchies—are much more protective of individual liberties than are democracies,[24] but did not extend the comparison to proclivities for war and peace. Had he done so, the monarchies would not have come off too well in the context of eighteenth-century Europe; however, the possibilities for a comparative study of political systems would have been slight, because of the prevalence of monarchy and the relative absence of participatory systems. It is more likely that he would have dwelled on a comparison of the moral character and political intelligence of individual monarchs.

In the absence of a systematic statement from John Wesley on the causes of war, it may be fair to say that war as an example served to prove the case for original sin better than original sin served as an explanation for particular wars. It is true, of course, that he believed original sin to be the source and undercurrent of the whole human system of conflict and violence. Therefore, inevitably it was involved in any instance of strife among human beings, whether as individuals or as groups. However, in his political interventions he discussed or alluded to war more in political than in theological terms. On those occasions he tended at times to place his arguments in the context of the balance of power, warning that failure to conserve the constitution or to maintain the integrity of the empire could weaken Britain to the point of inviting attack by its ever-watchful enemies.

War as Divine Judgment on Sin

The preceding analysis explains the phenomenon of war essentially in terms of human causation—the "bent to sinning" in human nature, or human calculations, institutions, and mistakes. When Wesley speaks in a more homiletical, pastoral, or prophetic mode, he insists that war is a work of God. Specifically, the misery of war is divine punishment for sin. It is a dramatic and painful call to repentance. If the people turn toward God and away from sin, the misery of war will come to an end. If they do not, they can expect more of the same. The essential point is that war is not simply a human contrivance or mistake. It is an event in the economy of God—an instrument of God's justice and redemption. Therefore it is neither arbitrary nor capricious nor intentionally cruel; however, the suffering and destruction it brings will continue unless and until the people return to God.

One finds this more specifically *theo*logical, less *anthropo*logical, interpretation whenever Wesley gives serious attention to particular wars. In "A Word in Season," published at the beginning of the Jacobite rebellion of 1745, he asks why we are "on the very brink of destruction," and answers, "Because of our sins; because we have well-nigh 'filled up the measure of our iniquities.' " To Sabbath breaking as an example of sin, he adds "the thefts, cheating, fraud, extortion; the injustice, violence, oppression; the lying and dissimulating; the robberies, sodomies, and murders," and "a thousand unnamed villanies."[25] He makes the same basic argument thirty years later in "National Sins and Miseries"—a sermonic attempt at the outset of the American rebellion to explain why war brings suffering on the innocent. As with Israel in King David's time, "General wickedness then occasioned a general visitation; and does not the same cause now produce the same effect?"[26] It appears also in the wartime correspondence with Thomas Rankin: "The universal corruption of all orders and degrees of men loudly calls for the vengeance of God; and inasmuch as all other nations are equally corrupt, it seems God will punish us by one another. What can prevent this but an universal, or at least a general, repentance?"[27] In "A Seasonable Address to the More Serious Part of the Inhabitants of Great Britain" he speaks of the conflict as a judicial action of God against the peoples, and offers a theory of the rise and fall of monarchies. "They rose by virtue; but they fell by vice." The principal vice of the English nation is the shedding of blood in Asia, Africa, and America, and especially the bloody and vicious enslavement of Africans. Ultimately, he sees the misery of this war as a "divine contention," of which the human contention is only an effect.[28]

Wesley may be correct in charging the people with this catalog of sins, but his explanation of war as divine judgment disconnects from serious political analysis. He offers political analysis of conflicts, and this particular theological analysis, but no integration of the two. The sins for which the people suffer the devastation and torments of war seem to have little or no political relevance. Repentance and reformation of life can end the war—evidence that human beings can affect the action of God—apparently without changing policies and converting the politics of war making. War is divine judgment on a catalog of sins, not self-evidently on the sinfulness of political actions and policies that provoked and prosecuted the hostilities. If Wesley thinks in terms of particular "sins of war" with massively destructive political and human consequences, he does not link them directly and causally with war as divine judgment. War is the punishment an entire nation draws for the multiplicity of sins, most of which have nothing to do with war.

In one respect, the manner in which he connects divine judgment and sin with war makes a useful contribution to thinking about political conflict. By seeing sin and guilt as *universal*, he provides a principled means for avoiding the destructive arrogance and self-righteousness of blaming one side for the conflict, and allowing the accuser to see itself as the instrument of divine vengeance. God punishes both sides, using each as the means of chastisement against the other. In the "Seasonable Address" referred to above, Wesley calls the partisans of both sides to "turn your eyes . . . from those you suspect to be the only authors of the present evil, and think seriously of a more secret but certain cause," namely, "universal sin."[29] With that diversion of attention, he then invites the advocates for both sides to examine themselves and to ask whether with their own impiety they contribute to the causes of the distress. That is something less than an open-minded and self-critical analysis of the political and economic sources of conflict. However, it is a theologically defined approach to human strife that provides the context for such analysis, and may encourage its realization in practice. In any event, it is an antidote to the *hybris* and self-righteousness that augment the violent and destructive tendencies inherent in the resort to war. Unfortunately, Wesley did not adhere strictly to this principled approach to war in his attitude to the American colonies. As the issues became clear to him, his partisanship sharpened, and his sentiments turned sour.

Is War a Sin?

So far as I am aware, there is no statement of John Wesley's in which he labels war a sin. Had he done so, he would have had to add it to the catalog of acts to be avoided—such as fornication, smuggling, lying, theft, and speaking evil of magistrates and ministers. That would have committed him to a pacifist position, to war rejection as aspect and evidence of moral cleanliness, to the refusal of any support to the government even in wars of self-defense, and to civil disobedience when confronted with orders from the king when such orders involved the king's subjects in the prosecution of the country's wars. Also, it would have included commitment to and refinement in pacifism in the process of "going on to perfection." That would mean that no Methodist Christian—even by the grace of God—could recover the moral image of God and thereby become holy without becoming a pacifist. It would mean also a new legalism in Wesleyan theology: becoming a pacifist is necessary to salvation.

Of course, Wesley did none of those things and believed none of them. He was not a pacifist himself, and did not require others to adopt that stance. He supported wars of self-defense, and placed a high premium on what he saw as the biblically grounded duty to obey the governing authorities. Some of his preachers were pressed into military service against their objections and his; however, the objections in most cases were not to military service as such, but to the illegality of press-gangs, and to the argument that they could be impressed legally on the grounds that Methodist preachers obviously were idlers with no employment.[30] Most of the impressed preachers fulfilled their duties as soldiers, but used the occasion to evangelize their comrades-in-arms.[31] Wesley certainly was convinced that many occasions of resort to war were sinful, but never suggested that resort to war *as such* was sinful.

For John Wesley, war was not a sin that belonged on a list of wrong acts to be avoided. War was horror and human catastrophe. With no direct experience of the wars of his century, he nevertheless had an acute sense of their terrors and devastation, and on several occasions portrayed them with graphic specificity. In his sermon on National Sins and Miseries, Wesley spoke of

> the fell monster, war! But who can describe the complicated misery which is contained in this? Hark! The cannons roar! A pitchy cloud covers the face of the sky. Noise, confusion, terror, reign over all! Dying groans are on every side. The bodies of men are pierced, torn, hewed in pieces; their blood is poured on the earth like water! Their souls take their flight into the eternal world; perhaps into everlasting misery. The ministers of grace turn away from the horrid scene; the ministers of vengeance triumph.[32]

It is a terrible picture—one replicated with different details in other sermons and tracts.[33] In this notable sermon Wesley deals with the relationship between war and sin, but never suggests that war itself is a sin. That is consistent with all of his writings that touch the problem of war. War is to be avoided, but when it happens apparently it is part of the burden of misery to be borne by human beings. Statesmanship and strategy, one supposes, are to be left to the statesmen, who wield the sword for purposes of punishment, order, and defense, with authority given to them by God. They are not charged with defiance of God for using office and national power to defend the country against its enemies. Subjects and citizens are to obey those set in authority over them. They do not forfeit the gifts of justifying and sanctifying grace by doing so even in the extreme case of war. They are admonished not to renounce war, but to repent of their sins—to renounce wickedness and impiety.

Should there be any lingering doubts on the matter, one need only recall that Wesley preached on numerous occasions to soldiers in their barracks, or to congregations with soldiers and their officers present, without ever suggesting to them—so far as we know—that their military calling put them in danger of hell's fire. On one occasion he recorded, "Abundance of soldiers and many officers came to the preaching. And surely the fear and the love of God will prepare them either for death or victory."[34] The following day, he noted, "I dined with Col. ____, who said, 'No men fight like those who fear God. I had rather command five hundred such than any regiment in his Majesty's army.' "[35] Wesley offered no comment on this incident, but apparently he took it as a compliment to his ministry. Wesley's sermons to military personnel were on God's love and pardoning grace, not on the sin of war. They were as empty of aspersions on the military office as was his "Advice to a Soldier." On some occasions he preached to them on "Render to Caesar the things that are Caesar's."[36] Those sermons were intended, of course, to reinforce their commitment to military duty, not to undermine it. His counseling with military personnel usually was on moral reform and education.[37] He objected strenuously to military drill exercises on the Sabbath. In fact, in August 1782 the Methodist Conference "adopted regulations under which any

Methodist who practised military exercises on Sundays, or witnessed them after warning, was to be expelled from membership."[38] However, such warnings carried no implication that Methodists should not be soldiers, or that war was a sin.[39] One of the most astonishing expressions of his positive feelings toward the military forces is found in his letter of 5 August 1779 to Samuel Bradburn: "You did well in lending the preaching-house to the Army. I would show them all the respect that is in my power."[40]

War and Divine Providence

It comes as no surprise that John Wesley understood war to be an arena of providential ordering.[41] God is active in all events—why not, therefore, in war also? Characteristically, Wesley's interpretation of providential engagement in human wars discloses the divine-human synergy, the movement of God into human struggles, shaping, ruling, overruling—illustrated most fully, perhaps, in the "wheels within wheels" analysis of the interactive "Late Work of God," in the rise and fall of piety, prosperity, and pride in the American colonies.[42] Divine interventions are purposive and commanding but not deterministic—God takes up the challenges of human wickedness when they appear, but always responds positively to penitence and to the return of the prodigals. The course of war turns around when the people turn to God. But no one can escape the presence of God in war, and those who act as though God were not there do so at their peril.

God's interventions in war can be discerned from every angle and at every level. God initiates particular wars as means to chastise the people for their sins, just as God employs natural disasters for the same purpose. God rules the course of war as Lord of Battles. "Know ye not yet there is a God that ruleth the world? What did ye see with your eyes? Was the 'race to the swift, or the battle to the strong?' Have ye forgotten Dettingen already? Does not England know that God was there? Or suppose your continuance in peace, or success in war, be the mere result of your own wisdom and strength; do ye command the sun and the clouds also? Can ye pour out or stay 'the bottles of heaven'? But let it all be nature, chance, anything—so God may have no hand in governing the earth!"[43] This portrayal of the controlling and efficacious power of God in war is reminiscent of the Holy War concept in the Old Testament: God fights the war and decides the outcome without reference to calculations of military force and strategic and tactical wisdom. The numbers of horsemen, chariots, and weapons; the weight of treaties with powerful allies; the shrewdness of strategy and tactics are meaningless if God the Warrior directs a different outcome. In Wesley's view, God also controls particular events in the war. The combined French and Spanish fleets, holding at sea off the port of Plymouth in 1779, easily could have destroyed docks and buildings and seized the city, but they did not. Why? "The plain reason was, the bridle of God was in their teeth; and he had said, 'Hitherto shall ye come, and no farther.' "[44]

Moreover, God intervenes to protect weak and vulnerable people who are faithful believers. When Newcastle was threatened by attack from Jacobite forces in September 1745, Wesley and the Methodists were warned to abandon their meetinghouse outside the walls, because the defending cannons would destroy it when the attack came. Wesley studied the placement of the cannons, and announced that he "could not but adore the providence of God. For it was obvious (1) they were all planted in such a manner that no shot could touch our house; (2) the cannon on Newgate so secured us on one side, and those upon Pilgrim Street Gate on the other, that none could come near our house, either way, without being torn in pieces."[45] The miraculous placement of the cannons to protect the Methodists demonstrated the adorable providence of God in war. That God providentially might arrange for the approaching enemy to be torn in pieces evidently was not a reproach.

Why does God intervene in wars and direct the course of battles? What are the providential intentions that are served thereby? Is God moved to intervene by discernment of a *just cause?* In writing about strife with the American colonies and considerations of balance of power, Wesley showed obvious interest in such matters as political goals, policies, strategies, defensive considerations, and material results. Wesley's God, although a deliberate intervener in wars, did not seem to have similar interests. God's interests were religious, not political. The larger context of divine action was the reconstitution of the fallen world. Political and military contexts were subordinate to that one. Apparently they were of interest to God mainly as particular venues and opportunities for redirecting individuals and whole peoples in their religious loyalties and moral practice. War was one of God's instruments for serving that transcendent purpose, chastising sinners and idolaters, and calling them to repentance.

In war, God responds favorably to evidences of religious and moral change. British forces fared poorly and even disastrously in the military contest with the Americans, until "At length the King published a Proclamation for a General Fast in England, that we 'might humble ourselves before God, and implore his blessing and assistance.' "[46] Following that devout but politically astute move, the tide turned. The British forces recovered their strength and assurance, and scored impressive victories over the rebels. The turn toward God won the day. Repentance and recovery of piety have their own religious rationale, but they also are instruments of military success. Once one understands the divine purpose and *modus operandi* in war, one recognizes that making friends with God can turn disaster into victory. Wesley gives no comparable attention to God's interest in changes in policies and methods relative to the issues and conduct of war.

If God were interested in the justice of the claims of contending forces, it did not show, or at least Wesley either did not discern the interest or did not give it much attention. God was interested in the restoration of peace, and could be encouraged by renewal of piety and reformation of life to shape the conflict to that end. However, the concept of peace as terminus of war was reconciliation and the recovery of order, not an agreement based on a just sorting out of disputed claims. Wesley knew that the British government was in the right in its contest with the American colonies. He tended to assume that his God saw matters the same way. However, when the ending of the war produced a contrary result, Wesley did not subject the divine mind to political and moral inquiry. Instead, he wrote to Francis Asbury and the American preachers that the outcome issued from "a very uncommon chain of providences."[47] Assuming that God engaged in political thinking about human events, the process of divine political-moral reasoning apparently was hidden even from Mr. Wesley. Nevertheless, the result was clear. Wesley did not rail against the injustice of the outcome, and he did not dispute its providential nature. Inasmuch as history had demonstrated the will of God, it was necessary to recognize that reality and move on. In the lens of theological interpretation, the connection between God's intervention and the program of religious and moral reform appeared self-evident; the connection with the issues of justice in the political and military struggle was obscure, if not nonexistent.

Wesley's certainties and speculations on divine intervention in war illustrate the logical difficulties of the Arminian providentialist: God must be shown to be in control of events, yet without overruling human free will. Although the interventions are designed to serve religious and moral ends, they do not always force the results. Sometimes results are favorable. Wesley noted that with the approach to Newcastle of the Pretender's army, the people were more attentive to his sermons—a development that served the religious purposes of God.[48] Sometimes results were not favorable. The imminent possibility of death in war did not make soldiers and sailors more devout or more righteous.[49] Often they were the worst offenders against piety and morality. Sometimes the work of God is much the worse off because of war. Writing to Thomas Rankin, Wesley observed, "When a land is visited with famine or plague or earthquake, the people commonly see and acknowledge the hand of God. But wherever war breaks out, God is forgotten, if He be not set at open defiance. What a glorious work of God was at Cambuslang and Kilsythe from 1740 to 1744! But the war that followed tore it all up by the roots and left scarce any trace of it behind; inasmuch that when I diligently inquired a few years after, I could not find one that retained the life of God!"[50]

Perhaps the most impressive sign of the failure or unwillingness of God to coerce the human will in war is the absence of evidence of enduring peace. God offers the gift of divine peace of the spirit in the midst of war, and works for and encourages a peaceful outcome to every war. Yet there is no suggestion by Wesley that peace flowers among the nations and spreads its presence through time as a cumulative result of divine leading and human response. There is no concept of *progress in peace* underlying these efforts and offering the promise of a world without war. Apparently the persistence of original sin is too strong even for God's efforts in the divine-human synergy.

"God is the Lord of war but not the author of war." I came across that statement more than fifty years ago, as a seminary student beginning to read about Wesley's politics. Unfortunately, I do not recall the particular source of the statement or the name of the writer. It reappears in 1960 in Egon Gerdes's study of Wesley's understanding of war.[51] The formula is designed to show that Wesley believed God to be active in wars, but not responsible for their occurrence. It absolves God from liability for wars, while leaving open a wide road for providential intervention. Wesley certainly believed the first part of the statement: God is the Lord of war. If he believed the second part, he failed to explain why God was not the author of a war brought on the people as divine vengeance for their sins, and without reference to the political and military sources of the war. God apparently chooses wars as instruments of judgment, just as God appoints floods, plagues, and earthquakes. Doesn't that make God the "author of war"?

Moreover, even the first part of the formula is left in a state of incompleteness by Wesley's failure to bring God into the political process in such a way as to take the human political struggle seriously. The lordship is largely external. God is not *Lord of the political process* in any integral sense, because God does not engage the process as a political enterprise but as an occasion for evangelism and moral reform. Wesley's God-in-war is a *demiurge,* taking the mess made by human beings and shaping it to divine purposes without respect to the internal dynamics arising from human purpose, social systems, and conflicting notions of justice. At times it is *deus ex machina,* interrupting the normal human course of events in an apparently mechanical fashion. However, it is not a *Creator,* doing something genuinely new in history in cooperation with human beings as they attempt to fashion, redefine, limit, and expand their communities.

One concludes from these reflections that Wesley's understanding of God's providential intervention into war is more a tool of evangelism than a theologically informed principle of political interpretation. Furthermore, it is not fully incarnational, and its supporting notion of divine-human synergy does not engage all aspects of war as both human catastrophe and human institution. Wesleyan thinking on the problems of war and peace requires a more specifically *political* approach to such matters than the one offered by John Wesley.

THE VOCATION OF PEACEMAKER

Peace with God is central to John Wesley's understanding of the blessings that come to a person who has been born anew through justifying grace and has entered the grace-filled process of becoming holy in love. It is an inward peace, a sure confidence of the presence of God amid all the sufferings and uncertainties of a threatening and uncertain world, an aim of the Christian believer for realization in time as well as in eternity.[52] Inward peace and joy in the Holy Ghost are so much a foretaste of blessings yet to come that they may be equated with the kingdom of God.[53] Such peace in one's own soul "is the foundation of the mission of a true gospel minister."[54] References of this sort abound in Wesley's writings, usually with rhetorical expansions on the nature of peace as a gift to those who have faith, and on the doubts and miseries of those who lose it. Yet only rarely does Wesley connect the peace that Christ gives with the peace that the world gives, except to underscore the superiority of the former and to remind his hearers and readers that it is *"Not as the world giveth*—Unsatisfying, unsettled, transient; but filling the soul with constant, even tranquillity."[55] Moreover, the peace of Christ actually is antithetical to worldly peace. In reference to Matthew 10:34—"Think not that I am come to send peace on earth: I came not to send peace, but a sword."— Wesley comments, "That is, think not that universal peace will be the immediate consequence of my coming: just the contrary. Both public and private divisions will follow, wherever my gospel comes with power."[56] When he suggests in the midst of a war that the war will end and peace will result from the repentance of the people and their turning to God, that seems contradictory to the "not peace, but a sword" prophecy—and if not a sheer contradiction, at least an inconsistency crying out for resolution.

A *work for peace* in the world, growing out of the experience of peace with God, certainly is of concern to Wesley—but not a matter on which he tends to reflect openly for public communication. One notable exception is his sermonic discourse on "Blessed are the peacemakers" (Matthew 5:9). In a relatively brief section of the sermon, Wesley expands the concept of *peacemaker* to make it central to, if not identical with, the vocation of a Christian.

> In its literal meaning it implies those lovers of God and man who utterly detest and abhor all strife and debate, all variance and contention; and accordingly labour with all their might either to prevent this fire of hell from being kindled, or when it is kindled from breaking out, or when it is broke out from spreading any farther. They endeavour to calm the stormy spirits of men, to quiet their turbulent passions, to soften the minds of contending parties, and if possible reconcile them to each other. They use all innocent arts, and employ all their strength, all the talents which God has given them, as well to preserve peace where it is as to restore it where it is not. It is the joy of their heart to promote, to confirm, to increase mutual goodwill among men, but more especially among the children of God, however distinguished by things of smaller importance; that as they have all "one Lord, one faith," as they are all "called in one hope of their calling," so they may all "walk worthy of the vocation wherewith they are called": "with all lowliness and meekness, with long-suffering, forbearing one another in love; endeavouring to keep the unity of the Spirit in the bond of peace."[57]

It seems clear from this statement that to be a Christian is to be a peacemaker. Peacemaking is a *vocational* concept—it is the very nature of the calling to gain the mind of Christ in all things. Moreover, the work of peacemaking is not limited.

> But in the full extent of the word a "peacemaker" is one that as he hath opportunity "doeth good unto all men"; one that being filled with the love of God and of all mankind cannot confine the expressions of it to his own family, or friends, or acquaintance, or party; or to those of his own opinions; no, nor those who are partakers of like precious faith; but steps over all these narrow bounds that he may do good to every man; that he may some way or other manifest his love to neighbours and strangers, friends and enemies.[58]

It is not limited in the scope of effort, because it is *equivalent to doing good*, and Wesley specifies that doing good to others includes their needs of both body and soul. Neither is it limited by the normal boundaries of kinship, friendship, religion, nationality, or like-minded people. Of greatest importance, the Christian as peace-maker is to love enemies as well as friends. That provision is echoed and at times extended in other writings of Wesley that are more prominent than this one sermon. In "The Character of a Methodist" he writes that a Methodist Christian " 'loves his ene-mies'; yea, and the enemies of God, 'the evil and the unthankful.' And if it be not in his power to do good to them that hate him, yet he ceases not to pray for them, though they continue to spurn his love and still 'despitefully use him and persecute him.' "[59] The admonition to "Love even the enemies of God" is offered also in his famous sermon "The Catholic Spirit."[60]

Wesley's understanding of the inclusiveness of the Christian vocation as peacemaker is evangelical in the best sense of the word, that is, it is a work of love undertaken in response to the love of God freely given. "You . . . believe this love of humankind cannot spring but from the love of God. You think there can be no instance of one whose tender affection embraces every child of man (though not endeared to him either by ties of blood or by any natural or civil relation) unless that affection flow from a grateful, filial love to the common Father of all; to God, considered not only as his Father, but as the Father of the spirits of all flesh; yea, as the gener-al parent and friend of all the families both of heaven and earth."[61] This assertion that Christian love is a work of divine grace—that it arises in and is shaped by divine love—is the fundamental motif of John Wesley's Christian ethic. That it should reach out to one's ene-mies, and even to the enemies of God, is nothing more or less than Wesley's reading the words of Jesus and taking them at face value.

On the other hand, the operative presence of divine grace neither eliminates nor excuses the Christian from the work of peacemaking as "doing good to all humankind." Speaking of service with regard to the needs of the soul, Wesley stresses the integral character of God's work and human work, while maintaining the primacy of grace.

This power indeed belongeth unto God. It is he only that changes the heart, without which every other change is lighter than vanity.

Nevertheless it pleases him who worketh all in all to help man chiefly by man; to convey his own power and blessing and love through one man to another. Therefore, although it be certain that "the help which is done upon earth, God doeth it himself," yet has no man need on this account to stand idle in his vineyard. The peacemaker cannot: he is ever labouring therein, and as an instrument in God's hand preparing the ground for his Master's use, or sowing the seed of the kingdom, or watering what is already sown, if haply God may give the increase.[62]

The synergism of Wesley's theological statement is clear, but so also is the initiating, commanding, and effecting role of God in this divine-human relationship. God works through human instruments to prepare and execute God's evocation and construction of peace. The human instruments, however, are not automatons, moving mechanistically to implement the divine will. They are responders, prompted by love, led by love to effect a loving result. Peacemaking is a work of love in the context of grace. It presupposes and continually depends on divine grace. The vocation of peacemaker is one that Christian believers cannot decline without losing the peace of God, and with it their sure knowledge of God and their ability to resist the power of sin.[63]

These comments amount to more than a sermonic advisory. *Peacemaker* is the image with which Wesley defined himself in situations of conflict. That is clear from the way he approached the strained relations between Britain and the colonial Americans, and the way he interpreted his own interventionary efforts.[64] At the outset, in his letter to Lords Dartmouth and North, he sought to dissuade the government from using military force against the Americans. He worried in letters to Thomas Rankin and others about the terrible cost to both sides, and hoped and prayed for a peaceful resolution. He saw the prospect of war as a judgment of God on all of the parties involved. He advised Rankin to keep the Methodist preachers in America out of politics, to admonish them to avoid partisan commitments, and to encourage them to devote themselves to prayer for divine deliverance. Even after Wesley involved himself in the politics of this struggle by publishing what others saw as propagandistic tracts on behalf of the government, he continued to see his own role as that of a peacemaker, as one who tried to calm the raging passions at home and abroad, to bring reason out of insanity, to "pour water, not oil, on the flames." His self-image to the contrary notwithstanding, however, he was not a neutral arbitrator but a partisan patriot—one whose politically defined idea of peace was submission to the constitutional authority of the government in London. Once the prospects for a peace of conciliation or submission were gone, he moved quickly to one side of the conflict. From that point on, as we have seen, his positive estimates of the Americans turned fundamentally negative, his negative readings of British military capabilities turned firmly positive, and he supported with peeved but sorrowed righteousness the efforts of the government to suppress the rebellion by forcible means.

PEACEMAKING, BUT NOT PACIFISM

If John Wesley equated peacemaking with Christian vocation, why didn't he insist on pacifism as the only defensible Christian attitude toward war? Or put differently, if peacemaking was his vocation, why didn't he protect himself from narrow and at times hostile partisanship in the American war by taking the pacifist route out of the conflict? Perhaps the answer is that there is no integral and exclusive connection between pacifism and peacemaking, and Wesley knew it. There is no reason to assume that nonpacifists cannot be peacemakers, or that pacifists, as such, are effective in peacemaking. As long as human beings are driven by original sin, worldly peace always will be a particular organization of power— some variable combination of force and consent. The art of peacemaking is to move hostile relations toward some denser combination of common consent, thereby reducing reliance on force while nevertheless presupposing its presence and persistence. Christian peacemaking, in practical terms, requires attention to the reordering and limitation of force in the reorganization of power. One must recall, also, that peacemaking is built into the criterion of *just intention* in the concept of justified war. The justifiable end of war is *peace*, not vengeance, expansion of empire, grandeur, or glory. The vocation of peacemaking invades the making of war, but not necessarily or most effectively as pacifism.

John Wesley was a peacemaker but not a pacifist. He could understand and advocate the possibilities of *reasoning* toward a solution of international or intra-empire conflict; he believed that war was a stupid way for rational beings to try to resolve their difficulties. Also, he was convinced of the possibilities of gaining peace by repenting and turning to God—even if done only by one party to the conflict. However, he did not advocate attempting to achieve peace by unilateral renunciation of power. His unwavering belief in the presence and persistence of original sin would have worked against such a proposal, had he chosen to reflect openly on it and especially on original sin as a limiting factor in peacemaking. Providing more immediate resistance was his conviction that governments were authorized by God to maintain order and provide defense. Failure to carry out this mandate would be dereliction of duty before God. Wesley thought in practical terms of governmental responsibility for protective use of power, apparently assuming that it was not to be questioned in principle. In his travels he took occasion to examine British fortresses and other defenses, commenting sometimes with admiration for their excellence and at other times in despair of their adequacy.[65] As I noted earlier, he also made policy and strategic recommendations with reference to the European balance of power. These are elements of realism in the thinking of a peacemaker who recognized the role of power in the making and maintaining of peace. They are not the calculations or the sentiments of a pacifist.

When the Methodist Conference met for the first time, in 1744, the question was asked, "Is it lawful to bear arms?" The answer was, "We incline to think it is: 1. Because there is no command against it in the New Testament; 2. Because Cornelius, a soldier, is commended there."[66] This answer is less than satisfying, because it relies on dubious proof texting, and because there is no record of supporting discussion. Also, it seems hesitant, given the use of the word *incline,* which may indicate a division of opinion.[67] Nevertheless, this minute of the Conference in effect grants permission for military service by Methodist Christians on the grounds that it is not contrary to the law of God (i.e., the meaning of *lawful* in this case). The decision does not suggest enthusiasm for military service, but it does not exclude it on religious and moral grounds. Moreover, the conclusion is consistent with Wesley's well-established attitude toward war and peacemaking. He pressed his disciples toward peacefulness, but never toward a principled rejection of military service. On at least one and possibly two occasions he actually offered to recruit companies of men to engage in military training for the purpose of helping defend England in case of foreign invasion.[68] One must assume that he would have turned first to the Methodist ranks as a source of recruits.

Nevertheless, there are curious omissions in Wesley's treatment of pacifism. Early in 1748 a Quaker (assumed to be Stephen Plummer) challenged Wesley to answer several propositions, including this one: "It is not lawful for Christians to swear before a magistrate, nor to fight in any case." Wesley answered, "Whatever becomes of the latter proposition, the former is no part of Christianity; for Christ Himself answered upon oath before a magistrate. Yea, He would not answer till He was put to His oath, till the high-priest said unto Him, 'I adjure thee by the living God.' "[69] Why Wesley declined to answer the question about fighting is not clear. He may have dodged it for the moment because he was troubled about how to respond. Or he simply may have felt that the issue of oaths was more pressing at the time. One cannot infer a conclusion to one side or the other from this single issue.

More puzzling is that in his *Explanatory Notes upon the New Testament*, Wesley offers no commentary at all or at times no revealing commentary on some of the texts most pertinent to the matter of fighting and military service. He offers no commentary on the question to John the Baptist and John's response: "And soldiers likewise asked him, saying, And what shall we do? And he said unto them, Do violence to no man, neither accuse *any* falsely; and be content with your pay" (Luke 3:14).[70] Historically, that text has been used to validate military service for Christians, on the grounds that John did not require the soldiers to renounce their military calling. Likewise, he offers no commentary on "if my kingdom were of this world, my servants would have fought, that I might not be delivered to the Jews" (John 18:36). That passage, of course, has been used historically to affirm pacifism. In commenting on "resist not the evil man; but whosoever shall smite thee on the right cheek, turn the other also" (Matthew 5:39), Wesley explains *resist* as "standing in battle-array, striving for victory," but passes up the opportunity to drive home (or deny) a pacifist conclusion. He explains "turn the other also" as a rejection of personal revenge—an interpretation congenial to the just war ethic. With regard to "Put up again thy sword into its place: for all they that take the sword shall perish by the sword" (Matthew 26:52), he comments, "*All they that take the sword—*Without God's giving it them; without sufficient authority." Wesley's comment is an undoubted reference to the authority of the government for using force. Again, it is a text used historically to confirm pacifism by claiming a repudiation of sword bearing, but Wesley chose not to interpret it as such. With Matthew 19:18, he translates the pertinent passage "Thou shalt do no murder," instead of "Thou shalt not kill." He offers neither explanation nor interpretation for translation or text. However, the distinction is important: *murder* refers not to any and all killing, but to *illegal* or *unjustifiable* killing.

Wesley does not seize on any one of these texts, or any combination of them, to establish a biblically grounded stance with regard to military service. The texts that might have supported pacifism are left without comment, for the most part. The comments affirming authority for using the sword and opposition to using it for personal vengeance, coupled with the translation as "murder" rather than "kill," support the case both for a biblically allowable use of military force and for its religious and moral limitation. Nothing in his review of these texts challenges the conclusion of the Conference of 1744: "There is no command against [bearing arms] in the New Testament."

One should not suppose that John Wesley stood first on one foot and then the other, trying to decide whether the use of force—physical force, even lethal force—was allowable according to Bible and moral law. Wesley believed that force, including military force, was a normal and natural ingredient of state power and responsibility. It was justified by its role in maintaining order and defending the rights, persons, and property of innocent and law-abiding societies and individual members of societies. Late in life he wrote in his journal: "At St. Peter's Church I saw a pleasing sight, the

Independent Companies, raised by private persons associating together without any expense to the government. They exercised every day and, if they answer no other end, at least keep the Papists in order, who were exceedingly alert ever since the army was removed to America."[71] The army is essential to the peace and security of the society. When the army is removed elsewhere, it is "pleasing" to see private citizens collectively take over this responsibility—even if the only effect is to "keep the Papists in order"! In Wesley's view, the role of the military or its surrogates is an important and indirect contribution to peacemaking.

What has been said about the role of authorized force in enforcing the law, protecting rights, and defending the country, is confirmed by what seems to be tacit approval of some occasions of spontaneous and unauthorized defensive force. Specifically with regard to riots against the Methodists, Wesley records numerous instances of private persons standing guard as physical protectors of the meetinghouses, or bashing the heads of rioters to stop their bullying and their disruptive actions. When public authorities declined to use their offices and resources to maintain order and provide protection, others with no office stepped forward to fulfill those responsibilities. These uses of force were exceptional, however. Wesley's standard practice was to confront his tormentors face-to-face, inquire as to their motives, reason with them, pray with them, and take large risks of being severely injured or even killed. The usual—but not unvarying—response of the Methodists to hostile authorities was passive obedience, followed by action in the courts. Nevertheless, when the spontaneous uses of defensive force occurred, Mr. Wesley did not seem to disapprove. A case in point involved a naval lieutenant who brought his press-gang ashore and seized two of Wesley's preachers. These they released after proper identification. Then they "seized upon a young man of the town. But the women rescued him by main strength. They also broke the lieutenant's head and so stoned both him and his men that they ran away with all speed."[72] As he did with other such instances, Wesley recorded this one without comment—but apparently with satisfaction, and clearly with no expression or sense of disapproval.

IN THE JUST WAR TRADITION

In a famous passage in "The Doctrine of Original Sin," Wesley launches a savage and sarcastic attack on justifications for the practice of war. Citing another author, he reviews a list of alleged causes of war, including princely ambitions, official corruption, differences of views on the sacraments and clothing, expansion of territory, imperial conquest, and considerations of balance of power. Wesley's attitude in offering the citation is one of ridicule and contempt for the "causes." He then continues, in what may or may not be his own words:

> But, whatever be the cause, let us calmly and impartially consider the thing itself. Here are forty thousand men gathered together on this plain. What are they going to do? See, there are thirty or forty thousand more at a little distance. And these are going to shoot them through the head or body, to stab them, or split their skulls, and send most of their souls into everlasting fire, as fast as they possibly can. Why so? What harm have they done to them? O none at all! They do not so much as know them. But a man, who is King of France, has a quarrel with another man, who is King of England. So these Frenchmen are to kill as many of these Englishmen as they can, to prove the King of France is in the right.[73]

This passage often is set forth as solid evidence of Wesley's rejection of all war, and therefore of a fundamentally pacifist attitude despite his many affirmations of soldiers, forts, armies, and defensive use of military power. The confirming fact is that in this portrayal war is inherently irrational, and precisely because of its irrationality can sustain no rational justification. Wesley's words here seem to contradict all the nonpacifist evidence shown to this point.

To put the matter in perspective, one must recognize in the first place that Wesley's intent was to produce a treatise on human nature, not on the problem of war. He is arguing in favor of the doctrine of original sin and against a Deistic, optimistic view of humanity that identifies reason as the central human attribute and claims human dignity on the grounds of inherent rationality. In critical response, Wesley puts forward a whole line of indictments against the role of rationality in human behavior. In this particular case, war is offered as evidence of sin-driven derangement. If human beings truly were guided by reason, they would not choose war as their means of settling disputes. War is proof of the predominance of original sin over other aspects of human nature, including reason, and therefore of the need for evangelical conversion and not simply rational enlightenment. However, war as such is not the focus of his polemic.

In the second place, Wesley does not proceed by raising a principled theological objection to war. What he does is *employ the just war criterion of just cause* to show that most of the reasons given for war *are not good reasons*. In other words, his approach to the problem of war in this passage is an example of just war reasoning, not of pacifist principled exclusion. Wesley's argumentation confirms that he is a just war thinker—one who uses the just war criteria properly to condemn and discredit unworthy arguments for resort to war. To get a principled exclusion of all uses of military force out of this passage, one would have to show that Wesley meant to exclude all possible causes, and did not simply choose some to suit his theological polemic.

As a rule, the only *just cause* Wesley allows is the right of self-defense.[74] The point is stated as a matter of principle in the words he borrowed from Judge Blackstone for his case against slavery: "War itself is justifiable only on principles of self-preservation."[75] Blackstone argued that the law of nations permits killing only in self-defense, and therefore prohibits the killing of prisoners taken in combat. That restriction itself is an important discriminating rule for the just conduct of war: no killing of prisoners, and by implication, no killing of noncombatants. Blackstone then extended this moral and legal limit to justification for resort to war. Wesley quoted him without comment, but obviously with approval. Wesley endorsed the cases of the Corsicans defending themselves against the Genoese, the United Provinces of Holland rebelling against the unrelenting tyranny of Spain, and the allied states of Italy fighting to avoid Roman domination.[76] He viewed the English wars of his time primarily in defensive terms, and almost never raised any justifying cause beyond self-defense. The '45 rebellion was an easy case for him, because King George II and his government were defending against illicit and unauthorized attacks from without and within. He supported the defense of England in the Seven Years' War, even though he seems to have had serious reservations concerning the provocative reasons for the war.[77]

The American War of Independence is a more complicated case, because for that one Wesley introduced the concept of reparations—a notion not reducible to a strict concept of self-defense. At one point he insists that the intention of British military action is " 'solely to gain reparation for injury,' from men who have already plundered very many of His Majesty's loyal subjects, and killed no small number of them."[78] That certainly is too narrow an explanation of British motives, but the notion of reparation and restoration appears also in this broader summary of British war aims: "to make them lay down their arms, which they have taken up against their lawful Sovereign; to make them restore what they have illegally and violently taken from their fellow-subjects; to make them repair the cruel wrongs they have done them, as far as the nature of the thing will admit, and to make them allow to all that civil and religious liberty whereof they have at present deprived them. These are the ends for which our Government has very unwillingly undertaken this war, after having tried all the methods they could devise to secure them without violence."[79]

Reparations, in this usage, is not a war aim that stands alone. Wesley employed it in an expanded concept of self-defense that served as the primary justification for British military action against the colonies. The British government was obligated to use force against the rebels to repress illegal and unauthorized force, to protect the integrity of the empire, to defend the true liberty of the Americans against the fanatics for liberty, and to shield the American population from marauding mobs liberated from the restraints of law and custom by false colonial leadership. Defense is not simply resistance and protection—it is restoration of the *status quo ante*. The full course of military action intends to restore royal authority, the wholeness of empire, the enjoyment of civil and religious liberty, the rule of law. It is a concept consistent with Wesley's notion of peacemaking. To seal the defensive character of British action, he included response in kind by British troops when attacked by rebel forces.

In the course of setting forth what he considered good reasons for the British action, Wesley also rejected what the Americans considered good reasons for their own action. The latter included taxation without representation, restraint of trade, trial of accused American smugglers in English (not American) courts, the alleged tyranny of King George III, the claim to independence, and the exchange of American liberty for English slavery. None of these, in his view, constituted justifiable causes for rebellion against royal authority and separation from the British Empire. On the other hand, at the beginning of the conflict with America, Wesley discouraged harsh action against the Americans partly on grounds of the absence of justifying cause—they were simply "an oppressed people asking for nothing more than their legal rights, and that in the most modest and inoffensive manner which the nature of the thing would allow."[80]

Just cause was by no means the only just war criterion to appear in Wesley's moral rhetoric in the context of war. The end of the quotation on the British aims of war—"after having tried all the methods they could devise to secure them without violence"—is an obvious and certainly intentional use of the criterion of *last resort.* The criterion of *competent authority* is central to the whole controversy, because it involves Wesley's assertion of the right of king and Parliament to make laws for all segments of the empire, as well as their sole authority to use military force. The correspondence with Lords Dartmouth and North implies the criterion of *reasonable hope of success,* inasmuch as it calls in question the British readiness for war by contrast with the adequate and enthusiastic readiness of the colonials to resist (an analysis reversed subsequently with a different application of this criterion). His observation at one point that the war is merely a "dispute relative to the mode of taxation" is a question posed by the criterion of *proportion* as well as that of *just cause.*[81] The fundamental criterion of *just intention* appears when he rejects the notion that the British mean "to acquire dominion or empire, or to gratify resentment."[82]

All of the instances cited above show evidence of Wesley's use of criteria concerning justification for resort to war, or *ius ad bellum.* There is not much in his war-related writings that is specific to moral limits to the conduct or war, or *ius in bello,* although Briane

Turley offers some pertinent citations from Wesley's *Concise Ecclesiastical History.*[83] The aforementioned reference to his rejection of the killing of prisoners, and by implication of noncombatants, is an important exception—although not one that Wesley expands on through doctrinal and moral reflection or specific application. However, his rage against what he believes to be the total breakdown in American practice of moral rules in warfare invokes by implication the principle of noncombatant immunity. In "A Calm Address to the Inhabitants of England" he wrote with reference to the American rebels, "they roar like a wild bull in a net. They tear up the ground with fierceness and rage; repentance is hid from their eyes. They revenge themselves—upon women and children; they burn—all behind them! O American virtue! Are these the men who are proposed as a pattern to all Europe?"[84]

It is not necessary, however, to dredge up every scrap of justificatory or condemnatory rhetoric to confirm the central point: John Wesley is rooted firmly in the just war tradition. Turley calls him a just war theorist.[85] The *just war* association is correct, but the term *theorist* is too strong for one who did no actual theorizing about the morality of war, but basically applied to particular situations elements of a general orientation. Turley does acknowledge that Wesley's war ethic is more implicit than explicit. We get a better understanding of that ethic if we think of Wesley as a person internal to the British community, but transcending it to some extent because of his witness of love and forgiveness. He loves his country, and he loves all humankind. He wants to see an end of all wars, but he knows that wars will occur, and that when they do, his government must exercise its responsibility under God to safeguard and defend its people and its material interests. However, when efforts to avoid violent conflict fail, love does not withdraw to a monastery until the fighting is over. It remains an operative principle in war, with its powerful mandate to love the enemy. In the Seven Years' War and again in 1779, Wesley showed great concern for and compassion toward French prisoners, even though France was the opponent of Britain.[86] The operative power of love would not allow Wesley's patriotism to exclude his awareness of the love of God for all humankind. That example, of course, is one of interpersonal relationships—of becoming a neighbor to the enemy whom the course of war has made powerless and vulnerable. Love is operative also in the moral methods of limiting and directing war: war must be avoided if at all possible; if military action is required, it must observe appropriate moral restraints; the aim of the war must be peace.

That is the attitude with which John Wesley confronted the moral challenges and responsibilities of war. In essence, it is the historic Christian tradition of testing the justification of particular wars without—on the basis of theological confession—either excluding war as instrument of national defensive policy or rejecting Christian participation in war. It is Wesley's position, but with him it did not have the status and presence of a fully articulated theory.

CHRISTIAN ATTITUDES TOWARD WAR IN THE CONTEXT OF PEACEMAKING

Although *just war* demonstrably is Wesley's own position, he never elevated it to the level of dogmatic necessity. The Conference Minute of 1744 "inclined" toward permission for military service, but was not used to discipline or to exclude any Methodist pacifist. Apparently there was a Methodist acceptance of military service, but no Methodist rule enforcing attitudes toward defensive war and Christian participation. Such issues may have been sufficiently marginal to Methodist interests in the eighteenth century as to leave the matter open to personal inclinations, and to allow the inclusion and prominence of persons with such divergent views as John Nelson and John Fletcher. Wesley copied into his journal entry of 12 December 1755, "a serious, sensible letter" from an unidentified correspondent. In the context of the Seven Years' War (not mentioned by name), the writer of the letter asks: "But what shall the Christians do if the storm come, if our country be actually *invaded?*" The writer then replies, "The general answer must be the same: Be still, look up, follow Providence. A particular answer is hard to give yet." The first part of the "particular answer" is that Christians must keep their focus on God. "The spirit of the Christians and the spirit of the world are entirely different." The second part is that "Everyone should deeply consider what he is called to do. Some may think it would be a sin to defend themselves. Happy are they if they can refrain from judging or condemning those that are of a different persuasion. Certain it is, some have fought and died in a just cause with a conscience void of offense. To some therefore it may be a matter of duty to repel the common enemy." The final particular is, "They who believe they are called to this should proceed in all things in a Christian spirit. They should if possible join in one body."[87]

This statement may lean slightly to the side of the just war ethic with its reservation of judgment to particular cases, but intentionally it is evenhanded. Dogmatically, it places the decision in the context of a Christian's calling, but clearly avoids a dogmatic stand for one side or the other. A Christian's decision with regard to war is made *in statu confessionis*—an expression of one's confession of faith, one's Christian calling. However, the confessional state is the vocation of peacemaking, not the person's stand with regard to war and participation. The latter stand is not part of the definition of what it means to be a Christian. That conclusion is established and underscored by the writer's call for persons of contradictory persuasions to respect each other's views and to remain in the same Christian body. Neither side should consider the other to be outside the church by reason of conscientious response to war.

Of course, these words are not John Wesley's, but there is nothing in the context to suggest that they do not represent his view. He chose to include the letter in his journal, and to introduce it with words of praise. Assuming his agreement, the clear inference is that he placed attitudes toward war in the category of *opinions on which Christians may differ sincerely,* but not in the category of central verities of the Christian faith.

One must keep these distinctions in mind when attempting to clarify church teaching on war and peace for later generations, including the present one.[88] The *Wesleyan* position, insofar as the reference is to John Wesley himself, is the *just war ethic*. It is not pacifism, and it most certainly is not a martial, nationalistic, crusading spirit. However, Wesley's just war position is not doctrinally necessary for Methodist Christians. Neither is any other attitude toward war. Wesley's own views were clear and definite. Yet his practice was to allow pluralism within the movement *on this particular question,* and not to enforce his own position or exclude others. In *Speak Up for Just War or Pacifism,* two eminent United Methodist theological ethicists—Paul Ramsey and Stanley Hauerwas—spoke up respectively for the Christian just war ethic and for Christian pacifism.[89] That kind of debate is entirely appropriate in the Wesleyan tradition, so long as it remains in the realm of advocacy and does not become a demand for doctrinal conformity. What is essential in Wesley's tradition is that one's stance with regard to war and military participation be placed in the context of the vocation of peacemaking. For the just war ethic, that means an emphasis on the criterion of just intention—which requires that war move toward the re-creation of political community and therefore toward a just and healing peace. For pacifism, it means serious attention to the requirements of peace as an organization of power. Wesley's insistence on the doctrine of original sin rules out any approach to peacemaking that makes renunciation of force into a sufficient method, and that draws conclusions for abolition of war, total and complete disarmament, and democratic world government from an overly optimistic understanding of human nature and the possibilities of historical progress.

The vocation of peacemaking can be brought to mature expression in Wesleyan thought only by drawing it into the larger political vocation implied in the concept of the *political image of God.* That Wesley failed to develop this concept explains in part his failure to provide political depth and integration to his understanding of war and peacemaking. Wesleyan thinking about war and the vocation for peace requires the recovery of the political image and its full *rapprochement* with Wesley's evangelical theology, as do all other aspects of Wesleyan thought and practice.

PART THREE

PROSPECTS FOR A WESLEYAN POLITICAL LANGUAGE

CHAPTER 12
RECOVERING THE POLITICAL IMAGE OF GOD

Historical research into John Wesley's political and social thought contributes to the quest for a Wesleyan political language at minimum by uncovering a more benign and acceptable political portrait than the one exposed in the concept of "John Wesley, Tory." It demonstrates that John Wesley was a *constitutionalist*, committed to structural limits to power and to the subordination of power to law at all governmental levels—not a divine right monarchist of the sort that would have pleased his mother, Susanna, but would make him politically irrelevant to later generations in the Wesleyan tradition. It discloses a fervent and unrelenting supporter of rights and liberties—not, perhaps, as an *emergent human rights liberal*, but also not in the nonhistorical, individualistic rights tradition of "possessive individualism," and clearly not an advocate of unqualified passive obedience. What no amount or kind of historical inquiry can do, however, is eliminate the dominant problem with Wesley's political thinking, that is, the one that supports the persistence of the Tory label: John Wesley defended a hierarchical, top-down concept of political authority and its consequent exclusion of the people from the political process. His belief that authority originated with God and not with the people was a basic tenet of his political thought—not one to be overturned by more historical research, no matter how thorough, learned, and at times artful. That problem can be dealt with to the advantage of a Wesleyan political language only by way of a theological transformation that incorporates the people into the processes of political authorization and participation without negating the sovereignty of God.

In general terms, the theological method for addressing this problem is to bring Wesley's politics into the order of salvation delineated in his evangelical theology. The two are not integrated in his thinking, and the concept of God undergirding his understanding of political authority seems to be different—or at least to function differently—from the one operative in the *ordo salutis*. As an evangelist, Wesley articulated an understanding of divine action and human response through a process of prevenient, justifying, and sanctifying grace. This process describes the movement from sinful ignorance of and alienation from God to redeeming holiness before God. It is a revelation of the fallen creation in the context of grace. For the most part, however, Wesley addressed the possibilities of the order of salvation to individual persons. When forced to develop political awareness, and when by choice he intervened in political conflicts of his day, he did not envision politics in the context of grace in the same way that he interpreted the plight and prospects of the lost sinner. The God of Wesley's politics appears to enter the *redemptive* process only when using war and other cataclysmic events to call the people to repentance, and even then without materially engaging the *political* process. In its imperial eminence this God seems different from the suffering, serving, and comforting God of the order of salvation. The latter is fully trinitarian; the former is not.

In specific terms, the method is the recovery of the *political image of God*. This concluding chapter will show how recovering the political image for Wesleyan theology draws politics into the order of salvation, thereby ending the exclusion of the people from the political process, and unifying the God of politics and the God of the *ordo salutis* as the Holy Trinity whose governing of a fallen world provides context and guidance for the political vocation of humankind. Also, it will serve the broader purposes of Wesleyan theological development by requiring attention to the *whole* image of God in place of the exclusive attention usually given to the moral image.

THE THREE IMAGES OF GOD

When Wesley extended his concept of the image of God to the fullest, characteristically he represented it in three dimensions:

"And God," the three-one God, "said, Let us make man in our image, after our likeness. So God created man in his own image, in the image of God created he him." Not barely in his *natural image,* a picture of his own immortality, a spiritual being endued with understanding, freedom of will, and various affections; nor merely in his *political image,* the governor of this lower world, having "dominion over the fishes of the sea, and over the fowl of the air, and over the cattle, and over all the earth"; but chiefly in his *moral image,* which, according to the Apostle, is "righteousness and true holiness." In this image of God was man made. "God is love": accordingly man at his creation was full of love, which was the sole principle of all his tempers, thoughts, words, and actions. God is full of justice, mercy, and truth: so was man as he came from the hands of his Creator. God is spotless purity: and so man was in the beginning pure from every sinful blot. Otherwise God could not have pronounced *him* as well as all the other works of his hands, "very good."[1]

The three images are interrelated yet dissimilar—a point of importance for our inquiry. The *natural* image is the structural constitution of human nature. It is the creature's essence, and its peculiar and distinctive characteristic is that the human creature is "capable of God, capable of knowing, loving, and obeying his Creator."[2] This capability alone distinguishes human beings from the beasts.[3] Therefore it determines the positioning of humankind in the graduated creational order known widely and anciently as the "Great Chain of Being," which Wesley termed the "scale of beings."[4] The *political* image is based on this positioning, and has a twofold character. It is an ordering of responsibility and stewardship in which humankind as a whole represents God in the governing of whatever else dwells on earth. This ordering is the *human* dominion that images *God's* dominion over the universe. It is also a connective link between God and nonhuman creation, which is essential to creation's well-being and to the relationship of human creatures to those lower in the "scale." "Man was God's vicegerent upon earth, the prince and governor of this lower world; and all the blessings of God flowed through him to the inferior creatures. Man was the channel of conveyance between his Creator and the whole brute creation."[5] Humankind does not simply occupy a superior place in the order of creation; it also stands between God and the "inferior creatures" as God's agent and representative.

The *moral* image is neither structural nor positional; it is simply a mirroring of God established in loving and willing obedience. It is "the continually seeing and loving and obeying the Father of the spirits of all flesh."[6] The love, justice, mercy, and truth that are the content of the moral image are not ingredients of human nature, but qualitative reflections of the divine nature. They are the perfection of the human creature in its imaging of the divine perfection. They are that "holiness without which no one can see God," but this holiness is possessed only in right relationship to God—not antecedent to that relationship, and not apart from it. If there is no right relationship to God, no loving and willing obedience, there is no holiness, no perfection, no love, mercy, justice, truth, no moral image. Character is relational, a contingency of the divine-human relationship; it is not a native endowment or an independent human enterprise.

All three modes of imaging God are affected profoundly by the Fall, but not all in the same way. The *moral* image is lost, because the constitutive relationship with God is lost. It is simply gone—not damaged, or present residually, to be renewed and refurbished—but gone. Moreover, it cannot be recovered by human efforts. That point is made forcefully, if not always clearly, in Article VIII ("Of Free Will") of the Articles of Religion of The United Methodist Church:

> The condition of man after the fall of Adam is such that he cannot turn and prepare himself, by his own natural strength and works, to faith, and calling upon God; wherefore we have no power to do good works, pleasant and acceptable to God, without the grace of God by Christ preventing us, that we may have a good will, and working with us, when we have that good will.[7]

The natural image is not lost, because it is the structure of human nature, but it is deprived of the functioning of what is most distinctively human—the "capability of God," of "knowing, loving, or obeying God."[8] Insofar as this capability does not function rightly, the human creature loses what distinguishes it from the other animals. "Whoever does not know, or love, or enjoy God, and is not careful about the matter—does in effect disclaim the nature of man, and degrade himself into a beast. . . . [They] are undoubtedly beasts—and that by their own act and deed. For they deliberately and wilfully disclaim the sole characteristic of human nature."[9]

The effect on the *political* image is more complicated. It would seem to be lost, because the sinful malfunctioning of "capability of God" implies lowering of rank in the "scale of beings," and consequent destruction of the constitutive political relationship. However, humankind retains its position of dominance over the rest of creation despite this moral and spiritual degradation. A form of dominion remains, which is at least analogical to the divine dominion in the universe. But this dominance is no longer the dominion of responsible stewardship and vicegerency. It has become an exploitative relationship, one characterized by hostility between the human creature and the other animals. It is not a relationship that allows for the conveyance of blessings, because humankind no longer is a channel of communication between God and the nonhuman elements of creation. Perhaps one can characterize the effect of the Fall by saying that the *constitution* of the political image has not been lost, but the *representational aspect* of imaging has been redirected. Humankind collectively retains the governance of the other creatures, and with it the collective responsibility, but in doing so it now represents human self-interest rather than God's will. Given these two perspectives, we can say that the political image of God is not lost, but it has become dysfunctional.

THE POLITICAL IMAGE AND THE TRINITARIAN FOUNDATION OF GOVERNMENT

Despite that ambiguity—or vagueness—the *political image* emerges as the central concept for reformulating Wesleyan political language. It presents the challenge and offers the possibilities to think through basic theoretical issues of politics with a theological orientation and method differing in important respects from other theological approaches to politics. These issues include the notorious stumbling block of Wesley's politics, namely, the problem of political authority, and the nature and purpose of political institutions. However, the starting point for reformulation must be the trinitarian political implications of the political image.

The concept of the political image grounds government theologically in the doctrine of God, or more specifically, in the governing relationship of God to the world. Government as disclosed in human nature as political image is *what God does* in ordering, preserving, and developing the creation. This theological notion of government is trinitarian. It is the government at once of Creator, Sustainer, Redeemer; of Father, Son, and Holy Spirit as unified divine personality. It is not a work located in and taking on the character of any single facet or dimension of the relationship of God to the world, but of all of them together in the simultaneity of governing the fallen creation. The theological foundation of government is the Trinity in being and action.

Government also is *what humankind does* through its being as agent and steward of God in the ordering, preserving, and developing of the parts of creation to which human beings have access. When their governing is done rightly, human beings *image the government of God.* Their work is performed in *imitation of God,* and is informed by *analogy of God.* Inasmuch as the God who is imaged or imitated is the trinitarian divine personality, the political ethic that emerges with the concept of the political image must be a trinitarian ethic—not one shaped exclusively by creation, fall, or even the work of redemption. Nevertheless, the trinitarian political ethic that provides substance and direction for the vocation of political imaging begins with the work of renewal of the fallen creation, that is, with the work of God in Christ, because neither the governing work of God nor the governing work of human beings can be understood rightly unless the grace of God opens the way to understanding. That is the point at which politics begins to be drawn into the order of salvation.

To speak of government or politics as God's governing of the world is reminiscent of Luther's metaphor of God ruling by means of the temporal and spiritual swords. However, the idea of the political image informed by a trinitarian ethic differs from Luther's view precisely because it draws politics into the order of salvation, whereas Luther rejected that move, especially in denying that gospel liberty had any political implications. The concept of the political image is transformationist in a way that Luther's political thought certainly is not.

A theory of government grounded in the doctrine of God also differs from Luther's government as *order of preservation*, not in renouncing its restraining and ordering functions, but in declining to explain government primarily as an institution invented by God to counteract the effects of the entry of sin into the world. In the Wesleyan concept of the political image, *government is human nature*, because humankind is created to image God, to represent God, to be God's stewards in the governing of the other elements of creation. To be sure, governmental institutions originate and function in history, but the primal understanding of government is drawn from the knowledge of the work of God and not from the problem that humankind has become and the problems it has produced since its expulsion from Eden.

It differs also from theories such as the Thomistic natural law tradition that derive government from the social and rational character of human nature. At first glance it would seem not to differ, because government is the activity of the political image, which is a constitutive element of original human nature. When one says *government is human nature*, it seems to imply that one can discover the nature of government by studying human nature. The difference, however, is that human nature as such tells us nothing of the meaning and work of government. Original human nature is a factor in governing only because it images the governing work of God. The fundamental reference of government therefore is to God, not human nature.

Moreover, the meaning of political image as human agency imaging divine agency is understood by faith through divine revelation. It is not a rational inference from human sociality. Inevitably, that requirement draws politics into the order of salvation. For example, the justice that gives substance and direction to political responsibility as imaging divine governance is dependent on the presence of the moral image. It is not a natural virtue discoverable by reason apart from faith. On this question there may be some difference with Wesley's thinking, because at some points—as, for instance, in the famous essay attacking slavery—he apparently concedes that there is a notion of justice that is visible and comprehensible to persons who are not guided by Christian faith. However, the fact that he refers to it somewhat disparagingly as a principle of "heathen honesty" implies that it occupies a lower level of moral discernment.[10] Wesley was not in principle a natural law thinker, and the dependence of political imaging on the recovery of the moral image and therefore on the presence and work of all persons of the Trinity demonstrates that the recovery of the political image for Wesleyan thinking does not support a concept of government that is primarily anthropological. It demonstrates also that nature is not separated from grace in a proper understanding of the political image.

If the political image of God establishes government theologically in a way that is reducible to neither of the two traditional Christian explanations for the origin of government (fall and creation), is it then established "in Christ"—as Karl Barth and Dietrich Bonhoeffer argued?[11] Certainly the christological element is essential to this theory of government, because the political image in fallen humanity cannot be restored to its proper orientation and mission apart from the recovery of the moral image. But the work of God in Christ in reintegrating the three images and therefore recovering the proper functioning of the political image presupposes the work of God the Creator and Sustainer, and depends for its continuance on God the Holy Spirit. The theological framework for this theory of government is the Trinity in its entirety, not one particular component thereof. No aspect of the Trinity is or can be absent from this process, which is the process of bringing politics into the order of salvation.

One must speak of the grounding of a Wesleyan theory of government in the doctrine of God in this trinitarian sense. The key to political understanding is the image of God in its fullness. The political image is the organizing concept. It defines the mission of government and the work of humankind in that mission. It draws on the natural image for rational clarification. It depends on illumination from the moral image for its understanding of justice, and on the recovery of the moral image for its own transformation.

THE PEOPLE AND THE POLITICAL IMAGE

Bringing politics into the order of salvation by recovering the political image for Wesleyan political language produces conflict with John Wesley's own political thought at the point where he was most unyielding, and where later Wesleyans have found it most objectionable: the exclusion of the people from politics. Wesley's unchanging view was that political responsibility belonged only to those who held political office. The rest of the people should obey those in authority over them, and go about their proper business, but not presume to involve themselves in matters of governance and public policy. For Wesley this hierarchical and exclusionary understanding of political authority was unalterable and beyond question because of its theological foundation. He added issues of competence in political judgment to the grounds for excluding most persons from the political process, but essentially his argument was that the Scriptures said clearly that authority to govern was handed down from God. With the restoration of the political image to its rightful place in Wesleyan theology, however, this conclusion becomes untenable—precisely on theological grounds. When humankind as a whole is defined essentially in a vocation of governance imaging God, it is no longer possible theologically to exclude the mass of humanity from the political process. Humankind as a whole is charged by God with the responsibility to govern. Wesley's formula—*from God and therefore not from the people*—must be revised to read *from God and therefore through the people.*

Political Responsibility

Once the concept of the political image is made foundational to politics, the resulting role of the people is altogether different. *Political image* is understood as both an authorization and a call to political participation. It is a corporate concept that pertains to the whole of humankind collectively, not simply to particular individuals, classes, or offices. Nothing human is excluded from the political imaging of God. The political image establishes political responsibility as common human responsibility, as responsibility shared by all humankind. The criterion for sharing responsibility for governance is not whether persons are fully competent or whether they hold particular offices, but whether they are human. Human beings are political by divine creation, in their imaging of God, in their common stewardship of the world, not by reason of office or competence.

This concept of collective responsibility does not exclude the creating of political institutions with particular offices and official duties and powers that may be different from what others have. Admittedly, it does not provide specifically for the articulation of offices in its basic theological charter, but neither does it reject it. The development of political institutions is a rational exercise of the *natural image* to fashion proper instruments for the fulfillment of the vocation of the *political image*. Different societies can use their own political imagination to create what is best for their own circumstances, so long as they do not offend against the principle of common and shared responsibility, and so long as they serve the assigned purpose of care of the creation. The absence of specification of offices actually is an advantage, because it removes the theological justification for monarchy in whatever form (including dictatorship and charismatic rule above the law) as a necessary imaging of God's relationship to the world, but without restricting the implications for democratic and representative institutions.

Of fundamental importance in this argument is the inference that there is no theologically grounded normative distinction between a political class and a nonpolitical class, between those for whom political affairs are their solemn and appropriate business and those for whom they are none of their business. There may be differentiations of function in political society, or even gradations of responsibility and power, but no theologically warranted differentiation between those with political responsibility and those with none. Human beings by divine creation are political. The words may sound Aristotelian, but the meaning is different. For Aristotle, the human being was *zoon politikon* (political animal), one who could realize human nature to its fullest extent only through life in the *polis*. For the Wesleyan concept of political image, human beings inherently are political by reason of their creation and authorization as agents of God in the governing of the world. They realize their full humanity in part through the exercise of that agency. They are denied it to the extent that they are excluded from political participation. They surrender it when they decline to accept political responsibility.

The Authorization of Governing Power

The question of the people in politics includes not only that of participation, but also that of the authorization of the exercise of political power. On this point, John Wesley's stand is clear: he denied that the people conferred authority on their governors. Authorization to rule descended from above, that is, from God; it did not rise up from below. He admitted no natural right either to participation in politics or to the authorization of power. Scriptural teaching could not be supplanted by natural rights philosophy, and on this point the word of Scripture was plain: rulers govern as lieutenants of God, not by consent of the people. He drove this point home again and again in various writings in the context of British domestic politics and the conflict with the American colonies, where the central issues were representation, extension of the electorate, self-rule, and independence.

If one looks at the question of political authority from the standpoint of Wesley's political image, one sees something quite different. In that theological construction, humankind as a whole is authorized to act politically. This authorization is more than a commission to act; it is a constituent of human nature as created. The passage does not say that the people confer authority, but that they are authorized and deputized as human beings to govern. It is clear that authority comes from God, but there is no suggestion that it is given to rulers who then delegate to others below them. That is not the pattern of political authorization in the political image. If the case for the political image is supportable theologically, it means that anyone exercising authority in political society through political office does so by some receiving of authority from the people, who corporately under God are given the task of governance. No one can govern authoritatively apart from this process of consent.

There are major elements in Wesley's political thinking that support this transposition of the source of political authority. His constitutionalism, in particular, places restraints on the hierarchical explanation. As we have seen, Wesley did not believe that the king could rule without Parliament, or that the king's will was valid apart from a supporting and confirming parliamentary law. He also did not believe that rulers should act in violation of the ancient constitution with its mutually limiting political institutions, its prescriptive rights, and its constraining traditions. What he apparently did not recognize was that these institutions and traditions were organic elements of authorization arising from the interactions of the English people over centuries of political history. The people authorized power through these social creations. Yet Wesley accepted them, and by implication accepted the notion of authorization from the people even while rejecting a liberal doctrine of direct consent. When one adds to this analysis the fact that he did not limit direct divine authorization to kings, but allowed the possibility that it could descend on aristocracies and even representative democracies, one discerns a Wesleyan approach to political authorization that calls in question his own insistence that authority comes down from God directly and does not in any sense rise from the people.

Wesley's argument for descending conferral of authority with its consequent exclusion of the people from the process is not the only theological possibility allowed by the concept of God as ultimate source of authorization. There is a long and honored Christian tradition that acknowledges God as ultimate source, but traces the route of authorization from God through the people to those who actually govern. A form of this teaching is found in Richard Hooker—the great theologian of Wesley's own Anglican tradition. Had Wesley chosen this route, he could have activated and recovered his own concept of the political image. That would have allowed him to include the people in the process of authorization without denying that God is the ultimate source of authority. Unfortunately, Wesley's motivation seems to have been more political than theological. His political intention was to exclude the people, not to include them. It would not have served his defense of constitution and united empire to review the broader reaches of his theology, searching for implications that would universalize the process of authorization.

It is possible, therefore, to reconstruct a Wesleyan understanding of political authority from the political image with its authorization of humankind as such to governance and political agency. This reconstruction rejects Wesley's belief in the direct divine conferral of authority on rulers. However, it draws upon fundamental elements in Wesley's political thinking that acknowledge the long-term process of authorization through the creation of organic and limiting political institutions. In these respects it is authentically Wesleyan, even though it parts company with Wesley on a point that he believed to be fundamental to political order and action. It is in accord also with the historic line of Christian thought that acknowledges the transmission of divine authority to governors by way of those whom they govern.

Self-government

In his note on Genesis 1:26-28, Wesley stated that "God's image upon man consists . . . [i]n his place of authority. Let us make man *in our image,* and *let him have dominion.* As he has the government of the inferior creatures, he is as it were God's representative on earth. Yet his government of himself by the *freedom of his will,* has in it more of God's image, than his government of the creatures."[12] This intriguing passage extends the political image to include the self-government of humankind, in addition to the government of the "creatures." In fact, self-government is said to be even more reflective of the divine image than other relationships of governance. The idea of the political in the concept of the political image therefore is comprehensive of human governance of humankind, and establishes self-government as the norm given in creation. If Wesley seriously believed what he wrote here (or copied from Matthew Henry and Matthew Poole and edited), it is strange that he should object so strongly to the role of the people in politics.

Without mentioning the political image at that point, Allen Lamar Cooper assumed an original capacity for self-government lost in the Fall. "Politically [the 'Fall'] meant for Wesley that just as man was incapacitated to act spiritually for himself in bringing about the restoration of the original State of Nature, he was incapacitated to govern himself."[13] That would explain why Wesley could acknowledge self-government in original creation yet exclude the people from politics and require them to be subordinate to their governors. The first problem with Cooper's argument is that Wesley himself never linked the Fall with incapacity to govern. He did link it with the need for restraining force, but that is a different matter. For Wesley, the relationships of governance were determined by divine conferral of authority, not by universal human loss of governing capability. When he talked of the incapacity of the people to participate in governmental deliberations and decisions, he attributed the condition to lack of knowledge, to inadequate socialization to responsibility, to the rowdiness of mobs—but not to sin as a sufficient explanation. All human beings are sinners. If some lack the capability for self-government because of original sin, presumably all do. But some persons know more and others know less, and some have acquired the sense and habits of responsibility more than others. What is most important, some are *authorized* to exercise power and others are not.

A second problem is that, according to Wesley, the political image is not lost in the Fall even though the moral image is. Wesley quotes (with agreement) Isaac Watts to the effect that the part of the image of God remaining after the Fall is "the natural image . . . not excluding the political image of God, or a degree of dominion over the creatures still remaining."[14] Nothing is said here of self-government, but if self-government is an aspect of the political image, and one that reflects the divine nature even more than government of the creatures, it surely must remain. That is unavoidably the case, because dominion over the creatures is a remaining characteristic of humankind as such, not a commission or privilege given to some persons but not to others. It may be, of course, that what Wesley meant by "his government of himself by the freedom of his will" was to be understood primarily with reference to the moral image, that is, to keeping the law of God in loving obedience. In that case, it would have been lost, but his comment on "government of himself" was made in the context of discussing the political image, not the moral image. Insofar as self-government is a dimension of the political image, it is affected by sin, but not destroyed by it.

This analysis is not meant to deny the derangement of governing capacity, including self-government, by reason of the entry of sin into the world. The turning of power to egoistic purposes and the inclusion of force as an element of power are hallmarks of political reality—in the most gentle and benign governance as well as in the most brutal and malevolent. However, it does mean to deny its loss in any absolute sense. What is not lost remains a factor in both the imaging of God and the determinations of political responsibility. The fundamental issue remains that of the authorization of power. Persistence of the political image through sin—especially the persistence of the capacity for self-government—means that the people are involved by theological necessity in the process of authorization of power as well as, to some extent, in its exercise.

POLITICAL INSTITUTIONS

How does one think theologically about the purpose(s) of political institutions in a theory of government shaped by the notion of the political image? The answer is that one regards human institutions as societal instruments of the purposes of God, inasmuch as the concept of *political image* is meaningless apart from the human vocation of imaging of God. A political ethic with this premise is an ethic of the *imitation of God*. The purposes of institutions must be decided with reference to an understanding of how God relates to the world. The formula is something like the following: God's political work consists in caring for the earth and its creatures, preserving them and enabling their development; human beings imaging God are to care for the earth and its creatures to the same ends; political institutions are the instruments of care that include not only the design of caring policy, but also the exercise of power to execute the design.

Programmatically, what stands out by way of implication from this line of thinking is the imperative of environmental protection and development. Human beings must live in the world into which God has placed them, and in order to live and prosper must make use of its natural resources. That is an implication of dominion over the creation that involves some necessary and unpredictable degree of invasion of the realm under protection by those charged with protecting it. There is an approach to environmental invasion that minimizes damage through respect and self-limitation. There are other approaches that damage excessively and extensively through negligence or mindless exploitation. An approach to environmental concern grounded responsibly and prudently in the political image will make these distinctions. Of course, that is a general and pervasive human responsibility, not only one to be implemented through governmental action. But the notion of *political image* clearly legitimates and imposes governmental responsibility for the environment. Legislation to protect the environment expresses in principle the preserving work of God. Legislation to overcome the damaging effects of human impact on the environment expresses the principle of the renewing and redeeming work of God. It is a fundamental and continuing task of government, not a peripheral and transient one, and not something to be left to the "environmentalists."

No one should suppose, however, that the concept of the political image of God pertains only to what popularly is known as "environmental concern." An understanding of political institutions framed by this concept is open-ended with regard to the kinds of purposes government might or must serve. It is responsive to the tradition in the history of Christian political thought that insists on order and defense as fundamental responsibilities of government. However, it refuses to limit political institutions to protective and preservative functions, thereby excluding or at least diminishing other purposes and allowing vast social needs to go unmet. To the contrary, it is quite comfortable with the broad purpose of government set forth in the Preamble to the Constitution of the United States of America: "to promote the general welfare." In that respect, it is in agreement with Wesley's use of the term "public good," and with the tradition in the history of Christian political thought that asserts the *common good* as the end of government. Political institutions fashioned in the image of God must concern themselves—in good conscience and with adequate resources—with education, the needs of the poor, public and private health, the arts, and other matters that enable the members of the community to fulfill their political vocation of imaging God. These purposes are not the responsibility of government only. They are the responsibility of family, community, church, education, economic enterprise—whatever groups or institutions influence human character and provide human beings with the material, intellectual, and spiritual means of fulfilling their political vocation of imaging God's work. However, they are no less the work of government in its role as the one institution to address the needs of the entire community and to enforce its expectations and requirements with authorized power.

This mode of thinking is vocational in that it is defined by the call of God to image the governing of God in the care of creation. It is attentive to human needs, but is not defined exclusively or primarily by human needs. It differs from theological approaches that think of government primarily in terms of human concerns—the creational approach that explains government with reference to human needs deriving initially from human nature as rational and social, and the preservationist approach that explains government with reference to human needs arising from the entry of sin into the world. That is not to say human needs do not function prominently in the work of governing—obviously they do. The point is that the serving of human needs through government is instrumental to the role of human beings in fulfilling a divinely given political vocation. Human needs are not the end of government apart from the divine work of governing the creation. If there is anthropocentrism in the identification of humankind as the agent of God's political action, it is not the anthropocentrism that takes title to the earth for the benefit of human beings. *Political image* keeps the focus of political institutions and their operators on God's political work, not on themselves.

It follows from what has been said concerning the political image that one does not grasp the true meaning of political institutions apart from faith in the clarifying, revelatory Word of God. If that sounds arrogant and imperious, let it be acknowledged that persons of other faiths—or no explicit faith—often reach similar conclusions concerning the range and types of purposes of government. However, the central issue is not whether persons of divergent religious views can come to agreement on one or more of such purposes, but whether their common or competitive efforts move political institutions toward their divinely intended role in the care of the earth, its living creatures, and its spatial home. How do they fit into and serve the whole-making work of God, expressed in the Old Testament as *shalom* and in the New Testament as reconciliation? Do they help bring God's creation to the fullness of its possibilities (a creational concept)? In a world deranged by sin, do they provide defense against further damage and disruption (the preservationist concept) and encourage and facilitate the overcoming of brokenness (the work of redemption and renewal)? The framing of these questions, and the possibility of answering them rightly, depend ultimately on trinitarian theology, not on natural law or common agreement or practical experience.

These dimensions of the political work of God shape the true meaning of political institutions in correspondence with the vocation of those who bear the political image (i.e., the entire human race). They are fully consonant with John Wesley's transformationist theological language: his vision of the restoration of all things in the ultimate fulfillment of God's activity, and his evangelical call for the recovery of the moral image. In broad terms they conceptualize his vocation of peacemaking. They disclose the social meaning of "going on to perfection."

REPRESENTATION AS ORGANIZATION FOR ACTION IN HISTORY

Does the recovery of the political image require commitment to a particular form of organization of a society for action in history? Specifically, does it commit contemporary Wesleyans to Wesley's constitutionalism modified by full popular participation, and institutions and leaders that are representative as agents of the people? For many persons that would be an easy and attractive requirement. For others it would set expectations far beyond what they could work for immediately in their cramped and repressive societies. In keeping with the contextual approach characteristic of John Wesley's political thinking, the political image does not posit an ideal of government but indicates a normative tendency for all governing. Bringing politics into the order of salvation is not a matter of exchanging the ideal for the actual, but of encountering government in its historical actuality and turning it in the direction of divine intentions. A government may be nothing other than the imposition of order by unanswerable force. In that case the tendency in governing introduced with the concept of political imaging is toward the creating and eliciting of counterforces, the initial formation of a consciousness of rights, and the attempt to begin the subordination of power to law. All of these efforts may seem minimal from the standpoint of a mature, constitutional, and representative system, but they constitute the beginnings of responsibility where the alternatives are chaos or arbitrary force. If a particular government concretely is mature, constitutional, and representative, the tendency in governing introduced by the political image monitors the inclusiveness of participation to be certain that no persons or groups are excluded arbitrarily from their vocation of the political imaging of God. It monitors also the responsiveness of officials and institutions, and the correlation of governmental policies and practices with the ends of care of the earth and its inhabitants.

To put the matter differently, no particular form of government is theologically necessary. What is theologically necessary is the activation in every government of the tendency to direct its processes, institutions, and personnel toward the care of the creation and the nurturing and enablement of members of the community in the fulfilling of their political vocation. That tendency will require the incorporation into the organic and structural reality of government of certain elements that are fundamental to John Wesley's political thinking: constitutional separation and balance of powers, the subordination of power to law, the guarantee of rights and liberties. However, the process of incorporation will have different agendas at different points of a society's history and political development. To reiterate: the theological issue is not the ideal, but the tendency that becomes an operational principle in the concreteness of government and governing. That is the proper mode of political thinking for drawing politics into the order of salvation.

RECONNECTING THE IMAGES OF GOD

The heart of John Wesley's evangelism is the message that God acts to restore the lost moral image, not for the few, but for the entire human race; not coercively, but through the empowerment of the Holy Spirit that enables the response to God's gracious gift. God opens our eyes to our condition of being without God in the world (prevenient grace), bestows forgiveness of sins (justifying grace), and encourages us lovingly to become more loving and to "have that mind which also was in Christ Jesus" (sanctifying grace, Christian perfection). Through this process, this grace-filled ordering of salvation, the moral image is restored, the "capacity for God" returns, true humanity is recovered, and the born-again creature comes to stand before God and to love other creatures in the holiness of grace. This is the good news, the evangelical tidings for lost sinners and for the rest of creation damaged through their sinning. It is the order of God's salvation for sinful humanity.

That is about as far as Wesley takes the project of recovering or restoring the image of God. His preoccupation is almost exclusively with the *moral* image. Apparently he found neither the natural nor the political images very interesting, except through extension of concern for the moral image, for he made no sustained effort to explore their meaning and implications and make them into important elements in his theology. In this section we must attempt to rectify that failure in part, first, by inquiring into the implications for the political image of the recovery of the moral image, and second, by pointing to the consequences for the moral image of its separation from and reconnection to the political image. Examination of the relationships of the natural image to the other two must be left to someone else.

Political Vocation in the Context of Grace

John Wesley's concentration on the moral image of God to the neglect of the political image assured that he would not develop a Wesleyan theoretical understanding of political reality reflecting the whole image of God. The individualism of his evangelical appeal kept institutional analysis outside the framework of theological interpretation. The love emphasis in "going on to perfection" compromised the possibilities for Christian thinking about power. It is not surprising, therefore, that Wesley the evangelist was able to hold views on political responsibility and authority that were at odds with the clear implications of his own full understanding of the image of God. Had he troubled himself to look closely at his own teaching on the political image, and to reckon with the fact that—by his own account—it was not lost in the Fall, he hardly could have missed seeing the conflict.

However, let us approach the matter through Wesley's own emphasis on the recovery of the moral image, and ask about the implications of the order of salvation for these questions of political responsibility and authority. With that approach one sees a confirmation of the claim that authority is from God through the people imaging God in their political vocation. One concludes also that Wesley's publicly stated position on political responsibility and authority is an aberration from his evangelical theology. The strongest argument on this point is that the concept of God that is foundational to Wesley's views on political authority is different from that which is operative in the fullness of the *ordo salutis*. The God of "Thoughts Concerning the Origin of Power" is an imperial first person of the Trinity, high above humankind, handing down decisions and decrees. In its process of authorization it separates rulers from the ruled, and establishes relationships of superordination and subordination. By contrast, the God of the *ordo salutis* is the second and ultimately third person of the Trinity—Emmanuel, God with us, the crucified suffering God, the One who takes human sin and guilt upon the divine self, and in doing so enables and empowers humankind to fulfill the human calling by imaging God. This view of God is incompatible with a top-down, hierarchical notion of political authority. It implies a concept of authority that associates governors and governed in a movement toward reciprocity and community, and requires the executors of community power to draw authorization from those over whom they exercise it. It is clear that the latter view affirms the political image—and therefore the unity of the divine image in humankind—whereas the former does not. It is clear also that the latter and not the former provides a viable theological basis for Wesley's constitutionalism. If a Wesleyan political language is to have a full trinitarian foundation, it will unite the moral image with the political image, and adopt a corresponding view of political responsibility and authority.

One should note also that the concept of the political vocation of humankind corresponds to Wesley's Arminian doctrine of universal grace, whereas his view of political authority corresponds to Calvinist doctrines of decrees and particular election: some receive authority to rule and others—in the inscrutable providence of

God—do not. In this sense also, his evangelical theology confirms the politics of the political image, and sets itself in conflict with the theology supporting his public political views.

Prevenient grace in the order of salvation testifies to the divine initiative in all action everywhere and at all times. God acts, and human beings are called upon and motivated to respond. God's initiative is necessary, because the effects of sin both obscure the intention of God for humankind and impair the ability to will what God wills. The work of God in caring for the creation establishes a context of grace within which humankind receives its nature as political image. God acts politically in governing the world, and humankind responds by fulfilling its political vocation. In human history as created by sinful humanity, we may take as evidences of prevenient grace those occasions when emerging public consciousness discerns the purpose of government to be service to the members of the political community and not to their rulers; when it discovers the notion of individual and group rights and perceives the need for protecting them with customs, laws, and structures of power; when it recognizes the necessity to draw the people into the political process—initially to serve their self-interest and draw upon their wisdom, but ultimately to create the possibility for them to fulfill their political vocation under God. Political understanding of these kinds is not universal, and it is not self-evident. Its appearance is an event in history that suggests divine intervention to overcome the distortions produced by sin.

Divine initiative as prevenient grace is the light and energy that gives hope for the opening of closed systems. It is the terminator of demonic projects, the revealer of God's image in the most despised and forgotten of human beings. It does not guarantee progress in the humanization of political systems, but it does guarantee that no political system will ever permanently shut out the light of God. Given the created and present reality of the political image, God's prevenient grace is diminished when confined to the order of salvation of individual persons.

Justifying grace as a component of the way of salvation declares the acceptance of all humankind for the vocation of imaging of God in the governance of the world. By the creative act of God, human beings are placed into that political relationship. By the entry of sin into the world, the relationship is obscured and distorted, even though not destroyed. When by prevenient grace any and all persons are turned toward God, they discover that the vocation to governance remains in force. By justifying grace they receive the gift of divine forgiveness, and are welcomed to renew the vocation on its original terms. The renewal of life that comes with God's justification therefore includes the renewal of political vocation. It is the beginning of the realization of the political image of God.

As we have seen, this vision has profound implications for political responsibility and authority, and for self-government as well as government of the "creatures." It bears implications also for exposing and undermining the sin that defines and drives the corporate conflicts of the human race. The defining corporate sin of humankind is the tendency to make provincial identities—memberships in tribe, nation, race, ethnic and religious groups—into criteria of justifying merit. That means to value ourselves in absolute terms by reason of a particular societal identity, and in doing so to devalue others not of our group by reason of their corporate memberships. It is Arab versus Jew, Serbs versus Muslims and Croats, Hutu versus Tutsi, Catholics in Northern Ireland versus Protestants in Northern Ireland. What justifying grace reveals to us in the new viewing of the political image is that the fundamental identity of human beings is given in and through the image of God *only*. It is an identity that all human beings share. Particular social identities have historic importance, and therefore are not to be discounted, but all of them are relativized in the light of the image of God. Justifying grace reestablishes all of humanity corporately in the political image of God. It is a gift, not something earned, and not something superseded by other memberships. The gracious renewal of the political vocation of all humankind is an essential aspect of drawing politics into the order of salvation.[15] It is the conjoining of the political image and moral image in discerning the full meaning of God's justifying work in Christ.

Similarly, one could explore at length and in depth the implications of *sanctification* for the political image, and of the political image for sanctification. With the political image fully in view, one cannot reduce the political implications of sanctification to positive changes in personal attitudes and behavior, however important they may be. The combination requires thinking of sanctification in terms of institutional developments that support and conserve the various goods to be served through political vocation, and of the organic social growth that provides continuity and predictable support. One thinks in terms of transforming power from predominance of force into predominance of consent, thereby encouraging the growth of community and authenticating the lines of authority. One thinks also of moving beyond the rhetoric of human rights, and even their articulation into charters and protocols, to their solid embodiment in laws, customs, and practice. These proposals move beyond what John Wesley thought politically. However, they incorporate the wisdom of his organic constitutionalism and explore the social meaning of his teaching on sanctification—but only when sanctification involves the recovery of the political image of God, and not the moral image only.

The Political Image and the Wholeness of Salvation

Obviously the moral image is fundamental to the total human experience, even though it is not related structurally to the natural and political images. The "capability of God" provides loving access to God when the moral image is intact. When it is not, the capability remains, but it becomes a capability for atheism and idolatry.[16] The political image, in the normative orientation provided by the moral image, is a benevolent and stewarding exercise of power based on loving consent. Absent the moral image, it is a self-serving, self-justifying exercise of power based on coercion and violence. Yet if the natural and political images depend on the moral image for their proper functioning, the moral image—as a reflection of God—works only in and through the natural and political images. Therefore the recovery of wholeness is an integrating project involving all three images and their reciprocal relationships. Wholeness or salvation cannot be reached through attention to one image only.

The neglect of the political image is especially significant, because it represents a victory of the individualistic over the universalist and corporate elements in Wesley's theology. When Wesley speaks of the political image in its pristine condition, he speaks in corporate, not individual terms. "Man was the great channel of communication between the Creator and the whole brute creation. . . . As man is deprived of *his* perfection, his loving obedience to God, so brutes are deprived of *their* perfection, their loving obedience to man."[17] He is speaking not of individual relationships, but of the perfection of the whole of humankind in relation to the perfection of the whole of the remaining animate world. The wholeness of the human race and the wholeness of the rest of creation reciprocate through the political image—a corporate concept. Perfection is in the political image, which relates humankind through the moral image to the rest of creation. It is not simply in the moral image restored to individual persons. This is the wholistic concept that derives from the fullness of Wesley's threefold understanding of image of God. It is the context of individual perfection in Christ, not merely an extension of it. The recovery of perfection therefore should be conceptualized primarily in the corporate terms of the relationships of the political image, not primarily in terms of individual salvation.

By concentrating on the moral image to the neglect of the political image, Wesley reduced the cosmic plan of redemption to a plan of individual salvation. When the full image of God is the object of salvation, the *ordo salutis* works necessarily through the political image to recover the whole of the fallen creation. When recovery of individual holiness before God is the object, the *ordo salutis* is constricted to the rescue of individual brands from the burning, and institutions and the despoiled creation are reached only by extension from individuals who have experienced the love of God in Christ and the breaking of the power of canceled sin. That explains in part why Wesley did not or could not develop his concept of the reconstitution of all things—the divine work of renewing the creation, damaged and disrupted by the Fall, not simply in its original purity, but in a higher state of excellence than before.[18] He knew that many persons would not accept the offered gift of salvation, and thereby would frustrate the divine plan. Therefore he sketched the eschatological fulfillment, but did not develop the connections between the salvation of the individual and the renewal of the *kosmos*. He could not develop it, because the connection goes by way of the recovery of the political image—which, as an evangelist focused on the saving of souls, he tended to ignore. It also helps explain why the theology that comes to expression in his politics is different in important respects from his theology of salvation.

CONCLUSION: THEOLOGICAL TRANSFORMATIONS

Developing a Wesleyan political language that remains Wesleyan in its theology while transcending the limitations of Wesley's political thought requires the recovery of the political image and the drawing of politics into the order of salvation. That is, it requires a work of theological transformation, and not simply a creative restatement of John Wesley's politics. No "improvement" on Wesley's political portrait through new historical research can overturn his hierarchical view of authority and its consequent exclusion of the people from all aspects of the political process. No accentuation of Wesley's commitment to rights and liberties can displace his confirmation of this view of authority by a patriarchal and autocratic concept of God and a secular concept of government as supreme power. The recovery of the political image and the drawing of politics into the order of salvation, however, establish the whole of humankind as responsible political actor in the context of grace, thereby reversing this view of authority and its supporting understanding of God. The line of authorization then runs from God through the people to the political leaders and institutions. God's presence as suffering servant, as redeemer and comforter, replaces God the patriarch and the autocrat.

Other elements of Wesley's political thought and ethics can be accommodated by incorporation into that framework: constitutional separation and balance of powers, subordination of office and power to law, an organic view of communal society, individual rights and liberties and their protection by custom and tradition, and the vocation of peacemaking. The outcome is a political language authentic in its Wesleyan theology, but free of the ideological and political encumbrances with which John Wesley fought the battles of the eighteenth century. It is conservative in its respect for tradition and community, but rejects a conservative defense of privilege and power. It is liberal in its passion for human rights, but avoids the abstractions and egoism of possessive individualism. This Wesleyan political language is the continuing language of the *political image,* and of its place in the recovering of the whole image of God by drawing politics into the order of salvation.

One must emphasize this point, however: bringing politics into the order of salvation is a *work of theological construction* whose purpose is to help Christians understand the God-defined reality of the world and their place in it. It is not a spatial concept implying that politics is a purely human or secular realm outside of the providence of God—something to be relocated into the arena of religion or rescued by "putting God into politics." Therefore it is not a plan to *Christianize* society according to a medieval Catholic ideal of church-state integration or a package of Scripture texts and principles selected by the religious right. Nor is it a program to *democratize* society along the lines of Walter Rauschenbusch's program for the Social Gospel, however appealing and pertinent that may be. Human politics takes place in the context of God's political care for and ordering of the world, not apart from it. The order of salvation discloses the context and therefore the nature of human politics. It discloses also the divine work of recalling and restoring humankind to its true vocation of imaging God in the care and nurturing of all that God has created. In those disclosures the sufferings of Christ and the powerful presence of the Holy Spirit are sublime expressions of God's political activity. It is the task of the church—before recommending or supporting any particular political activity—to understand and declare the political work of God and the political imaging for which humankind is created, and to make clear that Christian discipleship implies the vocational recovery of the political image.

Fundamentally, that is the meaning of *bringing politics into the order of salvation.* It is a theological transformation before it is a political transformation. In the light of that transformation, however, one should expect to see the fruits of the imaging of God in political vocation: tendencies toward the universalizing of political responsibility, more sensitive care of the environment and less exploitation, increased reliance on consent and less on force in the uses of power, the progress of justice over injustice, the protection and enhancement of rights and liberties, the feeding of the hungry and the clothing of the naked, the restraint of irresponsible political and economic power, reliable protection for the weak and vulnerable, small and large victories for liberation from the various forms of oppression, and the mutuality of peace over the hard self-interest of war.

This critical analysis of John Wesley's political thought and his use of image of God symbols generates issues that go well beyond the primary concerns of this book, and should be examined on other occasions. Obviously the recovery of the political image has major if not drastic implications for Wesley's understanding of Christian perfection. The wholistic use of *image of God*—by contrast with a reductionist focus on the *moral* image—requires us to understand the perfection of individuals in the context of the perfection of humankind. It forces attention to the corporate character of human existence and the social nature of the self, and thereby raises even more questions than exist already concerning the prospect of being "made perfect in love *in this life*" (emphasis added). It implies also that "going on to perfection" and "earnestly striving" for it are calls to political involvement—to participation in the common human responsibility for the care of creation, that is, to the imaging of God in our shared, interactive, public existence. However, the main point to be made in conclusion is that the development of a Wesleyan political language and the continuation of the Wesleyan theological project *per se* depend together on the recovery of the political image of God in Wesleyan thought and practice. That recovery will mandate thinking of "order of salvation" with reference to the entire fallen creation, instead of focusing so selectively on individual human beings. Also, it will open the concept of the *political* in Wesleyan understanding to rethinking in full trinitarian terms. After all, it is the "three-one God" who is imaged, and not only the first person of the Trinity.

POSTSCRIPT: CONSERVATISM, LIBERATION, AND REVOLUTION

The political language sketched out in this chapter will lack appeal to some persons because it does not focus on liberation and revolution, and because its central political symbol—organic constitutionalism—is frankly conservative. The first point to make in response is that the possibilities of political criticism are built into the notion of the political image when political vocation must express itself in a world where human beings turn power to their own advantage and use governance for exploitation. Political criticism is a constant element in the practice of political vocation, because no human enterprise of power and governance fulfills God's expectations. Whether political criticism should take the form of movements of liberation and revolution is in many respects a matter of contextual judgment, but in principle that could happen. The notions of constitutional arrangements of power and organic development in socially embedded political consciousness are, by definition, intended to establish continuity in societal existence. In that respect they are conservative. But the operative concern for political vocation conceptualized in Wesleyan theological terms is not primarily that prevailing institutions and customs should be maintained, but that they should bring to expression the normative substance of the political image. In a broken world that expression always will have some distortion, usually a great deal. But in the light of the political image, the distortion is not the norm. Political existence in the form of institutions and customs always must be under review, and frequently under severe challenge. To say more than this would be to inquire into the moral possibilities and limits of rebellion and revolution. A political theory derived from the notion of political image inevitably marginalizes rebellion and revolution (either of which may be the form that liberation takes), as do most political theories, but it does not exclude them on principle.

A second point in response is that liberation, rebellion, and revolution are not political theories. They are important questions on the margins of political theory. However compelling may be their case for overthrowing a given political structure, they cannot overthrow political structure *as such*. Every movement of radical change must deal with the question of how it will organize the society when it comes to power. The failure to do this, or to do it on terms that express the realities of human nature, is what leads to the tyranny of most successful seizures of power. Political theory is about the governance of the *polis*. By implication it must deal with problems of the pathology of the *polis*, but pathological analysis and radical surgery are not its central concern. That fact must be kept centrally in view when developing a Wesleyan—or any other—political language.

NOTES

PREFACE

1. Another writer on Wesley's politics whose interests and approach are similar to my own is Leon O. Hynson. I disagree with Dr. Hynson on some points (not widely, I think), but always with respect and appreciation for his contributions. Hynson's Ph.D. dissertation at the University of Iowa (1971), "Church and State in the Life and Thought of John Wesley," is an important study. Significant interpretations of Wesley can be found also in his published articles, especially "John Wesley and Political Reality," *Methodist History* 12 (October 1973): 37-42; and "Human Liberty as Divine Right: A Study in the Political Maturation of John Wesley," *Journal of Church and State* 25 (1983): 57-85.

2. For convenient access to these writings see *Political Writings of John Wesley,* edited with introduction by Graham Maddox (Bristol: Thoemmes Press, 1998).

3. Elie Halévy, *The Birth of Methodism in England,* trans. and ed. by Bernard Semmel (Chicago: University of Chicago Press, 1971); E. R. Taylor, *Methodism and Politics 1791–1851* (Cambridge: Cambridge University Press, 1935); Wellman J. Warner, *The Wesleyan Movement in the Industrial Revolution* (New York: Russell & Russell, 1930); E. P. Thompson, *The Making of the English Working Class* (New York: Vintage Books, 1966); Bernard Semmel, *The Methodist Revolution* (New York: Basic Books, 1973); John Walsh, "Methodism and the Mob in the Eighteenth Century," in *Popular Belief and Practice,* ed. G. C. Cuming and Derek Baker (Cambridge: Cambridge University Press, 1972), 213-27; David Hempton, *Methodism and Politics in British Society 1750–1850* (London: Hutchinson, 1984); and Hempton, *The Religion of the People: Methodism and Popular Religion 1750–1900* (London: Routledge, 1996). I suggest one begin with Hempton, who has the advantage of having read the others. Also, his research is thorough and cautious, and his writing is insightful and irenic.

4. Theodore R. Weber, "Political Order in *Ordo Salutis:* A Wesleyan Theory of Political Institutions," *Journal of Church and State* 37 (1995): 537-54.

5. I am not aware of any prior recognition of the possibilities offered by the political image, probably because Wesley himself largely ignored it. Allen Lamar Cooper in "John Wesley: A Study in His Theology and Social Ethics," (Ph.D. diss., Columbia University, 1962) seems to include it under the natural image (91), acknowledges that it was changed partially in the Fall (93), and contends that

"Even after this partial destruction of the political image, man still had the ability to rule over the lower creatures of the world" but "did not have the ability to partake in the rule of his fellow-man" (106). Loss of this ability made it necessary for a monarch to rule as God's representative. However, Wesley did not infer the origin of government from the partial loss of the political image, nor did he assume that only a monarch would be God's representative. Leon Hynson quotes the pertinent passage from Wesley in "War, the State and the Christian in Wesley's Thought" (*Religion in Life* 45 [1976]: 208), but without naming the political image as such. In "Church and State," he offers a brief statement on the political image, and makes the important observation that "Here Wesley particularly stresses the general government of man, rather than his particular governorship as a magistrate" (115). Neither Cooper nor Hynson examines the implications of Wesley's concept of the political image for other aspects of his political thought.

In 1998, Theodore Runyon published *The New Creation* (Nashville: Abingdon Press), in which he acknowledged the political image as one of the three elements of the image of God along with the natural image and the moral image (16-17). Runyon's exposition of the political image is much more extensive than the two writers mentioned previously. However, he limits his application of the political image to its implications for environmental stewardship (200-207).

1. THE PROBLEM OF A WESLEYAN POLITICAL LANGUAGE

1. The United Methodist Council of Bishops, *In Defense of Creation: The Nuclear Crisis and a Just Peace* (Nashville: The Graded Press, 1986).

2. Paul Ramsey, *Speak Up for Just War or Pacifism: A Critique of the United Methodist Bishops' Pastoral Letter "In Defense of Creation,"* Epilogue by Stanley Hauerwas (University Park: Pennsylvania State University Press, 1988).

3. Referred to often as the "Two Kingdoms" theory, it is Martin Luther's teaching that God rules the world with the two swords of spiritual and temporal authority.

4. Subtitle of Reinhold Niebuhr, *The Children of Light and the Children of Darkness* (New York: Charles Scribner's Sons, 1944).

5. English Methodist developments of this period are analyzed insightfully and often with rich detail in E. R. Taylor, *Methodism and Politics 1791–1851* (Cambridge: Cambridge University Press, 1935); Bernard Semmel, *The Methodist Revolution* (New York: Basic Books, 1973), 110-45; David Hempton, *Methodism and Politics in British Society 1750–1850* (London: Hutchinson, 1984); and Hempton, *The Religion of the People: Methodism and Popular Religion 1750–1900* (London: Routledge, 1996). Semmel observes that "Both the Establishment in Church and state and the Methodist leadership, conservative and Tory by predisposition, feared the translation of a liberal and egalitarian Methodist religious doctrine to the political sphere, and made strenuous efforts to inhibit such a development. The enemy was Disorder. . . . They worked to contain the Enthusiasm which was indispensable to their own evangelization within the bounds of order. They discouraged political

activity, enjoined the Biblical commands of obedience to the King as to God, and attempted, after Wesley's death, to divert evangelical Enthusiasm to the missionary movement. These efforts appeared to be successful: there seemed to be no direct or obvious translation of Methodist Enthusiasm and spiritual egalitarianism to the political realm" (5).

6. Hempton, *Methodism and Politics*, 59.

7. Semmel, *Methodist Revolution*, 124-27.

8. Ibid., 126-27.

9. Ibid., 131.

10. Ibid., 128, 135.

11. Hempton has shown the relationship between Methodist anti-Catholicism and Wesleyan Methodism's growing identification with the Tory Party (*Methodism and Politics*, 117-18, 130, 142).

12. The Articles of Religion of The United Methodist Church, No. XXIII, *The Book of Discipline of The United Methodist Church* (Nashville: The United Methodist Publishing House, 1996), par. 62, p. 63.

13. Taylor, *Methodism and Politics*, 14.

14. Ibid., 17.

15. Taylor (ibid., 203-4) gives an excellent account of the struggle of these two tendencies in British Methodism in the early nineteenth century: "The Wesleyan Tory was not so much a Tory by choice as by the necessity of circumstances. He was the most vigorous advocate of the 'No Politics' principle. Inheriting all the fear of John Wesley lest political activity should lead to spiritual sterility, he transmuted Wesley's advice into a repressive rule which defeated its own object, and divided Methodism into two political camps. Compelled by the circumstances of his daily life and contacts to take political sides, he applied the negative principles of his political quietism, and resisted the political philosophy of those who were working for social and constitutional change. Where his companions were inspired by Liberal and Radical ideals, he reacted against them and supported the existing régime. In effect he became a Tory. He might parade his hostility to 'Political Dissenters' and his own isolation from political factions, but his support of 'Church and King,' and his hatred of the Radicals, led him further and further into a tacit association with Conservative forces in the national life." Wesleyan Methodists were predominantly Tory, Free Methodists predominantly liberal.

Of Methodist liberals, Taylor wrote, "In refusing to separate religion and politics, or to keep politics out of Methodist pulpits . . . the Methodist Liberal gave to his political opinions a theological colouring. Inspired by his doctrines of Salvation and Assurance, he questioned all forms of ecclesiastical or political privilege. If men are equal in the sight of God, then, argued Griffith, they ought to share equally the privileges of social, religious, and political life. Universal Franchise, Disestablishment, and Anti-Clericalism were, for the Methodist liberal, all linked with his interpretation of the doctrine of Assurance, an interpretation which was a common constituent of Methodist Liberalism throughout the period from Kilham to Griffith" (207).

Taylor attributes the emergence and substance of Methodist liberalism more to Wesley's doctrines of salvation and assurance than to his social conscience and his own interventionary tendencies. By focusing on the political influences of these theological sources he clearly anticipates Bernard Semmel's thesis concerning the inherent democratic tendencies in Methodism.

16. See "On Human Liberty" (Libertas Praestantissimum), "On Civil Government" (Diuturnum), "On the Christian Constitution of States" (Immortale Dei), and "On the Rights and Duties of Capital and Labor" (Rerum Novarum).

17. Helmut Thielicke, Theological Ethics (Philadelphia: Fortress Press, 1969) 2:7-73.

18. Taylor, Methodism and Politics, 150.

19. Semmel shows that some Methodist writers attempted to combine the conservative and liberal elements. When I observe that the liberal elements forced the conservative elements out of their canonical status, I am referring to longer-range developments.

20. A notable and highly influential example of the conservative portrait is William Warren Sweet, "John Wesley, Tory," Methodist Quarterly Review 71 (1922): 255-68.

21. Semmel's central argument in Methodist Revolution is that Wesley's Arminianism turned Methodism into a liberal reformist and modernizing movement.

22. Leon O. Hynson, "Human Liberty as Divine Right: A Study in the Political Maturation of John Wesley," Journal of Church and State 25 (1983): 57-85.

23. For an excellent historical treatment of the ancient constitution and other modes of political authorization in eighteenth-century England, see Harry T. Dickinson, Liberty and Property: Political Ideology in Eighteenth-Century Britain (New York: Holmes & Meier, 1977).

24. "Word to a Freeholder," Works (Jackson) 11:197-98.

25. Henry Rack, for example, states that Wesley's "Word to a Freeholder" advocated voting for government candidates; Rack, Reasonable Enthusiast: John Wesley and the Rise of Methodism (Nashville: Abingdon Press, 1993), 373.

26. For this insight into Wesley's sense of the British community, I am indebted to the late Professor Raymond P. Morris, former librarian of the Yale Divinity School and a Methodist layman with an extraordinary range of knowledge of Wesley and Methodist history. We had several conversations about John Wesley early in 1949, when I was doing research on the paper for Professor H. R. Niebuhr mentioned in the preface.

27. Semmel wrote that "By striking at 'Antinomian' doctrines held by the evangelical sects, masses of enthusiasts that had posed such a danger to state and church in the past, Wesley was seeking to counter the ideological forces that had helped lead to the practical Antinomianism of civil war in the preceding century, and which, he feared, might be leading in the same direction in his own lifetime. In so doing, he was, as we shall see, more and more consciously setting forth a libertarian and egalitarian doctrine couched in constitutional (i.e., rational and contractual) forms suitable for a modern society" (Methodist Revolution, 54). As I shall

show subsequently, it is a fundamental mistake to interpret Wesley's constitutionalism in rational and contractual rather than organic terms.

28. "Thoughts Concerning the Origin of Power," *Works* (Jackson) 11:46-53.

2. READING THE POLITICAL RECORD

1. See Leon O. Hynson's critique of W. W. Sweet's "John Wesley, Tory" in "John Wesley and Political Reality," *Methodist History* 12 (October 1973): 37-42.

2. Bernard Semmel, *The Methodist Revolution* (New York: Basic Books, 1973); Leon O. Hynson, "Human Liberty as Divine Right: A Study in the Political Maturation of John Wesley," *Journal of Church and State* 25 (1983): 57-85.

3. See Wesley, "Free Thoughts on The Present State of Public Affairs," *Works* (Jackson) 11:14-33; Letter to Thomas Rankin (1 March 1775), *Letters* (Telford) 6:143; and "How Far Is It the Duty of a Christian Minister to Preach Politics?" *Works* (Jackson) 11:154-55.

4. For excellent brief summaries and historical interpretations of Wesley's politics, see Henry D. Rack, *Reasonable Enthusiast: John Wesley and the Rise of Methodism* (Nashville: Abingdon Press, 1993), 370-80; and David Hempton, *The Religion of the People: Methodism and Popular Religion 1750–1900* (London: Routledge, 1996), 77-90.

5. Letter of Susanna Wesley to Lady Yarbrough (7 March 1702), *Writings SW,* 35. For an account of this incident, based on the uncovering of these letters, see Robert Walmsley, "John Wesley's Parents: Quarrel and Reconciliation," *Proceedings of the Wesley Historical Society* 29 (1953): 50-57, here 52.

6. Wesley, "An Account of the Disturbances in my Father's House," §8, *Works* (Jackson) 13:504.

7. Walmsley, "Wesley's Parents," 50.

8. Letter to Lady Yarbrough (7 March 1702), *Writings SW,* 35-36.

9. Wesley, "An Account of the Disturbances in my Father's House," §8, *Works* (Jackson) 13:504.

10. Walmsley, "Wesley's Parents," 56.

11. Journal entry in *Writings SW,* 204; Walmsley, "Wesley's Parents," 57.

12. The following works provide thorough treatments of the Sacheverell case: Abbie Turner Scudi, *The Sacheverell Affair* (New York: Columbia University Press, 1939); Geoffrey Holmes, *The Trial of Doctor Sacheverell* (London: Eyre Methuen, 1973); and G. V. Bennett, *The Tory Crisis in Church and State* (Oxford: Clarendon Press, 1975), 98-118.

13. *Concise History of England* 4:75.

14. For discussions of the authorship of Sacheverell's speech see Scudi, *Sacheverell Affair,* 90; Holmes, *Trial of Sacheverell,* 196; and Bennett, *Tory Crisis,* 116. Robert Southey wrote, "Wesley has asserted, and his biographers have repeated it after him, that Dr. Sacheverell's defense was composed by his father. It has been usually ascribed to Atterbury, and very possibly he may have employed his young friend in the task—a task by no means consonant with the father's principles."

Robert Southey, *The Life of Wesley and the Rise and Progress of Methodism*, 2nd American ed. (New York: Harper & Bros., 1847) 1:64 n.

15. "When the Revolution was effected, [Samuel] Wesley was the first who wrote in its defense: he dedicated the work to Queen Mary, and was rewarded for it with the living of Epworth, in Lincolnshire." Southey, *Life of Wesley* 1:57.

16. "Years after, in 1730, when Samuel, now an old man of nearly seventy, was trying to get permission to dedicate his monumental opus on the Book of Job to Queen Caroline, he boasted to his son Samuel of his loyalty. He told how he had written 'the first thing that appeared in defence of the Government after the accession of King William and Queen Mary to the crown,' and declared that 'I ever had the most tender affection and deepest veneration for my sovereign and the royal family; on which account (it is no secret to you, though it is to most others,) I have undergone the most sensible pains and inconveniences of my whole life, and that for a great many years together; and have still, I thank God, retained my integrity firm and immovable, till I have conquered at the last' " (Walmsley, "Wesley's Parents," 57). Henry Rack writes that "Father and son transferred their loyalism to the Hanoverian monarchy, though Wesley's mother did not" (*Reasonable Enthusiast*, 8). In fact, Samuel Wesley Sr. seems to have transferred his loyalty to William and Mary in 1689, and maintained it with all their royal successors—including the Hanoverians—until he died.

17. Atterbury's career and politics are reviewed with considerable thoroughness in Bennett, *Tory Crisis*.

18. Letter to editor of the *Gentleman's Magazine* (24 December 1785), *Letters* (Telford) 7:305-6.

19. Southey wrote that Samuel Jr. "took orders under the patronage of Atterbury. But he regarded Atterbury more as a friend than a patron, and holding the same political opinions" (*Life of Wesley* 1:63). John S. Simon comments that Samuel's "warm affection for Atterbury, and his readiness to defend him, brought him under great suspicion of being a Jacobite. When Atterbury was banished for being implicated in the great Jacobite plot he expressed his admiration for him in a poem overflowing with eulogy. Samuel Wesley was not a Jacobite, but his advocacy of his friend was so ardent that he often seemed to be one" (Simon, *John Wesley and the Religious Societies* [London: Epworth Press, 1921], 84). G. V. Bennett reports that "Samuel Wesley, elder brother of John and Charles, came to be a master at Westminster School on the Bishops' recommendation, and was subsequently ordained by him" (Bennett, *Tory Crisis*, 201).

20. Elie Halévy, *The Birth of Methodism in England*, trans. and ed. Bernard Semmel (Chicago: University of Chicago Press, 1971), 44.

21. Semmel, *Methodist Revolution*, 17.

22. Ibid., 57.

23. V. H. H. Green, *The Young Mr. Wesley* (New York: St. Martin's Press, 1961), 78.

24. Rack, *Reasonable Enthusiast*, 371-72.

25. Cf. Green, *Young Wesley*, 78-79; and Martin Anton Schmidt, *John Wesley: A Theological Biography*, 2 vols. (London: Epworth Press, 1962) 1:102-3.

26. Green, *Young Wesley*, 202-3.

27. For influential discussions of these trends and conditions see Norman Sykes, *Church and State in England in the XVIII Century* (Cambridge: Cambridge University Press, 1934); and Basil Williams, *The Whig Supremacy 1714–1760* (Oxford: Clarendon Press, 1939).

28. For political attitudes, pressures, and developments in Oxford University after 1714, see Green, *Young Wesley*, 20-27.

29. Martin Schmidt, *John Wesley: A Theological Biography*, vol 1. (New York: Epworth Press), 102-3.

30. Green, *Young Wesley*, 78.

31. Ibid.

32. Ibid., 28 n. 2.

33. Ibid., 79.

34. Ibid.

35. Ibid., n. 1.

36. Hynson, "Human Liberty," 58.

37. Luke Tyerman, *The Life and Times of the Rev. John Wesley, M.A.* (London: Hodder & Stoughton, 1870) 1:99.

38. See Introductory Comment to Sermon 146, "The One Thing Needful," *Works* 4:351-52.

39. Sermon 146, "The One Thing Needful," §1, §III.1, *Works* 4:352, 358.

40. "Court" and "Country" were common modes of political differentiation and identification that cut across Whig and Tory party lines. Lawrence Stone, in *The Past and the Present* (London: Routledge and Kegan Paul, 1981), 183, states that "the Court is easy enough to define: all those ministers, courtiers, officials, servants and financiers of the crown. However, it also presumably includes the titular aristocracy, the bishops, and those merchants who benefited from royal monopolies and who controlled local corporations by virtue of restrictive royal charters. In short it is what today we would vaguely call 'the Establishment.' " Stone sees "Country" as a more comprehensive concept. It was an ideal of "rustic peace, simplicity and virtue," a sentiment of community loyalty both local and national together with institutional means of expressing it, and a political program—much of it having to do with decentralization (184-88). During the period of Whig domination (1714–60), most persons identified as "Court" were drawn—not surprisingly—from Whig ranks, although not all Whigs were "Court." Whigs out of power sometimes made alliances—usually transitory—with Country Tories. Country complaints against the "Establishment" included corruption, use of patronage to increase control of Parliament, and opposition to a peacetime standing army (but support for a militia). We have no evidence that John Wesley opposed a peacetime standing army, but his sermon reflects Country critiques of corruption and patronage (in ecclesiastical terms, "preferment"). It should not surprise if Court Loyalists should find it politically threatening, and label it "Jacobite."

41. Cf. Richard P. Heitzenrater, ed., *Diary of an Oxford Methodist: Benjamin Ingham, 1733–1734* (Durham: Duke University Press, 1985). There is nothing polit-

ical in this diary. Two entries record the visit of the Prince of Orange and his receiving an honorary degree, but without commentary. Of course, Ingham may have been playing it safe by saying nothing with political meaning. More likely, his utterly nonpolitical diary reflects faithfully the absence of political interest and commitment among the Oxford Methodists.

42. Letter to Susanna Wesley (18 December 1724), *Works* 25:153-56.

43. Maximin Piette, *John Wesley in the Evolution of Protestantism* (London: Sheed & Ward, 1937), 290. See Simon, *Wesley and Religious Societies*, 99-103, for an account of Thomas Deacon's influence on John Wesley. According to Simon, Deacon was a bishop in a separate church formed by a small group of nonjurors. Simon's recording of actual influence seems inconclusive, but his discussion of Deacon is wholly liturgical, theological, and ecclesiological. He mentions nothing of a political nature. According to this account, Wesley evidently was selective in accepting Deacon's influence. For example, Deacon encouraged Wesley to study the *Apostolic Constitutions,* of which Wesley wrote in his journal of 20 September 1736, that "I once thought more highly than I ought to think" (*Works* 18:171-72).

44. Rack, *Reasonable Enthusiast,* 26.

45. Wesley's letters to William Law of 14 May and 20 May 1738, and Law's curt reply later that month, pertain to Wesley's faulting Law for not telling him of salvation through the blood of Christ (see *Works* 25:540-42, 546-48). Wesley's Letter to William Law (6 January 1756), *Letters* (Telford) 3:332-70, discusses basic theological themes of creation, sin, justification, new birth, and so forth. There is nothing political in any of this correspondence—specifically, no references to Law's Jacobitism or to the matter of taking oaths to a king not of the line of James II. J. Brazier Green's *John Wesley and William Law* (London: Epworth Press, 1945) shows no interest in any political influence of Law on Wesley.

46. Piette, *John Wesley,* 293.

47. Some members of the Grand Jury in Savannah, Georgia, defended Wesley on this point: "The third we do not think a true bill, because several of *us* have been his hearers when he has declared his adherence to the Church of England, in a stronger manner than by a formal declaration; by explaining and defending the Apostles', the Nicene, and the Athanasian Creeds, the Thirty-nine Articles, the whole Book of Common Prayer, and the Homilies of the said Church." Cited in *Journal* (31 August 1737), *Works* 18:192.

48. Semmel, *Methodist Revolution,* 57. The passage continues: "3. That the church is subject to the jurisdiction of God alone, particularly in matters of a religious nature. 4. That, consequently, Sancroft and the other bishops, deposed by King William III, remained, notwithstanding their deposition, true bishops to the day of their death; and those who were substituted in their places were the unjust possessors of other men's property" (*Concise Eccles. History* 4:116).

49. Semmel, *Methodist Revolution,* 57.

50. Hynson, "Human Liberty," 63.

51. *Concise Eccles. History* 4:169.

52. Ibid., 115.

53. See note 43.

54. Sykes, *Church and State*, 28-29.

55. Green, *Young Mr. Wesley*, 246. Wesley reported, according to Dr. Clarke, that Queen Caroline commented, "It is very prettily bound," and then laid it down without opening it. He rose up, bowed, walked backwards, and withdrew. The Queen bowed and smiled, and immediately resumed her sport (reported in Luke Tyerman, *Samuel Wesley* [London: Simplin & Marshal, 1866]).

56. In a letter to the author, Professor Rack stated, "It is difficult to separate the religious from the political in the circles in which Wesley moved and the 'politics' were seen as religious in a very real sense." That is true, of course. The question here is whether Wesley saw the religious attitudes and practices as necessarily and inevitably entailing particular political commitments on his part.

57. Gordon Rupp, "Son to Samuel: John Wesley, Church of England Man," in *Just Men* (London: Epworth Press, 1977), 113.

58. Simon, *Wesley and Religious Societies*, 99-101.

59. Hynson, "Human Liberty," 71.

60. Semmel, *Methodist Revolution*, 58.

61. William Higden, *A View of the English Constitution, With Respect to the Sovereign Authority of the Prince, and the Allegiance of the Subject. In Vindication of the Lawfulness of taking the Oaths to Her Majesty, by Law Required. To which is added, A Defence, by way of Reply, to the several Answers that have been made to it*, 4th ed. (London: S. Keble and R. Gosling, 1716). Higden was prebend of Canterbury and late rector of St. Paul Shadwell.

62. Hynson, "Human Liberty," 67.

63. Ibid, 69. For Wesley's full reply see Letter to Samuel Brewster (22 February 1750), *Works* 26:410-11. Brewster apparently inquired also as to why Wesley had not written against the Oath of Abjuration, which would have required persons who had taken oaths of loyalty to the Stuarts to renounce their oaths. After his commendation of Higden's book, Wesley wrote, "Yet I do not approve of the imposing that oath, no more than of many other things which yet are not mentioned in the *Appeal*. The design of that tract not only did not require but did not admit of my mentioning them. For I was there arguing with every man on his own allowed principles—not concerning the principles of any man. Besides, my conscience not only did not require, but forbade my mentioning this in a tract of that nature. I dare not thus speak evil of the rulers of my people, whether they deserve it or not." Wesley was opposed to requiring persons to act against their consciences by renouncing their loyalty, but he was unwilling to criticize the government for imposing this requirement. When the letter was printed, Wesley added a note: "And could Mr. Brewster think that I had no better work than to write against the Oath of Abjuration? Truly it never once came into my mind!"

64. Hynson, "Human Liberty," 69. There is no reason why Wesley would have had to read Higden in order to learn the distinction between monarchs *de jure* and *de facto*. Ever since 1689 it had been in common use in discussions over how to interpret the authority and claims to obedience of English monarchs. More important for Wesley's "maturation" is Higden's argument from the ancient constitution, which could have helped Wesley develop and clarify his political thinking.

65. Higden establishes the constitution in its antiquity and persistence as the context for his argument: "That of all these who liv'd in many different Reigns, to think there should be none who understood the Constitution and their Duty, or had Virtue enough to suffer for it; is to entertain a very mean, or a very hard Opinion of our Ancestors. In Modesty, we cannot but allow them to understand what the Constitution was in their own times, at least better than we can at this distance, and in Charity believe that they acted agreeable to it. And if it was the Constitution from the Conquest to Henry the VII. as this universal Practice and common usage of all Orders and Degrees of Men, must at least induce a strong Presumption that it was, it will be found, I believe, that the Constitution has descended the same to us; for there has no Law been made, since that time, concerning this matter, but that of the Eleventh of Henry the VII. which justifies this Practice, and enacts the Usage into a Statute of the Realm" (Higden, *English Constitution*, 6-7). Higden argues that the ancient constitution endorses the sovereignty of *de facto* kings—or "kings for the time being"—by acknowledging their legislative authority. However, he never refers to a legislative authority of the king separate from that of Parliament. His concept of the legislative aspect of the constitution is that of king and Parliament together. This also was John Wesley's view.

66. John Wesley to Samuel Wesley Jr. (22 May 1727), *Works* 25:221. John asks: "What you understand as spoken of rulers, I expressly say of private men: 'As well every ruler as every private man must act in a legal way.' "

67. Letter to Archibald Hutchinson (23 July 1736), *Works* 25:468. Cf. Letter to James Vernon (23 July 1736), *Works* 25:469: "Here is an Act of the King in Council, passed in pursuance of an Act of Parliament, forbidding unlicensed persons to trade with the Indians of Georgia."

68. See note 18.

69. "Some Remarks on Article X. of Mr. Maty's *New Review*, for December, 1784" (11 January 1785), §9, *Works* (Jackson) 13:411.

70. Although he did not level this accusation at John Wesley, H. Broxap apparently thought most Jacobites were practicing sycophants and hypocrites. He wrote, "The Jacobite was a believer who dissembled, who frequently took oaths of allegiance to the Government in being, and not seldom occupied positions of importance under the Government. The Nonjuror . . . was a 'whole-hogger.' His conscience forbade him to take the oaths, and there was an end of it. *Ruat coelum*, Let the sky fall in, he could not be moved" (H. Broxap, "Jacobites and Non-Jurors," in *The Social and Political Ideas of Some English Thinkers of the Augustan Age*, ed. F. J. C. Hearnshaw [London: George G. Harrap, 1928], 99-100). Maurice Woods had a strict definition of the Jacobites, and apparently accorded them more integrity than did Broxap: "No one could be fairly so described unless he was a believer in the Divine Right of Kings, held that Charles Edward was the legitimate sovereign, and that to make conditions with him for his return, whether in religious or civil matters, was treason and blasphemy" (Woods, *A History of the Tory Party* [London: Hodder & Stoughton, 1924], 166). Woods saw very few Tories as holding this position. If his definition is correct, John Wesley clearly was not a Jacobite, and therefore would not have to "dissemble" or be sycophantic.

71. For studies of Susanna Wesley, see Grace Elizabeth Harrison, *Son to Susanna* (Nashville: Cokesbury Press, 1938); and Rebecca Lamar Harmon, *Susanna, Mother of the Wesleys* (Nashville: Abingdon Press, 1968). See also Charles Wallace Jr., ed., *Susanna Wesley: The Complete Writings* (New York: Oxford University Press, 1996).

72. Hynson, "Human Liberty," 58.

73. Semmel, *Methodist Revolution,* 59.

74. *Concise History of England* 1:189. These volumes contain the substance of works by Oliver Goldsmith, Paul de Rapin Thoyras, and Tobias Smollet, "only with various corrections and additions." See Wesley's introduction, 1:vi-vii (reprinted in *Works* [Jackson] 14:272-75). I do not know whether these genealogical accounts derive from one of these authors or from Wesley himself.

75. Harry T. Dickinson, *Liberty and Property: Political Ideology in Eighteenth-Century Britain* (New York: Holmes & Meier, 1977), 164-65.

76. Tyerman, *Life of Wesley* 1:42-43.

77. The woman was Sophia Hopkey, and her uncle was Thomas Causton. The story has been told in many places. See, for example, Rack, *Reasonable Enthusiast,* 124.

78. See the sermon list for 1725–35 in Appendix II to Richard P. Heizenrater, "John Wesley and the Oxford Methodists, 1725–1735" (Ph.D. diss., Duke University, 1972), 431-32.

79. Wesley's youthful politics, to the extent that one can discern and describe it, shows some similarities to Country attitudes. Nevertheless, I am reluctant to press the Wesley-as-Country identification too far, for the reasons given in this sentence, and also because the definition of "Country" was not precise. See note 40 of this chapter.

80. The classic statement of the history and components of the divine right concept is J. N. Figgis, *The Divine Right of Kings* (Cambridge: Cambridge University Press, 1914).

3. *Public Political Controversies I*

1. F. J. McLynn, "Issues and Motives in the Jacobite Rising of 1745," *The Eighteenth Century* 23 (1982): 97.

2. George Hilton Jones, *The Main Stream of Jacobitism* (Cambridge: Harvard University Press, 1954), 228, 234-39; "Britain from 1742 to 1754," *Britannica Online* 97.1.1.

3. *Works* 20:9.

4. *Works* 20:10-14. Wesley cites a report from James Jones as the source of information on these riots against the Methodists.

5. See John Walsh, "Methodism and the Mob in the Eighteenth Century" in *Popular Belief and Practice,* ed. G. C. Cuming and Derek Baker (Cambridge: Cambridge University Press, 1972). Walsh discusses the Jacobite accusations only at the end of his article, and then in sketchy fashion. The implication is that these accusations played only a minor and occasional role in mob riots against the Methodists.

6. *Works* 20:15.

7. *Works* 20:16. Also published in *Works* 26:104-6.

8. See Charles's journal entry for 6 March 1744, *Journal CW* 1:354-55.

9. *Works* 20:23.

10. Luke Tyerman, *The Life and Times of the Rev. John Wesley, M.A.* (London: Hodder & Stoughton, 1870) 1:440.

11. *Works* 20:17.

12. *Works* 20:22.

13. *Works* 20:25.

14. *Works* 20:78.

15. See *Journal* (8 November 1745), *Works* 20:105.

16. *Works* 26:152-53.

17. *Works* 26:162.

18. *Works* 26:162-64.

19. "Advice to the People Called Methodists," §§8-15, *Works* 9:125-28.

20. "A Word in Season," §§2-3, *Works* (Jackson) 11:182-83.

21. *Works* (Jackson) 11:187.

22. "Farther Appeal to Men of Reason and Religion, Part III," §III.34, *Works* 11:315.

23. Ibid., §IV.15-16, *Works* 11:323.

24. There are numerous references in Wesley's *Journal* of this period to the activities of press-gangs in attempting to force Methodist preachers into military service. Some of these attempts were successful. As a result, Methodist preachers served in the British army in continental wars. Press-gangs were authorized to force into military service any adult male who appeared to be idle and unemployed. In the eyes of the authorities, Methodist preachers—by definition—fit that description. For examples, see the entry for 11 May 1744 (*Works* 20:28), which refers to the impressment of John Downes and the threatened impressment of all men in the Methodist congregation at Sykehouse, and that for 15 May (*Works* 20:29-30), which records the case of John Nelson. Nelson was arrested just after finishing his sermon at Adwalton. Wesley wrote, "Many were ready to testify that he was in no respect such a person as the Act of Parliament specified. But they were not heard. He was a preacher; that was enough. So he was sent for a soldier at once." Legal action for the impressment of Thomas Maxfield is recorded in the entries of June 19, 21, and 22, 1745 (*Works* 20:69-71). Assaults on Wesley himself for this purpose are noted in the entries for July 2 and 3, 1745 (*Works* 20:73-75).

25. *Works* 20:144.

26. In an obscure entry for 1 April 1747 (*Works* 20:165-66), Wesley reports that he "rode to Winlaton Mills, a place famous above many, and called the rebels to lay down their arms and be reconciled to God through his Son." He does not make clear whether he is referring to persons who are religiously rebellious, or to die-hard Jacobites who refused to give up the armed struggle even after the defeat at Culloden.

27. *Journal* (5 June 1739), *Works* 19:64. The particular form of the Conventicle Act effective in Wesley's time forbade unauthorized (non-Church of England)

gatherings for worship of more than five persons who were not members of the same family.

28. Henry D. Rack, *Reasonable Enthusiast* (Nashville: Abingdon Press, 1993), 278-81. Glenn Burton Hosman Jr. contends that Bishop Edmund Gibson's *Observations upon the Conduct and Behavior of a certain Sect usually distinguished by the name of Methodism* (1744) reflects the context of the Jacobite hysteria; see "The Problem of Church and State in the Thought of John Wesley as Reflecting His Understanding of Providence and His View of History" (Ph.D. thesis, Drew University, 1970), 222.

29. Linda Colley, *In Defiance of Oligarchy: The Tory Party 1714–60* (Cambridge: Cambridge University Press, 1982), 171-72.

30. Ibid., 172.

31. Bernard Semmel, *Methodist Revolution* (New York: Basic Books, 1973), 58. In "Human Liberty as Divine Right," *Journal of Church and State* 25 (1983): 57-85, Leon O. Hynson agrees that there was a major shift in loyalty from Stuart to Hanover, but traces its origin to Wesley's reading of William Higden's *A View of the English Constitution*. He knows Semmel's position, but does not—at least in this article—review the impact of the '45 rebellion on Wesley's politics.

32. *Works* 26:253.

33. *Works* 21:3.

34. *Letters* (Telford) 3:166. Telford gives the candidate's name but not his party. Hosman cites Simon (*Wesley* 3:318) as the source for identifying Spenser's party as Whig. "Simon says that Latimer's *Annals of Bristol in the Eighteenth Century* is proven incorrect by this letter to Ebenezer Blackwell. Latimer had suggested that Wesley gave energetic support to the Tory candidate, Jarrit Smith. This aftermath of Jarrit Smith's victory and the open display of Jacobite sympathy would have been particularly abhorrent to Wesley" (Hosman, "Church and State," 288-89). Hosman's citation of John S. Simon actually is from Simon's *John Wesley and the Advance of Methodism* (London: Epworth Press, 1925), pp. 317-18.

35. *Works* (Jackson) 9:172-78.

36. *Works* 9:175-76.

37. *Journal* (27 May 1750), *Works* 20:340-41 (and *Works* 26:427-28).

38. *Journal* (5 January 1761), *Works* 21:297.

39. Ibid., 298.

40. See Letter to the Editor of the *Gentleman's Magazine* (24 December 1785), *Letters* (Telford) 7:305-6; and my discussion in chapter 2, note 16.

41. "Americanus" [Caleb Evans], *A Letter to the Rev. Mr. John Wesley, Occasioned by his Calm Address to the American Colonies* (London: Printed by William Pine, 1775), 11.

42. H. Broxap, discussing the reaction of Scottish Jacobites to the claims of Henry Stuart, states that "The prayers for Henry IX are reported to have been made on one knee only" ("Jacobites and Non-Jurors," in *The Social and Political Ideas of Some English Thinkers of the Augustan Age,* ed. F. J. C. Hearnshaw [London: George G. Harrap, 1928], 109).

43. *Works* (Jackson) 4:420.

4. PUBLIC POLITICAL CONTROVERSIES II

1. John Brewer, *Party Ideology and Popular Politics at the Accession of George III* (Cambridge: Cambridge University Press, 1976) studies the politics of transition in considerable detail. Harry T. Dickinson, *Liberty and Property: Ideology in Eighteenth-Century Britain* (New York: Holmes & Meier, 1977) is interested primarily in the development and clash of ideologies.

2. Dickinson, *Liberty and Property,* 195.

3. Brewer, *Party Ideology,* 207, 250-52; Dickinson, *Liberty and Property,* 196.

4. Dickinson, *Liberty and Property,* 197-205.

5. *Works* (Jackson) 11:14-33. The letter was published first in 1768. Wesley published a revised edition in 1770.

6. *Works* (Jackson) 11:34-46.

7. *Works* (Jackson) 11:46-53.

8. Accounts of the Wilkes affair are found in countless sources. See Brewer, *Party Ideology,* pp. 163-200; Dickinson, *Liberty and Property,* pp. 210-15; and George Rudé, *Wilkes and Liberty; A Social Study of 1763 to 1774* (London: Clarendon Press, 1962). For Wesley and Wilkes see, *inter alia,* C. T. Winchester, *The Life of John Wesley* (New York: Macmillan, 1906), 223-27.

9. "Free Thoughts," *Works* (Jackson) 11:21.

10. Ibid., 25-26.

11. Ibid., 20.

12. Ibid., 32.

13. Ibid., 28.

14. Ibid., 33.

15. Ibid., 24.

16. Leon O. Hynson wrote, "In Wesley's orchestration of liberty, the monarchy was considered the most adequate instrument, but it was only an instrument. The political system, whatever it may be, must preserve human rights" ("Human Liberty as Divine Right: A Study in the Political Maturation of John Wesley," *Journal of Church and State* 25 [1983]: 64).

17. "Free Thoughts," *Works* (Jackson) 11:24.

18. Ibid., 15.

19. Ibid., 19.

20. Ibid.

21. Brewer, *Party Ideology,* 190.

22. "Thoughts upon Liberty," §24, *Works* (Jackson) 11:44. The "Letters of Junius" were anonymous journalistic attacks on the king and other prominent public persons. They were brilliantly written, savage in their sarcasm, devastating in their effect—and highly popular.

23. Ibid., §26, *Works* (Jackson) 11:45.

24. Ibid., §2, *Works* (Jackson) 11:34.

25. Ibid., §16, *Works* (Jackson) 11:37.

26. Ibid., §21, *Works* (Jackson) 11:41.

27. Ibid., §19, *Works* (Jackson) 11:40.

28. Ibid.

29. "Thoughts Concerning the Origin of Power," §11, *Works* (Jackson) 11:49.

30. In his "Concise History of England" Wesley appears to recognize a functional role for the popular source of royal authority. Concerning the six hundred years of Saxon monarchy, he wrote, "The crown, during this period, was neither wholly elective, nor yet totally hereditary" (75). Also, William I, according to Wesley, "accepted the crown upon the terms that were offered him, which were, that he should govern according to the established customs of the country. Though he had it in his power to dictate his own conditions, he chose to have his election considered rather as a gift from his subjects, than a measure extorted by him. He knew himself to be a conqueror, but was willing to be thought a legal king. In order to give his invasion all sanction possible, he was crowned at Westminster by the Archbishop of York, and took the oath usual in the times of the Saxon and Danish kings, which was to defend the church, to observe the laws of the realm, and to govern the people with impartiality" (78). One implication of this example is that the people express their will through customary and traditional practices and codes, and not only through direct conferral of authority.

31. According to Maldwyn Edwards, Wesley had great admiration for Locke's limited government, but attributed to Parliament authority equivalent to that of Hobbes's sovereign. "The cumulative effect of his sayings leads one inevitably to the contemplation of a Parliament with powers that are virtually absolute"; Edwards, *John Wesley and the Eighteenth Century* (London: Epworth Press, 1933), 31. This surely is an exaggeration on Edwards's part. Wesley spoke on several significant occasions of the mixed and balanced authority of all elements of the limited government.

32. See for example Wesley's citation of Lord Chief Justice Mansfield, in objecting to Lord Chatham's proposal that the House of Lords reverse the resolution of the Commons in the Wilkes-Luttrel case. Mansfield argued strenuously that one house should not interfere in the affairs of the other. Wesley quoted Mansfield with obvious approval ("Free Thoughts," *Works* [Jackson] 11:22-23).

33. Dickinson, *Liberty and Property*, 272.

34. See ibid., 272 for a broader discussion of the elements of conservative ideology.

5. PUBLIC POLITICAL CONTROVERSIES III

1. Most biographies of Wesley and other related historical accounts review the stages and details of his response to the American War of Independence. They agree that early on he was sympathetic to the Americans, but turned sharply critical when he realized they wanted independence from Britain, not simply a redress of grievances. See Lynwood M. Holland, "John Wesley and the American Revolution," *Journal of Church and State* 5 (1963): 199-213. More thorough, insightful, and useful is Allan Raymond, " 'I fear God and Honour the King': John Wesley and the American Revolution," *Church History* 45 (1976): 316-28. Raymond charges Holland with inaccuracy in some dates and citations.

2. "Free Thoughts on the Present State of Public Affairs," *Works* (Jackson) 11:24.

3. Ibid. "But whose measures were these? If I do not mistake, Mr. George Grenville's. Therefore the whole merit of these measures belongs to him, and not to the present ministry."

4. *Letters* (Telford) 6:156. See pp. 155-64 for the full texts of the letters to Dartmouth and North.

5. Wesley's letter of 23 August 1775 to Lord Dartmouth repeats his somber view of social conditions in Britain (*Letters* [Telford] 6:175-76). More that two years earlier—on 20 January 1773—he had written similar observations in "Thoughts on the Present Scarcity of Provisions," *Works* (Jackson) 11:53-59.

6. *Letters* (Telford) 6:159.

7. Ibid., 159-60.

8. John Brewer argues that the Americans did not originate the debate over taxation and representation, but they did formalize and familiarize it, and therefore made it attractive to domestic British politics; Brewer, *Party Ideology and Popular Politics at the Accession of George III* (Cambridge: Cambridge University Press, 1976), especially chapter 10, "American ideology and British radicalism; the case for parliamentary reform," 201-16.

9. *Works* (Jackson) 11:80-90. The pamphlet was published in September 1775.

10. "A Calm Address to Our American Colonies," §9, *Works* (Jackson) 11:85.

11. Ibid., §1, *Works* (Jackson) 11:82.

12. Ibid., §5, *Works* (Jackson) 11:83-84.

13. *Works* (Jackson) 11:46-53.

14. "Calm Address," preface, *Works* (Jackson) 11:81. Earlier on Wesley had the right to vote, and voted in several parliamentary elections. Presumably he had this right as a fellow of Lincoln College, Oxford University, but lost it when he resigned his fellowship following his marriage.

15. Ibid.

16. See my discussion of Wesley's views on rights and liberties in chapter 10.

17. "Calm Address," §10, *Works* (Jackson) 11:86.

18. Brewer, *Party Ideology*, 201.

19. "Calm Address," preface, *Works* (Jackson) 11:80. *Taxation no Tyranny; an Answer to the Resolutions and Address of the American Congress*, 3rd ed. (London: Printed for T. Cadell, 1775), was written by the eminent Dr. Samuel Johnson, who was an acquaintance of John Wesley.

20. Numerous writers have reported Johnson's favorable reaction to Wesley's use of his *Taxation no Tyranny*. Allan Raymond (" 'I Fear God and Honour the King': John Wesley and the American Revolution," *Church History* 45 [1976]: 321) notes that Johnson sent Wesley a letter complimenting him. He states further that James Boswell, Johnson's biographer, was convinced that Johnson wrote the pamphlet in response to a request from the government. George Otto Trevelyan, writing much earlier than Raymond, states that Dr. Johnson was recruited by the government to write pamphlets supporting government policy, and in fact, government officials reviewed his writings before publication. Trevelyan insists, however, that Johnson's words were his own. The main purpose of such censor-

ship was to tone down the explosive rhetoric of this ardent patriot and Tory, in order to render the pamphlets less provocative and offensive (*The American Revolution* [New York, London: Longmans, Green & Co., 1928] 3:256). Public critiques of Wesley's "Calm Address" are listed as items 475 and 479-86, in Richard Green, *Anti-Methodist Publications Issued During the Eighteenth Century* (London: C. H. Kelly, 1902).

21. Mr. [David] Parker, *An Argument in Defence of the Exclusive Right claimed by the Colonies to Tax Themselves* (London: Brotherton & Sewell, 1774).

22. "Americanus" [Caleb Evans], *A Letter to the Rev. Mr. John Wesley, Occasioned by his Calm Address to the American Colonies* (London: Printed by William Pine, 1775). The letter is dated Bristol, 2 October 1775. It is No. 482 in Green, *Anti-Methodist Publications*. Trevelyan reports that "Wesley's change of attitude bordered on the grotesque, and to some of his followers was perfectly bewildering. At the general election of the previous year he had advised Bristol Methodists to vote for the candidates who were in favour of conciliation with America" (*American Revolution* 3:261). That Wesley should favor conciliation is not surprising, so long as he did not urge support of the American cause. He continued to press for conciliation at the time of the writing of "Calm Address" and for several months thereafter.

23. "Calm Address," preface, *Works* (Jackson) 11:81-82.

24. *Letters* (Telford) 6:186.

25. *Letters* (Telford) 6:187-88. Cited in Telford's editorial note.

26. Letter to James Rouquet (8 November 1775), *Letters* (Telford) 6:188.

27. See *Letters* (Telford) 6:189.

28. Letter to Charles Wesley (31 July 1775), *Letters* (Telford) 6:170.

29. Letter to James Rouquet (12 November 1775), *Letters* (Telford) 6:188-89.

30. Letter to Caleb Evans (9 December 1775), *Letters* (Telford) 6:194-95.

31. Wesley's comment and the letter to Evans are in Journal (9 December 1775), *Works* 22:476-77. His accusation of Evans of plagiarism has less credibility than Evans's accusation of him. Evans cited Parker by name and publication and used quotation marks, neither of which Wesley did in using Johnson's work.

32. *Taxation no Tyranny*, 58.

33. "Calm Address," §11, *Works* (Jackson) 11:86.

34. *Works* (Jackson) 11:14-33.

35. *Works* (Jackson) 11:34-46.

36. "Calm Address," §12, *Works* (Jackson) 11:87.

37. *Works* (Jackson) 11:90.

38. *Letters* (Telford) 6:142.

39. Ibid., 148.

40. Ibid., 152

41. Ibid., 168.

42. William Warren Sweet, *Religion in the Development of American Culture, 1765–1840* (New York: Charles Scribner's Sons, 1952), 31.

43. Coen G. Pierson writes, "It was not until after American independence was achieved that any considerable migration of American loyalists to Canada

occurred. But a few had left the thirteen colonies while the Revolution was in progress. Deprived of their property and facing a hopeless future in the United States, thousands upon thousands of Tories finally fled to British territories, including the future colony of Upper Canada, or Ontario. This fact became significant for Methodism" ("Mission and Revolution," in *The History of American Methodism*, ed. Emory S. Bucke [New York, Abingdon, 1964] 1:152).

44. Francis Asbury, *Journal and Letters*, ed. Elmer T. Clark et al. (Nashville: Abingdon Press, 1958) 1:181.

45. *Works* 22:465.

46. *Letters* (Telford) 6:179.

47. Letter to Thomas Rankin (20 October 1775), *Letters* (Telford) 6:182.

48. In "A Calm Address to the Inhabitants of England" (1777), Wesley stated that "within a few months, fifty, or perhaps an hundred thousand copies, in newspapers and otherwise, were dispersed throughout Great Britain and Ireland" (*Works* [Jackson] 11:129). He could not send them to America, as he had planned, because the Americans had closed their ports. However, some arrived there and were distributed—at times by his enemies.

49. Letter to Thomas Rankin (20 October 1775), *Letters* (Telford) 6:182.

50. *Letters* (Telford) 6:188.

51. Ibid., 199.

52. Sermon 111, "National Sins and Miseries," *Works* 3:566-76.

53. Ibid., §4, *Works* 3:567-68.

54. Ibid., §I.2, *Works* 3:569-70.

55. Ibid., §I.4, *Works* 3:570-71.

56. *Letters* (Telford) 6:192.

57. Ibid., 193.

58. Ibid.

59. Wesley's journal entry for 2 January 1776 (*Works* 22:479) records that he was "pressed to pay a visit to our brethren at Bristol, some of whom had been a little unsettled by the patriots, so called." But that says nothing about changes in his thinking.

60. *Works* 23:8. The full title of Richard Price's publication is "Observations on the Nature of Civil Liberty, the Principles of Government, and the Justice and Policy of war with America."

61. *Works* (Jackson) 11:90-118.

62. "Some Observations on Liberty," §3, *Works* (Jackson) 11:91.

63. Ibid., §14, *Works* (Jackson) 11:96-97.

64. Ibid., 97.

65. *Works* (Jackson) 11:46-53.

66. "Some Observations on Liberty," §40, *Works* (Jackson) 11:108-9.

67. Ibid., §43, *Works* (Jackson) 11:111.

68. Ibid., §51, *Works* (Jackson) 11:114-15.

69. Ibid., §50, 114.

70. "A Seasonable Address," *Works* (Jackson) 11:119-28.

71. Ibid., 121.

72. Ibid., 122.
73. Ibid.
74. Ibid., 125.
75. Ibid., 126.
76. Ibid., 127.
77. Ibid., 128.
78. *A Union Catalogue of the Publications of John and Charles Wesley,* 2nd rev. ed., compiled by Frank Baker (Stone Mountain, Ga.: George Zimmermann, 1991), Sec. 1, p. 22.
79. *Works* (Jackson) 11:129-40.
80. "Calm Address to the Inhabitants of England," §2, *Works* (Jackson) 11:129.
81. Ibid., §7, 131.
82. Ibid., §9, 131-32.
83. Ibid., §16, 134.
84. Letter of 24 December 1775, *Letters* (Telford) 6:198-99.
85. "Calm Address to the Inhabitants of England," §16, *Works* (Jackson) 11:135.
86. Ibid., §19, 135-36.
87. Ibid., §21, 137.
88. Ibid., §17, 135.
89. Sermon 113, *Works* 3:595-608.
90. For secondary sources on Wesley's economic ethics, see Theodore W. Jennings, *Good News to the Poor* (Nashville: Abingdon Press, 1990); Kathleen W. MacArthur, *The Economic Ethics of John Wesley* (New York: Abingdon Press, 1936); and Thomas W. Madron, "John Wesley on Economic Ethics," in Theodore Runyon, ed., *Sanctification and Liberation* (Nashville: Abingdon Press, 1981).
91. Sermon 113, "The Late Work of God in North America," §II.1, *Works* 3:601.
92. *Works* (Jackson) 11:140-49.
93. *Works* (Jackson) 11:149-54.
94. "Compassionate Address to the Inhabitants of Ireland," §4, *Works* (Jackson) 11:150-51.
95. Ibid., §5, 151.
96. Ibid., §8, 152.
97. Ibid., §9, 152.
98. Ibid., §11, 153
99. Ibid., §13, 154.
100. *Works* 23:43-44.
101. *Works* 23:64.
102. *Works* 23:157-58.
103. See *An Account of the Conduct of the War in the Middle Colonies. Extracted from a Late Author* (London: n.p., 1780); *Reflections on the Rise and Progress of the American Rebellion* (London: Paramore, 1780); *An Extract from a Reply to the Observations of Lieut. Gen. Sir William Howe, on a Pamphlet entitled, Letters to a Nobleman* (London: Paramore, 1781); *An Extract of a Letter to the Right Honourable Lord Viscount H—e on his Naval Conduct in the American War* (London: Paramore, 1781). This listing of Wesley's published extracts is taken from Oliver A.

Beckerlegge, "Charles Wesley's Politics," *London Quarterly and Holborn Review* 182 (October 1957): 291. Most, if not all, of the works extracted were by Joseph Galloway, whom Wesley knew, and who supplied him with negative impressions of the American leaders and the war. Wesley wrote in his journal for 13 November 1779, "I had the pleasure of an hour's conversation with Mr. G., one of the members of the first Congress in America. He unfolded a strange tale indeed! How has poor K. G. been betrayed on every side! But this is our comfort: there is One higher than they. And He will command all things to work together for good" (*Works* 23:153). For Joseph Galloway's own unedited writings, see *Letters to a Nobleman on the conduct of the American war* (London: G. Wilkie, 1779); and *Historical and political reflections on the rise and progress of the American rebellion, in which the causes of that rebellion are pointed out, and the policy and necessity of offering to the Americans a system of government founded in the principles of . . .* (London: G. Wilkie, 1780).

104. ST Kimbrough Jr., and Oliver A. Beckerlegge, eds., *The Unpublished Poetry of Charles Wesley* (Nashville: Kingswood Books, 1988) 1:41.

105. Ibid., 57.

106. *Letters* (Telford) 7:238.

107. Ibid., 239.

108. *Works* 23:388.

109. "Calm Address to the Inhabitants of England," §23, *Works* (Jackson) 11:137.

110. *Journal* (18 October 1775), *Works* 22:470.

111. "Calm Address to the Inhabitants of England," §23, *Works* (Jackson) 4:138-40.

112. *Journal* (10 November 1776), *Works* 23:36.

113. *Journal* (3 May 1777), *Works* 23:47.

114. *Journal* (16 April 1778), *Works* 23:80.

115. *Journal* (26 July 1778), *Works* 23:101.

116. *Works* (Jackson) 11:59-79.

117. "Americanus" [Caleb Evans], *Letter to the Rev. John Wesley*, 11.

118. "Calm Address to the Inhabitants of England," §21, *Works* (Jackson) 11:137.

119. Harry T. Dickinson (*Liberty and Property: Political Ideology in Eighteenth-Century Britain* [New York: Holmes & Meier, 1977], 233) refers to a sermon by Andrew Kippis in commemoration of the Revolution, in which "he rejected the conservative claim that the liberties of Englishmen were first established in 1688." The "conservatives" in this case were establishment Whigs, who sought to protect their position by arguing the primacy of Revolution-based rights over those grounded in the ancient Constitution. Wesley accepted both the Ancient Constitution and the Revolution, and did not argue one against the other. In this context, however, he was contending for the constitutional settlement of 1689 in opposition to natural rights arguments, and seized on the Whiggish rhetoric to make his point.

In his *Concise History of England*, Wesley offers evidence of his belief that English liberties were much older than 1689. Writing of Henry II, he observed, "He gave charters to several towns, by which the citizens claimed their privileges, independent of any superior but himself. These charters were the groundwork of English liberty" (1:136).

120. "Calm Address to the Inhabitants of England," §21, *Works* (Jackson) 11:137.

121. "Calm Address to Our American Colonies," §8, *Works* (Jackson): 11:85.

122. Letter to Charles Wesley (8 June 1780), *Letters* (Telford) 7:21.

123. John Fletcher, *American Patriotism farther Confronted with Reason, Scripture, and the Constitution: Being Observations on the Dangerous Politicks Taught by the Rev. Mr. Evans, M.A., and the Rev. Dr. Price with a Scriptural Plea for the Revolted Colonies* (Shrewsbury: J. E. Drowes, 1776), 17.

124. "Doctrine of Original Sin," Part I, §II.11, *Works* (Jackson) 9:224.

125. "Most of those who gave [his brother Samuel] this title [Jacobite] did not distinguish between a Jacobite and a Tory; whereby I mean, 'one that believes God, not the people, to be the origin of all civil power.' " Letter to the editor of *The Gentleman's Magazine* (24 December 1785), *Letters* (Telford) 7:305. See supra, chapter 2.

126. *Letters* (Telford) 6:192.

127. William Warren Sweet, *Methodism in American History* (New York: Methodist Book Concern, 1933), 80.

128. *A Vindication of the Rev. Mr. Wesley's "Calm Address to our American Colonies": in some letters to Mr. Caleb Evans* (London: Strahan, 1776).

129. Fletcher, *American Patriotism*, 2 n.

130. See *Letters* (Telford) 6:197.

131. Letter to Lord Dartmouth (24 December 1775), *Letters* (Telford) 6:198.

6. *POLITICAL AUTHORITY I*

1. See especially "Thoughts Concerning the Origin of Power," *Works* (Jackson) 11:46-53.

2. See Wellman J. Warner, *The Wesleyan Movement in the Industrial Revolution* (New York: Russell & Russell, 1930), 74.

3. Eric Voegelin, *The New Science of Politics* (Chicago: University of Chicago Press, 1952).

4. Ibid., 1.

5. Quoted in Brian Tierney, *The Crisis of Church and State 1050–1300* (Englewood Cliffs, N.J.: Prentice-Hall, 1964), 14-15.

6. J. N. Figgis, *The Divine Right of Kings* (Cambridge: Cambridge University Press, 1914).

7. Ibid., 137-50.

8. Theodore W. Jennings, *Good News to the Poor: John Wesley's Evangelical Economics* (Nashville: Abingdon Press, 1990). See the appendix: "Wesley on Politics," 199-222.

9. Ibid., 202.

10. Ibid., 205.

11. Ibid., 206.

12. The edition of the Homilies used here is *Certain SERMONS or HOMILIES*

Appointed to be Read in Churches in the Time of the Late QUEEN ELIZABETH of Famous Memory. And now Thought Fit to be Reprinted by Authority from the King's Most Excellent Majesty. A New Edition (Oxford: Clarendon Press, 1822).

13. "Good Order and Obedience," *Certain SERMONS,* 104.

14. Ibid., 104-5.

15. "Wilful Disobedience," *Certain SERMONS,* 506.

16. Ibid., 507.

17. Ibid., 507-8.

18. Ibid., 508.

19. Ibid., 509-10.

20. *Works* (Jackson) 11:46-47.

21. *Patriarcha and Other Writings,* ed. Johan P. Somerville (Cambridge: Cambridge University Press, 1991).

22. Ibid., 52.

23. Ibid., 35.

24. Ibid., 44.

25. Ibid., 57.

26. Ibid., 55.

27. Ibid., 57.

28. For background information on Filmer and *Patriarcha,* see J. P. Somerville's introduction (ibid., ix-xxiv). For a discussion of authorship and dating, see xxxii-xxxvii.

29. John Locke, *Two Treatises of Government,* ed. with intro. by Peter Laslett (New York: New American Library, 1960), 169.

30. Robert Hole writes: "One of the most important themes of J. C. D. Clark's *English Society* is the continuing importance of Filmer, and the relative neglect of Locke in the eighteenth century; the pervasion of patriarchialist and the rarity of contractarian thought." *Pulpits, Politics and Public Order in England 1760–1832* (Cambridge: Cambridge University Press, 1989), 61.

31. Peter Lee, "The Political Ethics of John Wesley" (Yale University Ph.D. thesis, 1940), 220. Lee does not give the source of the quote concerning "the learned Sir Robert," which does not seem to be from Wesley.

32. Hole, *Pulpits, Politics, and Public Order,* 79-80. Hole does not show that Wesley took the argument directly from Filmer. Wesley, for his part, does not quote Filmer.

33. However, Wesley did not lean as far toward Parliament as Maldwyn Edwards claimed. Edwards contended that Wesley ceded all power to the Parliament, which for him became Hobbes's sovereign. See chapter 4, note 31.

34. Sermon 96, "On Obedience to Parents," §I.6, *Works* 3:365.

35. "A Word to a Smuggler," §II.3-4, *Works* (Jackson) §11:174-75.

36. Hole, *Pulpits, Politics, and Public Order,* 24.

37. Quoted in William Ebenstein, ed., *Great Political Thinkers; Plato to the Present,* 3rd ed. (New York: Holt, Rinehart & Winston, 1951), 349.

38. William Warren Sweet, "John Wesley, Tory," *Methodist Quarterly Review* 71 (1922): 262.

39. Bernard Semmel, *The Methodist Revolution* (New York: Basic Books, 1973), 93.

40. Leon O. Hynson, "John Wesley and Political Reality," *Methodist History* 12 (1973): 38. Elsewhere Hynson states that Wesley "moved from an early emphasis on the 'divine, indefeasible hereditary right' of the monarchy to an emphasis on the divine right of human rights" ("Human Liberty as Divine Right: A Study in the Political Maturation of John Wesley," *Journal of Church and State* 25 [1983]: 85). However, there is no uncontrovertible evidence that Wesley ever supported the divine, hereditary indefeasible right of the monarchy. If he did not hold that view, he could not have moved from it to something else. Whether Hynson is right in ascribing to him an emphasis on the "divine right of human rights" is a matter yet to be considered.

41. Figgis, *Divine Right of Kings*, 5-6.

42. "A Short Address to the Inhabitants of Ireland," §11, *Works* 9:284.

43. "A Word to a Freeholder," *Works* (Jackson) 11:197.

44. Wesley believed that both Richard III and Mary of Scotland were "greatly injured characters" who had been falsely accused (*Journal* [14 January 1776], *Works* 23:3). He believed that Charles I brought his troubles on himself by "persecuting the real Christians" (*Journal* [30 January 1785], *Works* 23:342), but did not approve the idea of executing a monarch.

45. *Journal* (29 October 1781), *Works* 23:227.

46. *Journal* (11 January 1768), *Works* 22:118.

47. "Thoughts upon Liberty," 16, *Works* (Jackson) 11:37.

48. "A Calm Address to Our American Colonies," §8, *Works* (Jackson) 11:85.

49. Hynson, "Human Liberty," 70.

50. Semmel, *Methodist Revolution*, 93.

51. In a letter to John Mason (13 January 1790), Wesley penned his famous comment: "We are no republicans, and never intend to be," *Letters* (Telford) 8:196. The remark was a repudiation of the choosing of stewards and other leaders by the Methodist societies, instead of their being appointed by Mr. Wesley himself. It characterized with equal strength his attitude toward republicanism in civil politics.

52. "Observations on Liberty," §34, *Works* (Jackson) 11:105.

53. "Origin of Power," §21, *Works* (Jackson) 11:52-53.

54. Ibid., §§15-18, *Works* (Jackson) 11:50-52. See also "Observations on Liberty," §§16-17, *Works* (Jackson) 11:98. Wesley acknowledges the popular transfer of power to Thomas Aniello by the people of Naples in the preceding century, but saw it as an isolated historical example. Filmer also noted the absence of historical evidence, but without referring to the Naples incident.

55. "Origin of Power," §17, *Works* (Jackson) 11:51.

56. Ibid., §18, *Works* (Jackson) 11:51-52.

57. "Free Thoughts on Public Affairs," *Works* (Jackson) 11:19.

58. In fact, on one occasion Wesley argues in his journal that subjects can be industrious, happy, and virtuous under an absolute monarch, and cites the examples of Peru and China. The point is made in fierce rebuttal of Abbé Raynal's

History of the Settlements and Trade of the Europeans in the Indies (see *Journal* [27 April 1778], *Works* 23:83). One presumes from Wesley's diatribe that Raynal apparently attacked both monarchy and Christianity, and associated the harmful effects of each with the other. Although Wesley does not provide sufficient detail or commentary to make the issue clear, he seems to be defending the benign possibilities of the extreme case in order to defend monarchy itself. Nowhere else does he offer a comparable argument. All of his comments about Tudor and Stuart absolutism are critical of their policies and practices.

59. Allen Lamar Cooper, "John Wesley: A Study in Theology and Social Ethics," (Ph.D. diss., Columbia University, 1962), 93.

60. For excellent comprehensive coverage of Wesley and the church, see Frank Baker, *John Wesley and the Church of England* (Nashville: Abingdon Press, 1970). For an extended study of Wesley's views on church and state, see Leon O. Hynson, "Church and State in the Thought and Life of John Wesley," (Ph.D. diss., University of Iowa, 1971).

61. *Works* (Jackson) 11:197-98.

62. Maurice Henry Woods, *A History of the Tory Party in the Seventeenth and Eighteenth Centuries* (London: Hodder & Stoughton, 1924), 15.

63. Sermon 102, "Of Former Times," §16, *Works* 3:450. For other passages setting forth Wesley's complaints about Constantine's conversion and its effects on the church, see Sermon 61, "The Mystery of Iniquity," §27, *Works* 2:462-63; Sermon 66, "The Signs of the Times," §II.7, *Works* 2:529; Sermon 89, "The More Excellent Way," §2, *Works* 3:263-64; Sermon 104, "On Attending the Church Service," §14, *Works* 3:470; and Sermon 121, "Prophets and Priests," §8, *Works* 4:77.

64. "Minutes" (17 June 1747), Qq. 7-8, in Albert Outler, ed., *John Wesley* (New York: Oxford University Press, 1964), 173.

65. Sermon 49, "The Cure of Evil Speaking," §III.1, *Works* 2:259.

66. Sermon 74, "Of the Church," §I.15-17, *Works* 3:51-52.

67. Frank Baker, *John Wesley and the Church of England* (London: Epworth Press, 1970), 137.

68. See *Works* 9:567-80 for the full text of the document. The form in which we have the document is a copy made partly by Charles Wesley, partly by John Nelson, from John Wesley's original paper.

69. "Ought We to Separate," §II, *Works* 9:568-70.

70. Ibid., §III.1, *Works* 9:570.

71. Ibid., §III.4-5, *Works* 9:571.

72. Wesley's comments critical of the Constantinian settlement come mainly from the latter part of his life. It is possible that he was growing out of the contradiction in a direction prompted by the pressures of the sectarian movement that he led. If so, that would fit the evident secularization in his manner of arguing public political questions, especially those pertaining to political authority. It might support also the claims that increasingly he gave his attention to human rights and less to the traditional interests of Tories and Jacobites. The problem with this argument is that he never renounced or even criticized the church-state arrangements prevailing in England, or said anything to suggest less than the full

support he always had given. He continued to share with Richard Hooker and Edmund Burke the organic sense of national community with its enmeshed components of crown, church, and people.

73. Hynson, Jennings, Runyon, and Semmel offer forms of the human rights/natural rights argument. See chapter 10, "Rights and Liberties."

7. POLITICAL AUTHORITY II

1. "Origin of Power," §1, *Works* (Jackson) 11:46.
2. Ibid., §7, *Works* (Jackson) 11:47.
3. "Concerning our Governors in England, you teach, 'A Parliament forfeits its authority by accepting bribes.' If it does, I doubt all the Parliaments in this century, having accepted them more or less, have thereby forfeited their authority, and, consequently, were no Parliaments at all: It follows, that the Acts which they enacted were no laws; and what a floodgate would this open!" "Observations on Liberty," §35, *Works* (Jackson) 11:105-6.
4. "A Calm Address to Our American Colonies," postscript, *Works* (Jackson) 11:89.
5. "Origin of Power," §2, *Works* (Jackson) 11:46.
6. See chapter 2 for a discussion of the "genealogical flaw" (Semmel's term) for which Wesley questioned the right of the Stuarts to inherit the throne. Had he followed the logic of this claim, he would have been bound to consider them as monarchs *de facto* but not *de jure*. Given his agreement with William Higden on the authority of *de facto* rulers, he would have had to consider them authoritative monarchs nonetheless. However, he elected not to press the point.
7. "Origin of Power," §7, *Works* (Jackson) 11:47-48.
8. "A Calm Address to Our American Colonies," §3, *Works* (Jackson) 11:83. See also "Observations on Liberty," §10 & §14, *Works* (Jackson) 11:94, 96.
9. Perhaps the most explicit natural law limitation is expressed in his "Thoughts upon Slavery," §IV.2 (*Works* [Jackson] 11:70): "The grand plea is," Wesley observes, " 'They are authorized by law.' But can law, human law, change the nature of things? Can it turn darkness into light, or evil into good? By no means. Notwithstanding ten thousand laws, right is right, and wrong is wrong still. There must still remain an essential difference between justice and injustice, cruelty and mercy. So that I still ask, Who can reconcile this treatment of the Negroes, first and last, with either mercy or justice?"
10. "A Calm Address to Our American Colonies," postscript, *Works* (Jackson) 11:89.
11. "Observations on Liberty," §5, *Works* (Jackson) 11:92.
12. Ibid., §34, *Works* (Jackson) 11:105.
13. Ibid., §5, *Works* (Jackson) 11:92.
14. "Thoughts upon Liberty," §16, *Works* (Jackson) 11:37-38.
15. See the discussion in chapter 2 of William Higden's views on the legitimacy of *de facto* monarchs, and Wesley's agreement with him.

16. That was the traditional Whig interpretation; see Harry T. Dickinson, *Liberty and Property: Political Ideology in Eighteenth-Century Britain* (New York: Holmes & Meier, 1977), 140.

17. In chapter 2 (note 42), I refer to a letter written by John Wesley to his mother in 1742 when he was an Oxford student. In the letter he referred to the "abdication" of King James II. To speak of the king having abdicated was a popular means of dismissing the fact that he was forced from the throne. It is not clear whether Wesley intended his use of that term as a justification for the king's removal and replacement, or whether it was simply an offhand remark. Certainly it would not have pleased his mother. In any event, John did not use the term again in any surviving document. Therefore it did not figure in any public attempts on his part to discuss the justification for the events of 1688–89.

18. "Origin of Power," §18, *Works* (Jackson) 11:51-52. See chapter 6 (note 56).

19. Ibid., 52.

20. Wesley recognized—in the case of Henry II—an earlier example of a combination of elements of authorization: "Henry Plantagenet had now every right, both from hereditary succession, from universal assent, from power, and personal merit, to make sure of the throne, and to keep its prerogatives unimpaired." *Concise History of England* 1:135.

21. Leon O. Hynson, "Human Liberty as Divine Right: A Study in the Political Maturation of John Wesley," *Journal of Church and State* 25 (1983): 80.

22. Ibid., 81.

23. Ibid., 82.

24. "Observations on Liberty," §14, *Works* (Jackson) 11:96.

25. "A Calm Address to Our American Colonies," §4, *Works* (Jackson) 11:83.

26. "Observations on Liberty," §14, *Works* (Jackson) 11:97.

27. "A Calm Address to Our American Colonies," §4, *Works* (Jackson) 11:83.

28. *Works* 20:492.

29. *Works* 21:24.

30. "Observations on Liberty," §34, *Works* (Jackson) 11:105.

31. Ibid., §55, *Works* (Jackson) 11:117.

32. Ibid., §53, *Works* (Jackson) 11:116.

33. Richard Hooker, "Of the Lawes of Ecclesiasticall Politie," book I, chapter 10.4, in *The Works of Richard Hooker*, vol. I, ed. Georges Edelen and W. Speed Hill (Cambridge, Mass.: Harvard University Press, 1977), 98. Hooker also uses the term "supreme power," as do other English writers, but Wesley's manner of using it shows the influence—though indirect—of the Frenchman Jean Bodin.

34. Ibid., 99.

35. Ibid., book I, chapter 10.8 (p. 102).

36. Ibid., 102-3.

37. Ibid., 103.

38. See Sermon 45, "The New Birth," §I.4, *Works* 2:190.

39. Richard Hooker, "Of the Lawes of Ecclesiasticall Politie," book VIII, chapter 3.1 in *The Works of Richard Hooker*, vol. III, ed. Paul G. Stanwood and W. Speed Hill (Cambridge, Mass.: Harvard University Press, 1981), 336.

8. POLITICAL AUTHORITY III

1. Matthew 22:15-22; Mark 12:13-17; Luke 20:20-26.

2. For various perspectives on exegetical controversies over Romans 13, see Oscar Cullmann, *The State and the New Testament* (New York: Scribner, 1956); Clinton Morrison, *The Powers That Be* (London: SCM Press, 1960); and John H. Yoder, *The Politics of Jesus* (Grand Rapids, Mich.: Eerdmans, 1972).

3. Richard Allestre, *The Whole Duty of Man* (London: Printed by R. Norton for George Pawlet, 1686).

4. *Letters* (Telford) 6:267.

5. "A Farther Appeal to Men of Reason and Religion, Part III," §III.34, *Works* 11:315.

6. The full texts of the letters to Lords Dartmouth and North are found in *Letters* (Telford) 6:155-64.

7. See Sermon 96, "Obedience to Parents," §I.5-6, *Works* 3:364-65; and Sermon 97, "Obedience to Pastors," *Works* 3:374-83.

8. "Ought We to Separate," §II.4, *Works* 9:570.

9. Ibid., §II.1, *Works* 9:568-69.

10. Sermon 97, "On Obedience to Pastors," §III.6, *Works* 3:380.

11. Wesley insisted that the choice of one's pastor was a personal decision, not a matter of inheritance or geographical location. "Everyone must give an account of himself to God. Therefore every man must judge for himself; especially in a point of so deep importance as this is, the choice of a guide for his soul" (ibid., §II.2, *Works* 3:377-38). The fundamental issues of religious faith and practice were not simply subjective, but they rested ultimately on personal accountability before God.

12. *Letters* (Telford) 4:146-47.

13. Ibid., 147.

14. *Journal* (25 July 1747), *Works* 20:184.

15. *Journal* (25-26 August 1748), *Works* 20:241-43.

16. *Journal* (20 May 1750), *Works* 20:337.

17. Letter to the Mayor of Newcastle (12 July 1743), *Works* 26:100-101.

18. *Journal* (3 September 1750), *Works* 20:360.

19. Letter to the Earl of Dartmouth (10 April 1761), *Letters* (Telford) 4:147-48.

20. Ibid., 148.

21. Ibid., 152.

22. For a review of Wesley's severe criticisms of lawyers and the law, see Theodore W. Jennings, *Good News to the Poor: John Wesley's Evangelical Economics* (Nashville: Abingdon Press, 1990), 76-78. Jennings contends that when Wesley views the legal system from the standpoint of the poor, he sees lawyers as thieves and charlatans, and the law as an instrument of injustice.

23. William Stephens, *Journal of the Proceedings in Georgia, beginning October 20, 1737, The Colonial Records of the State of Georgia,* ed. Allen D. Candler (Atlanta: The Franklin Printing and Publishing Co., 1906) 4:19. Henry Rack also notes Stephens's account of Wesley's legal problems and activities in Georgia, but his

report differs in some details from Stephens's journal (*Reasonable Enthusiast: John Wesley and the Rise of Methodism* [Nashville: Abingdon Press, 1993], 131).

24. The editor and compiler of Stephens's *Journal* notes this bias also. He wrote, "Since it is apparent that Col. Stephens was in sympathy with that faction headed by Mr. Causton, which was opposed to Mr. Wesley, the compiler has deemed it not amiss to present in a footnote Wesley's own account of the matter" (15 n.).

25. *Journal* (9 August 1737), *Works* 18:187.

26. *Journal* (2 December 1737), *Works* 18:195.

27. Ibid.

28. Stephens, *Journal*, 24.

29. *Works* 25:412-13.

30. *Journal* (20 June 1743), *Works* 19:327.

31. *Journal* (25 January 1742), *Works* 19:246-47.

32. Cf. *Journal* (3-4 March 1745) *Works* 20:55 (18 September 1746), 20:142, and (7 May 1747) 20:173.

33. On 2 November 1748 Wesley wrote William Grimshaw, advising him to pay the lawyers early and regularly, and to make haste to take and send affidavits. "The judges often put off a cause which comes before them at the latter end of a term" (*Works* 26:340). On 17 November 1748 he advised John Bennet, "If they proceed you must immediately remove the cause into the King's Bench, which will tear them all to pieces. Let them send him to prison, if they see good" (ibid., 341). See also Letter to George Merryweather (20 December 1766), *Letters* (Telford) 5:33-34; and Letter to the Commanding Officer at Lowestoft (30 November 1782), *Letters* (Telford) 7:151-52.

34. Letter to James Hargrove (26 August 1748), *Works* 26:327.

35. *Letters* (Telford) 5:22.

36. Sermon 96, "On Obedience to Parents," §I.6, *Works* 3:365. In his journal for 1 June 1777 Wesley wrote, "The *will* even of the king does not bind any English subject, unless it be seconded by an express law" (*Works* 23:52).

37. See Letter to Revd. Westley Hall (27-30 December 1745), *Works* 26:174.

38. Norman Sykes, *Church and State in England in the XVIII Century* (Cambridge: Cambridge University Press, 1934), 29.

39. J. N. Figgis, *The Divine Right of Kings* (Cambridge: Cambridge University Press, 1914), 96: "In more than one of Latimer's Sermons and in two famous homilies, that of the reign of Edward VI, entitled An Exhortation concerning Order and Obedience, and that of Elizabeth's collection directed Against Wilful Rebellion, the religious basis of non-resistance is asserted. Doubtless it is true, as the popular party afterwards claimed, that it is non-resistance to law which is here set forth in general terms; and that no guidance is given by the Homilies for the case of a monarch, like James II, arbitrarily violating the laws."

40. Leon O. Hynson, "Human Liberty as Divine Right: A Study in the Political Maturation of John Wesley," *Journal of Church and State* 25 (1983): 61-62.

41. "Thoughts upon Slavery," §11, *Works* (Jackson) 11:69.

42. "Observations on Liberty," §46, *Works* (Jackson) 11:112.

43. *Journal* (27 May 1758), *Works* 21:149-50.

44. "General Rules," §4, *Works* 9:71. This rule, incidentally, is still in *The Book of Discipline of The United Methodist Church* (Nashville: The United Methodist Publishing House, 1996), Par. 62, p. 70.

45. Sermon 49, "The Cure of Evil-speaking,"§1, *Works* 2:252.

46. Luke Tyerman, *The Life and Times of the Rev. John Wesley, M.A.* (London: Hodder & Stoughton, 1870), 1:431.

47. Tyerman's dating is supported by the new critical edition of Wesley's *Works* (see note 16 on 9:71).

48. "How Far Is It the Duty of a Christian Minister to Preach Politics?"§2, *Works* (Jackson) 11:154.

49. "An Answer to Mr. Rowland Hill's Tract, entitled, 'Imposture Detected' " (28 June 1777), §21, *Works* (Jackson) 10:451.

50. Vivian Green, *The Young Mr. Wesley* (New York: St. Martin's Press, 1961), 78. Professor Green deciphered Wesley's early diary. I am indebted to him for this quotation and the subsequent ones. An updated rendering of the diary is forthcoming in the Bicentennial Edition of Wesley's works.

51. "Thoughts upon Slavery," §V.1, *Works* (Jackson) 11:75.

52. "Free Thoughts on Public Affairs," *Works* (Jackson) 11:33; "Thoughts upon Liberty," §§24-28, *Works* (Jackson) 11:43-46.

53. "How Far Is It the Duty of a Christian Minister to Preach Politics?" §6, *Works* (Jackson) 11:155.

54. Ibid., §4, *Works* (Jackson) 11:155.

55. Lynwood M. Holland and Ronald F. Howell, "John Wesley's Concept of Religious and Political Authority," *Journal of Church and State* 6 (1964): 306.

56. Sermon 52, "The Reformation of Manners," §1, *Works* 2:301.

57. Ibid., §3, *Works* 2:302.

58. Ibid., §I.2-4, *Works* 2:304-5.

59. Ibid., appendix, *Works* 2:323.

60. Doubtless Wesley's retention of the framework of authority was of considerable importance also to the maintenance of his own authority within the Methodist movement.

9. GOVERNMENT IN CONTEXT

1. The United Methodist Council of Bishops, *In Defense of Creation: The Nuclear Crisis and a Just Peace* (Nashville: Graded Press, 1986), 12.

2. See chapter 7.

3. Letter to Harman Verelst (10 November 1736), *Works* 25:485-86.

4. Letter to the Georgia Trustees (4 March 1737), *Works* 25:497. The Mr. Causton praised so highly in this report is the same one with whom Wesley was involved so bitterly and destructively in the Sophia Hopkey affair.

5. Sermon 52, "The Reformation of Manners," *Works* 2:301-23.

6. "Calm Address to the Inhabitants of England," §23, *Works* (Jackson) 11:137.

7. "Ought We to Separate," §II.4, *Works* 9:571.

8. John Calvin, "On Civil Government," *Institutio Christianae Religionis,* book IV, chapter 20, section 2. The citation is from *Luther and Calvin on Secular Authority,* trans. and ed. Harro Höpfl (Cambridge: Cambridge University Press, 1991), 49. The bracketed dates refer to changes in the text in different editions. FV refers to the French Version.

9. Ibid., Section 3; p. 50.

10. Ibid., Section 9; p. 58.

11. See Sermon 34, "The Original, Nature, Properties, and Use of the Law," *Works* 2:4-19. In the introductory section, Wesley restates the distinctions—prominent in Calvin, although not his exclusive property—among moral, ceremonial, and judicial law in the Old Testament. In §IV.1-3, he offers his own adaptation of the three uses of the law.

12. Calvin, "On Civil Government," *Institutio Christianae Religionis,* book IV, chapter 20.1.

13. Cf. Roland Bainton, *Hunted Heretic; The Life and Death of Michael Servetus, 1511–1553* (Boston: Beacon Press, 1953).

14. "Ought We to Separate," §II.1-4, *Works* 9:568-72.

15. Ibid., 571.

16. I am aware, of course, that Calvinists of one sort or another were elements in English religious diversity, and therefore important factors in the struggle to define the role of the church in political society. However, the resulting establishment was not what they wanted. John Wesley, by contrast, supported it with enthusiasm.

17. Robert C. Monk, *John Wesley: His Puritan Heritage* (Nashville: Abingdon Press, 1966).

18. See chapter 8.

19. Karl Barth, "Church and State," in *Community, State, and Church,* ed. Will Herberg (Garden City, N.Y.: Doubleday, 1960), 101-48; Dietrich Bonhoeffer, *Ethics,* ed. Eberhard Bethge (New York: Macmillan, 1955), 332-53.

20. *OT Notes,* vol. 1, Genesis 1:26-28. That Wesley is using the words of Matthew Henry and Matthew Poole in *OT Notes* is of no contrary consequence, because Wesley revised their work at points where he disagreed; therefore what we have here is what he believed himself. Moreover, he used the concept of the political image with the same meaning in other places.

21. Augustine's argument was that dominion *as such* was unnatural, because (following Cicero) it was not right that one rational being should have dominion over another. Therefore, government as well as slavery was an institution of the fallen order, not the created order.

22. *NT Notes,* Romans 13:6.

23. "Free Thoughts," *Works* (Jackson) 11:32.

24. "A Calm Address to Our American Colonies," §1, *Works* (Jackson) 11:82.

25. The principle of subsidiarity holds that higher levels of political organization should take on only those responsibilities that cannot be managed adequately by lower levels. Wesley might see the merit of such a proposal, and yet contend that the authority to make such judgments is at the higher level, not the lower.

Such reasoning has to do in part with his hierarchical understanding of authority, but also with the need in some situations to impose burdens and restrictions on the lower levels because of the overriding importance of the public good.

26. "Of the Lawes of Ecclesiasticall Politie," book VIII, chapter 3.4 in *The Works of Richard Hooker*, ed. Paul G. Stanwood and W. Speed Hill (Cambridge, Mass.: Harvard University Press, 1981), 349.

27. The scant use of such corporate terminology by Wesley does not mean that it played no significant role in his thinking. One supposes—rightly, I believe—that he found the notion of "public good" to be self-evident conceptually and often in its content, and not requiring theoretical explanation or justification.

28. Sermon 34, "The Original, Nature, Properties, and Use of the Law," §I.1-2, *Works* 2:6.

29. Ibid., §I.3-4, *Works* 2:7.

30. Ibid., §II.3, *Works* 2:9.

31. Ibid., §II.4-6, *Works* 2:9-10.

32. Ibid., §I.4, *Works* 2:7.

33. Ibid., §I.4-6, *Works* 2:7-8.

34. See Wesley's *OT Notes* commentary on Genesis 1:26-28; and Sermon 60, "The General Deliverance," §I.1-2, *Works* 2:438-39.

35. See Sermon 44, "Original Sin," §II.2-4, *Works* 2:176-77; and Sermon 45, "The New Birth," §I.2, *Works* 2:189.

36. For Calvin's distinction among the three types of law, see *Institutio Christianae Religionis*, book IV, chapter 20.14-15.

37. "Thoughts upon Slavery," §IV.2, *Works* (Jackson) 11:70.

38. Ibid.

39. Ibid., §II, *Works* (Jackson) 11:61-65.

40. Wesley's use of scriptural argument against slavery in "Thoughts upon Slavery" is almost nonexistent. That fact may reflect his awareness that some passages in the Old Testament accept and legislate for the holding of slaves, and not only his skepticism concerning the Christian receptivity of the persons to whom his arguments against the institution are directed.

41. Hooker's treatment of law is found in book I of "Of the Lawes of Ecclesiasticall Politie." He follows fairly closely Aquinas's distinctions among eternal, natural, divine, and human law. Book VIII, of course, is an important statement of his political theory, and especially of his treatment of church-state relations. See chapter 3.4, book VIII, for his statement on the common good as the end of government, and the need for centralized management of society to pursue that end. Hooker's case for the supremacy of the monarch over the church certainly does not follow Aquinas, but reflects the religious struggles in England to which Hooker's book made a significant—if belated—contribution.

42. Luther's "On Secular Authority" can be found in numerous collections and editions. It is the principal text for Luther's political thought, but not a sufficient one. Luther focused the work of government on the protective and punitive functions, but did not set dogmatic limits to what governments should and should not do. For a highly useful treatment of Luther's social ethics, including his under-

standing of state and government, see George W. Forell, *Faith Active in Love* (Minneapolis: Augsburg, 1959). Forell notes, among other things, that the predominantly Lutheran Scandinavian societies developed extensive state-supported educational and welfare systems, thereby calling in question the claim that Lutheran theology limits the responsibilities of government to order and defense.

43. *Journal* (2 December 1737), §2, *Works* 18:202.

44. Sermon 69, "The Imperfection of Human Knowledge," §II.6, *Works* 2:580.

45. "A Letter to the Rev. Mr. Baily of Cork," §III.15, *Works* 9:313.

46. Sermon 15, "The Great Assize," §IV.1-2, *Works* 1:371-72.

47. In Wesley's comment on Romans 13:4 in *NT Notes*, he writes of *"The Sword*—The instrument of capital punishment, which God authorizes him to inflict." See also his *OT Notes* comment on Genesis 9:6: *"By man shall his blood be shed*. That is, by the magistrate, or whoever is appointed to be avenger of blood. Before the flood, as it should seem by the story of Cain, God took the punishment of murder into his own hands. But now he committed this judgment to men, to masters of families at first, and afterwards to the heads of countries."

48. *Journal* (20 April 1752), *Works* 20:418.

49. *Journal* (27 March 1753), *Works* 20:449.

50. Ibid.

51. See especially Leon O. Hynson, "Human Liberty as Divine Right: A Study in the Political Maturation of John Wesley," *Journal of Church and State* 25 (1983): 57-85.

52. Wesley's complaints against persons who shout and write passionately about liberty without regard to the societal consequences of their crusades, and without regard for the institutional embodiment of liberty, are recorded in numerous writings, including Sermon 111, "National Sins and Miseries," *Works* 3:566-76.

53. Sermon 44, "Original Sin," *Works* 2:172-85; and "Doctrine of Original Sin," *Works* (Jackson) 9:191-464.

54. I have been influenced in this analysis of Wesley's view of politics and original sin by C. B. Macpherson's interpretation of Thomas Hobbes. Macpherson argues that Hobbes did not reason from the state of nature to the condition of organized society, but abstracted his understanding of the state of nature from what he believed to be present in civilized men—tendencies that would reveal themselves starkly were the trappings of civilization to be stripped away. *The Political Theory of Possessive Individualism* (Oxford: Oxford University Press, 1962), 19-29.

55. "Politically [the Fall] meant for Wesley that just as man was incapacitated to act spiritually for himself in bringing about the restoration of the original State of Nature, he was incapacitated to govern himself" (Allen Lamar Cooper, "John Wesley: A Study in Theology and Social Ethics," [Ph.D. diss., Columbia University, 1962], 93). To my knowledge, Wesley never drew such an inference. We shall return to this point in the concluding chapter.

56. *Works* (Jackson) 11:53-59.

57. Wesley made a distinction among alcoholic beverages between beer and wine, which he saw essentially as beverages to be used mainly with meals and in

moderation, and spirituous liquors, principally whiskey and gin. He drank beer and wine himself (except for a short period in his life when someone convinced him to abstain from wine, also), but rejected distilled spirits. His reasons for doing so: distilled spirits often were poisonous, they used up scarce bread grains thereby depriving the poor of food, they induced drunkenness quickly and easily, and the money spent on them could be used to feed the poor.

58. George Soros, an extraordinarily successful and influential capitalist financial manager, offers a critique of the negative effects of free market ideology in *The Crisis of Global Capitalism [Open Society Endangered]* (New York: Public Affairs, 1998).

59. For a notable and inspired treatment of Wesley's concern for the poor and his suspicion of economic power, see Theodore W. Jennings, *Good News to the Poor: John Wesley's Evangelical Economics* (Nashville: Abingdon Press, 1990).

60. "Advice to the People Called Methodists," §2, *Works* 9:123-24.

61. Sermon 60, "The General Deliverance," §III.10, *Works* 2:449.

62. Sermon 15, "The Great Assize," §IV.1, *Works* 1:371

63. In chapter 6, I commented on the use of the analogy of God in the Homily of 1570. I noted there that Wesley's use of analogy is similar to that of the Homily in suggesting the behavior of God as a model for the behavior of public officials, but not in using the monarchy of God to establish the institution of kingship theologically. In any event, Wesley does not cite or comment on this Homily, nor does he seem to have it or the earlier Homily in mind when writing on political matters.

10. RIGHTS AND LIBERTIES

1. Cf. Bernard Semmel, *The Methodist Revolution* (New York: Basic Books, 1973); Leon O. Hynson, "Human Liberty as Divine Right: A Study in the Political Maturation of John Wesley," *Journal of Church and State* 25 (1983): 57-85; Theodore Jennings, *Good News to the Poor* (Nashville: Abingdon Press, 1990); and Theodore Runyon, *The New Creation: John Wesley's Theology Today* (Nashville: Abingdon Press, 1998), 170-84. At the opposite extreme one finds Maldwyn Edwards, who wrote, "Wesley vested people with no natural rights of their own. . . . The only rights they possess are the privileges they have in assisting to fulfil the divine mission of the State" (*John Wesley and the Eighteenth Century: A Study of His Social and Political Influence* [London: Epworth Press, 1955], 33-34). Edwards is wrong on both counts, although he is closer to being right if he is referring only to natural political rights.

2. Semmel, *Methodist Revolution*, 93.

3. Jennings, *Good News to the Poor*, 200.

4. C. B. MacPherson, *The Political Theory of Possessive Individualism: Hobbes to Locke* (Oxford: Clarendon Press, 1962).

5. "Thoughts upon Liberty," §1, *Works* (Jackson) 11:34.

6. Sermon 60, "The General Deliverance," §I.1, *Works* 2:439.

7. "Thoughts upon Liberty," §§3-4, *Works* (Jackson) 11:34-35.
8. Ibid., §6, *Works* (Jackson) 11:35.
9. Ibid., §16, *Works* (Jackson) 11:37.
10. "A Calm Address to Our American Colonies," §4, *Works* (Jackson) 11:83.
11. Theodore Runyon wrote concerning Wesley's comparative usage of natural and positive rights concepts, "And Wesley knew how to appeal to 'the rights of an Englishman' when it was necessary" (*New Creation*, 171). Actually, the appeal to rights of Englishmen was fundamental to Wesley's understanding of rights. The *necessity* of such rights was established by existence in society. It was not an occasional matter, as Runyon's comment suggests. It would be truer to Wesley's view to say that he knew how to appeal to natural rights when necessary.
12. "Calm Address," §6, *Works* (Jackson) 11:84.
13. Ibid., §7, *Works* (Jackson) 11:84.
14. "Thoughts Concerning the Origin of Power," §§11-13, *Works* (Jackson) 11:48-50.
15. Ibid., §1, *Works* (Jackson) 11:46.
16. In his *Journal* of 21 July 1739, Wesley records the seizure of one of his hearers by a press-gang. As a parenthetical aside, he asks, "(Ye learned in the law, what becomes of Magna Charta, and of 'English liberty and property'? Are not these mere sounds, while, on any pretence, there is such a thing as a press-gang suffered in the land?)" *Works* 19:81-82. His reference to the Magna Carta of 1215 marks his conviction concerning the antiquity of English liberty. His "mere sounds" comment is a critique of governmental practice in the light of the ancient tradition of liberty. It implies that at least in 1739 he was not fully satisfied that English liberties had been established by the revolution of 1688-89.
17. "Observations on Liberty," §14, *Works* (Jackson) 11:97.
18. Sermon 111, "National Sins and Miseries," §I.4, *Works* 3:570.
19. *Works* (Jackson) 11:59-79. Inasmuch as I am interested at this point only in Wesley's use of the natural rights concept, I shall not discuss the history of his stand on slavery, or examine the arguments of this tract in detail. The available evidence indicates that from early on he saw persons of all races as equally objects of divine redeeming grace, and therefore equally objects of his evangelistic ministry. However, he did not translate this theological insight into active opposition to the institution of slavery until fairly late in life—except for his support of General Oglethorpe's refusal to allow slavery in the colony of Georgia in the 1730s. Clearly Wesley was influenced in the development of his thinking by the antislavery writings of the Hugenot Quaker, Anthony Benezet. Wesley's very favorable reporting of the character of Africans in their native Africa, drawn largely from Benezet's writings and indirectly from others, contrasts dramatically with the starkly negative portrayal in "The Doctrine of Original Sin, According to Scripture, Reason, and Experience," Part I, §II.2, *Works* (Jackson) 9:209-10.
One can be misled as to the dating of Wesley's antislavery attitudes by the text of "The Nature, Design, and General Rules of Our United Societies" as it appears in the 2000 *Book of Discipline of The United Methodist Church* (Nashville: The United Methodist Publishing House, 2000). That text prohibits "Slaveholding; buying or

selling slaves" (p. 73). I have not found this particular prohibition in any English publication of the General Rules during Wesley's lifetime. It was added by the Methodist Episcopal Church in America. See the editorial commentary in *Works* 9:70-71, note 11.

20. "Thoughts upon Slavery," §1, *Works* (Jackson) 11:59.

21. Ibid, §2, *Works* (Jackson) 11:59-60.

22. Ibid., §IV.2, *Works* (Jackson) 11:70.

23. Ibid., §IV.3, *Works* (Jackson) 11:71.

24. Blackstone's arguments are quoted by Wesley without citation of source, in ibid., *Works* (Jackson) 11:70-71.

25. "Thoughts upon Slavery," §V.6, *Works* (Jackson) 11:79.

26. Ibid., §III.8, *Works* (Jackson) 11:68.

27. Ibid., §III.11, *Works* (Jackson) 11:69.

28. On 24 November 1787 John Wesley wrote to Thomas Funnell, "Whatever assistance I can give those generous men who join to oppose that execrable trade, I certainly shall give. I have printed a large edition of the *Thoughts on Slavery*, and dispersed them to every part of England. But there will be vehement opposition made, both by slave-merchants and slave-holders; and they are mighty men: But our comfort is, He that dwelleth on high is mightier" (*Letters* [Telford] 8:23). Wesley's famous last letter, written on 26 February 1791—four days before his death—urged on William Wilberforce in his campaign against slavery. "Unless the divine power has raised you up to be as *Athanasius contra mundum*, I see not how you can go through your glorious enterprise, in opposing that execrable villany, which is the scandal of religion, of England, and of human nature. Unless God has raised you up for this very thing, you will be worn out by the opposition of men and devils. But, 'if God be for you, who can be against you?' Are all of them together stronger than God? O 'be not weary in well doing!' Go on, in the name of God and in the power of his might, till even American slavery (the vilest that ever saw the sun) shall vanish away before it" (*Letters* [Telford] 8:265). Thomas Jackson's note to this letter (*Works* [Jackson] 12:153-55) is worth reading for even more evidence of Wesley's awareness of the enormous weight of economic interest and power supporting the institution of slavery and opposing its abolition.

29. "Observations on Liberty," §41, *Works* (Jackson) 11:109.

30. "Thoughts upon Liberty," §16, *Works* (Jackson) 11:37-38.

31. "Earnest Appeal," §17, *Works* 11:50.

32. See Sermon 60, "The General Deliverance," §I.1, *Works* 2:438-39.

33. *Letters* (Telford) 5:22.

34. Letter to the Commanding Officer in Lowestoft (30 November 1782) *Letters* (Telford) 7:151-52.

35. "Thoughts upon Liberty," §17, *Works*, (Jackson) 11:38.

36. These were two of the four acts that constituted the Clarendon Code, passed by the Cavalier Parliament during the period 1661–65. The other two were the Corporation Act (1661), which excluded from public—specifically municipal—office persons who did not receive the sacraments in a Church of England parish, and the Five-Mile Act (1665), which prohibited

Nonconformist ministers from living or approaching within five miles of any place where they had served. To my knowledge, Wesley does not mention either of these acts.

John Wesley may not have treated King Charles II fairly in this regard. The Clarendon Code was the work essentially of a Parliament intent on restoring rigid Anglican conformity. The king apparently disapproved of such severity, preferring a broader and more comprehensive settlement. Charles's First Minister and chief advisor, the Earl of Clarendon, also was not enthusiastic for these acts, which were named for him.

37. "Thoughts upon Liberty," §17, *Works* (Jackson) 11:39.

38. C. T. Winchester records that "Bartholomew Wesley lived to a ripe old age, supporting himself by the practice of physic after the church was closed to him; but John, who was subjected to repeated imprisonments after his ejection, broke down under the hardships of his lot, and died at the early age of thirty-four" (*The Life of John Wesley* [New York: Macmillan, 1906], 2).

39. "Thoughts upon Liberty," §17, *Works* (Jackson) 11:39.

40. Letter to William Wilberforce (July 1790), *Letters* (Telford) 8:231.

41. Sermon 39: "The Catholic Spirit," §I.10, *Works* 2:86.

42. Letter to the Printer of the *Public Advertiser* (12 January 1780), *Letters* (Telford) 6:370-73. Several items pertaining to Wesley's views on Roman Catholicism, including this letter and the O'Leary correspondence, are found in *Works* (Jackson) 10:80-177.

43. See the two letters to the editors of the *Freeman's Journal* (23 March 1780), *Letters* (Telford) 7:3-8, and (31 March 1780), ibid., 9-16. David Hempton contends that Father O'Leary deliberately misrepresented Wesley's relationship to the Gordon Riots. "For, by cleverly manipulating his title pages, O'Leary made it appear that Wesley not only wrote the letters to the *Public Advertiser* and the *Freeman's Journal*, but was also responsible for the *Defence of the Protestant Association*. By extension, O'Leary alleged that Wesley was the publicist for the Association in the build-up to the Gordon Riots" (*Methodism and Politics in British Society 1750–1850* [London: Hutchinson, 1984], 41).

44. Cf. *Journal* (16-19 December 1780), *Works* 23:189-90.

45. *Journal* (29 December 1780), *Works* 23:190. Wesley may have been naive or willfully ignorant concerning Gordon's actual role. See Christopher Hibbert, *George III* (New York: Basic Books, 1998), chapter 26, "The Gordon Riots," 215-25.

46. Letter to the Printer of the *Public Advertiser* (12 January 1780), *Letters* (Telford) 6:371.

47. Ibid., 372. Of course, these Roman Catholic activities that Wesley found so threatening were precisely the activities for which the Methodists were persecuted and accused of subverting both church and state, and for the pursuit of which he demanded religious liberty as a natural right.

48. Ibid., 371.

49. See his list of objectionable Catholic doctrines in "A Word to a Protestant," *Works* (Jackson) 11:188-89.

50. *Letters* (Telford) 3:7-14.

51. The vigor of Wesley's criticism of "papism" had much to do with his own struggle against salvation by works, and his efforts to repudiate accusations that he was a papist himself.

52. See Sermon 113, "The Late Work of God in North America," §I.1, *Works* 3:596.

53. For example, in a letter to a Roman Catholic priest apparently written in May 1735, Wesley made clear that he did not trust the "Romanists" to quote accurately from classical texts or to refrain from leaving out passages that did not serve their purposes (*Works* 25:428-30). In the same letter, however, he maintained that he "could by no means approve the scurrility and contempt with which the Romanists have often been treated. I dare not rail at or despise any man, much less those who profess to believe in the same Master" (429).

54. Basil Williams, *The Whig Supremacy, 1714–1760* (Oxford: Clarendon Press, 1962), 73.

55. "Advice to the People Called Methodists," §23, *Works* 9:130.

56. Cf. "A Word to a Protestant," §13, *Works* (Jackson) 11:191.

57. Letter to the Editors of the *Freeman's Journal* (31 March 1780), *Letters* (Telford) 7:15-16.

58. "Observations on Liberty," §48, *Works* (Jackson) 11:113-14.

59. Ibid., §46, *Works* (Jackson) 11:113.

60. Ibid., §48, *Works* (Jackson) 11:114.

61. Ibid., §§46-47, *Works* (Jackson) 11:112-13.

62. In replying to Price's *Observations on the Nature of Civil Liberty, the Principles of Government, and the Justice and Policy of the War with America,* Wesley wrote: "We come now to more matter entirely new: 'No country can lawfully surrender their liberty, by giving up the power of legislating for themselves, to any extraneous jurisdiction; such a cession, being inconsistent with unalienable rights of human nature, would either not bind at all, or bind only the individuals that made it.' This is a home thrust. If this be so, all the English claim either to Ireland, Scotland, or America, falls at once. But can we admit this without any proof?" "Some Observations on Liberty," §38, *Works* (Jackson) 11:107-8. No mention is made of Wales.

The statement is puzzling for several reasons. First, one would expect Wesley to agree with Price on the principle of a people's not giving up a natural right to legislate for itself. Second, Wesley's statement seems to imply that Ireland and Scotland voluntarily ceded their right of legislation to England, and did not have it taken from them by force of English arms. Third, Wesley groups Ireland and Scotland with America, and contends that America never had a right of self-government. Could he seriously make the same claim for the other two countries? Lest one forget the original point, it was that Wesley made a strong case for the right of national independence of several countries under foreign domination, but did not make the same case for countries under English domination.

63. Sermon 98, "On Visiting the Sick," §III.1-2, *Works* 3:392-93.

64. Ibid., §III.7, *Works* 3:395-96.

65. See Earl Kent Brown, "Women of the Word: Selected Leadership Roles of

Women in Mr. Wesley's Methodism," in Hilah E. Thomas and Rosemary Skinner Keller, eds. *Women in New Worlds* (Nashville: Abingdon Press, 1981) 1:69-87; and Paul Wesley Chilcote, *John Wesley and the Women Preachers of Early Methodism* (Metuchen, N.J.: Scarecrow Press, 1991).

66. "Some Observations on Liberty," §5, *Works* (Jackson) 11:92.

67. In Sermon 113, "The Late Work of God in North-America," §II.15 (*Works* 3:607) Wesley contrasts independency with "liberty—real, legal liberty." He defines "true civil liberty" as "a liberty from oppression of every kind; from illegal violence; a liberty to enjoy their lives, their persons and their property—in a word, a liberty to be governed in all things by the laws of their country."

68. "A Calm Address to Our American Colonies," §4, *Works* (Jackson) 11:83.

69. "Thoughts Concerning the Origin of Power," §20, *Works* (Jackson) 11:52.

70. "A Calm Address to the Inhabitants of England," §21, *Works* (Jackson) 11:137.

71. Reference was made in earlier chapters to Wesley's call for such measures in "Free Thoughts on the Present State of Public Affairs," *Works* (Jackson) 11:33, and "Thoughts upon Liberty," §27, *Works* (Jackson) 11:45.

72. Wesley sets forth this concept of stewardship in Sermon 51, "The Good Steward" (*Works* 2:282-98) and numerous other writings. For a thoughtful and provocative interpretation of Wesley's view of stewardship and its implications, see Jennings, *Good News to the Poor,* chapter 5, "Stewardship: The Redistribution of Wealth," 97-117. See also Thomas W. Madron, "John Wesley on Economics and Ethics" in *Sanctification and Liberation,* ed. Theodore Runyon (Nashville: Abingdon Press, 1981). Wesley did allow that one should use income and property to provide modest support for oneself and one's family. Beyond that, one should see to the needs of members of the household of faith, and what remained should be given to the poor.

73. Jennings offers numerous examples of Wesley's advocacy of surrendering and sharing property in *Good News to the Poor*. Jennings prefers the term "communalism" to "communism" in order to avoid confusion with violent and dehumanizing twentieth-century forms of communism, with which it has almost nothing in common. Many persons have noted that the communism of the book of Acts was a matter of common sharing and distributing, not a communism of productive property and production itself. That was true also of Wesley's "communalism."

Richard Cameron reports a pertinent entry in the diary of Richard Viney, an associate of Wesley. On 22 February 1744, Viney wrote: "He [Wesley] told me of an intention he and some few have of beginning a Community of goods, but on a plan which I told him I doubted could not succeed. 'Tis this; each is to bring what cash they have and put it together. If any owe small debts, they are first to be paid. Then each abiding in their Dwellings and following their Business as they do now, are to bring weekly, what they earn and put into the common box, out of which they are again to receive weekly, as much as is thought necessary to maintain their Families, without Reflecting whether they put much or little into Ye Box" (*Methodism and Society in Historical Perspective* [New York: Abingdon, 1961], 70).

Cameron took this quotation from R. F. Wearmouth, *Methodism and the Working Class Movements of England, 1800–1850* (London: Epworth Press, 1937), 203.

74. Wesley also advocated celibacy as the optimum commitment for serving God. The communities he praised for their communal provisions for property were also celibate communities. If one is going to require a Methodist commitment to common ownership on the basis of Wesley's early vision, one also should require a Methodist commitment to celibacy. See his "Thoughts on a Single Life," *Works* (Jackson) 11:456-63, and "A Thought upon Marriage," *Works* (Jackson) 11:463-65.

75. MacPherson, *Political Theory of Possessive Individualism*, 270.

76. Sermon 50, "The Use of Money," §III.2, *Works* 2:277.

77. My reference here is to the alleged influence of Wesley's evangelical theology on his own political thinking, not to the influence of his theology on political attitudes in the Methodist movement. For the latter, Bernard Semmel's historical examination in *The Methodist Revolution* remains a very important study.

78. That, it seems to me, is exactly what Semmel does. In his interpretation, Wesley becomes "libertarian and egalitarian," and his constitutionalism "rational and contractual": "By striking at 'Antinomian' doctrines held by the evangelical sects, masses of enthusiasts that had posed such a danger to state and church in the past, Wesley was seeking to counter the ideological forces that had helped lead to the practical Antinomianism of civil war in the preceding century, and which, he feared, might be leading in the same direction in his own lifetime. In so doing, he was, as we shall see, more and more consciously setting forth a libertarian and egalitarian doctrine couched in constitutional (i.e., rational and contractual) forms suitable for a modern society." Semmel, *Methodist Revolution*, 54.

79. Interpretations of Wesley that claim more intentionality for societal transformation can be found in Jennings, *Good News to the Poor;* and Theodore Runyon, "Introduction: Wesley and the Theologies of Liberation," in *Sanctification and Liberation*, 9-48.

80. For a discussion of the three generations of rights, with references to other pertinent literature, see Darryl M. Trimiew, *God Bless the Child That's Got Its Own: The Economic Rights Debate* (Atlanta: Scholars Press, 1997), 19-30.

81. See the discussion of this tract in chapter 9.

82. "Thoughts upon Liberty," §16, *Works* (Jackson) 11:37-38.

83. Sermon 113, "The Late Work of God in North-America," §II.15, *Works* 3:607.

11. WAR AND PEACEMAKING

1. Roland Bainton's *Christian Attitudes Toward War and Peace* (New York: Abingdon Press, 1960) classifies historic Christian attitudes into the threefold typology of pacifism, the just (or justified) war, and the crusade. Subsequent writers have criticized and revised Bainton's typology, but it remains the standard for analysis and interpretation. For sympathetic studies of the just war ethic by United Methodist scholars, see Joseph L. Allen, *War: A Primer for Christians*

(Nashville: Abingdon Press, 1991); Paul Ramsey, *The Just War: Force and Political Responsibility* (New York: Charles Scribner's Sons, 1968); Ramsey, *War and the Christian Conscience: How Shall Modern War Be Conducted Justly?* (Durham, N.C.: Duke University Press, 1961); and Theodore R. Weber, *Modern War and the Pursuit of Peace* (New York: Council on Religion and International Affairs, 1968). Roland Bainton, a Quaker pacifist, was the teacher of all three of these United Methodist scholars.

2. Quoted from Donald W. and Lucille S. Dayton, "An Historical Survey of Attitudes Toward War and Peace Within the American Holiness Movement," in *Perfect Love and War*, ed. Paul Hostetler (Nappanee, Ind.: Evangel Press, 1974), 135. Citations are from John Nelson, *An Extract of John Nelson's Diary* (Bristol, 1767), reprinted as the first "life" in Thomas Jackson, ed., *The Lives of the Early Methodist Preachers* (London: Wesleyan Conference Office, 1865) 1:109. The incident also provoked an earlier publication of *The Case of John Nelson Written by Himself* (2nd ed.; London, 1745).

3. John Fletcher, *The Bible and the Sword* (London: R. Hawes, 1776).

4. Ibid., 6.

5. Ibid., 6-7.

6. *Works* (Jackson) 11:198-202.

7. *Works* (Jackson) 11:179-82.

8. The 1781 *Arminian Magazine* carried an article titled "On War"(4:658-60). The main point of the article was to denounce the notion that war was beneficial, and especially to deny that it brought providential blessings. It specified *offensive* hostility, and criticized "papist men-killing crusades." The 1782 *Arminian Magazine* published "The Causes and Cure of War" (5:39-43). It argued against fighting by *choice*, not *necessity*, and criticized the Americans, French, Spanish, and Dutch for *choosing* war mainly to gain wealth, and accused the French additionally of fighting to "waste the lives of hated Protestants" (5:40). The articles are antiwar but not evidently pacifist, inasmuch as they appear to allow defensive wars and wars fought of necessity. Both are unsigned. It is highly unlikely that either article was written by John Wesley, although he may have approved their contents.

9. That does not mean Wesley wrote nothing on the subject of peace and war. His views come to piecemeal expression in various other tracts, sermons, journals, and commentaries, especially writings having to do with the colonial American War of Independence.

10. Doubtless that is why there has been so little writing on Wesley's understanding of war. The most extensive study is Egon W. Gerdes's "John Wesley's Attitude Toward War" (Emory University Ph.D. diss., 1960). Shorter works of note include Leon O. Hynson, "War, the State, and the Christian Citizen in Wesley's Thought," *Religion in Life* 45 (1976): 204-19; Samuel J. Rogal, "John Wesley on War and Peace," *Studies in Eighteenth Century Culture* 7 (1978): 329-44; and Briane K. Turley, "John Wesley and War," *Methodist History* 29 (January 1991): 96-111.

11. See Wesley's *Journal* entries for 31 March, 5 April, and 9 April 1756 (*Works* 21:47-49).

12. In "A Word in Season, or, Advice to an Englishman" (*Works* [Jackson]

11:182-86). Wesley projects a picture not only of the destructiveness of war but also of the disastrous results for English people and their liberties should England come under the rule of a Catholic monarch supported by France. John appended two of Charles's hymns to this tract (186-87). The first speaks of the sword as a plague abroad and at home, and prays for repentance to turn away the wrath of God. The second is "For His Majesty King George," praying for divine protection and help, and—in effect—for victory. For a full treatment of Wesley and the '45 rebellion, see chapter 3.

13. "Doctrine of Original Sin," Part I, §II.10, *Works* (Jackson) 99:222.

14. Wesley and George Whitefield initially planned to raise a company of five hundred volunteers, but Whitefield backed away from the proposal. Wesley went ahead with a scaled-down version. On 1 March 1756 he wrote to the Hon. James West: "I am constrained to make the following independently of [Whitefield]: To raise for His Majesty's service at least two hundred volunteers, to be supported by contributions among themselves; and to be ready in case of invasion to act for a year (if needed so long) at His Majesty's pleasure; only within . . . miles of London"(*Letters* [Telford] 3:165). Wesley then requests that they be supplied with arms out of the Tower, and that a sergeant be assigned to train them. It should be noted also that in 1755 Charles Wesley reissued his *Hymns for Times of Trouble and Persecution* (1745). However, Charles later ridiculed John's proposal to raise troops.

15. Kenneth N. Waltz, *Man, the State, and War* (New York: Columbia University Press, 1954, 1959).

16. *Doctrine of Original Sin*, Part I, §II.15, *Works* (Jackson) 9:237-38.

17. "A Seasonable Address to the More Serious Part of the Inhabitants of Great Britain," *Works* (Jackson) 11:127.

18. "Doctrine of Original Sin," Part I, §II.10, *Works* (Jackson) 9:221-22.

19. Furthermore, the inclination toward war is not equally characteristic of all states. Some seem bent toward aggression as a matter of historical vocation; others are content to be at peace. At times the roles reverse: international bullies become model international citizens; previously peaceful states flex their muscles and intimidate their neighbors. In this case also, the doctrine of original sin is not sufficient as an explanatory principle.

20. This is a principle of international law, meaning that treaties are to be observed.

21. "Free Thoughts on Public Affairs," *Works* (Jackson) 11:19.

22. *Journal* (19 September 1790), *Works* (Jackson) 4:494.

23. "A Compassionate Address to the Inhabitants of Ireland," §§6-8, *Works* (Jackson) 11:151.

24. "Some Observations on Liberty," §34, *Works* (Jackson) 11:105.

25. "A Word in Season," §4, *Works* (Jackson) 11:183.

26. Sermon 111, "National Sins and Miseries," §4, *Works* 3:567-68.

27. Letter to Thomas Rankin (28 July 1775), *Letters* (Telford) 6:168.

28. "Seasonable Address," *Works* (Jackson) 11:119-28.

29. Ibid., *Works* (Jackson) 11:127.

30. Wesley's objection to the legality of such impressments appears as early as 1739. He records that "in the middle of the sermon the press-gang came and seized on one of the hearers (Ye learned in the law, what becomes of Magna Charta, and of 'English liberty and property'? Are not these mere sounds, while, on any pretence, there is such a thing as a press-gang suffered in the land?); all the rest standing still, and none opening his mouth or lifting up his hand to resist them" (*Journal* [22 July 1739], *Works* 19:81-82). In this case, the person seized was a hearer, not a preacher. The meaning of the concluding comment is unclear. It could express passive obedience, or cowardice, or unwillingness to give the authorities an excuse for breaking up the meeting.

31. Wesley's *Journal* for 14 May 1752 reports the case of a Highlander recruiting officer who had been warned to stay away from the Methodists. At one point he ignored the admonition, and drew in two or three of the Methodists. They stayed close to him and converted him. "A fortnight after," Wesley wrote, "he was ordered to follow the regiment to Berwick, where he is continually exhorting his comrades to be 'good soldiers of Jesus Christ.' And many already have listed under his banner" (*Works* 20:423).

32. Sermon 111, "National Sins and Miseries," §I.4, *Works* 3:571.

33. See, for example, "A Seasonable Address to the Inhabitants of Great Britain," *Works* (Jackson) 11:120-21.

34. *Journal* (24 February 1756), *Works* 21:41.

35. *Journal* (25 February 1756), *Works* 21:41.

36. For example: "The commanding officer ordered all the soldiers to be present, and attended himself with the rest of the officers, while I explained, 'Render unto Caesar the things that are Caesar's, and unto God the things that are God's' " (*Journal* [16 April 1778], *Works* 23:80).

37. *Journal* (17 May 1749) states, "I met the class of soldiers, eight of whom were Scotch highlanders. Most of these were brought up well, but evil communications had corrupted good manners. They all said from the time they entered into the army they had grown worse and worse. But God had given them another call, and they knew the day of their visitation" (*Works* 20:273). Again, there is no suggestion of conflict between God's call and the military vocation.

38. Wesley defends this decision in his Letter to Lord Shelburne (7 December 1782), *Letters* (Telford) 7:152.

39. D. Stephen Long, in *Living the Discipline: United Methodist Reflections on War, Civilization, and Holiness* (Grand Rapids, Mich.: Eerdmans, 1992), contends that war as such is a sin, and that it is inconsistent with "going on to perfection." That was not John Wesley's view, as this section demonstrates, and as Dr. Long appears to concede on pages 83-84 of his book.

40. *Letters* (Telford) 6:352. By contrast, consider the comment on King Egbert in Wesley's *Concise History of England*: "He was doubtless a great warrior, that is, a great robber and murderer. Thereby he acquired the forename of Great, such is the wisdom of the world!" (33).

41. Egon W. Gerdes offers an extensive and insightful study of Wesley's views on providence and war in "John Wesley's Attitude Toward War," 52-78.

42. Sermon 113, "The Late Work of God in North-America," *Works* 3:595-608.

43. "A Farther Appeal to Men of Reason and Religion," Part II, §28, *Works* 11:240. The Battle of Dettingen (27 June 1743), during the War of the Austrian Succession, was the last occasion on which a British monarch commanded troops in combat. George II led British, Hanoverian, and Austrian troops to victory over a French and Bavarian army. An attack on France itself was dissuaded by the reentry of Prussia into the war against Austria, thereby shifting the balance of power.

44. *Journal* (1 September 1779), *Works* 23:148.

45. *Journal* (22 September 1745), *Works* 20:92.

46. "A Calm Address to the Inhabitants of England," §16, *Works* (Jackson) 11:134.

47. Letter to "Our Brethren in America" (10 September 1784), *Letters* (Telford) 7:238.

48. See *Journal* entries for September 18, 22, 29, and October 23, 1745 (*Works* 20:90-93, 96).

49. "Are our countrymen more effectually reclaimed when danger and distress are joined? If so, the *army,* especially in time of war, must be the most religious part of the nation. But is it so indeed? Do the soldiery walk as those who see themselves on the brink of eternity? *Redeeming* every opportunity of glorifying God, and doing good to men, because they know not the hour in which their Lord will require their souls of them? So far from it, that a 'soldier's religion' is a byword, even with those who have no religion at all; that vice and profaneness in every shape reign among them without control; and that the whole tenor of their behaviour speaks, 'Let us eat and drink, for tomorrow we die' " ("A Farther Appeal to Men of Reason and Religion," Part II, §II.30, *Works* 11:242). Wesley proceeds to offer similar comments on sailors, and follows with the familiar inference of the certainty of divine vengeance on the people, unless they repent and turn to the Lord.

50. Letter to Thomas Rankin (19 May 1775), *Letters* (Telford) 6:150-51.

51. Gerdes, "John Wesley's Attitude Toward War," 67.

52. Sermon 114, "On the Death of John Fletcher," §II, *Works* 3:613-14.

53. See Sermon 7, "The Way to the Kingdom," §I.10-11, *Works* 1:223-24.

54. *NT Notes,* John 20:21.

55. *NT Notes,* John 14:27.

56. *NT Notes,* Matthew 10:34.

57. Sermon 23, "Sermon on the Mount, III," §II.3, *Works* 1:517-18. Wesley's comment on Matthew 5:9 in *NT Notes* restates briefly the broad definition of peacemakers that is spelled out in more detail in the sermon: *"The peacemakers*—They that, out of love to God and man, do all possible good to all men. Peace, in the Scripture sense, implies all blessings, temporal and eternal."

58. Ibid., §II.4, *Works* 1:518.

59. "Character of a Methodist," §9, *Works* 9:38.

60. Sermon 39, "The Catholic Spirit," §I.17, *Works* 2:89. In "The Principles of a Methodist" Wesley responds to Josiah Tucker's public attack on the Methodists. In a preface "To the Reader," §3 (*Works* 9:49), he restates the "love neighbor as myself" theme. Wesley makes clear that he does not withdraw love from one who is of a

different opinion, and in that spirit will respond to Tucker. He will strike at the ideas, not the person.

61. "Advice to the People Called Methodists," §3, *Works* 9:124.

62. Sermon 23, "Sermon on the Mount, III," §II.6. *Works* 1:519.

63. For Wesley's comments on the loss of the peace of God, see Sermon 46, "The Wilderness State," §I.4-5, *Works* 2:207-8.

64. See chapter 5.

65. Wesley records in his journal of 24 April 1752, that he was "surprised at the miserable condition of the fortifications, far more ruinous and decayed than those at Newcastle, even before the Rebellion. 'Tis well that there is no enemy near" (*Works*, 20:419). On 25 May 1756 he offers similar comments on the disrepair of the Fort at Kinsale (*Works* 21:55).

66. See "Minutes" (29 June 1744), Q. 17, as cited in Richard Cameron, ed., *The Rise of Methodism* (New York: Philosophical Library, 1954), 360.

67. Martin Schmidt (*John Wesley: A Theological Biography*, vol. 1 [New York: Epworth Press, 1962], 115) claims that there was some pressure toward pacifism because of the influence of the Moravians. However, the conference based the right and duty of bearing arms on what they perceived to be the attitude of primitive Christianity. If that indeed was the basis of their decision it is somewhat curious, inasmuch as the early church was "inclined" strongly toward pacifism—at least well into the third century.

68. Wesley's offer in the 1 March 1756 letter to the Hon. James West was noted earlier (note 14). A second offer around 1779 is referred to in the Letter to Joseph Benson (3 August 1782), *Letters* (Telford) 7:133.

69. Letter to Thomas Whitehead (?) [now assumed to be Stephen Plummer, see *Works* 26:664] (10 February 1748), *Letters* (Telford) 2:127.

70. In commenting on verse 10 of this chapter, Wesley states that the responses to the questions are not from John but from the Holy Ghost.

71. *Journal* (26 April 1778), *Works* 23:81-82.

72. *Journal* (4 July 1759), *Works* 21:207.

73. "Doctrine of Original Sin," Part I, §II.10, *Works* (Jackson) 9:222. There is some question as to whether these are Wesley's own words, or those of the person from whom he borrowed much of this treatise. In "A Seasonable Address to the Inhabitants of Great Britain," *Works* (Jackson) 11:121, Wesley states that he "would leave to present to your view in a piece of fine painting, done by an abler master." The words that follow—by this "abler master"—are an obvious paraphrase of the passage quoted here from "Doctrine of Original Sin." He changes the issue from a quarrel between the king of France and the king of England to a "dispute relative to the mode of taxation."

74. Inasmuch as Wesley does allow defensive war, it is incorrect for Gerdes to conclude that "the divine right over life and death, delegated to man, does for Wesley not justify war either because it is no right at all. . . . Consequently there remains only one kind of war, the war without any right whatsoever" ("John Wesley's Attitude Toward War," 55). Leon O. Hynson acknowledges that Wesley accepted the right of defensive war, but claims he did not believe it was justified

for Christians ("War, the State, and the Christian Citizen in Wesley's Thought," *Religion in Life* 45 [1976], 216). To my knowledge, there is no evidence that Wesley excluded Christians from participating in justifiable wars.

75. "Thoughts upon Slavery," §IV.3, *Works* (Jackson) 11:71.

76. "Observations on Liberty," §§46-47, *Works* (Jackson) 11:112-13.

77. In the passage previously cited from "Doctrine of Original Sin," Wesley is severely critical of certain "causes" of this war. The facts probably justified his sarcastic criticism; however, this form of theological polemic is not equivalent to sober political and ethical analysis. At those points where this war threatened English territory, he supported the defense of his homeland.

78. "Observations on Liberty," 52, *Works* (Jackson) 11:115.

79. Ibid., 43, *Works* (Jackson) 11:111.

80. Letter to the Earl of Dartmouth (14 June 1775), *Letters* (Telford) 6:156.

81. "A Seasonable Address to the More Serious Part of the Inhabitants of Great Britain," *Works* (Jackson) 11:121.

82. "Observations on Liberty," 52, *Works* (Jackson) 11:115. Wesley's opposition to imperial expansion is manifest in his severe criticisms of commercial policy in India and the African slave trade. However, he does not seem to be troubled by the British invasion of the New World of North America.

83. "How guilty so ever an enemy may be, it is the duty of brave soldiers to remember that he is only to fight an opposer and not a suppliant." *Concise Eccles. History* 4:227 (quoted in Briane K. Turley, "John Wesley and War," *Methodist History* 29 [1991], 111). Turley sees Wesley's repudiation of war motives of resentment and expansion of territory as an example of the principle of discrimination in *ius in bello*, whereas it seems clear that the proper category is *ius ad bellum*, and the appropriate just war criterion is just intention. A contrary bit of evidence from Wesley's *Concise History of England* is the reference to Danish revenge for Ethelred's slaughter of Danish settlers in Britain: "their suffering the just indignation of the conqueror" (57).

84. "A Calm Address to the Inhabitants of England," §18, *Works* (Jackson) 11:135.

85. Turley, "John Wesley and War," 98.

86. See *Journal* entries for 1 October 1759 (*Works* 21:231), 18 April 1760 (*Works* 21:250), 24 October 1760 (*Works* 21:285), and 4 October 1779 (*Works* 23:150), and the Letter to the Editor of *Lloyd's Evening Post* (20 October 1759), *Letters* (Telford) 4:73-74. Wesley arranges collections to provide food, clothing, blankets, and mattresses. In the letter he defends the prison administration against the charge that the prison is not clean and that the prisoners lack sufficient food and medical care. However, he observes that they are clothed inadequately to survive the coming winter.

87. *Journal* (12 December 1755), *Works* 21:37-38.

88. In *Living the Discipline*, D. Stephen Long argues that pacifism is the official position of The United Methodist Church, and that members should be disciplined into that belief and its accompanying practice, and not be allowed to plead pluralism or "freedom of individual conscience" should they disagree. Until the General Conference of 2000, the Social Principles of The United Methodist Church

rejected without qualification "war as an instrument of national foreign policy," and offered only a grudging acknowledgment of "persons who conscientiously choose to serve in the armed forces. . . . " (*The Book of Discipline of The United Methodist Church, 1996* [Nashville: The United Methodist Publishing House, 1996], Par. 69C, pp. 104-5; Par. 68G, p. 103). These statements encouraged Long and others to infer (mistakenly) that the church was in fact officially pacifist by action of its highest legislative body. In the year 2000, the General Conference changed the language of the paragraph on "War and Peace" (Par. 65C, p. 121) to state a rejection of "war as a *usual* instrument of national foreign policy . . . ." (italics added). Also, it revised the paragraph on "Military Service" (Par. 164G, pp. 119-20) to give more evenhanded treatment to pacifists and nonpacifists, and incorporated language on resort to war that reflects clearly the historic *justified war* ethic (*The Book of Discipline of The United Methodist Church, 2000* [Nashville: The United Methodist Publishing House, 2000]). The two paragraphs continue to reflect an optimistic view of human nature that John Wesley would have questioned, given his commitment to the doctrine of original sin. This view implies that United Methodism is not yet *Wesleyan* in its anthropological assumptions concerning international possibilities, even though it evidently allows the attitude toward war that Wesley himself held. Nevertheless, the revisions make clear that General Conference does not consider the church to be a *pacifist* denomination. Therefore, there is no justification for a call to discipline Methodist members into pacifism. This discipline, rather, should be toward a vocation of *peacemaking*.

89. Paul Ramsey and Stanley Hauerwas, *Speak Up for Just War or Pacifism* (University Park: Pennsylvania State University Press, 1988). Paul Ramsey, a United Methodist layman and son of an itinerant Mississippi Methodist preacher, was Harrington Speare Paine Professor of Religion at Princeton University. He died the year the book was published. Stanley Hauerwas, a Texas United Methodist, is Professor of Ethics in the Divinity School of Duke University. The book is by Ramsey, with epilogue by Hauerwas, and is subtitled *A Critique of the United Methodist Bishops' Pastoral Letter "In Defense of Creation."* Both writers are severely critical of the document on biblical, theological, and logical grounds, and for failures in ethical, military, and political analysis—often for the same reasons. I agree with most of their criticisms.

12. RECOVERING THE POLITICAL IMAGE OF GOD

1. Sermon 45, "The New Birth," §I.1, *Works* 2:188.
2. Sermon 60, "The General Deliverance," §I.2, *Works* 2:439.
3. Ibid., §III.11, *Works* 2:449.
4. Ibid., §III.6, *Works* 2:448.
5. Ibid., §I.3, *Works* 2:440.
6. Ibid., §I.2, *Works* 2:439.
7. *The Book of Discipline of the United Methodist Church* (Nashville: The United Methodist Publishing House, 2000), 61.

8. Sermon 60, "The General Deliverance," §I.5, *Works* 2:441.

9. Ibid., §III.11, *Works* 2:449-50.

10. "Thoughts upon Slavery," §IV.1, *Works* (Jackson) 11:70. I discuss the role of natural law in John Wesley's thinking in chapter 9.

11. Cf. Karl Barth, "Church and State" in *Community, State, and Church*, ed. Will Herberg (Garden City, N.Y.: Doubleday, 1960), 101-48; and Dietrich Bonhoeffer, *Ethics*, ed. Eberhard Bethge (New York: Macmillan, 1955), 332-53.

12. *OT Notes*, Genesis 1:26-28.

13. Allen Lamar Cooper, "John Wesley: A Study in Theology and Social Ethics" (Ph. D. diss., Columbia University, 1962), 93.

14. "Doctrine of Original Sin," Part IV, introduction, question 2, *Works* (Jackson) 9:381.

15. See Theodore R. Weber, "Breaking the Power of Canceled Sin: Possibilities and Limits in a Wesleyan Social Theology," *Quarterly Review* 11 (1991): 4-21.

16. Sermon 44, "Original Sin," §II, *Works* 2:176-82.

17. Sermon 60, "The General Deliverance," §II.1-2, *Works* 2:442-43.

18. The deficiencies of the sermon on "The General Deliverance" are manifest at this point.

SELECT BIBLIOGRAPHY

Bready, John Wesley. *Wesley and Democracy.* Toronto: Thorn Press, 1939.

Cameron, Richard M. *Methodism and Society in Historical Perspective.* New York: Abingdon Press, 1961.

Cooper, Allen Lamar. "John Wesley: A Study in Theology and Social Ethics." Ph.D. diss., Columbia University, 1962.

Copplestone, John T. "John Wesley and the American Revolution." *Religion in Life* 45 (1976): 89-105.

Edwards, Maldwyn. *John Wesley and the Eighteenth Century: A Study of His Social and Political Influence.* London: Epworth Press, 1955.

Eli, R. George. *Social Holiness: John Wesley's Thinking on Christian Community and Its Relationship to the Social Order.* New York: P. Lang Publishers, 1993.

Gerdes, Egon W. "John Wesley's Attitude Toward War: A Study of the Historical Formation, the Theological Determination, and the Practical Manifestation of John Wesley's Attitude Toward War and Its Place in Methodism." Ph.D. diss., Emory University, 1960.

Haywood, Clarence Robert. "Was John Wesley a Political Economist?" *Church History* 33 (1964): 314-21.

Hempton, David. *Methodism and Politics in British Society 1750–1850.* London: Hutchinson, 1984.

———. *The Religion of the People: Methodism and Popular Religion, 1750–1900.* London: Routledge, 1996.

Hoffman, Thomas G. "The Moral Philosophy of John Wesley: The Development and Nature of His Moral Dynamic." Ph.D. diss., Temple University, 1968.

Hole, Robert. *Pulpits, Politics, and the Public Order in England, 1760–1832.* Cambridge: Cambridge University Press, 1989.

Holland, Lynwood M. "John Wesley and the American Revolution." *Journal of Church and State* 5 (1963): 199-213.

Holland, Lynwood, and Ronald F. Howell. "John Wesley's Concept of Religious and Political Authority." *Journal of Church and State* 6 (1964): 296-313.

Hosman, Glenn Burton, Jr. "The Problem of Church and State in the Thought of John Wesley as Reflecting His Understanding of Providence and His View of History." Ph.D. diss., Drew University, 1970.

Howard, Harry L. "John Wesley: Tory or Democrat?" *Methodist History* 31 (1992): 38-46.

Hynson, Leon Orville, *Church and State in the Thought and Life of John Wesley*. Ph.D. diss., University of Iowa, 1971. Ann Arbor, Mich.: UMI Dissertation Services, 1998.

————. *To Reform the Nation: Theological Foundations of Wesley's Ethics*. Grand Rapids: Francis Asbury Press, 1984.

————. "Human Liberty as Divine Right: A Study in the Political Maturation of John Wesley." *Journal of Church and State* 25 (1983): 57-85.

————. "Implications of Wesley's Ethical Method and Political Thought." In *Wesleyan Theology Today: A Bicentennial Theological Consultation*, 373-88. Ed. Theodore Runyon. Nashville: Kingswood Books, 1985.

————. "John Wesley and Political Reality." *Methodist History* 12.1 (1973): 37-42.

————. "John Wesley's Concept of Liberty of Conscience." *Wesleyan Theological Journal* 7 (1972): 36-46.

————. "War, the State, and the Christian Citizen in Wesley's Thought." *Religion in Life* 45 (1976): 204-19.

Jennings, Theodore W., Jr. *Good News to the Poor: John Wesley's Evangelical Economics*. Nashville: Abingdon Press, 1990.

Kapp, John Ruse. "John Wesley's Idea of Authority in the State." Ph.D. diss., Boston University, 1938.

Kingdon, Robert Maccune. "Laissez-faire or Government Control: A Problem for John Wesley." *Church History* 26 (1957): 342-54.

Kirkham, Donald H. "John Wesley's 'Calm Address': the Response of the Critics." *Methodist History* 14 (1975): 13-23.

Lee, Peter. "The Political Ethics of John Wesley." Ph.D. diss., Yale University, 1941.

MacArthur, Kathleen Walker. *The Economic Ethics of John Wesley*. New York: Abingdon Press, 1936.

McNulty, Frank John. "The Moral Teaching of John Wesley." S.T.D. diss., Catholic University of America, 1963.

Madron, Thomas W. "The Political Thought of John Wesley." Ph.D. diss., Tulane University, 1965.

————. "John Wesley on Economic Ethics." In *Sanctification and Liberation*, 102-15. Ed. Theodore Runyon. Nashville: Abingdon, 1981.

Marquardt, Manfred. *John Wesley's Social Ethics: Praxis and Principles*. Nashville: Abingdon Press, 1992.

Raymond, Allan. " 'I Fear God and Honor the King': John Wesley and the American Revolution." *Church History* 45 (1976): 316-28.

Rogal, Samuel J. "John Wesley on War and Peace." *Studies in Eighteenth-Century Culture* 7 (1978): 329-44.

Semmel, Bernard. *The Methodist Revolution*. New York: Basic Books, 1973.

Sweet, William Warren. "John Wesley, Tory." *Methodist Quarterly Review* 71 (1922): 255-68.

Thompson, David D. *John Wesley as a Social Reformer*. Freeport, N.Y.: Books for Libraries Press, 1971.

Thompson, E. P. *The Making of the English Working Class*. New York: Vintage Books, 1966.

Turley, Briane K. "John Wesley and War." *Methodist History* 29 (1991): 96-111.

Walsh, John. "Methodism and the Mob in the Eighteenth Century." In *Popular Belief and Practice*, 213-27. Ed. G. C. Cuming and Derek Baker. Cambridge: Cambridge University Press, 1972.

Warner, Wellman J. *The Wesleyan Movement in the Industrial Revolution*. New York: Russell & Russell, 1930.

Wearmouth, Robert F. *Methodism and the Common People of the Eighteenth Century*. London: Epworth Press, 1945.

_____. *Methodism and the Working Class Movements of England, 1800–1850*. London: The Epworth Press, 1937.

Weber, Theodore R. "Breaking the Power of Canceled Sin: Possibilities and Limits in a Wesleyan Social Theory." *Quarterly Review* 11 (1991): 4-21.

———. "Political Order in *Ordo Salutis:* A Wesleyan Theory of Political Institutions." *Journal of Church and State* 37 (1995): 537-54.

INDEX OF NAMES

Verelst, Mr. Harman, 264, 265, 300, 449 n. 3

Vernon, James, 430 n. 67

Viney, Richard, 458 n. 73

Voegelin, Eric, 159, 441 n. 3

Wallace, Charles, Jr., 431 n. 71

Walmsley, Robert, 425 n. 5, 425 n. 7, 425 n. 10, 425 n. 11, 426 n. 16

Walpole, Robert, 47, 50, 65, 66, 253

Walsh, John, 14, 421 n. 3, 431 n. 5

Waltz, Kenneth W., 358, 360, 461 n. 15

Wanley, Francis, 248, 325

Warner, Wellman J., 14, 158, 421 n. 3, 441 n. 2

Watson, Richard, 20

Watts, Isaac, 404

Wearmouth, Robert, 459 n. 73

Weber, Theodore R., 421 n. 4, 460 n. 1, 467 n. 15

Wesley, Bartholomew, 326, 456 n. 38

Wesley, Charles, 52, 53, 54, 73, 81, 120, 121, 123, 126, 145, 309, 426 n. 19, 432 n. 8, 441 n. 122, 444 n. 68, 461 n. 12, 461 n. 14

Wesley, John (grandfather), 326

Wesley, Samuel, Sr., 43, 44, 45, 46, 47, 54, 61, 65, 71, 235, 325, 339, 426 n. 15, 426 n. 16

Wesley, Samuel, Jr., 46, 54, 60, 61, 66, 84, 426 n. 16, 426 n. 19, 420 n. 66, 441 n. 125

Wesley, Susanna, 43, 44, 47, 53, 57, 60, 62, 63, 64, 215, 235, 247, 325, 339, 425 n. 5, 428 n. 42, 431 n. 71

West, James, 461 n. 14, 464-68

Whitefield, George, 56, 461 n. 14

Wilberforce, William, 327, 455 n. 28, 456 n. 40

Wilkes, John, 88, 90, 91, 92, 98, 99, 100, 103, 251, 254, 308

William and Mary, 47, 108, 215, 216, 217, 218, 220, 426 n. 16

William I, 95, 101, 188, 214, 435 n. 30

William III, 42, 43, 44, 53, 57, 60, 62, 161, 163, 188, 213, 214, 215, 428 n. 48

Williams, Basil, 333, 427 n. 27, 457 n. 54

Winchester, C. T., 434 n. 8, 456 n. 38

Woods, Maurice, 192, 430 n. 70, 444 n. 62

Yoder, John Howard, 447 n. 2

SUBJECT INDEX